NATIVE TIME

NATIVE TIME

A Historical Time Line
of Native America

LEE FRANCIS

 ST. MARTIN'S GRIFFIN ✦ NEW YORK

Design by Janet Tingey

Library of Congress Cataloging-in-Publication Data

Francis, Lee
    Native time : a historical time line of native America / Lee Francis
        p.   cm.
    ISBN 0-312-18141-8
    1. Indians of North America—History—Chronology.
2. America—History—Chronology   I. Title
E98.C55F73   1995
970.004'97'00202—dc20   95-8027
                                                          CIP

First St. Martin's Griffin Edition: February 1998

10   9   8   7   6   5   4   3   2   1

For my great-grandmother Meta, grandmother Agnes,
mother Ethel, and Mary, my spouse,
four women of the People who have nurtured and helped me grow.
Máh-meh tou-y-eh niyah hanno.

CONTENTS

Acknowledgments   ix
Remembering Ourselves: An Introduction   1

I JOURNEY TIME   200,000 B.C.–A.D. 1679   7
  Journeys of the People   9
  Perspective 1400–1540   27
  Perspective 1540–1620   39
  Perspective 1620–1660   56
  Perspective 1660–1700   69

II COMBAT TIME   1680–1777   81
  A Pox upon Their Houses   83
  Perspective 1700–1740   95
  Perspective 1740–1780   115

III CEREMONY TIME   139

IV TREATY TIME   1778–1871   163
  This Land Was Ours—First   164
  Perspective 1780–1820   168
  Perspective 1820–1860   196
  Perspective 1860–1900   232

V BUREAU TIME   1872–1994   247
  The Earth Is Our Reservation   248
  Perspective 1900–1940   263
  Perspective 1940–1980   283
  Perspective 1980–1994   314

Prologue   1994 and Beyond   328
Endnotes   330
About the Author   331
Wordcraft Circle   332
Index   334

ACKNOWLEDGMENTS

There are so very many people to whom I owe a debt of gratitude for all their help and support. First and foremost, I thank my grandmother Agnes who told me when I was a little boy to "always remember you are Laguna." To my mother, Tdu-u-eh-t'sah (Like A Song), or Ethel, who passed over in November 1991, because she always believed in me and always expected that I would do no less than my best. To my spouse of twenty-four years, Mary, for all the proofreading, good counsel, coffee pouring, and absolute unconditional love. To my son, Lee IV, for teaching me so much in the past eighteen years.

To the late Diane Cleaver, literary agent par excellence, go my special thanks for gently guiding me through the maze of the book-publishing world. My heart grieves at her sudden passing over on April 10, 1995. Native writers have lost a truly good advocate. This book would not have "happened" were it not for her patient care and I offer my prayer-song to her spirit for she will always remain in the hearts of the People. To Robert Weil at St. Martin's Press I also give my thanks-blessing for his kindness and good advice. Not to be forgotten are Becky Koh, assistant editor at St. Martin's, who kept track of everything, including the photos, and Hazel Rowena Mills, a most wonderful and diligent copy editor extraordinaire.

My grateful thanks to LaDonna Harris (Comanche), president and founder of Americans for Indian Opportunity (AIO), and Norbert Hill Jr. (Oneida), executive director of the American Indian Science and Engineering Society (AISES), and to all the leaders among the People of the sovereign Native nations and tribes for their dedication to the nurturing of Native students throughout Indian country.

Blessings and special thanks to Joseph Bruchac III (Abenaki), Robert J. and Evelyn Conley (Cherokee), Patricia Penn Hilden (Nez Percé), Paulette Fairbanks Molin (White Earth Chippewa), Bill Penn (Nez Percé), and Cliff Trafzer (Wyandot)—Wordcraft Circle mentors one and all—for their comments and suggestions about the manuscript and their advice from the heart.

Finally, to all Wordcrafters whose unconditional care and concern got me past the self-doubt and grief, and all those whose good thoughts and gentle prodding kept me at the task, I ask a special blessing from Sitch-tche-na-ko.

A substantial portion of the royalties from this publication will be given to Wordcraft Circle of Native Writers and Storytellers to ensure that the voices of Native writers and storytellers—past, present, and future—are heard throughout the world.

. . . And so, Sitch-tche-na-ko, or Thought Woman, who always had existed, drew a line of cornmeal from north to south and then crossed it with another line running east to west. Then Sitch-tche-na-ko began to sing, and after awhile E-yet-e-co appeared. E-yet-e-co is the mother of life, who brought forth the People from Shi-pahpu and told them to go out into the world. The People went out into the world, and it is said that on their travels they had many wonderful adventures.

REMEMBERING OURSELVES: AN INTRODUCTION

. . . And so,[1] it is said, in the time before, all the People[2] came together for a great powwow.[3] There was one sacred drum, and the People sang and danced for a long time. After a while, everyone knew the thousand thousand songs of the one great drum. They had heard the songs so often they had memorized them.

After a while, some of the People got tired of singing the same songs and decided to do something different. They began to build a great tower to climb up so they could see and talk with Grandfather Sky. As the tower got taller and taller and the People climbed higher and higher, they were not able to hear the great drum or the People still singing far below.

The People at the bottom of the tower, who had agreed to keep it steady for those who were climbing up to see and talk with Grandfather Sky, soon lost interest, and one by one began to drift away.

Finally, there was no one to hold the tower steady, and it came crashing down.

All the People who were climbing the tower were dazed and disoriented from their long fall to the ground. The People who had not climbed the tower rushed to help their fallen relatives. They asked, "Are you hurt?" but the relatives who had fallen couldn't understand the words. They listened to the great drum and the singers, but they were able to understand only one or two of the songs.

And that is how it came to be that the People were no longer able to understand one another. The great powwow ended with the People leaving and the circle of unity fragmented. Some went east, some south, others west, and the remainder went north. And although they parted to the four directions,[4] they all still carried in their hearts the beat of the great drum which reminded them of their common link to Mother/Grandmother Earth.

After a while, the People of the four directions began to make their own drums, and soon a thousand thousand drums began to beat. As the thousand thousand drums continued to beat, the People remembered themselves and their duties. They remembered that it is important to continue to hold on to the tower for their relatives who want to do something different. They remembered, as we do today, that it is important to sing our songs clearly so our relatives who are climbing the tower will not forget their harmonious place in the order of things.[5]

This book provides a glimpse of the many adventures of the Native People of Turtle Island, otherwise known as the People of the sovereign Native nations and tribes of the western hemisphere. Specifically, this book concentrates on the history, literature, art, heroes, legends, wisdom, and philosophy of the Native People of what is now known as America.

Beginning with the arbitrary date of 200,000 B.C., the time line provides a chronologically organized perspective about the People all across Turtle Island, who have lived here for more than two hundred centuries. It is a series of images about the People, their respective sovereign Native nations and tribes, their heroic words and deeds. It is about the events that affected—and affect—their lives and the lives of their non-Native immigrant relations, who came to the land of the People of the sovereign Native nations and tribes from Norway, Scotland, Russia, Sweden, France, Italy, England, Spain and Portugal, Egypt and Africa. It is about the People of Turtle Island from the perspective of an individual who is a proud descendant of a sovereign tribe. Most important, this time line is to help the People of the sovereign nations and tribes to continue to hold on to the tower, and to sing our songs clearly so that our non-Native relations who are climbing the tower will not forget their harmonious place in the order of things.

Among all the People of the sovereign nations and tribes, the number four is sacred because it is associated primarily with the sacred directions—east, south, west, north—as well as the four aspects of human beings—spirit, mind, heart, body. Because the number four is central to all People of the sovereign nations and tribes, the time line is composed of four major divisions.

Journey Time is the first division, which begins with the year 200,000 B.C. and ends with A.D. 1679. During that period, the People of the sovereign nations and tribes traveled all across Turtle Island. Toward the end of that period, they traveled to other lands across the ocean, sometimes as slaves and sometimes as heads of state—more often the former than the latter.

The ending date for the first division was chosen because it is the year before one of the most significant events in the adventures of the People of the sovereign nations and tribes—the Great Revolt of the People in what is now the southwestern United States.

Encompassing more than two hundred thousand years, the entries in the first division clearly emphasize the point that the People of the sovereign nations and tribes always have lived on Turtle Island. Admittedly, the chronological entries in the beginning are sketchy. For example, the first entry is for the years 200,000 B.C. to 50,000 B.C. As the time line progresses, the interval narrows from thousands of years to centuries and finally to a year-by-year account.

Combat Time, the second division, begins with the Great Revolt of the People in A.D. 1680 and ends in 1777. Although the sovereign nations and tribes throughout Turtle Island had gone to war against their non-Native relations, after having been provoked beyond reason, as early as A.D. 1500, the People of the Southwest (now New Mexico and Arizona) were the first to defeat the conquerors completely and keep them out of their homelands for a decade.

The period from 1680 through 1777 was a time when the sovereign nations and tribes, in the belief that their cause was righteous and just, engaged in battle with the non-Native immigrants to their lands. In that time period—just short of a century—the confidence and pride exhibited by the People of the sovereign nations and tribes were gradually replaced by fear and distrust. Treaties initially between equals gave way to treaties imploring peace between the victor and the vanquished, with the landholdings of the defeated People of the sovereign nations and tribes being the prize. The People gained hard-won victories over their non-Native adversaries at the expense of long-held traditional values, attitudes, and beliefs. Guns, rum, and the Christian Bible became the weapons used to defeat and destroy the People of the sovereign nations and tribes and their ways.

Sadly, all the treaties between the People of the sovereign nations and tribes and the colonies in the beginning, as well as the treaties concluded with Great Britain at the end of the eighteenth century, did little to satisfy the voracious appetite of the non-Native colonists for land and resources belonging to the People of the sovereign nations and tribes. The final disaster for the People of the eastern sovereign nations and tribes came with the defeat of the English in the American Revolutionary War and the establishment of a new government called the United States of America.

Combat Time ends with the year 1777, on the eve of the first treaty between the new government of the United States and the People of the sovereign nations and tribes.

The third division, **Treaty Time,** begins in 1778 and ends with the declaration by the United States Congress in 1871 that it will not sign any more treaties with the People of the sovereign nations and tribes. Yet despite that declaration, the government of the United States continued to sign "treaties" until the early 1900s. The only difference was that the name of the legal document was changed from "treaty" to "agreement." Although such sleight of hand, or word games, continues to be a common practice among our non-Native immigrant relations, the fact remains that the intent and format used in the agreements are identical to those of the treaties and have the same legal effect.

When reading this section, it is important to understand that treaty law is as essential to the United States as are constitutional law and civil law. Unfortunately, in a vast majority of schools in this country at the elementary, secondary, postsecondary, and graduate levels, only constitutional and civil law are taught. Teachers in America need to teach their students at the elementary and secondary levels about the area where the schools are located in terms of which of the sovereign nations held it as their ancient homelands, and the treaties that ceded the land to the United States. Professors in research universities need to teach American history, social policy, and environmental science, to list only a few topics, in terms of the treaties (treaty law) related to a particular area or historical event or social policy shift.

What most people fail to understand is that the treaties between the People of the sovereign nations and tribes of Turtle Island and the United States are as legally binding under international law as are treaties between the United States and Israel or the United States and England. Moreover, to specify only a few of the treaties between the People of the sovereign nations and tribes, for whatever reason, is an odious minimalization of the history of the Native People. What is also critically important is the number of treaties entered into by the United States with the sovereign nations and tribes across Turtle Island. The terms of the treaties almost always pertain to cession of land by the People of the sovereign nations and tribes to the United States. Only a relatively few treaties are about "friendship" or repudiation of a previous treaty.

Bureau Time, the final division, begins in 1872 and ends in 1994. During that time, the Office (later Bureau) of Indian Affairs exercised control over the lives and destinies of the People of the sovereign nations and tribes.

In the early decades, the office's policies, directives, rules, and regulations were devised with one goal in mind—obliteration of the People of the sovereign nations and tribes. Strategies included forcible removal of the People from their ancestral homelands to desolate reservations, with armed United States soldiers eager to kill any who dared to leave. Smallpox-infected blankets were sent to the cold and starving People of the sovereign nations and tribes confined to reservations. Still, the People of the sovereign nations and tribes continued to survive.

A more "enlightened" bureau then undertook a mission to "civilize" the People of the sovereign nations and tribes by forcible abduction of children from their families and homes to be placed in boarding schools hundreds or thousands of miles away. The idea was simple. At the boarding schools, the minds, hearts, and souls of the children systematically were raped.

The horror of the Holocaust endured by the Jewish people of Nazi Germany does not begin to compare with the millions of people of the sovereign nations and tribes who died as a direct result of such "civilizing" policies imposed by their non-Native relations under the guise of the national interest of the United States. And still the People of the sovereign nations and tribes continued to survive.

With the Vietnam War and the Nixon era of the 1960s and 1970s, the bureau's power over the lives of the People of the sovereign nations and tribes dimmed. The memory, however, remains.

Again, because of the significance of the number four to the People of the sovereign nations and tribes, each major division of the timetable is separated into four areas: History/Law/Politics, Literature/Art/Legends and Stories, Heroes/Leaders/Victims, and Elder Wisdom/Philosophy.

The first area, **History/Law/Politics,** focuses on historical accounts from the perspective of the People. For example, although standard texts present the immigrant explorer first, I present the People of the sovereign nations and tribes first.

Also incorporated in this area are the treaties agreed to by the People of the sovereign nations and tribes. Although many of the People entered into treaties with France, Spain, and possibly Russia, only treaties between the People and Great Britain, the

American colonies, and later, the American government are included.

Treaties are of critical importance to the People of all the sovereign nations and tribes. The treaties, as noted legal historian Vine Deloria Jr. (Hunkpapa Lakota) points out, "record the numerous instances during which the tribes expressed their sovereign capacity as nations. . . ." Although the People of the sovereign nations and tribes entered into more than one thousand treaties and "agreements" with the immigrant explorers and colonists, brief details concerning what the treaties provided for are given only for those with Great Britain and a limited number with the United States of America. For the majority of entries, only the dates of the treaties are presented, because their principal focus was the ceding of land by the People of the sovereign nations and tribes to the government of the United States of America.

Entries concerning activities between sovereign nations and tribes, as well as actions by the immigrant government currently in power, are included as part of the politics segment.

Taken together, **History/Law/Politics** permits a wider perspective concerning the triumphs and defeats of the People of the sovereign nations and tribes all across Turtle Island.

The second area, **Literature/Art/Legends and Stories,** highlights the written literature, artistic contributions, legends, and stories of and by the People of the sovereign nations and tribes.

Great care has been taken in retelling the legend-stories. The phrase *it is said* is used because it is the respectful form when repeating a legend-story. Legend-stories given in this area were selected to enhance the time segment in which they are placed. For example, in the **Journey Time** division, many of the legend-stories are creation stories of the People of a particular sovereign nation or tribe. The creation legend-stories among the People of the sovereign nations and tribes are no less important than the creation story of our non-Native Judeo-Christian relations, which they call Genesis.

Heroes/Leaders/Victims is the third area in each division. The heroes, leaders, and victims among the People include the women and men who were visionaries, prophets, poets, explorers, slaves, civil and religious leaders, holy people, "wordkeepers," or writers, visual artists, Olympic athletes, military strategists and war leaders, politicians elected to the U.S. Congress, and others. The diversity of heroes, leaders, and victims profiled in this area is by no means complete. For every hero, leader, or victim highlighted, the People of that individual's sovereign nation or tribe could cite an additional fifty. The purpose is to go beyond the overdone fare of superstars regularly chosen by non-Native writers by citing the names of the heroes, leaders, and victims by which they were known among their respective sovereign nations and tribes. For example, Cooweescoowee was the Cherokee name of John Ross, principal chief of the Cherokee Nation, or the Tsalagi.

The final area, **Elder Wisdom/Philosophy/Songs,** presents the words of the People of the sovereign nations and tribes. It is important to understand that the wisdom spoken by a noted individual from among the People is not confined to words spoken at that specific time. This is because time is a fluid concept among the People. Therefore, the reflections or wisdom transcend arbitrary time boundaries. Also, the words of the earliest known heroes among the People are translations from their respective languages into the common language of the time. Thus, although the words spoken give a sense of what the People were thinking and feeling, no actual word-for-word translations exist. However, the same thoughts and feelings, the same words, the same truths spoken by the People from the earliest times still are spoken today. The reflections within each chronological period are universal truths spoken by the People which apply throughout time—spirituality, the land, the environment, honoring of elders, respecting all life. These are a few examples of the universal truths about which the People of the sovereign nations and tribes have spoken. And although the actual words may have been spoken centuries earlier or later, their timeless applicability is intended to give a sense of the mind-heart wisdom of the elders of the sovereign nations and tribes.

Ceremony Time, a special section, is a seasonal time line which draws from the diverse traditions and cultures of the sovereign nations and tribes of Turtle Island. Containing spiritual and secular components, **Ceremony Time** provides a perspective into the traditional cultural lifeways of the People of the sovereign nations and tribes.

Within the spiritual component are twelve prayers, one for each month; four festivals, spring equinox, summer solstice, autumn equinox, and winter solstice; four seasons which center on the broken treaties, powwows and sacred dances, the prophets, dreamers, and holy ones among the People of the sovereign nations and tribes, and the season of tears and despair; four solemn times, which focus on the Heyoka, the sacred drum, the sacred fire and the sacred directions; eight honorings, which focus on infants and children, the Red Earth our mother, scholars and learners, dancers and singers, artisans and workers, the fallen, storytellers and the sacred word bundles, and all our relations; and four celebrations that emphasize our languages, our sovereignty, our heritage, and our traditions.

The secular component of **Ceremony Time** cites social events held throughout the year all across Turtle Island, such as powwows, cultural heritage events, and public ceremonial dances. In addition to the social events, an important aspect of tribal life is highlighted each month, such as traditions, education, health, and government. To emphasize the fact that the sovereign nations and tribes on Turtle Island are vital communities, the names and locations of the federally recognized sovereign nations and tribes are given.

Finally, like my great-granduncle John M. Gunn, who in 1917 wrote the book *Schat-Chen: History, Traditions and Narratives of the Queres Indians of Laguna and Acoma*, I too pray that I "may be guided and guarded by Sitch-tche-na-ko (Thought Woman), the spirit of reason" in organizing and writing down the historical facts that "have survived the obliterating influence of time" in the hope that all the People may live and prosper.

JOURNEY TIME

200,000 B.C.–A.D. 1679

JOURNEYS OF
THE PEOPLE

Once, while visiting a respected Lenape teacher, I mistakenly asked the word, "Why?" I was scolded immediately and told that I sounded just like a "sha-wa-nuk" or "white person" because "white people" are always asking "why this" or "why that." The teacher instructed me to be like my clan, the Turtle. "Just listen; it takes the turtle a long time to get somewhere, but it knows where it has been. Listen!!"[6]

Contrary to popular opinion, the People of the sovereign nations have traveled extensively all across Turtle Island for considerably more than two hundred thousand years. The earliest chronology is that of the *Wallam Olum* of the Lenni Lenape, or Lenape, which begins with their *return* journey from Asia to their original homelands in what is now Delaware. The word *return* is emphasized because archaeologists have uncovered evidence which provides proof that toolmaking peoples were living in the Mojave Desert region of California in about 200,000 B.C.

The first division follows the return journey of the Lenape from Asia to the East Coast of North America, where the sun first touches the land. Listen to the stories of the People of the sovereign nations and tribes.

	HISTORY/LAW/ POLITICS	LITERATURE/ART/ LEGENDS AND STORIES
200,000 TO 50,000 B.C.	Prehistoric stone tools discovered at Calico Hills in the Mojave Desert east of Los Angeles, California, provide evidence that Calico Native toolmakers were living in the region two hundred thousand years ago. Stone Age tools uncovered in the area now known as San Diego, California, provide evidence of Native People living in that region one hundred thousand years ago.	Among the Ak-mul Au-authm (known as the Pima people of what is now Arizona and southeastern California) is the creation story of the Great Mystery, who takes light and hurls it into the void and creates the stars, the Woman Moon, and the Man Sun. It is said that the Great Mystery then creates Coyote, who is composed of laughter and mischief.
50,000 TO 30,000 B.C.	Excavations at Santa Rosa Island in California reveal that Native people lived in the area approximately forty thousand years ago. China Lake in California is one of the earliest sites where Native people lived, approximately thirty-seven thousand years ago.	The Keres, living in what is now New Mexico, tell of E-yet-e-co, the mother of all life, who calls the People from their lodging deep inside a pit to live on the earth. Led by Mausay and Oyoyave, the hero brothers, the People come out from the place they call Shi-pahpu and visit strange lands. It also is said that the People have many adventures during their journey.
30,000 TO 10,000 B.C.	Native Peoples are living in th e area now known as southern New England. Native Peoples are living in the southwestern region of Turtle Island, now known as Nevada, Utah, Arizona, Colorado, New Mexico, Kansas, Oklahoma, and Texas. The Lenni Lenape, or Lenape, begin their return journey from Asia to Turtle Island (now known as the United States).	The *Wallam Olum*, the oldest known historical record, depicts the journey of the Lenape to the East Coast of Turtle Island (now known as the Delaware area).
10,000 TO 5,000 B.C.	Corn (maize), beans, squash, pumpkins, tomatoes, and other food plants not found anywhere else in the world are cultivated first on Turtle Island. Agricultural and sedentary village life becomes widespread. Native Peoples in various areas across Turtle Island invent and build elaborate irrigation projects for agricultural use. In what is now western Minnesota, the Browns Valley Native People hunt for food with spears whose points are made of chipped flint.	Native Peoples, called Old Copper people living in what is now the western Great Lakes area from northern Illinois to Lake Superior, are the first workers of metal anywhere in the world. They develop the process of annealing—heating and then cooling metal. Working with pieces of raw copper, they create decorative art such as beads, finger rings, and bracelets. They also make knives, axes, and spear points.

At the beginning, the sea everywhere covered the earth. Above extended a swirling cloud, and within it the Great Spirit moved. Primordial, everlasting, invisible, omnipresent—the Great Spirit moved. Bringing forth the sky, the earth, the clouds, the heavens. Bringing forth the day, the night, the stars. Bringing forth all of these to move in harmony.7

Wallum Olum

200,000 TO 50,000 B.C.

I say there are many paths and how can you know the best path unless you have walked them all? I am one hundred and one, and I know that sometimes many paths go to the same place.

White Calf (Piegan Blackfoot States)

50,000 TO 30,000 B.C.

Cliff Palace

COURTESY OF THOMAS E. ALLEN

There is a place where the sacred records [of the Lenape] are deposited in the Indian country. These records are made on one side of bark and board plates, and are examined once [every] fifteen years, at which time the decaying ones are replaced by new plates. . . . The guardians had for a long time selected a most unsuspected spot, where they dug fifteen feet, and sunk large cedar poles around the excavation. In the center was placed a large hollow cedar log, besmeared at one end with gum. The open end is uppermost, and in it are placed the records after having been enveloped in the down of geese or swans.

Kahgegagahbowh, or George Copway (Ojibwa)

30,000 TO 10,000 B.C.

Nothing lives long except the earth and the mountains.

Black Kettle (Southern Cheyenne)

10,000 TO 5,000 B.C.

	HISTORY/LAW/ POLITICS	LITERATURE/ART/ LEGENDS AND STORIES
5,000 TO 3,000 B.C.	Red Paint people occupy what is now Blue Hill Bay in Maine. The Lenape are victorious in war with their enemies, who are confined to the coastal areas of what is now Alaska. This enables the Lenape to move deeper into the evergreen land of the Alaskan and Canadian interior. Anasazi people living in what is now the southwestern United States develop the mano and metate for grinding.	Olmec people of what is now Mexico and Central America create a variety of sculptures (or sculpted objects) from jade.
3,000 TO 2,000 B.C.	The victorious Lenape continue their journey farther up the Yukon valley. The Hopi and other Native Peoples across Turtle Island are visited by Ta-Chang and Shu-Hai, assistants of the Great Yu of China, who had sent them to survey the world. Evidence in a rock shelter in what is now west-central New Mexico confirms that Native People occupying the cave were engaged in agricultural projects.  *Nompeyo, or Harmless Snake (Hopi)* <small>COURTESY OF SMITHSONIAN</small>	Poverty Point people in what is now known as the lower Mississippi valley create pendants, buttons, beads, carvings, and other decorative art using such stones as limonite, galena, quartz, green and red talc, amethyst, feldspar, and red jasper. Native artisans living in what is now Georgia and Florida make fired earthenware ceramics. Beads from marine shells are made by Native artisans living in what is now western New York state.
2,000 TO 1,500 B.C.	The first people inhabiting the Ashiwi, or Zuñi area, in what is now western New Mexico, hunt big and small game, collect wild plants, and engage in agricultural projects.	Evidence of pottery made by Native People in the southwest area of Turtle Island is confirmed. The culture referred to as "pottery culture" spreads throughout Turtle Island.

Among the Iroquois, the storyteller was often an older relative, perhaps a grandparent, an aunt or uncle, someone who remembered the stories from long ago. Although young people learned stories at an early age, it was almost always one of the older men or women who did the actual telling, since elders were always treated with great deference.

Joseph Bruchac III (Abenaki)

5,000 TO 3,000 B.C.

Wapallanewa, or the White Eagle (Lenape), is the visionary explorer who crosses the Bering Strait and leads the People on their return journey to Turtle Island to their new home in the Yukon River valley, which they call Akomen (c. 3000 b.c.).

Kolawil, or Noble Elder (Lenape), is selected Great Sachem, or leader, of the Lenape. He is the first in a succession of ninety-six great sachems listed in the *Wallam Olum.* Kolawil is the leader when the Lenape engage in war with their enemies in what is now Alaska (c. 2800 b.c.).

Wapagokhos, or the White Owl (Lenape), becomes the Great Sachem and leads the Lenape up the Yukon valley (c. 2600 b.c.).

Janotowi Enolowin, or Keeping Guard (Lenape), is selected Great Sachem of the Lenape after Wapagokhos. Along with the People, Janotowi Enolowin is wary and watchful of the Snakes—the enemies of the Lenape (c. 2400 b.c.).

Chilili, or Snow Bird (Lenape), becomes Great Sachem after Janotowi Enolowin and persuades half of the People to move south down the Pacific coastline to what is now the Northwest Coast, where the Lenape encounter the Tlingit and Haida. Tamakwi leads the remaining half east and travels upstream into what is now the Yukon valley of the Canadian Rockies (c. 2200 b.c.).

Ayamek, or the Seizer (Lenape), becomes the next Great Sachem of the Lenape after Chilili. He makes war on the Peoples called Snakes, Charlatans, Blackened Ones, and Stony Ones living in the region, and kills all of them (c. 2100 b.c.).

We do not walk alone. Great Being walks beside us. Know this and be grateful.

Polingaysi Qoyawayma, or Elizabeth Q. White (Hopi)

3,000 TO 2,000 B.C.

Northern Drum COURTESY OF THOMAS E. ALLEN

Little Man, all things you see around you—on earth, in the sky, and in the waters—have life in them.

Itireitok (Inuit)

2,000 TO 1,500 B.C.

	HISTORY/LAW/ POLITICS	LITERATURE/ART/ LEGENDS AND STORIES
1,500 TO 1,000 B.C.	The civilization established by Olmec people along the Gulf Coast of southern Mexico thrives and flourishes. Colored clay of red, purple, yellow, and blue, as well as white, orange, and brown sand, is used in geometric patterns on the buildings in the Olmec ceremonial centers.	Olmec artisans create highly polished concave iron mirrors which are worn as pendants by the elite of their society.
1,000 TO 500 B.C.	The technique of acid etching of designs by Hohokam peoples in what is now southwestern Arizona predates the technique in Europe by more than three hundred years. The People of the Longhouse, often referred to as the League of the Five Great Fires, or Iroquois Confederacy, is created. The Peacemaker establishes the Great Law of Peace, which is agreed to by the Mohawk, Oneida, Seneca, Cayuga, and Onondaga. Non-Native historians give a.d. 1570 as the date of the league's founding because that is when the immigrant Europeans first learned of its existence. Oral history among the People of the Longhouse places the origin of the league at about 900 b.c.	The history and genealogy of the Lenape are preserved in a form of symbol writing. Anasazi artisans develop textiles and basketry with the introduction of corn from Mexico (c. 1000 b.c.). Among the Inuit people, it is said that in the very earliest time when both people and animals lived on earth, a person could become an animal and an animal could become a human being. It is also said that the animals and people spoke the same language and that words were like magic. No one could explain how a word, spoken by chance, suddenly came alive so that all that needed to be done to make something happen was to say it.

HEROES/LEADERS/ VICTIMS	ELDER WISDOM/PHILOSOPHY/ SONGS	
Langundowi, or the Peaceful One (Lenape), is the eleventh Great Sachem listed in the Wallam Olum after Ayamek. The intervening centuries (c. 2100 to c. 1200 b.c.) are a time of great confusion among the Lenape, and none of the ten other Great Sachems is given (c. 1260 b.c.). Tasukamend, or the Blameless One (Lenape), is the next Great Sachem identified after Langundowi. Tasukamend is described as an honest and upright person (c. 1200 b.c.). Pemoholend, or Constant Love (Lenape), is the next Great Sachem after Tasukamend. He brings goodness to the Lenape (c. 1150 b.c.). Matemik, or House Maker (Lenape), is the next Great Sachem after Pemoholend (c. 1090 b.c.). Pilsohalan, or Chaste Loving (Lenape), is identified as the next Great Sachem after Matemik (c. 1030 b.c.).	We went through places where long ago my people once lived and now it is deserted with trees, weeds, growing here and there. *Lenora Palmer (White Mountain Apache)*	1,500 TO 1,000 B.C.
Gunokeni, or Long Lineage (Lenape), is the next Great Sachem of the Lenape after Pilsohalan (c. 980 b.c.). Mangipitak, or Big Teeth (Lenape), is the Great Sachem of the Lenape after Gunokeni (c. 900 b.c.). Olumapi, or History Man (Lenape), becomes the Great Sachem after Mangipitak. Olumapi is identified as the one who originates a way to preserve the history and genealogy of the Lenape in a form of symbol writing (c. 870 b.c.). Taquachi, or Frozen One (Lenape), is selected Great Sachem after Olumapi. Taquachi leads the People south from what is now the Saskatchewan River in Canada to a warmer climate in the Great Plateau region near the Snake River (c. 810 b.c.). Huminiend, or Hominy Man (Lenape), is the next Great Sachem identified after Taquachi who leads the People in raising crops and gathering food (c. 750 b.c.). Alkosohit, or the Subdivider (Lenape), becomes Great Sachem after Taquachi and is described as being helpful in ensuring an abundance of food for the People (c. 700 b.c.). Shiwape, or Shriveled Man (Lenape), is named Great Sachem after Alkosohit and builds on the good fortune of his predecessors in raising and harvesting crops (c. 650 b.c.). Penkwonwi, or Drought (Lenape), becomes the civil leader of the People. A drought of epic proportion results in starvation and death for many of the Lenape (c. 600 b.c.). Wekwochella, or Exhaustion (Lenape), is chosen civil leader as the People continue to die from starvation. The People are unable to plant or harvest any crops because there is no rain and the rivers have dried up (c. 550 b.c.). Hienwatah (not Hiawatha) is the principal speaker for the Peacemaker. Jigonsaseh (Iroquois), the most powerful of all Iroquois women, supports the efforts of the Peacemaker and Hienwatah in bringing together the five sovereign nations which always had been at war with one another.	. . . whenever they shall assemble for the purpose of holding a council . . . [they] . . . shall make an address and return thanks to the earth where [the People] dwell, to the streams of water, the pools, the springs, and the lakes, to the maize and the fruits, to the medicinal herbs and trees, to the forest trees for their usefulness, to the animals that serve as food and give their pelts for clothing. . . . *The Peacemaker*	1,000 TO 500 B.C.

HISTORY/LAW/ POLITICS	LITERATURE/ART/ LEGENDS AND STORIES
500 TO 400 B.C. Lenape survivors of the continuing drought journey east in search of a new home beyond the Rocky Mountains with the hope of finding food and animals for hunting. The Adena culture, or Mound Builders, flourishes in what is now Ohio, Indiana, Kentucky, West Virginia, and Pennsylvania.	Adena artisans create wood engravings, of which more than two hundred are discovered in 1845, about twenty-three centuries later.
400 TO 300 B.C. Hopewell peoples residing in the Ohio valley region build immense geometric earthworks. The ceremonial complex near what is now Newark, Ohio, covers four square miles. The enclosures, or buildings, which are circular, square, and octagonal, are connected by wide, walled avenues.	Adena artisans create pots and other household objects decorated with incised geometric designs.
300 TO 200 B.C. Adena peoples institute the practice of entombing their dead in conical earthen mounds. Native People of the Southwest (now New Mexico and Arizona) live in villages of three- and four-story apartmentlike houses.	Adena artisans create artistic objects from exotic materials. The objects are distinctive in design, such as wolf masks, polished stone tablets, tubular stone pipes, beads made from shells, and ornaments cut from sheets of mica. Native artisans living in what is now Colorado, New Mexico, and Arizona make pottery with highly artistic designs.
200 TO 1,100 B.C. The influence of Ohio valley Adena culture and traditions spreads east to what is now Delaware, Maryland, and New York.	Adena artisans carve elaborate stone effigy pipes and effigy figures for burial ceremonies.

Tdu-u-eh-t'sah, or Like-A-Song, or
Ethel Gunn Haynes Gottlieb Franics (Laguna Pueblo/Chippewa)

HEROES/LEADERS/ VICTIMS	ELDER WISDOM/PHILOSOPHY/ SONGS	
Chingalsuwi, or the Hardened One (Lenape), is the next civil leader after Wekwochella who leads the starving Lenape to the east (c. 500 b.c.). Kwitikwand, or the Denouncer (Lenape), is the next civil leader after Chingalsuwi. Some of the People who are angry with Kwitikwand's leadership leave secretly and journey east (c. b.c. 440).	The great sea has sent me adrift. It moves me as the weed in a great river. Earth and the great weather move me. Have carried me away. And move my inward parts with joy. *Uvavnuk, Eskimo holy woman*	500 TO 400 B.C.
Wakaholend, or the Beloved One (Lenape), becomes the Great Sachem and leads the People who remained under the leadership of Kwitikwand on a journey to the Yellow River (Yellowstone). In that fertile area, the People hunt and grow and harvest abundant crops (c. 390 b.c.). Tamanend, or Tamanend I (Lenape), is identified as the next Great Sachem after Wakaholend. Tamanend I is the first of three leaders by that name among the Lenape (c. 340 b.c.).	It is from the land that each true Hopi gathers the rocks, the plants, the different woods, roots, and his life, and each in the authority of his rightful obligation brings to our ceremonies proof of our ties to this land. *Religious leaders of Shongopovi (Hopi)*	400 TO 300 B.C.
Maskansisil, or Mighty Bison (Lenape), becomes the Great Sachem after Tamanend I. Maskansisil is also known as the Pathmaker (c. 290 b.c.). Machigokhos, or the Great Owl (Lenape), becomes the Great Sachem after Maskansisil (c. 240 b.c.).	There is the world that is in the mind, heart and soul that each of us carries with us at all times. It is a beautiful place where I feel the joy and gratitude for the sun which appears each morning . . . a joy of being, when the smell outdoors is fresh, clean, and quivering with the expectancy of what is to come . . . the gradual warming of the earth and the smell of its richness and fertility. This is the world I treasure. *Tdu-u-eh-t'sah (Laguna)*	300 TO 200 B.C.
Wapkicholen, or White Crane (Lenape), is identified as the next Great Sachem after Machigokhos (c. 190 b.c.). Wingenund, or the Willing One (Lenape), the Great Sachem after Wapkicholen, is also an herbalist who presides over great festivals (c. 140 b.c.).	. . . the earth is our mother. She nourishes us. That which we put into the ground she returns to us. *Bedagi, or Big Thunder (Wabnakis)*	200 TO 1,100 B.C.

	HISTORY / LAW / POLITICS	LITERATURE / ART / LEGENDS AND STORIES
100 B.C. TO 0 A.D.	The ideas and practices of the Hopewell people are adopted widely in the eastern half of what is now the United States, from Canada to Florida.	Highly skilled artisans of what is known as the Hopewell culture create delicate artwork, including spool-shaped earrings from copper, as well as ornaments made from mica, silver, and tortoiseshell.
A.D. 1 TO 100	Pit houses, quadrangular and rounded, known as kivas are occupied by Native People in what is now Colorado, Oklahoma, New Mexico, Texas, Arizona, and Utah. Kivas of today are almost identical to those built almost two thousand years ago.	Native potters of the southern New England region create ceramic vessels of clay with delicate decorative motifs.
100 TO 200	Hohokam peoples create massive irrigation projects to grow crops in what are now the lowland deserts of Arizona. Mogollon peoples are the first to adopt the bow and arrow in the Southwest.	The Hohokam mold rubber from the Mexican lowlands into a ball to play a game like a combination of soccer and basketball on an elaborate playing field constructed on the desert sand of what is now Arizona. Among the Tlingit, it is said that Raven created West Wind, and no matter how hard it would blow, West Wind would not hurt anyone. Raven then created South Wind, who climbed on top of a rock and never stopped blowing. After that, Raven made North Wind, and on top of a mountain made a house for North Wind with ice hanging down the sides. This is why, it is said, that mountains are white with snow.
200 TO 300	The Lenape continue their journey across the Great Plains until they reach the Mississippi River, which they follow downstream to where it meets the Missouri River, near what is now St. Louis, Missouri. It is here, at the great city of the Mound Builder culture known as Cahokia—the spiritual, political, and business center often described as a combination of New York, Washington, D.C., and Jerusalem—where the Lenape meet the peoples they call the Talega, in about 280.	Hohokam artisans create pottery of brown and smudged plain ware. Among the Skagit, it is said that Suelick created four powers—Schodelick, Swadick, Hode, and Stoodke. It is said that Schodelick came to Skagit country (upper Washington state), where he created a man, a woman, and some land. Schodelick put fish in the rivers and lakes and showed man and woman how to catch, clean, and eat the fish. After Schodelick completed his work, he dived into the water, where he still lives.
300 TO 400	The Talega grant permission to the Lenape to pass through Talega land in the search for a new homeland. As the Lenape peacefully begin to cross the Mississippi, Talega warriors attack and massacre those who already had crossed. Iroquois from the North unite in an epic battle with the Lenape against the Talega. The allies attack and capture many of the Talega villages in about 370.	Anasazi artisans create pottery for trade with their Hohokam neighbors.

HEROES/LEADERS/ VICTIMS	ELDER WISDOM/PHILOSOPHY/ SONGS	
Lapawin, or Rich Again (Lenape), is listed as the next Great Sachem after Wingenund (c. 100 b.c.). Wallama, or Painted Red (Lenape), becomes Great Sachem after Lapawin (c. 50 b.c.). Waptipatit, or White Chick (Lenape), is the Great Sachem identified after Wallama. The golden age under Tamanend I ends in civil war, with bloodshed in the south and north (c. 2 b.c.).	The earth is referred to as our Mother. . . . Everything that the Hopi survived with came from the earth . . . everything for sustaining life came from the earth. . . . When you still go out and plant a field, you talk to your cornfield just like you talk to your mother. Because these things come from her. Just like a child gets nourishment from its mother, the Hopi—and humans—get nourishment from the earth. *Elders of the Reed and Snake (Hopi)*	**100 B.C. TO 0 A.D.**
Tamaskan, or Mighty Wolf (Lenape), is Great Sachem. He is described as crafty and strong. He kills Strong Stone, the leader of the Stonies (c. a.d. 45). Messissuwi, or Whole Hearted (Lenape), is Great Sachem of the Lenape who fights the Snakes (c. a.d. 90).	And how does it feel to be Indian? That may well be the most important question of the day. Let me ask you a question in return. Hopefully, your answer will be the same as mine. Do you enjoy being a human being? *Roy A. Young Bear (Mesquakie)*	**A.D. 1 TO 100**
Chitanwulit, or Strong Is Good (Lenape), is Great Sachem who leads the people in battle against the Wyandot (c. 140). Alokuwi, or Poor One (Lenape), is Great Sachem who leads the Lenape warriors against the invaders thought to be Athabascan- or Siouan-speaking Peoples (c. 190).	. . . you should leave one bite of food on your plate and offer it to the spirits. That way you will always have enough to eat. You must remember your ancestors so they will remember you. *Carol Lee Sanchez (Laguna Pueblo)*	**100 TO 200**
Opekasit, or East Looking (Lenape), is Great Sachem who has a vision and leads the People on the long journey east across the Great Plains, where they first meet and become friends with the Iroquois people (c. 230). Yagawanend, or the Lodge Man (Lenape), is the Great Sachem who leads the People from the Great Plains to the Mississippi River and down it until it meets the Missouri (c. 280).	Respect for elders was taught from the beginning and it didn't take a teacher to teach these values. We just watched, learned, and followed our elders. *Alfred Stalker (Noatak Inupiat)*	**200 TO 300**
Chitanitis, or Strong Ally (Lenape), is Great Sachem who asks the grand leader of the Talega for land on which the Lenape may settle, but the request is denied. Chitanitis leads the People east across the Mississippi River in search of a new homeland (c. 330). Kinehepend, or Sharp One (Lenape), is Great Sachem who leads the war of revenge against the Talega (c. 370).	The Great Spirit made the flowers, the streams, the pines, the cedars—takes care of them . . . lets a breeze go through there, makes them breathe it, waters them, makes them grow. *Peter Catches (Oglala Lakota)*	**300 TO 400**

	HISTORY/LAW/ POLITICS	LITERATURE/ART/ LEGENDS AND STORIES
400 TO 500	The bow and arrow are introduced into the Plains area and used by the Blackfeet, Cree, and Arapaho, who are all descendants of the Lenape.	Hohokam and Mogollon artisans exchange artistic ceramics. Hopewell artisans create highly prized art objects of obsidian from what is now Wyoming, shells from what is now the Florida coasts, galena from what is now the Missouri Ozarks and upper Mississippi valley, copper from what is now the Lake Superior area, mica from what is now North Carolina, and chalcedony from what is now North Dakota.
500 TO 600	The Wyandot Iroquois, with their allies the Lenape, after winning the battle against the Talega people, take the land north around the Great Lakes, and the Lenape take the land south in the Ohio valley.	Anasazi artisans carve art objects made of turquoise at Chaco, in what is now the Four Corners region of Utah, Colorado, Arizona, and New Mexico.
600 TO 700	Hohokam peoples of what is now Arizona continue construction of houses around a central courtyard in what is known as the pioneer period, Estrella phase.	Hohokam artisans create ceramic bowls decorated on the exterior in what is called Estrella red-on-gray style. Other ornaments include rings, pendants, beads, nose and lip plugs, and carved effigy containers.
700 TO 800	Hohokam peoples of Gila Butte, during what are referred to as the colonial period, construct housing in clusters, with two to four structures centered on a common courtyard work area.	Hohokam artistry during the Gila Butte phase becomes more elaborate with the creation of the first mosaic plaques or mirrors decorated with shell and turquoise.

Ray A. Young Bear (Mesquakie)
COURTESY OF LEE FRANCIS III

HEROES/LEADERS/ VICTIMS	ELDER WISDOM/PHILOSOPHY/ SONGS	
Pimokhasuwi, or Stirring (Lenape), is the Great Sachem who continues to fight the Talega throughout what is now the Ohio valley in about 422. Said to be extremely fierce and strong, the Talega had built an earthwork stronghold now known as Fort Ancient which could hold more than ten thousand people. It had walls more than twelve feet high and five miles long. Tenchekensit, or Breaking Open (Lenape), is the Great Sachem who captures all the great towns of the Talega and leads the Lenape to victory over their enemies in about 469.	it came in various forms from the Creek & the Navajo but the message is always clear white men will come (they did) they will take the land (they did) they will nearly destroy the People (they tried) they will waste the land (they have) then they will go away (we wait). *Robert J. Conley (United Keetoowah Band Cherokee)*	400 TO 500
Paganchihilla, or the Crusher (Lenape), is the Great Sachem after Tenchekensit who drives the defeated remnants of the Talega south in about 516. The descendants of the Talega who flee to the south become the Natchez. Hattanwulaton, or Having Possession (Lenape), is Great Sachem after Paganchihilla. Hattanwulaton takes possession of the new homeland in about 563 and divides it with the Wyandot Iroquois, who were allies of the Lenape during the war with the Talega.	. . . Even a break in the cardinal balance may be restored to wholeness and harmony. Broken strands in the web of life may be repaired, as a basket out of kilter may be returned to balance if one unweaves it back to the original error, corrects it and reweaves from there. Hope strengthens the will to survive. Determination and work make survival possible. *Awiakta (Cherokee)*	500 TO 600
Gunitakan, or Long-in-the-Woods (Lenape), is the Great Sachem of the Lenape after Hattanwulaton. While Gunitakan is Great Sachem, the Iroquois initiate treacherous attacks against the Lenape, in about 610. Linniwulamen, or Truthful Man (Lenape), is Great Sachem after Gunitakan. Linniwulamen successfully stops the attacks and punishes the Iroquois for their actions, in about 657.	For more than seventy years I have hunted in this grove and fished in this stream, and for many years I have worshipped on this ground. Through these groves and over these prairies in pursuit of game our fathers roamed, and by them this land was left to us as a heritage forever. *Senachwine (Potawatomi)*	600 TO 700
Shakagapewi, or Righteous (Lenape), becomes Great Sachem after Linniwulamen, in about 705. The Iroquois greatly fear Shakagapewi. Tamaganend, or the Pathmaker (Lenape), is Great Sachem after Shakagapewi. Tamaganend leads the People into a new age of peace and abundance in about 752. The People settle in their new homeland, which they call Talega country. Wapashuwi, or White Lynx (Lenape), becomes Great Sachem after Tamaganend, in about 799. Under the leadership of Wapashuwi, the Lenape grow abundant crops and raise families.	Plants are thought to be alive, their juice is their blood, and they grow. The same is true of trees. All things die, therefore all things have life. Because all things have life, gifts have to be given to all things. *William R. Benson (Pomo)*	700 TO 800

	HISTORY/LAW/ POLITICS	LITERATURE/ART/ LEGENDS AND STORIES
800 TO 900	Mississippian culture emerges in what are now the central and lower Mississippi, lower Ohio, and Red River valleys.	Decorated pottery of the Hohokam people during the Santa Cruz phase reaches its peak. It features tightly packed and carefully rendered patterns.
900 TO 1000	The Ashiwi, or Zuñi, build the Village of the Great Kivas, about sixteen miles north of Zuñi in what is now New Mexico. The Village of the Great Kivas consists of six kiva centers or clusters. The Great Center at Cahokia, at what is now East Saint Louis, Illinois, is established. It covers approximately 125 square miles.	Anasazi artisans of the Four Corners region of what is now New Mexico, Arizona, Utah, and Colorado create art objects from turquoise and shells.
1000 TO 1100	Eight Native People of what is now Nova Scotia are killed by Thorvald, the Viking son of Erik the Red. Cahokia peoples build Monks Mound, located at what is now the outskirts of East St. Louis, across the Mississippi River in St. Clair County, Illinois, which is seven miles northeast of Cahokia, Illinois, which covers approximately forty acres. It is the most massive completely earthen monument on Turtle Island. Etowah, in what is now northern Georgia, is settled by Cahokia peoples.	Mogollon artisans living in what is now New Mexico, along the Mimbres River, begin to create highly artistic pottery with designs painted in black on white (1000). *Robert J. Conley* *(United Keetowah Band Cherokee)* COURTESY OF DAN AGENT
1100 TO 1200	Anasazi people, in a mass exodus, abandon Pueblo Bonito, in what is now New Mexico's Chaco Canyon (1150).	Cahokian artists at Moundville, near present Tuscaloosa, Alabama, create pottery, effigy pipes, and statues in addition to making beads and copper ornaments.

HEROES/LEADERS/ VICTIMS	ELDER WISDOM/PHILOSOPHY/ SONGS	
Wulitshinik, or Fine Forests (Lenape), becomes Great Sachem after Wapashuwi. The families of the People continue to grow (c. 846). Lekhihitin, or the Author (Lenape), is Great Sachem after Wulitshinik. Working with records dating as far back as Olumapi, or History Man, Lekhihitin adds the recent adventures to the *Wallam Olum* (c. 893).	If you are to be a leader . . . you must listen in silence to the mystery, the spirit. *Leaf Dweller (Kaposia Sioux)*	**800 TO 900**
Kolachuisen, or Pretty Bluebird (Lenape), is identified as Great Sachem after Lekhihitin, in about 940. The People continue to have great harvests while Kolachuisen is their leader. Pematilli, or Always There (Lenape), becomes Great Sachem after Kolachuisen. In about 987, while Pematilli is Great Sachem, the People build many new towns to house the rapidly growing Lenape population.		**900 TO 1000**
Pepomahemen, or Navigator (Lenape), becomes Great Sachem after Pematilli. The Lenape travel in canoes on the Ohio and Mississippi Rivers, along with other traders in about 1034. Tankawon, or Little Cloud (Lenape), is Great Sachem after Pepomahemen. Drought and hunger become widespread when harvests fail, and many of the People move south to what is now Kentucky. They became the Nanticoke and Shawnee. The Nanticoke journey through the Cumberland Gap into what is now Virginia and eventually settle in the Maryland tidelands. The Shawnee travel deep into the South and settle in the Appalachian valleys (c. 1081).	We must be united; we must smoke the same pipe; we must fight each other's battles; and more than all, we must love the Great Spirit. . . . *Tecumtha, or Tecumseh (Shawnee/Muscogee)*	**1000 TO 1100**
Kichitamak, or Great Beaver (Lenape), is Great Sachem after Tankawon. Kichitamak leads the People in their desperate effort to recover from the drought by moving to hunting areas that have salt licks, where animals congregate (c. 1128). Onowutok, or the Prophet (Lenape), is the visionary of the people who travels west to visit those who remained when the Lenape continued their journey to the East about twenty generations previously. Onowutok also visits the Anasazi peoples of what is now New Mexico and Arizona (c. 1176).	My people say that the earth is the mother of all things. Plants grow from the earth. Animals live on plants. The sun shines down on them and makes them grow. . . . When springtime comes all the plants turn green. . . . The Earth Mother is good to us, for we have corn, beans, squash and fruit. *E-yeh-shur, or Blue Corn, or Louise Abeita (Isleta Pueblo/Laguna Pueblo)*	**1100 TO 1200**

**1200 TO
1300**

Acoma, the Sky City, atop a high mesa in what is now western New Mexico, is a thriving village. It becomes the oldest continuously occupied town or settlement on Turtle Island.

Cahokian artisans of the center at what is now Spiro, Oklahoma, create stone effigy figurines, copper breastplates, intricately engraved shell cups, headdresses, and masks.

Among the Haida is a story of the origin of ten supernatural beings. It is said that one day ten brothers went hunting with their dogs, and as they began to climb up a steep mountain, a very thick fog surrounded them. Unable to see through the fog to return home, the brothers made a fire. It is said that the youngest brother threw his bow into the fire, and when it was completely burned, he and his brothers were astounded to see the bow on the ground below. The youngest brother threw himself into the fire and was burned up quickly. Like the bow, the youngest brother appeared, completely unharmed, on the ground below. So following their youngest brother's example, the other nine brothers also threw themselves into the fire one by one. As each was consumed quickly by the flames, he appeared on the ground below with his other brothers. It is said that after all the brothers were on the level ground below, they returned home.

**1300 TO
1400**

The Cahokian center at Spiro, Oklahoma, becomes a major ceremonial center in the early 1300s, but declines, along with the other great Cahokian centers, in about 1400.

Hohokam artisans of the Tucson basin create red-on-buff pottery, and art objects of obsidian, such as figurines.

It is said among the Ojibwa that Waubun was the guardian of youth and knowledge. As Waubun became more knowledgeable, he challenged Ningobianong, the guardian of age and wisdom, to a contest of powers. It is said that although Waubun's powers were great, Ningobianong completely nullified them, and this is when the struggle between youth and age, knowledge and wisdom began.

The Indian Fort Sasquesahanok and Map of Delaware
COURTESY OF SMITHSONIAN

1200 TO
1300

Pawanami, or Rich Turtle (Lenape), is Great Sachem after Kichitamak. While Pawanami is leader, the People survive a great flood (c. 1201).

Lokwelend, or Traveler (Lenape), becomes Great Sachem after Pawanami. Lokwelend leads the People in battle against their old enemies from the Great Plains and Rockies, who are now referred to as the Shoshone and the Sioux (c. 1238).

Mokolmokom, or Canoe Master (Lenape), identified as the Great Sachem after Lokwelend, leads the warriors among the People against their enemies. Their canoes carry the warriors in all directions. Those traveling north go as far as what is now the Great Lakes of Michigan and Wisconsin. The Lenape who settle in the North become what are known now as the Menominee, Odawa, or Ottawa, Sauk, Mesquakie, or Fox, and Potawatomi peoples (c. 1266).

Winelowich, or Hunter-in-Snow (Lenape), is Great Sachem when the People continue their expansion to the Far North beyond the Great Lakes which is now Canada. While there, the People encounter those now known as the Cree, Montaignais, and Canadian Algonkian (c. 1283).

Pleasant it looked, this newly created world. Along the entire length and breadth of the earth, our grandmother, extended the green reflection of her covering and the escaping odors were pleasant to inhale.

Ho'Chunk prayer song

Linkwekinuk, or the Beholder (Lenape), is Great Sachem during the time when two-thirds of the People travel through the Alleghenies. A third of the People remain in the land of the Talega (c. 1304).

Wapalawikwan, or Eastern Home (Lenape), becomes Great Sachem after Linkwekinuk. Wapalawikwan is leader of the People who settle in the land of plenty and have no enemies (c. 1323).

Gikenopalat, or Trailblazer (Lenape), is Great Sachem who leads the People north (c. 1342).

Hanaholend, or River Loving (Lenape), is identified as Great Sachem who leads the People along the Susquehanna (c. 1360).

Gattawisi, or Near Fulfilled (Lenape), is Great Sachem after Hanaholend. Gattawisi leads the People to the abundant, green region of what is now eastern Pennsylvania (c. 1379).

Makhiawip, or Red Arrow (Lenape), becomes Great Sachem after Gattawisi. The People finally reach the place from which they began their journey hundreds of thousands of years before—the great salt sea of the East Coast, somewhere near what is now New Jersey or Delaware (c. 1397).

1300 TO
1400

. . . these white men . . . [were] . . . always telling us of their great Book which God had given them. . . . While they held the big Book in one hand, in the other they held murderous weapons—guns and swords— . . . to kill us poor Indians. . . . They killed those who believed in their Book as well as those who did not.

Delaware Chief (Delaware)

Enchanted Mesa, Acoma, New Mexico
COURTESY OF LEE FRANCIS III

PERSPECTIVE

1400 — 1540

Prior to the arrival of immigrants from across the great waters of the East there were, by conservative estimates, at least thirty million People of the sovereign nations and tribes living all across Turtle Island from what is now Alaska to Florida, from Newfoundland to the Baja, from Canada to Mexico. From 200,000 B.C. through A.D. 1400, the records of the *Wallam Olum* and archaeological evidence clearly point to the fact that the People of the sovereign nations and tribes were not a sedentary people confined to a limited geographical area.

From the limited amount of remaining evidence, it is possible to trace the sweeping movements of the People of the sovereign nations and tribes all across Turtle Island from the earliest of times.

By the beginning of the 1400s, stories handed down from generation to generation by the People tell of the times they had encountered the very first strangers exploring their ancient lands. The stories were passed from sovereign nation to sovereign nation and eventually, no doubt, became exaggerated in the telling. The point is that the People of the sovereign nations and tribes were well aware of the "strange white beings" who visited the lands of the People or those of their neighbors near or far. Those strangers did not stay for any length of time and had only brief contact with the People.

The Island Arawak were the first people of a sovereign nation to endure the continuous presence of the strangers, led by that erstwhile entrepreneur, Christopher Columbus. This enterprising young man had sold his vision for a new sea route to "India," where he planned to buy spices and other luxuries treasured by the folks back home for resale. As the story goes, Columbus journeyed by boat to "the New World," where he and his cohorts promptly began to despoil the land and enslave the people.

A decade later, the Portuguese captured and enslaved shiploads of the People who had lived in what is now Labrador and Newfoundland for untold generations. Thus began the tragedy in earnest. Explorers, traders, merchants, and mercenaries from the "Old World" came to the lands of the People of the sovereign nations and tribes with one thought in mind—conquer and kill the People and possess their lands in the name of the immigrants' god, monarch, and country.

For the most part, the People of the sovereign nations and tribes were initially curious but unconcerned about the arrival of the strange beings. As the enslavement, massacres, land possession, and disease began to exact a toll on the People, the curiosity turned to distrust and reluctant accommodation whenever possible. Yet even with accommodation, the horrors inflicted by the conquerors on the People all across Turtle Island continued unabated.

By the 1530s, the People began to understand that accommodation of the strangers from across the ocean was more costly than they had thought possible. Devastated by smallpox, measles, cholera, starvation, massacres, slavery, and kidnapping, the People replaced hospitality toward the immigrant strangers with stoic reserve and toleration, or frantic determination to stop the immigrants from establishing permanent settlements. Such determination merely delayed the inevitable.

	HISTORY/LAW/ POLITICS	LITERATURE/ART/ LEGENDS AND STORIES
1400 TO 1500	The Taino (Island Arawak) encounter Christopher Columbus at what is now Watling's Island in the Bahamas, which Columbus names San Salvador. The population of the island is estimated at 125,000. The North American continent at that time is estimated to have more than 30 million People of the sovereign nations and tribes (October 1492).· Micmac people living in what is now Maine encounter John and Sebastian Cabot, who kidnap three Micmac and take them back to England. 	Creative artwork by People of the sovereign nations and tribes living in population centers throughout Turtle Island continues to flourish. Among the Cherokee, it is said that in the beginning there was no fire and the world was cold until the lightning from the Thunders created fire in the bottom of a hollow sycamore tree which grew on an island. It is said that Water Spider created a tusti, or small bowl, and then she crossed over to the island. When Water Spider reached the place where the fire was burning in the sycamore tree, she put a coal of fire into her bowl and then brought fire to the People. It is said that Water Spider still keeps her tusti.
1501	Two shiploads of Native People living in the area now known as Labrador and Newfoundland are captured and sold into slavery by Portuguese explorer Gaspar Côrte-Real.	Among the Wyandot, it is said that once some small boys danced for several days and nights without being given anything to eat. It is said that they were very hungry but no one would feed them, so they just kept dancing and began to float into the sky. When the People saw this, they brought some food for the boys, but it was too late and the People cried in despair. It is said that as one of the boys looked back, he fell from the sky and became a cedar tree. The others appeared in the sky as the seven stars which are now called "the Cluster."
1502–1503	Micmac living in the area now known as Newfoundland encounter more explorers from Europe of the Anglo-Portuguese Syndicate. People of the sovereign nations and tribes of what is now Honduras and Panama encounter Christopher Columbus on his fourth and final voyage.	Among the Seneca is the story of the grandmother and her grandson who challenged the mysterious being of the West. It is said that the mysterious being was determined to harm the young man and his grandmother. After many encounters with the mysterious being of the West, the young man finally discovered that a green frog in the middle of a dried-up lake was the mysterious being who had been tormenting him and his grandmother. It is said that the young man traveled west to the dried-up lake and with a quick blow of a stick, killed the creature. From that time on, the grandmother lived in peace and quiet.

HEROES/LEADERS/ VICTIMS	ELDER WISDOM/PHILOSOPHY/ SONGS	
Wolumenap, or Good Inscribed (Lenape), is Great Sachem after Makhiawip. The People continue to travel to the great falls, now called Niagara Falls (c. 1416). Wulitpallat, or Good Fighter (Lenape), becomes Great Sachem after Wolumenap and leads many of the people north to what is now the New England region. These people eventually become known as the Massachuset, Nipmuc, Narraganset, Pequot, Wampanoag, Montauk, and Mahican (c. 1434). Lippitamenend, or Tamanend II (Lenape), is Great Sachem after Wulitpallat. Lippitamenend brings all the Lenape tribes together in peace. The capital of the People is near Shackamaxon, by the Delaware River, close to what is now Philadelphia (c. 1450). Kichitamak, or Great Beaver (Lenape), is Great Sachem after Lippitamenend. Kichitamak lives in what is now eastern Pennsylvania (c. 1477). Wapahakey, or Dawn Ground (Lenape), becomes Great Sachem. He settles along the eastern shore of Turtle Island (c. 1486). Elangomel, or Harmonizer (Lenape) is selected Great Sachem after Kichitamak. Elangomel does much good among the People (c. 1495).	When most people think of slavery in the United States, they think only of the [African-American]. Christopher Columbus initiated the enslavement of Native Americans by Europeans in 1494 by sending more than 500 of them to Spain to be sold. *Jack D. Forbes (Rappahannock/Delaware)*  *Alice Hatfield Azure (Mi'kmaq)* <small>COURTESY OF HOLLYWOOD GLAMOUR PORTRAITS</small>	**1400 TO 1500**
	Columbus goes back to Europe and claims that he found a New World. This world was not "lost." *Pablo Abeita (Isleta)*	**1501**
Hatuay (Island Arawak), it is said, curses the day that Christopher Columbus came to the Arawak homeland.	In school I was taught the names Columbus, Cortez, and Pizarro and a dozen other filthy murderers. . . . No one mentioned the names of even a few of the victims. *Jimmie Durham (Cherokee)*	**1502–1503**

	HISTORY/LAW/ POLITICS	LITERATURE/ART/ LEGENDS AND STORIES
1504–1507		Among the Ashiwi, or Zuñi, is the story of how Awonawilona is created. It is said that the Creator gave the sea part of the Creator's essence and then hatched it with the Creator's heat, and green scums were formed which became Earth and Sky. It is said that from Mother Earth and Father Sky came all the creatures.
1508–1512	People of the sovereign nations and tribes living along the East Coast from what is now Florida to Charleston, South Carolina, encounter English explorers seeking possible sites for establishing colonies. Native People of the Yucatán coast discover Spanish survivors of a shipwreck. Two men, Aguilar and Guerrero, are made slaves by Mayan people.	Among the Pawnee is the story of the boy who grew up to become a bear man. It is said that before the boy was born, his father, who was hunting, came upon a small bear cub. The father placed some sacred tobacco around the cub and asked that Tiráwa—the Great Spirit—take care of the small animal. When the father returned home, he told his pregnant wife about the bear cub. She kept thinking about the cub every day until her son was born. That is why, it is said, the boy became more and more like the bear as he continued to grow and become a man.
1513–1518	Timucua peoples encounter Juan Ponce de León, who had been on Columbus' second voyage. Ponce de León arrives April 3 near what is now Daytona Beach, Florida. He gives the name of Florida to what he thinks is an island. He captures Timucua people and keeps them as slaves, to work with slaves imported from Africa, on the plantations and ranches on the larger islands of the Caribbean—Hispaniola, Puerto Rico, Jamaica, and Cuba. The Taino (Island Arawak) Nation is decimated by disease brought by Columbus and other Spanish conquerors. Of an estimated population of 250,000, only 14,000 remain by 1513. Island Arawak living on the island now known as Cuba encounter Diego de Velázquez, who establishes the settlement of Santiago in 1514. Native People living in Hispaniola are slaves of Spanish conquerors brought by Columbus in 1515. A smallpox epidemic sweeps over Yucatán, killing Mayan people by the thousands in 1516.	Among the Ojibwa is a story of Nakomis, or Sky Woman, who was the first mother of the People. Residing all alone in the heavens, she asked Kitche Manitou for a companion. A companion was sent for Sky Woman, and after she conceived, the companion left her. It is said that Nakomis eventually gave birth to twins who destroyed each other, and she was alone once again.

HEROES/LEADERS/ VICTIMS	ELDER WISDOM/PHILOSOPHY/ SONGS	
Pitenumen, or Mistaken (Lenape), is Great Sachem after Elangomel. During the time of Pitenumen, the Lenape record the arrival of the Europeans.	The people that live here have both minds and hearts and good sense. Our only idea has been to live here in peace and do that which is good for the future of our people. *Black Coal (Arapaho)*	**1504–1507**
Guarionex (Arawak), principal leader at Capa, near what is now Utaudo, Puerto Rico, grants an audience to Juan Ponce de León.	When you first came we were very many and you were few. *Red Cloud (Sioux)*	**1508–1512**
	When I was a boy, I saw the white man afar off, and was told that he was my enemy. I could not shoot him as I would a wolf or a bear, yet he came upon me. My horse and fields he took from me. He said he was my friend. He gave me his hand in friendship; I took it, he had a snake in the other; his tongue was forked; he lied and stung me. *Coacoochee, or Wild Cat (Seminole)*	**1513–1518**

Goyathlay, or Geronimo (Chiricahua Apache)

HISTORY/LAW/ POLITICS	LITERATURE/ART/ LEGENDS AND STORIES
1519–1520	

<table>
<tr><td>1519–1520</td><td>Native Peoples along the western coast of Florida observe Alonso Alvarez de Piñeda's sailing ships, which travel along the Gulf Coast from Florida to the port of Vera Cruz.

The conquest of Mexico begins, and more than 120,000 people die at the hands of the Spaniard Hernán Cortés. He enters the great city of Tenochtitlán, capital of the Aztec Empire under Moctesuma, on November 8.</td><td>Among the Maidu, it is said that Kodoyanpe the Creator discovered the world, along with Coyote. With the help of Coyote, the earth is made habitable for the People. It is said that Coyote and Kodoyanpe made people out of wood but they were not suitable, and so they were turned into animals. After a while, Kodoyanpe began to suspect that Coyote was causing the problems with the wooden people. The two began to fight, and Coyote defeated Kodoyanpe. It is said that Kodoyanpe had hidden many of the wooden people, and at the end of the battle between Kodoyanpe and Coyote, the wooden people emerged from their hidden places and became the Original People.</td></tr>
<tr><td>1521</td><td>The Timucua fatally injure Juan Ponce de León when he returns to their homelands in Florida, in retaliation for his capturing and selling into slavery several shiploads of Timucua.</td><td>Among the Algonkian is the story of Glooskap and his brother Malsum, who were twins. It is said that their mother died giving birth to the twins and that Glooskap formed the sun, moon, animals, fishes, and the People from out of his mother's body. It is also said that Malsum made the mountains, valleys, serpents, and other things which would be a nuisance or trouble for the People.</td></tr>
<tr><td>1522–1523</td><td></td><td>David Boxley (Tsimsian) performing Raven Dance
<small>COURTESY OF CAROL LEE SANCHEZ</small></td></tr>
<tr><td>1524–1527</td><td>Wampanoag and Narraganset peoples are visited by Giovanni da Verrazano, a Florentine sailing on behalf of the French. His crew abducts a child from a woman elder after entering what is now New York harbor. They attempt to kidnap a young, beautiful woman of the People. She screams and successfully resists their efforts.</td><td>The Wallam Olum records the arrival of Giovanni da Verrazano, who first sights land south of what is now Cape Fear, North Carolina. He sails north along the Carolina Outer Banks, then to what is now known as New York harbor and Newfoundland, after which he returns to France.</td></tr>
</table>

HEROES/LEADERS/VICTIMS	ELDER WISDOM/PHILOSOPHY/SONGS	
Moctesuma (Aztec) dies a few days after having been wounded in battle. Cuauhtémoc (Aztec), nephew and son-in-law of Moctesuma, becomes the new ruler of the Aztec people.	. . . before the advent of the European . . . wise men foretold the coming of a strange race from the sunrise, as numerous as the leaves upon the trees, who would eventually crowd them from their fair land possessions. *Waun-na-con, or John Quinney (Stockbridge Mahican)*	**1519–1520**
	I remember the old men of my village. These old, old men used to prophesy about the coming of the white man. They would go about tapping their canes on the adobe floor of the house and call to us children. . . . Such things have come true. . . . *Flaming Arrow, or James Paytiamo (Acoma)*	**1521**
Francisco de Chicora (Yamasee) is one of sixty Yamasee captured and enslaved by Lucas Vásquez de Ayllón. On the journey from what is now Edisto Beach, Georgia, to Santo Domingo, one of the ships sinks. Of the Yamasee who survive, one is baptized under the name Francisco de Chicora. He learns Spanish and accompanies Ayllón to Spain.	I foresaw that our rule began to be destroyed. I went forth weeping that it was to bow down and be destroyed. *Aztec prophecy of obliteration* Once there was an Indian who became a Christian. He became a very good Christian; he went to church, and he didn't smoke or drink, and he was good to everyone. He was a very good man. Then he died. First he went to the Indian hereafter, but they wouldn't take him because he was a Christian. Then he went to Heaven, but they wouldn't let him in—because he was an Indian. Then he went to Hell, but they wouldn't admit him there either, because he was so good. So he came alive again and he went to the Buffalo Dance and the other dances and taught his children to do the same thing. *Mesquakie*	**1522–1523**
Francisco de Chicora (Yamasee) escapes in 1526 when Lucas Vásquez de Ayllón returns to the area near what is now Edisto Beach, Georgia, where he had abducted de Chicora in 1522.	It is better that one man should perish than that a whole nation should be destroyed. *Bender of the Pine Bow (Lenape)*	**1524–1527**

	HISTORY / LAW / POLITICS	LITERATURE / ART / LEGENDS AND STORIES
1528–1533	Apalachee people forcibly prevent the attempt by Pánfilo de Narváez, accompanied by four hundred Spaniards, to establish a colony near what is now Tampa Bay, Florida. The colonizers depart on their ship, which is shipwrecked and blown ashore onto what is now the Gulf Coast of Texas. Karankawa people living in the vicinity of what is now Galveston Island, Texas, are horrified as they watch the four survivors of Pánfilo de Narváez's sailing ship eat the dead bodies of the men washed up on the beach. One of the survivors is Álvar Núñez Cabeza de Vaca and another is an African slave named Estevánico.	Among the Shawnee is the story about a powerful people they called the Stone Giants. It is said that at one time the Stone Giants, even though powerful, lived peacefully in the area of what is now the lower Ohio valley. It is also said that they were gentle and hospitable with their neighbors. Then the Stone Giants became restless and migrated to the far Northwest—probably to Asia—where the extreme cold froze them and they became people of icy hearts. The Stone Giants were unable to stand the harsh climate and became wanderers. It is said that for untold generations, as they traveled back to their original homelands, they ravaged sovereign nations and tribes before they descended on the Iroquois, who defeated them.
1534	Micmac traders traveling in forty to fifty canoes greet French explorer Jacques Cartier at the north entrance to Chaleur Bay in what is now New Brunswick on about July 14. The Micmac, experienced in trading with Europeans, barter all their furs for knives, iron kettles, and other goods. Stadacona Iroquois in what is now the Saint Lawrence valley encounter Jacques Cartier on about July 22. Bringing their canoes alongside Cartier's sailing ship at what is now Gaspé harbour, the Stadacona Iroquois are given glass beads, combs, knives, and other goods by the French sailors.	The first list of Iroquoian words translated into French is compiled by a Jesuit priest. The list is the oldest recorded Iroquoian vocabulary.
1535	The Algonkian, Huron, and Montagnais encounter Jacques Cartier, who returns to the area in three sailing ships in mid-July and spends about eight weeks exploring what is now known as the Saint Lawrence. Stadacona settlements of Ajoaste, Starnatum, Tailla, and Sitadin, on the north shore of what is now the Saint Lawrence near Québec City, are viewed by Jacques Cartier. He anchors his ships just north of Stadacona, where the Lairet River meets the Saint Charles River. Cartier is greeted by the Stadacona (September). Stadacona peoples witness the building of a small fort by sailors left by Cartier at the Saint Charles River landing site. He continues his explorations to the town of Hochelaga, and then returns to Stadacona in early November. More than fifty Stadacona die from disease.	Stadacona artisans create collars made of shell beads, and other artistic objects such as knives of red copper.  *Marilou Awiakta (Cherokee/Appalachian)* COURTESY OF STEPHANIE HARROVER

HEROES/LEADERS/ VICTIMS	ELDER WISDOM/PHILOSOPHY/ SONGS	
Makelomush, or Much Honored (Lenape), is the Grand Sachem identified after Pitenumen. During this time, the Lenape are prosperous and happy.	Men have visions. Women have children. *Adeline Wanatee (Mesquakie)*	**1528–1533**
Donnacona (Stadacona Iroquois), leader of the fishing and trading Stadacona, is seized by Cartier, and everyone in Donnacona's canoe is forced to board the French sailing ship. In exchange for knives and small axes, Cartier forces Donnacona to send his two sons, Taignoagny and Domagaya, to France, where they learn to speak French.	The Creator made the Web of Life and into each strand put the law to govern it. Everything in the universe is part of the web. *Awiakta (Cherokee)*	**1534**
Taignoagny and Domagaya, forcibly taken by Jacques Cartier to France the previous year, return in early September and are met by their father, Donnacona. He leaves with them after a brief gathering on Cartier's sailing ship. Donnacona, principal leader of the Stadacona living in the area of what is now Québec City, tries unsuccessfully in October to prevent Cartier from continuing on a journey up the so-called Saint Lawrence to the Hochelaga, who are competitors of the Stadacona. Domagaya becomes ill from disease, which kills more than fifty of the people in mid-December. Gathering the fronds of northern white cedar (*Thuja occidentalis*), he brews a curative drink and recovers. Domagaya shows the French how to brew the drink, and they too recover from the illness, as well as from syphilis.	Culture has its beginnings in the roots and traditions which are passed from one generation to another, from elder to youth. Those elements which make up one's cultural background do not depend on where an individual lives but rather on how an individual lives. *Jacque Winter (Pohlik-lah, or Yurok/Tolowa)*	**1535**

	HISTORY/LAW/ POLITICS	LITERATURE/ART/ LEGENDS AND STORIES
1536	Several hundred Karankawa accompany the four Spanish survivors of the shipwreck off the Texas coast on their walk to western Mexico, across what is now the southwestern United States and northern Mexico. Ten Stadacona are captured on May 3 by Jacques Cartier, who forcibly takes them to France.	
1537–1538	The People of the sovereign nations and tribes of the Southwest die in massive numbers of smallpox, measles, cholera, and starvation. Their Roman Catholic Spanish conquerors continue to make slaves of the People, even though Pope Paul III outlaws slavery in all forms in his papal bull, Sublimis deus. The great pronouncement does not halt the continued enslavement of the People of the sovereign nations and tribes by Roman Catholic conquerors. The Ashiwi or Zuñi people are visited by Franciscan Fray Marcos de Niza, who give him and his small party well-tanned buffalo hides around 1538.	The Iroquois, or Haudenausaunee, or People of the Longhouse, tell of Hahnunah, the Turtle, who agreed to bear Oeh-da, the earth, on his back. It is said that earthquakes happen when Hahnunah is restless, and when Turtle moves, the oceans rise and fall in great waves.
1539	The Ashiwi, or Zuñi, execute Estevánico, the African from the west coast of Morocco who had survived the shipwreck at Galveston Island, Texas, in 1528. Estevánico had demanded women and turquoise when he arrived at Haw:kuh, the westernmost of Ashiwi towns. Estevánico's companion, Fray Marcos de Niza, flees to Mexico and tells exaggerated stories about the "Seven Golden Cities of Cibola." Apalachee people endure the presence of Hernando de Soto and six hundred soldiers who come ashore at Tampa Bay on March 25. Karankawa people living in what is now Texas die in a cholera epidemic.	Among the Siksika, or Blackfeet, it is said that Na'pi, or Old Man, made animals and birds as he traveled from south to north. Old Man made the mountains, prairies, timber, and brush first, and then after resting, Na'pi made a woman and a child of clay.

HEROES/LEADERS/ VICTIMS	ELDER WISDOM/PHILOSOPHY/ SONGS	
Donnacona (Stadacona Iroquois), his two sons, Taignoagny and Domagaya, and seven others are captured by Jacques Cartier's forces and forcibly taken to France to live at Saint-Malo. After four years, only one of the ten captives survives, but she never returns to her homeland. Wulakeningus, or Well Praised (Lenape), is Grand Sachem after Makelomush. Wulakeningus wins fame in battle against the Cherokee and Tutelo living to the south in the area now known as the Carolinas, Georgia, and Tennessee. Wulakeningus' victories gave protection to the Lenape tribes of what is now Virginia, as well as the Shawnee, by keeping the Cumberland Gap and Alleghenies open and accessible for western Lenape peoples.	Europeans always profess to have great wisdom and understanding from above, at the same time, they deceive us at will, for they regard us as fools. [Their spiritual wisdom and justice are merely a scheme] . . . to deceive Indians, to defraud them of their lands. *Gischenatsi (Shawnee)*	**1536**
	For each tribe . . . Usen created, He also made a home. In the land for any particular tribe He placed whatever would be best for the welfare of that tribe. *Goyathlay, or Geronimo (Chiricahua Apache)*	**1537–1538**
Donnacona (Stadacona Iroquois) dies in France after having been baptized a Christian.	You should say nothing against our religion, for we say nothing against yours. *Tatanka Iyotake, or Sitting Bull (Hunkpapa Lakota)*	**1539**

PERSPECTIVE
1540 — 1620

Few practicing fundamentalists—be they Muslim, Jew, or Christian—are unable to recount the more significant occurrences of their historical past. Jews, for example, can speak at length about the Exodus out of Egypt, and about their leader Moses. Muslims can tell long stories about Abraham. Christians can speak at length about the birth of Jesus of Nazareth, and the ministry of Paul and other leaders who lived and died nearly two thousand years ago. The People of the sovereign nations and tribes also remember their past with equal clarity.

What is interesting is that whatever the People remember and speak about always has been (and continues to be) disregarded by others and demeaned as "simple stories by simple people." And so we tell our stories to one another, and we remember. For the most part, the stories of the People of the sovereign nations and tribes were not written. We did not construct sentences, paragraphs, monographs, or historical compendiums. The remembering of the history of the People of a particular sovereign nation or tribe was entrusted to a particular clan or family. They were the record keepers, the historians, if you will, for their respective people.

Larger stories that impacted People of other sovereign nations and tribes—regardless of the distance—were interwoven within the stories kept by the record keepers. As an example, while the Lenni Lenape were making their return journey from Asia to the East Coast of what is now the United States, other People of the sovereign nations and tribes told about their visit to their lands. As a person who grew up among the Laguna Pueblo people in what is now western New Mexico, I remember being told a story about the People from the North who came to trade. These northern People were, according to the Lenape story, the Lenape. Although I did not know the "identity" of the northern People of the story I was told, nonetheless I knew that those People had come to our land to trade and tell their stories.

These ancient stories of the journeys of the Peoples all across Turtle Island reached their nadir with the arrival of the strange people from across the great waters of the East who are able to tell their stories by looking at a "book" with "strange markings." The People of the sovereign nations and tribes easily understood the concept. Many of the eastern peoples had wampum belts that accomplished the same purpose. The difference between the wampum belts and books was that the books left no room for individual interpretation. The story was always the same, regardless of who told it, when read from a book.

The stories told by the record keepers were equal in detail except that depending on the speaker, some details were emphasized more than others. Not until highway signs, with their pictures of what a driver is permitted to do or not do (e.g., a circle with a slash means NO) has there been any way to equate the record keeping of the People of the sovereign nations and tribes with that of our non-Native relations.

The arrival of the immigrants, with their books and writing, provided the information for much of what we now know about the Peoples of the sovereign nations and tribes, from a non-Native perspective. Coupling this with our own stories, we are able to correlate our experiences with those "written" by our non-Native relations. As a result, telling about the encounters of the People of the sovereign nations and tribes with their non-Native relations becomes an easier process from 1540 to the present.

Again, as in the times when there were no "written records," it is a matter of interpretation of the story about a particular event or person as perceived by the People, in comparison to that same event or person as perceived by our non-Native relations. They tell the story of 1540 through 1620 as a great adventure and time of great excitement. With envy, they tell of the great exploits of their explorers, of their conquistadores, their skillful traders.

The People of the sovereign nations and tribes tell the story of 1540 through 1620 as a time of massacres, rapes, murders, pillaging, kidnapping, degradation, and enslavement of the People by the strangers from across the great water. We tell of the epidemics in which thousands of People all across Turtle Island die from cholera, smallpox, and measles—diseases brought to our lands by our non-Native relatives. The events and people are the same. It is the perspective which is different.

In the first decade (1540–1550), the fanatic lust for gold and treasure resulted in the deaths of thousands of women and children among the Edisto, Cusabo, Yamasee, Muscogee or Creek, Natchez, Choctaw, and others living in what is now the southeastern United States. The Hopi, living in what is now Arizona, were defeated in battle and became psychological prisoners of war, bowing to the will of the Spanish conquerors. Absolutely all their clothing, including what they were wearing, was stripped from the Tiguex people, living near what is now Alburquerque, New Mexico, by the Spanish conquistadores so they could keep themselves warm. The Stadacona living in what is now Québec, in Canada, are the notable exceptions to devastation. They thwarted French attempts to establish a colony. The decade ended with the Illinois, Shawnee, and Conoy—all Lenape tribes—coming together for a great council.

From 1550 through 1580, the rapes of the spirits, minds, hearts, and bodies of the People by the French, Spanish, English, Portuguese, and others continued. Although it is true that civil authorities attempted to protect the "rights" of Native Peoples, they continued to be enslaved, and died by the thousands at the hands of the immigrant conquerors. The French claimed land for their god, monarch, and country. The English did the same. At no time were the People of the sovereign nations and tribes aware of what was going on. It was much like the visitor declaring that he owns the house of the person he is visiting because that person is on vacation somewhere else.

The People of the sovereign nations and tribes were confounded. Like their Jewish relations of the 1930s, they were convinced mistakenly that no one in his right mind would continue to commit horrors directly resulting in the deaths of hundreds of thousands of the People. Like their docile Jewish relations who went to the death camps run by Hitler's Nazi death squads in the 1940s, the People of the sovereign nations and tribes failed to unite all across Turtle Island and expel the invaders once and for all. Instead, they permitted the English invaders to attempt the establishment of a colony at Roanoke, North Carolina.

The decade of 1590 through 1600 began with the revealing of the Iroquois League of the Five Fires to the immigrant colonists from across the sea. The invading colonists learned about the Great Law of Peace and about the Peacemaker. They heard but did not understand. On January 23, 1599, the Massacre at Acoma resulted in the deaths of fifteen hundred men, women, and children at the hands of Spanish conquerors.

Still attempting some sort of accommodation with the immigrant colonists, the leaders of the Powhatan Confederacy assisted the English colonists in establishing the first permanent settlement, at Jamestown, Virginia. The English settlers "crowned" Wahunsenacawh, Grand Sachem of the Powhatan Confederacy, and called him "King Powhatan."

From 1560 through 1620, the People of the sovereign nations and tribes were decimated by smallpox, bubonic plague, and yellow fever brought to them by their non-Native relations. The massacres, rapes, murders, pillaging, kidnapping, degradation, and slavery continued.

1540

Yuma peoples help Hernando de Alarcón as he travels up the Colorado River by boat.

The Ashiwi, or Zuñi, at Haw:kuh unsuccessfully battle against the forces of Francisco Vásquez de Coronado, who captures the town within two hours. The settlement is occupied from July to early December.

Stadacona living in the area now known as Québec City, Québec, Canada, are agitated when Jacques Cartier returns to their homeland without Donnacona and the nine other captives, as Cartier had promised four years earlier.

The Edisto, Cusabo, Yamasee, Yuchi, Muscogee, Hitchiti, Alabama, Mobile, Biloxi, Choctaw, Chickasaw, Tunica, Natchez, Chitimacha, Atakapa, Caddo, and Quapaw in what is now South Carolina, Georgia, Alabama, Mississippi, Louisiana, and Arkansas defend themselves against Hernando de Soto and his explorers. The explorers pillage, rape, kidnap, and murder on their journey from what is now Florida to Texas in search of gold and other treasures lusted after by Spanish conquerors.

Black African soldiers desert from Hernando de Soto's forces and settle in the land of the Muscogee, where they marry Muscogee women and raise families.

Tascaluza warriors fight valiantly against the forces of Hernando de Soto at their town of Mabila, near what is now Selma, Alabama, on October 18. Twenty-five hundred men, women, and children are killed in the fierce battle, which lasts one day. De Soto later dies of a fever on the banks of the Mississippi River.

Among the Keres, it is said that in the long-ago time, the People endured many hardships. Corn would not grow because there had been no rain and the land was dry. It is said that to save themselves from starvation, the People decided to move south to a place called Qeya pu kowak.

1541

The Mescalero Apache, Apache, Diné (Navajo), Tohono O'odham (Papago), and Ak-mul Au-authm (Pima) encounter Francisco Vásquez de Coronado. He is exploring the southwestern region in the vain hope of discovering the "Seven Cities of Cibola," whose streets are reputed to be paved with gold.

The Hopi are unsuccessful in their battle against Francisco Vásquez de Coronado. The defeated Hopi submit and bring presents to the invaders. The Hopi guide the Spaniards to the Grand Canyon, in what is now Arizona.

Plains Apache living in what are now known as the high plains of the Texas Panhandle encounter Coronado and his group, who are guided by Turk (Pawnee).

Quivira people, now known as the Wichita, living along what are now known as the Arkansas and Smoky Hill Rivers in central Kansas encounter Coronado's forces in search of gold, with Ysopete (Wichita) as guide.

An Alcanfor Tiguex woman is raped by the brother of a high Spanish official in Mexico. The rapist goes unpunished.

And so, it is said that in the long-ago time, crows were all white and could speak like human beings. One day, E-yet-e-co warned the crows not to pick out the eyes of dead people because they would be punished severely if they did. One crow did not listen to her and picked out an eye of a dead person. At that instant, all the crows turned black and lost the power of speech.

(continued)

1540

Bigotes (Cicúye) and Cacique (Cicúye), principal leaders of about five hundred warriors, lead a delegation from Cicúye to meet with Coronado. Cicúye, strongest of all settlements (located in what is now New Mexico), has fifty apartmentlike houses five stories high grouped around eight central squares. Bigotes and Cacique guide Coronado east to the Plains.

Agona (Stadacona Iroquois) becomes principal leader of the Stadacona after learning that Donnacona had died in France. During Donnacona's absence, Agona had been "temporary" principal leader.

The paramount leader of Cofitachique (at what is now Camden, South Carolina) successfully defends herself against Hernando de Soto's attempt to kidnap her when he arrives at her town on the Savannah River.

Comomo (Altamaca Muscogee, or Creek) is presented with a white feather adorned with silver by Hernando de Soto, who arrives with six hundred Spaniards searching in vain for gold, at Altamaca, near what is now Abbeville, Georgia (March 28).

Cooso Cacique and his sister are captured by Hernando de Soto who uses them as hostages to ensure his safe passage through Cooso lands. The main Coosa town is near what is now Cartersville, Georgia.

If you have one hundred people who live together, and if each one cares for the rest, there is One Mind.
Shining Arrows (Crow)

1541

Ysopete, or Sopete (Wichita), and Turk (Pawnee), captive slaves of the Cicúye, guide the Spaniards east to the high plains of what is now the Texas Panhandle. Hernando de Alvarado puts Bigotes, Cacique, Ysopete, and Turk in chains and returns to Alcanfor, a Tiguex settlement in what is now Bernalillo, near Albuquerque, New Mexico.

Bigotes (Cicúye), Cacique (Cicúye), Ysopete (Wichita), and Turk (Pawnee) are taken to the Tiguex settlement conquered by López de Cárdenas to witness the horror of the resistance fighters being burned alive.

I heard that long ago there was a time when there were no people in this country except Indians. After that the people began to hear of men that had white skins. Before I was born they came out to our country and visited us.
Curly Chief (Pawnee)

(continued from page 40)

1541

Tiguex people are stripped of the clothes they are wearing by Spanish conquerors collecting food and warmer clothing for themselves. The Tiguex begin to plot resistance against the Spanish invaders.

The Tiguex build palisades around distant settlements (pueblos) and begin to attack Spanish herds of horses. García López de Cárdenas storms the fortified settlements and captures resistance fighters who are fastened to stakes and burned alive.

Tiguex people abandon most of their settlements and move into two fortified settlements. Coronado leads a siege against the two, and thousands of Tiguex men, women, and children die. Afterward, Coronado burns all the settlements. The remaining survivors, mainly women and children, are captured and become slaves. The Tiguex Nation ceases to exist.

Jicarilla Apache reservation scene at Dulce, New Mexico
COURTESY OF SMITHSONIAN

	HISTORY/LAW/ POLITICS	LITERATURE/ART/ LEGENDS AND STORIES
1542	Tipai-Ipai, or Jamul Digueño, and the Peoples of the sovereign nations and tribes living in what is now San Diego, California, encounter explorer Juan Rodríguez Cabrillo when his ship sails into the area. Cabrillo, a Portuguese in the service of Spain, meets the Peoples of the sovereign coastal nations and tribes as he continues his journey north up the coast to Point Reyes, California. Chickasaw living in the area now known as Tennessee, outraged by Hernando de Soto's demands for women and carriers, attack and kill eleven invaders and most of their horses. Native Peoples of the sovereign nations and tribes along the coast of what is now California and Oregon encounter Juan Rodríguez Cabrillo, who travels as far north as the Rogue River in southern Oregon.	The Diné, or Navajo, tell of Atse'hastquin, or First Man, and Atse'esdza, or First Woman, and how they were formed in the First World. It is said that when First Man was formed, a perfectly shaped white corn with kernels covering the entire ear was formed also. When First Woman was formed, it is said, a perfect ear of yellow corn was formed along with the white shell, turquoise, and yucca plant.
1543–1554	The Stadacona thwart French attempts to establish a successful colony in the area of what is now Québec City, Québec, Canada. Explorer Jean-François de La Rocque de Roberval's colony of France-Roy is abandoned and he returns to France. French colonization of the Saint Lawrence valley does not resume until 1600.	Among the Wyandot, it is said that there was a man sitting by a river making bows and arrows. One day he saw a giant approaching and jumped into his canoe and paddled across the river. The giant, it is said, waded across, and on reaching the shore discovered the man had crossed back to the other side. It is said that the giant and the man went back and forth across the river but the giant could not catch the man.
1555–1564	Indigenous Peoples who are slaves in Mexico are freed from forced labor in the mines. The Spaniards establish a special court in Mexico in 1556 to protect the rights of Native People. Despite that, Native Peoples continue to be made slaves and continue to die by the thousands at the hands of the conquerors.	 *Clara Sue Kidwell (Choctaw/Chippewa)* <small>COURTESY OF LEE FRANCIS III</small>

HEROES/LEADERS/ VICTIMS	ELDER WISDOM/PHILOSOPHY/ SONGS	
	I love this country as I love my mother, for it is my mother. I love it as I love my father. I love its hills and mountains, and its valleys and trees and rivers, and everything that is in this country. *Osway Porter (Chickasaw)*	**1542**
Wapagamoshiki, or White Otter (Lenape), is Grand Sachem after Wulakeningus. Wapagamoshiki travels north from the Lenape homeland in what is now Delaware to establish trade with the Wyandot. Wapashum, or White Horn (Lenape), is the Grand Sachem after Wapagamoshiki who lives in the Talega country. Wapashum brings together the Illinois, Shawnee, and Conoy—all Lenape tribes—to a great council around 1549.	The Great Spirit desires that we come by another way than that used by the white people for we do not share the same path. *Scattameck (Delaware)*	**1543–1554**
Nitispayat, or Friend Coming (Lenape), is Grand Sachem after Wapashum at what is now known as the Great Lakes around 1555. Pakimitzin, or Cranberry Eating (Lenape), Grand Sachem after Nitispayat, lives in the Great Lakes area. The Lenape become good friends with the Odawa, or Ottawa, peoples of what is now Canada around 1561. Maccoa (Cusabo) is principal leader of the band that lives on what is now the south coast of South Carolina near Saint Helena Island. Maccoa cautiously receives Jean Ribault, who arrives from France in three ships with approximately 150 men. Ribault claims the land for France, unknown to the Cusabo in April 1562.	As a blond Indian, I often get . . . a sort of what's-wrong-with-this-picture reaction. I carry my own mixed metaphors into my writing, the mixed metaphors of my Norwegian-lineage blood and the mixed metaphors of the reservation I have lived on most of my life: dream messages and windowless Buicks, Salish prayers and banty roosters in '52 Chevy wagons, sun offerings and sweet, sweaty lovemaking, seven generations of memory and hope and as many generations of broken promises and broken lives. And maybe it is, finally, that in these mixed metaphors we will begin to recognize the center of our pain and passion: our humanity. *Annie Hansen (Lenape/Norwegian)*	**1555–1564**

1565–1578

People of the sovereign nations living in the area of what is now St. Augustine, Florida, witness the establishment of a permanent colony by European immigrants in September.

Robert B. Haynes (Cheppewa/Métis)
COURTESY OF LEE FRANCIS III

Miwok peoples living in the area now known as Drake's Bay, north of San Francisco, California, encounter English explorer Francis Drake as he and his group travel up the California coast by boat. Drake takes possession of the country in the name of Queen Elizabeth I of England and her successors. The Miwok people have no idea that they have given away all their land.

The People of the sovereign tribes in what is now New Mexico stoically endure the attempts of about thirty-one Roman Catholic missionaries, under the leadership of lay brother Friar Augustin Rodríguez and military aide Francisco Chamuscado, to convert them to Catholicism.

Exploring conquerors from Spain estimate that Acoma, in what is now New Mexico, has more than six thousand people living in approximately five hundred homes three to four stories high.

Tiwa, Jémez, Zia, and Acoma peoples are visited by Antonio de Espejo, a wealthy citizen of Mexico, and Fray Bernaldino Beltran. The Acoma welcome Espejo with ceremonial dances and juggling acts.

Canonicus (Narraganset), who will become Great Sachem, is born around 1565.

Passaconaway (Pennacook), who will become Grand Sachem and holy man, is born around 1565.

Ensenore (Secotan), principal leader, an ardent friend of the English whose homeland is in what is now North Carolina, prevents his son, Wingina, from going to battle against the English. Ensenore's other son, Granganemeo, is friendly with the English in 1565.

Lowaponskan, or North Walker (Lenape), is Grand Sachem after Pakimitzin at what is now Niagara Falls. It is a recognized neutral trade zone and gathering center where the Lenape act as mediators in conflicts between tribes and nations around 1567.

Olotaraca (Saturiba Timucua), military leader, joins the French in their attacks on Spanish forts at the mouth of what is now the St. Johns River in Florida in 1568.

Tashawinso, or Quite Ready (Lenape), Grand Sachem after Lowaponskan, is living what is now known as the Delaware River. While Tashawinso is Grand Sachem, the Lenape divide into three major groups—Unami, Munsee, and Turkey.

Tisquantum, or Squanto (Patuxet Wampanoag), who will teach the immigrant Pilgrims how to survive in the wilderness, is born at about this time.

Massasoit (Wampanoag), who will become Grand Sachem of the People, is born at about this time.

Epallahchund, or Calling Retreat (Lenape), is Grand Sachem after Tashawinso. Epallahchund fights the Iroquoian Susquehanna, or Andaste. The Lenape are forced to retreat as the Andaste slowly conquer the Susquehanna valley around 1584.

When the Spanish conquistadors stopped looking for gold long enough to talk to the natives, the Mayan priests showed them packets of thin wooden slabs. . . . The Mayan priests said these packets were the means by which the Mayan/Aztec culture preserved its thoughts, including its history and the details of its religion. The I@#&! Spanish priests promptly burned every Mayan book they could capture with lance and pistol.

Charles Brashear (Cherokee)

Charles Brashear (Cherokee)
COURTESY OF PER BRASHEAR

Nothing can change what has happened, but history is what we make of what happened, and that means trying to see not just how we came to be where we are, but also where we seem to be headed.

Nompehwahthe, or Carter Revard (Osage)

Show respect for all men, but grovel to none.
Tecumtha, or Tecumseh (Shawnee)

	HISTORY/LAW/ POLITICS	LITERATURE/ART/ LEGENDS AND STORIES
1585–1586	The Wingandacoa people observe Sir Walter Raleigh's attempt to establish the first English settlement at Roanoke Island, in what is now North Carolina. The colony lasts one year.	
1587–1592	The Wingandacoa people observe the second attempt by the English to establish a permanent settlement or colony at Roanoke Island, in what is now North Carolina. The colony fails with the disappearance of all the colonists.	
1590–1592	The Iroquois League of the Five Fires is revealed to non-Native explorers around 1590. The hope is that the Europeans will turn away from war and live under the Great Law of Peace. The league consists of the Cayuga, Mohawk, Onondaga, Oneida, and Seneca. Native tribes of the Southwest in what is now New Mexico reluctantly tolerate Gaspar Castano de Sosa's attempts to colonize all Pueblo villages without permission from Spain. De Sosa is taken back under guard to Mexico by Captain Juan Morlete in 1590.	
1593–1597	San Ildefonso Pueblo, in what is now New Mexico, is occupied by Antonio Gutiérrez de Humana and Francisco Leyba de Bonilla. Humana kills Bonilla. Eastern Plains people kill the remaining conquerors while they are on an exploring trip.	
1598	Native People living along the lower Rio Grande near what is now El Paso, Texas, are informed that Juan de Oñate has taken formal "possession" of the land (an area including what is now Texas, New Mexico, Arizona, and lower California) in the name of Spain on April 30. Pueblo peoples are not impressed. The All Indian Pueblo Council (AIPC) is founded when thirty-eight leaders from the tribes of what is now New Mexico observe the establishment of the first permanent white settlement, San Gabriel de los Espanoles, by Oñate at what is now San Juan Pueblo on July 11. Acoma people attack the Spanish conquerors led by Captain Juan de Zaldivar on December 4. Among the thirteen Spaniards killed are Zaldivar, Diego Núñez, and Felipe de Escalante.	Among the Keres, it is said that Pustsmoot was famous for his skill with a bow but that he looked like a monster and not a man. Then, it is said, he married Kochi-ni-nako, who told his mother that she was content even though her husband had a horrible deformity and was very poor. Pustsmoot's mother took Kochi-ni-nako to a small room and told her to look inside. It is said that when she did, Kochi-ni-nako saw that the room was filled with beautiful clothing, ornaments, turquoise beads, and dresses. Then she was taken to another room and saw a hideous mask hanging on the wall. The mask reminded Kochi-ni-nako of her husband. As she looked at the mask, a very handsome young man came into the room. Then, it is said, the mother told Kochi-ni-nako that the handsome man was Pustsmoot and the mask was his deformity. And so, it is said, Pustsmoot and Kochi-ni-nako lived together happily ever after.

Adawosgi, or Swimmer Wesley Snell (Cherokee)
COURTESY OF EVELYN B. CONLEY

HEROES/LEADERS/VICTIMS	ELDER WISDOM/PHILOSOPHY/SONGS	
	We have to look at the way we were in the past, hang on to it in our hearts and at the same time change; accept we're always changing to survive. *Dorothy Haberman (Yurok)*	**1585–1586**
	The issue of Native people's survival is dependent on the notion of cooperating more than leading people. *Agnes Williams (Seneca)*	**1587–1592**
		1590–1592
Langomuwi, or Kindred (Lenape), Grand Sachem after Epallahchund, continues to fight the Andaste. The Lenape are defeated and are cut off from their relatives in what is now Ohio. Matoaka, or Pocahontas (Mattaponi), is born in about 1595.	Crisis changes people and turns ordinary people into wiser or more responsible ones. *Wilma P. Mankiller (Cherokee)*	**1593–1597**
Coomo, Chaamo, and Ancua (Acoma) leaders pledge allegiance and vassalage to the Spanish Crown in October.	What the hell are you doing to this land? My grandfather hunted here, prayed, dreamt; one day there was a big jolt, flame, and then silence, just the clouds forming. *Simon J. Ortiz (Acoma)*	**1598**

	HISTORY/LAW/ POLITICS	LITERATURE/ART/ LEGENDS AND STORIES
1599–1606	The Massacre at Acoma begins on January 23 by Spanish conquerors led by Juan de Oñate's brother, Vicente de Zaldivar Mendoza, in retaliation for the attack by Acoma people the month before. During the three-day battle, fifteen hundred Acoma men, women, and children are murdered. The survivors are forced to submit to Spanish rule. Mendoza takes five hundred men, women, and children prisoner. In February, the prisoners' hands or feet are cut off as punishment. The prisoners are made personal slaves of the Spanish captains and soldiers for twenty years. Sixty to seventy young Acoma women are sent to Mexico and delivered to the viceroy. Oñate is recalled to Mexico, where he and Mendoza are punished for crimes against the Acoma people. Oñate is sentenced to perpetual banishment from what is now New Mexico and is exiled for four years from Mexico City. Mendoza also is convicted and banished. Native Peoples living in the Monterey Bay area of what is now California encounter Sebastián Vizcaíno, who is exploring the region in 1602.	Among the Lenape, it is said that the Lenape ambassador Mottschujinga, or Little Grizzly Bear, fearlessly went out to meet the Iroquois. Nude in the ancient way of the Lenape, Mottschujinga carried a black wampum belt containing a declaration of war in one hand, and in the other hand he carried a pipe of peace. It is said that he waited for the strangers to make their choice.  *Clifford E. Trafzer (Richard Red Hawk) (Wyandot)* COURTESY OF LEE ANN SMITH TRAFZER
1607	The Powhatan Confederacy, composed of about thirty sovereign tribes, including the Powhatan, Pamunkey, and Mattaponi, in association with the Chickahominy Nation, assists the English colonists in establishing the first permanent English settlement, at Jamestown, Virginia. The Powhatan Confederacy enters into a treaty that provides for friendship and peace with the Jamestown colony of Virginia.	Among the Huron peoples, it is said that in the beginning there was nothing but water, which was occupied by animals that live in and on the water. Then it is said that a woman who was pregnant with twins fell down from the upper world. It is said that one of the twins was good and was born in the usual manner, but the other twin was bad and burst through the mother's side, killing her. It is said that from her body came the pumpkin vine, the corn, and the bean.
1608	The Nanesmond enter into a peace treaty with the English colony of Virginia. The Rappahannock and representatives of the British colony of Virginia negotiate and sign a peace treaty. The Mannahock and representatives of the British colony of Virginia conclude a friendship treaty. The Powhatan Confederacy enters into a treaty that provides for friendship and peace with the British colony of Virginia.	

Wangomend, or Saluted, or Wahunsenacawh, or Powhatan (Powhatan tribe), is Grand Sachem who unites the People of the sovereign tribes living in what is now Virginia.

Skidwaros (Abenaki) is captured by sea captain George Waymouth, who forcibly takes him to England, where he is interrogated about Abenaki lands in 1605.

I ask you in the name of justice for repose, for myself and my injured people. Let us alone—we will not harm you. We want rest. We hope, in the name of justice, that another outrage may never be committed against us.

George W. Harkins (Choctaw)

Ron Andrade (La Jolla Luiseno)
COURTESY OF RON ANDRADE

1599–1606

Skidwaros (Abenaki) returns to his homeland as the reluctant guide for English colonizers who plan to establish a colony on what is now known as the Kennebec River.

The English release Tisquantum, or Squanto (Patuxet Wampanoag). They had captured him and taken him to England to be interrogated for information about the "New World." He returns to his homeland.

Wahunsenacawh, or Powhatan (Powhatan tribe), Great Leader of the Powhatan Confederacy, provides corn to the English settlers of the Jamestown colony and teaches them how to plant and grow tobacco. Jamestown becomes the first successful English colony to be established on Turtle Island, with 120 colonists.

Storytelling has always been a Native American art that was practiced communally, and although there were some "specialists" in the field, nearly everyone engaged in the art. Mothers, grandmothers, aunts, and sisters told stories to the children of creation, power, and medicine, particularly during the winter when people huddled around a fire to hear the words. Fathers, grandfathers, uncles and brothers told stories of love, hunts, and heroes who had saved the people, emphasizing that an individual was not set apart from the whole but was part of a community that required the assistance of those who could contribute most to the well-being of the family, band, or tribe.

Clifford E. Trafzer (Wyandot)

1607

Ocaninge (Chickahominy), a noted orator, strongly advocates on behalf of the People during treaty negotiations with the colonists of Virginia.

Why will you take by force what you may obtain by love? Why will you destroy us who supply you with food?. . . We are . . . willing to give you what you ask, if you come in a friendly manner. . . .

Wahunsenacawh, or Powhatan (Powhatan)

1608

	HISTORY/LAW/ POLITICS	LITERATURE/ART/ LEGENDS AND STORIES
1609	The people of the Iroquois Confederacy residing along what is now known as the Hudson River and New York Bay encounter Henry Hudson, who sails into the area for the Dutch East India Company. Hudson brings the People of the sovereign nations such items as liquor and firearms. The Manhattan attack Hudson on his return from exploration of the river later named for him.	
1610–1614	The Lenape peoples living along what always has been known as the River of the Lenape encounter Captain Samuel Argall. Argall names the river the Delaware after Thomas West, Baron De La Warr, governor and captain general of Virginia. The Lenape come to be known as the Delaware by non-Native peoples. The Spanish abandon San Gabriel de Yongue. La Villa Real de Santa Fe de San Francisco Assisi, now known as Santa Fe, New Mexico, is established by the third Spanish governor, Pedro de Peralta. Work is started on the Palace of the Governors, in Santa Fe. It is completed in 1614. Epidemics of cholera, tuberculosis, smallpox, and measles decimate the Timucua in what is now Georgia and Florida, from 1613 to 1617. The Iroquois initiate a treaty of friendship with a Dutch trader at Tawagonshi in 1613. The Powhatan Confederacy and the British colony of Virginia enter into a treaty which provides for friendship and allegiance. The Chickahominy Nation and the British colony of Virginia enter into a treaty which provides for friendship and alliance. The Chickahominy are allowed to keep their tribal form of government. Each council member is presented with a copper medallion with an engraving of King James I of England on it.	
1615	The French under Samuel de Champlain attack the Onondaga, breaching their defense fortifications and conquering their villages. The Odawa, or Ottawa, and Neutrals engage in battle against the Huron.	
1616	The Narraganset Nation, in what is now the Rhode Island area, asserts authority over the Nipmuc, Niantic, Shawamet, Wampanoag, and Massachuset. A smallpox epidemic brought by the Europeans almost wipes out Narraganset living in the area now known as Boston Bay, in Massachusetts.	

HEROES/LEADERS/ VICTIMS	ELDER WISDOM/PHILOSOPHY/ SONGS	
English settlers "crown" Wahunsenacawh, or Powhatan (Powhatan), as "King Powhatan."	We think if the Great Spirit had wished us to be like whites, he would have made us so. We believe he would be displeased with us to try and make ourselves different from what he thought good. *Daykauray (Winnebago)*	**1609**

Wapachikis, or White Crab (Lenape, or Delaware) is Grand Sachem who presides in the homeland of the People in what is now Delaware.
   Captain Edward Harlow kidnaps Epanow, or Apannow (Plymouth), and forcibly takes him to England. Epanow eventually escapes.
   Matoaka, or Pocahontas (Mattaponi), marries John Rolfe in April.
	That our earth mother may wrap herself in a fourfold robe of white meal; that she may be covered with frost flowers; that on all the mossy mountains the forests may huddle together with the cold; that their arms may be broken by the snow, in order that the land may be thus, I have made my prayer sticks into living beings.
	
	Ashiwi, or Zuñi, offering song
	
	We saw the Great Spirit's work in almost everything: sun, moon, trees, wind, and mountains. Sometimes we approach the Great Spirit through these things. Did you know that trees talk? Well, they do. I have learned a lot from trees: sometimes about the weather, sometimes about animals, sometimes about the Great Spirit.
	
	Tatanga Mani, or Walking Buffalo (Stoney Assiniboin)
		1610–1614

	I do wonder If she is truly humiliated— The Sioux woman— Whose head I have cut off? *Ojibwa prayer song*	**1615**
	Then, the children would be bedded down and my late grandfather would tell tales of Coyote. He would say to us, Listen well. Afterwards, with his elderberry flute, he used to sing Indian songs. . . . All of you listen very closely, he would say to us, I am talking in the ancient manner. Then he would talk and tell us many things of long ago. *Maym Hannah Gallagher (Maidu)*	**1616**

	HISTORY/LAW/ POLITICS	LITERATURE/ART/ LEGENDS AND STORIES
1617	Moor's Charity School is founded at what is now Lebanon, Connecticut, as a training school for students from the sovereign nations and tribes as well as English students.	
1618	Disastrous epidemics of measles, smallpox, cholera, and tuberculosis continue to rage among the People of the sovereign nations and tribes throughout what is now the New England region (1616–1619).	
1619	Smallpox, bubonic plague, and yellow fever decimate nearly nine-tenths of the People of the sovereign nations and tribes living along what is now the coast of Massachusetts and New York, including the Abenaki, Wampanoag, Massachuset, and Pawtucket. A treaty provides for an alliance between the Powhatan Confederacy and the British colony of Virginia.	

HEROES/LEADERS/ VICTIMS	ELDER WISDOM/PHILOSOPHY/ SONGS	
Matoaka, or Pocahontas (Mattaponi), dies.	Kitche Manitou, the Great Spirit, has been generous to you. He has allowed you to see all of life in a dream. He grants this privilege to only a few. *Chejauk, or Crane (Ojibwa)*	**1617**
Nenachihat, or Watching Closely (Lenape, or Delaware), is the final Grand Sachem identified in the Wallam Olum. While he is Grand Sachem, "from north and south, the white people came." The Lenape believe the invaders arriving in great ships are friendly. Wahunsenacawh, or Powhatan (Powhatan), dies. Opechancanough (Powhatan) succeeds his brother Wahunsenacawh as great leader of the Powhatan Confederacy.	Mother, I am going to the other world. I will tell the gods of you. Mother, love all my people. Protect them. They are your children; you are their mother. *We'wha (Ashiwi, or Zuñi)*	**1618**
Epanow, or Apannow (Plymouth), leads an attack on the English Captain Thomas Dormer's forces when they attempt to land at what is now Martha's Vineyard, in Massachusetts. Nanespasket, or New Moon (Nipmuc), principal leader of the Nipmuc, is killed. Squaw Sachem (Massachuset) becomes principal leader of the Nipmuc on the death of her husband, Nanespasket, or New Moon.	The Great Spirit has given you many advantages, but he has not created us to be your slaves. We are a separate people. *Old Tassel (Cherokee)*	**1619**

PERSPECTIVE
1620–1660

During the forty-year period—approximately one generation—from 1620 through 1660, many changes came to the People of the sovereign nations and tribes throughout Turtle Island. The English established Plymouth colony. Massasoit, great leader of the Wampanoag, helped them to survive. At the colony of Jamestown, in Virginia, the great leader of the Powhatan Confederacy led a war against the colonists which lasted for more than eight years.

During lulls between battles, the People across the eastern area of what is now the United States entered into more than twenty treaties with colonists in that forty-year period. The treaties centered mainly on establishing peace and friendship between two equals. Committed to keeping their part of the treaties, the People of the sovereign nations and tribes repeatedly were forced to engage in battle against the colonists, who failed in every instance to observe their part of the treaty agreement.

For example, the Powhatan Confederacy concluded a treaty in which the colonists agreed to remain within a certain geographic area. Within months, if not days, afterward, the colonists encroached on areas specifically delineated as belonging to the Powhatan people. The repeated disregard of agreements between the People and the immigrant colonists or conquerors or traders or explorers resulted in stories among the People of the sovereign nations and tribes that emphasized the treacherous and dishonest character of white people.

The core belief system concerning good and evil and walking in harmony and balance held in common by all the People of the sovereign nations and tribes across Turtle Island presented a dilemma of massive proportions for them. What the People utterly failed to understand was the immigrants' core belief system. For the immigrant colonists, owning a particular plot of land made perfectly good sense. For the People, such a concept was absurd. For example, the story about Peter Minuit "purchasing" Manhattan Island is true for the non-Native. The People, on the other hand, thought he was "renting" the land for a time. When the People came back some time later expecting their "yearly fee" for the land, the colonists became violent because they already had "purchased" the land. They *owned* it. It finally began to dawn on the People of the sovereign nations and tribes that the immigrant colonists believed that a person could *own* land.

As the People of the sovereign nations and tribes continued to travel back and forth across Turtle Island visiting and trading, they told stories to one another about the strange idea of land ownership. Many of the People of the sovereign nations and tribes adopted a "go along, get along" strategy of accommodation with the whites. Others "just said no." The battles between the People of the sovereign nations and tribes and the immigrant colonists began to escalate. What also began to escalate were the battles among different sovereign nations and tribes. It is true that wars among sovereign nations and tribes had occurred with frequency long before the arrival of the immigrant colonists. The difference in those wars between ancient enemies and the ones that began to occur in the mid-1600s was that a third party (the immigrant colonists), in many instances, caused the fight between two sovereign nations or tribes and/or allied itself with one side.

In essence, the People no longer were able to walk in balance and harmony, as they had for untold millennia previously. By 1660, the People had become factionalized and the sacred hoop had begun to splinter.

	HISTORY / LAW / POLITICS	LITERATURE / ART / LEGENDS AND STORIES
1620	Nauset and Wampanoag peoples observe the establishment of an English settlement at Plymouth, Massachusetts.	
1621	The Wampanoag and the newly established British colony of Plymouth enter into the Treaty of Amity at Plymouth on September thirteenth. It provides for friendship and land cession by the Wampanoag.	*Velma Garcia Mason (Acoma Pueblo)* COURTESY OF GLORIA MORA
1622	The Powhatan Confederacy declares war against Jamestown colonists after African immigrant servants murder one of the People in retaliation for the killing of their master by a Powhatan.	
1623	Pennacook people living in what is now Little Harbor, near Rye, New Hampshire, endure the establishment of a permanent settlement by the English under the leadership of David Thomas. The Chiskiack tribe of the Powhatan Confederacy, living in what is now the Potomac River area, and the British colony of Virginia conclude a peace treaty. Two hundred Chiskiack, including the principal leader and his sons, die from having drunk poisoned brandy. The English soldiers kill the remaining Chiskiack.	
1624–1625	The Iroquois negotiate a trade treaty with New France. The Mohawk engage in war against the Mahican, who are aided by the Dutch from Fort Orange (Albany, New York).	

HEROES / LEADERS / VICTIMS	ELDER WISDOM / PHILOSOPHY / SONGS	
Tisquantum, or Squanto (Patuxet Wampanoag), educates the English settlers of the New England Bay colony, at Plymouth, in planting corn and constructing houses. Because of his efforts, the colony survives.	. . . the first evening after dark, each one goes off in some direction . . . to pray. . . . We pray to the mountain lion, eagles, hawks, wolves, and other wild beasts. . . . Then [we] sing . . . through the night until dawn. *Flaming Arrow, or James Paytiamo (Acoma)*	**1620**
Massasoit (Wampanoag) is Great Sachem of the People without whose help the Pilgrims at Plymouth colony would not have survived. In March, Massasoit visits the colony and concludes a treaty in which he generously grants large parcels of land to the immigrant European colonists. Hobomok (Wampanoag) and Squanto (Patuxet Wampanoag) teach Pilgrims at Plymouth colony how to plant crops. It is said that Massasoit and more than one hundred of the People gather at Plymouth to share a meal with the Pilgrims, as the colonists are known. Chickataubut, or House Afire (Massachuset), reluctantly submits to English authority.	It is customary with us to make a present of skins, whenever we renew our treaties . . . but your horses and cows have eaten the grass our deer used to feed on. *Canassatego (Onondaga)*	**1621**
Opechancanough (Mattaponi), great leader of the Powhatan Confederacy, leads the People in battle against the English colony of Jamestown, Virginia, on March 22. In the battle, one-fourth (350) of the colonists are killed. The conflict, known by non-Native peoples as the Powhatan War, continues for nine years.		**1622**
Iyanough (Wampanoag) and Aspinet (Nauset Wampanoag) make plans to engage in war against the European immigrant colonists, but are thwarted by Massasoit (Wampanoag), who warns Miles Standish of the plan. Aspinet (Nauset Wampanoag), principal leader of the Nauset while Massasoit is principal leader of the Wampanoag Confederacy, dies of disease brought by Europeans. Massasoit (Wampanoag) becomes ill and is treated by doctors sent by Plymouth colony Governor William Bradford.		**1623**
Tisquantum, or Squanto (Patuxet Wampanoag), contracts smallpox and dies while voluntarily acting as a guide for the Pilgrims, who are forced to land their ship, *Swan*, in what is now Chatham Harbor of Cape Cod.	They could not capture me except under a white flag. They cannot hold me except with a chain. *Osceola (Seminole)*	**1624–1625**

	HISTORY/LAW/ POLITICS	LITERATURE/ART/ LEGENDS AND STORIES
1626–1627	Manhattan people of the Wappinger Confederacy sell to Peter Minuit, Dutch governor of New Amsterdam (now known as New York) the island of what is now Manhattan, on May 6, 1626. The Dutch pay sixty guilders (about twenty four dollars) and establish a colony on what is now the Hudson River. The Manhattan people think the payment is to "rent" the land for a year. They and the other People of the sovereign nations and tribes living on Turtle Island have no concept of "owning" land.	
1628	The Mohawk are victorious in war against the Mahican and the Dutch. The Iroquois Confederacy drives the Mohegan to the valleys of what is now New England.	
1629	Ashiwi, or Zuñi, Hopi, and Acoma people reluctantly tolerate the establishment on their lands of the first missions by Spanish Roman Catholics.	
1630	The Huron develop and perform new sacred ceremonies in response to the dreams and visions of their holy people. The ceremonies reinforce the shared belief of the Huron (and all the People of the sovereign nations and tribes living on Turtle Island) in the importance of maintaining harmony and balance with all of creation.	
1631	The defeated Powhatan Confederacy and the British colony of Virginia conclude a treaty of peace.	
1632	The Pequot make their first contact with the English. The Powhatan Confederacy declares a truce with the Jamestown colonists.	
1633	The Iroquois negotiate a trade treaty with the French. The Wappinger people endure the establishment of a Dutch settlement in what is now Connecticut.	

HEROES/LEADERS/ VICTIMS	ELDER WISDOM/PHILOSOPHY/ SONGS	
	From the West Indies to California and from Newfoundland to Oregon tens of thousands of Native Americans died from the effects of diseases introduced by the Europeans. Without the "aid" of this secret weapon the various European groups would have been hard-pressed indeed in their conquest of America. *Jack D. Forbes (Rappahannock/Delaware)*	**1626–1627**
Uncas (Mohegan), principal leader, is buried at what is now Norwich, Connecticut.	The Great Spirit, in placing men on the earth, desired them to take good care of the ground and to do each other no harm. *Young Chief (Cayuse)*	**1628**
Passaconaway (Pennacook), great leader of the People, is present at the marriage of his daughter to Winnepurget, the sachem of Saugus.	A small portion of food is being prepared for many hungry people. To it we add sand as a prayer for abundance. Sand, whose grains are without number, has in it this essence. What is more plentiful than the sand of Mother Earth in its endlessness? We remember that as we mix our food in its lack of muchness. *Sevenka (Hopi)*	**1629**
Adario, or Kondiaronk (Huron), who will become a noted orator speaking on behalf of the People, is born. Chitomachen, or Tayac (Conoy), is known as "emperor" of the Conoy, an Algonkian tribe closely related to the Lenape, or Delaware. While Chitomachen is "emperor," he converts to Christianity (c. 1620–1650).	Contemporary people can only heal the wrongs of the past by creative empathizing and feeling the pain of those who suffered, not by putting the past behind us. Cultural memory . . . rather than cultural amnesia, provides our best hope for approval. Lying and covering up threaten democracy, not truthtelling. *Craig S. Womack (Creek/Cherokee)*	**1630**
	I grew up believing that Whites are wicked, deceitful people. It seemed that most of them were soldiers, government agents, or missionaries. . . . *Don C. Talayesva (Hopi)*	**1631**
Massasoit (Wampanoag), principle leader, escapes from his main village near what is now Bristol, Rhode Island, to avoid capture by Narraganset forces by their principle leader, Canonicus.		**1632**
Chickataubut, or House Afire (Massachuset), principal sachem, dies of smallpox.		**1633**

	HISTORY/LAW/ POLITICS	LITERATURE/ART/ LEGENDS AND STORIES
1634	Pequot attack the Hope, a Dutch trading post near what is now Hartford, Connecticut. The murder eventually leads to the so-called Pequot War two years later. The Mohawk nation declares a truce with the sovereign nations of Canada. The Pequot and the British colony of Massachusetts enter into negotiations for a treaty which provides for land cession by the Pequot. The Pequot council does not ratify the treaty. "Indians" (sovereign nations and tribes unknown) and representatives of the British colony of Maryland conclude a treaty which provides for land cession by the "Indians." The Narraganset enter into a treaty with the British colony of Providence Plantations (Rhode Island) which provides for land cession by the Narraganset.	 *Janice Gould (Koyangk'auwi/Maidu)* COURTESY OF MARGARET RANDALL
1635–1639	The Oneida, Onondaga, Mohawk, and Dutch hold a trade council at Oneida, in what is now New York. During the winter of 1636–1637, Pequot warriors lay siege to the English Fort Saybrook, in what is now Connecticut. A massacre of the Pequot occurs on May 25, 1637. At dawn, about six hundred to one thousand men, women, and children are murdered in a surprise attack by the English of the Plymouth colony, led by Captain John Mason. The two hundred or so survivors are sold into slavery, and many of them are sent to the West Indies. The *Wallam Olum* (Red Record) notes the arrival in 1638 of non-Native peoples from the north and south in great ships. The record asks: "Who are they?"	
1640	The Mohegan and the British colony of Connecticut enter into a treaty which provides for land cession by the Mohegan. Disease, famine, and war decimate the Huron Confederacy, consisting of the Huron, Tionontati, and neutral peoples. Their population of 160,000 before contact with whites drops to approximately 25,000.	
1641	The Potawatomi people endure the establishment of a French settlement in what is now Michigan.	

HEROES/LEADERS/ VICTIMS	ELDER WISDOM/PHILOSOPHY/ SONGS	
Dutch traders kill Tatobam (Pequot), honored sachem of the People, in retaliation for the killing of Narraganset who were trading with the Dutch.	There is an important Indian woman in virtually every major encounter between Europeans and Indians in the New World. As mistresses or wives, they counseled, translated, and guided white men who were entering new territory. While men made treaties and carried on negotiations and waged war, Indian women lived with white men, translated their words, and bore their children. *Clara Sue Kidwell (Choctaw/Chippewa)*	**1634**
Sassacus (Pequot), Grand Sachem of the Pequot, is the leader of what is referred to as the Pequot War against the colonists of New England. He is beheaded in 1637. Canonicus (Narraganset), Grand Sachem of the People, generously grants land to Roger Williams, who founds Providence after having been banished from the Massachusetts Bay colony in 1636. The Powhatan Confederacy enters into a treaty with the British colony of Virginia which provides for boundary revisions in 1636.	. . . he was overcome with an instant horror at the inhumanity of his captors, their cold indifference to human suffering, their casual acceptance of so much misery and terror, and their ready participation in its creation. *Robert J. Conley (United Keetoowah Band Cherokee)*	**1635–1639**
	Upon the continent of North America prior to the landfall of the first white man, a great league of peace was formed, the inspiration of a prophet called The Peacemaker. He was a spiritual being, fulfilling the mission of organizing warring nations into a confederation under the great law of peace. . . . The Peacemaker came to our lands, bringing the message of peace, supported by Hienwatah (not Hiawatha). He began the great work of healing the twisted minds of men. *Oren Lyons (Onondaga)*	**1640**
		1641

1642	Dutch soldiers under the leadership of Governor Willem Kieft and Sergen Rudolph massacre Walwaskik Wappinger people who had come to live in peace among the Dutch in what is now northern New Jersey. More than 120 men, women, and children asleep in their homes are murdered brutally during the night. Bayonets are run through the stomachs of babies, men's hands are cut off, women are cut open with swords. The Dutch then torch the entire village. There are no survivors among the Walwaskik Wappinger.	
1643	The Mohawk and the Dutch agree to a treaty of trade and peace which forges an alliance between the two nations. The Wappinger Confederacy of what is now eastern New York is defeated in war against the Dutch. More than fifteen hundred people of a population of five thousand die during the war.	
1644	The Chickahominy Nation and the Powhatan Confederacy attack the Jamestown settlement, in Virginia, killing more than five hundred colonists. The Huron and Algonkian attack the Iroquois near the mouth of what is now the Richelieu River in Québec, Canada.	
1645	The Mohawk, Algonkian, Huron, and French agree to a treaty at Three Rivers (July and September). The Mahican and Mohawk negotiate a treaty with Dutch Governor Willem Kieft at Fort Orange, now Albany, New York (July). Algonkian peoples negotiate a treaty ending war with the Manhattan Dutch at Fort Amsterdam, now New York City, in the presence of Mohawk ambassadors asked by the Dutch to be mediators (August). The Narraganset and Niantic enter into a treaty with the New England Confederation. The terms provide for peace and the return of captives.	*Roberta M. Lewis (Zuñi/Cherokee)* COURTESY OF ROBERT M. LEWIS
1646	The Wampanoag Nation and the British colony of Providence Plantations enter into a treaty which provides for peace and land cession. The Powhatan Confederacy enters into a treaty with the British colony of Virginia. The terms provide for peace, land cession, and the return of captives.	

HEROES/LEADERS/VICTIMS	ELDER WISDOM/PHILOSOPHY/SONGS	
Ahatisistari (Huron), leader of the Huron against the Iroquois, is captured and held prisoner by Mohawk who then kill him. Miantonomo (Narraganset), principal leader of the Narraganset, meets with his noted enemy, Waindance, at Meaticut, near present Norwich, Connecticut, while Uncas is principal leader of the Mohegan. Miantonomo signs the tripartite agreement among the British colony of Connecticut, the Narraganset, and the Mohegan. Although respected and loved by everyone, he is executed by Wawequa, brother of Uncas, by order of the English, who had tried, condemned, and sentenced him.	Since these Englishmen have seized our country, they have cut down the grass with scythes, and the trees with axes. Their cows and horses eat up the grass and their hogs spoil our bed of clams; and finally we shall all starve to death. *Miantonomo (Narraganset)*	**1642**
Squaw Sachem (Massachuset) enters into a covenant with the British colony of Massachusetts in which the Nipmuc come under the rulership of the English.	My Indian mother, Pretty Face in her humble way, helped to make the history of her race. For it is the mothers, not the warriors, who create a people and guide their destiny. *Luther Standing Bear (Oglala)*	**1643**
Opechancanough (Powhatan), great leader of the Powhatan Confederacy and almost one hundred years old, leads an attack against the English. He is captured and dragged before royal Governor Sir William Berkeley. An angry guard shoots and kills Opechancanough while he is in prison. Passaconaway (Pennacook), great leader of the People, formally submits to English rule. He dies at an advanced age shortly afterward.	Sometimes they tore the clothes off the women and girls. All the time the white men were laughing and making fun of them. Do you wonder now that the people of Hotévilla tremble when they see white people coming to our village? *Violet Pooleyama (Hopi)*	**1644**
Kiosaton (Iroquois), principal leader, pleads with French Governor Charles-Jacques de Huault de Montmagny of Canada for the release of two Iroquois prisoners held by the French. Montmagny releases the captives.	We do not know what the designs of the Master of Life toward us may be. Is it the Master of Life who inspires our brothers to war? *Teata (Huron)*	**1645**
Necotowance succeeds Opechancanough as principal leader of the Powhatan Confederacy. Necotowance signs a peace treaty in which the People of the confederacy submit to the English Crown as its subjects		**1646**

1647–1659

The Yuchi, or Chisca, living in what is now Florida, revolt against the Spaniards, who are tyrannical rulers.

The Seneca attack and destroy the town of the Aondiron, of the Neutral Confederacy, in what is now western Ontario. The Aondiron had broken their code of neutrality (from which came their name of Neutrals) by allowing the Huron to capture a Seneca leader who was visiting the Neutrals.

The Seneca and Mohawk continue joint attacks on the Huron in 1649, resulting in destruction of the Huron Confederacy, consisting of the Huron, Tionontati, and Neutrals.

On May 30, 1650, counterfeiting of wampum ("money" used by the People of the sovereign nations and tribes) is prohibited by an ordinance passed by the Dutch director of council of New Netherlands. The purpose is to stop the making in Europe of imitation wampum which is used to defraud the People of the sovereign nations and tribes of Turtle Island.

The Iroquois massacre the Nipissing in 1650 near what is now Lake Nipissing, in Ontario, Canada.

A treaty is concluded in 1650 between Indians and representatives of the British colony of Maryland that provides for land cession.

The Iroquois Confederacy attacks the Neutrals in 1651.

The Susquehanna enter into a treaty with the British colony of Maryland in 1652. The terms provide for land cession by the Susquehanna.

Each of the Iroquois Five Nations negotiates a peace treaty at Montréal with the French in 1653.

The Illinois, who later become known as the Miami, encounter French fur traders Pierre Esprit Radisson and Médard Chouart Groseilliers in 1654. The Illinois capture and adopt Radisson (1652–54). The Illinois consist of the Wea, Piankashaw, Atchatchakangouen, Kilatika, Pepicokia, and Mengakonkia, who live northwest of what is now Green Bay in Michigan.

The Ojibwa attack the Iroquois in 1655 near what is now Sault Sainte Marie, Michigan.

The Iroquois engage in war against the Illinois in 1656. More than three hundred Illinois die in the assault.

The Seneca peoples regarded as nondistinct "Upper" Iroquois, west of the Mohawk Nation, enter into treaty negotiations with the Dutch in 1657.

The Plymouth peoples enter into a land-cession treaty with the British colony of Plymouth Plantation in 1658.

The Mohawk and Dutch in 1659 renew an alliance made sixteen years earlier, in a conference at Kahnawakeh, the first Mohawk citadel.

Canonicus (Narraganset), Grand Sachem of the Narraganset, dies at age eighty-two, in 1647, on Canonicus Island opposite what is now Newport, Rhode Island.

The Erie kill Annenraes (Onondaga), principal leader who was involved in negotiations with the Huron in 1654 before the Seneca and Mohawk invasion of Huronia.

Juan Cuna (Hopi), martyr of the Hopi, is beaten until he is "bathed in blood" by Franciscan missionary Friar Salvador de Guerra in 1655. He then drags Cuna into the church at the Hopi First Mesa and beats him again, pours turpentine over him, and sets him on fire. Cuna dies as a result.

Wannalanset (Pennacook), principal leader of the Pennacook Confederacy, son of the highly regarded Passaconaway, and a lifelong friend of the English colonizers, signs the Treaty of Dover, in what is now Delaware, in 1659. The English subsequently imprison him for debt.

They are so convinced that Whites are the only superior human beings that they can never believe that non-Whites can have a creative thought or achieve greatness. I feel so sorry for these people.

Egon Pleyel (Alabama-Coushatta/Tonkawa)

Craig S. Womack
(Muscogee, or Creek/Cherokee)
COURTESY OF PHILIP CAMPBELL

PERSPECTIVE
1660—1700

The twenty years from 1660 through 1679 were instructive and continue to be remembered by the People of the sovereign nations and tribes. Two events were especially significant. One occurred in what is now Virginia, and the other in what is now Arizona and New Mexico.

Government-sanctioned discrimination against a people is one of the more significant events. It occurred, ironically, in the Virginia colonies, which became the home of that advocate of democracy, Thomas Jefferson, a century later. The assembly at James City, Virginia, passed an ordinance "prohibiting the entertainment of Indians without badges" (silver and plated plaques to be worn by Native people around their necks) in any of the Virginia settlements. There was no hue and cry against such vileness in 1662. There was no hue and cry when Hitler imposed the same vileness on the Jewish people of Germany, either.

The other significant event occurred in 1661. Roman Catholic Spaniards destroyed more than sixteen hundred sacred religious objects of the Native People in what is now New Mexico and Arizona.

What is important in both instances is that the People of the sovereign nations and tribes still remember these and similar contemptible acts of their non-Native relations.

It should come as little surprise that after nearly two centuries of such treatment, the People of the sovereign nations and tribes finally would rise up in rage. They did so in the Great Revolt of 1680. It marks the beginning of the second part of this timetable—**Combat Time**.

From 1680 through 1700, the People of the sovereign nations and tribes waged more and more battles against the invaders of their ancestral homelands. And the People continued to die.

	HISTORY/LAW/POLITICS	LITERATURE/ART/LEGENDS AND STORIES
1660	Dutch leader Peter Stuyvesant takes Delaware children hostage to control the Delaware Nation's "behavior." In the early 1660s, Esopus people agree to a treaty with the Dutch at Wiltwick, in what is now New York, at the coercion of the Mohawk, Susquehanna, and Mahican principal leaders. Algonkian peoples living in the area now known as Natick, Massachusetts, tolerate the establishment of the first Christian church by John Eliot, an Englishman. Eliot later publishes the first Christian Bible in North America, translated into Algonkian.	
1661	Kivas, the sacred ceremonial houses of the Native Peoples in what is now New Mexico and Arizona, are raided by Spanish authorities bent on suppressing the religious practices of the sovereign People. The Spaniards destroy more than sixteen hundred sacred kachina masks, as well as other ceremonial religious objects.	
1662	An ordinance "prohibiting the entertainment of Indians without badges" (silver and plated plaques to be worn by Native People) when they visit English settlements is passed by the assembly at James City, Virginia. This law is like the one Chancellor Adolf Hitler of Nazi Germany imposes almost three hundred years later requiring Jews to display the Star of David stitched to their clothing or worn as an armband. The Ojibwa, Odawa, or Ottawa, and Nipissing defeat the Iroquois at what is now Point Iroquois, Michigan.	*Valerie Red-Horse (Cherokee/Cheyenne River Sioux)* COURTESY OF VALERIE RED-HORSE
1663		
1664	The Mohawk and Seneca negotiate a treaty of friendship, trade, and mutual aid with the English at what is now Albany, New York (September). Jersey peoples enter into a treaty ceding their land to the British colony of New Jersey.	

HEROES/LEADERS/ VICTIMS	ELDER WISDOM/PHILOSOPHY/ SONGS	
Harquip (Chickahominy) is one of the more prominent mungai, or principal elders, among the People.		**1660**
	Their numbers were small, they found friends and not enemies. They told us they have fled from their own country for fear of wicked men and come here to enjoy their religion. *Sagoyewatha, or Red Jacket (Seneca)*	**1661**
Wamsutta (Wampanoag), who succeeded his father, Massasoit, as Grand Sachem of the Wampanoag Confederacy, dies. Wamsutta's brother, Metacomet, known as "King" Philip, succeeds him.		**1662**
The death of Juan Cuna (Hopi), who was tortured and then set afire in 1655, is the subject of a detailed report by a soldier at a hearing held by the Inquisition in Mexico City. The missionary responsible for Cuna's death, Friar Salvador de Guerra, is moved to Santa Fe, where he continues physical abuse of the sovereign Pueblo people without being punished. The policy of the Roman Catholic Church in North America to keep secret the child molestation and physical abuse by its priests continues for another 330 years, until 1993.		**1663**
		1664

	HISTORY/LAW/ POLITICS	LITERATURE/ART/ LEGENDS AND STORIES
1665	The Iroquois hold a conference with the governor of New France at Québec at which peace is proposed. The Narraganset enter into a treaty with the British colony of Massachusetts. The terms provide for land cession by the Narraganset.	
1666	The French attack the Mohawk Nation at Tionontoguen, near what is now Canajoharie, New York (January). Articles of peace negotiated the previous year between the Mohawk and the French (with the Oneida speaking on behalf of the Mohawk) are confirmed (July). The Dutch at Albany force the Mahican to be at peace with the Mohawk (September).	
1667–1668	The Iroquois and the French hold a council at Montréal in 1667 after the destruction of Mohawk settlements by the Marquis Alexandre de Prouville Tracy.	
1669	The Chickahominy provide several guides to assist John Lederer on his first expedition in search of a passage through the Appalachians to what he thought would be the East Indies. The Mohawk defeat the Mahican near what is now Schenectady, New York.	
1670	The Illinois Confederacy has a total population of more than eleven thousand. The confederacy consists of the Chepoussa, Moingwena, Peoria, Espminkia, Michigamea, Kaskia, Coiracoentanon, Cahokia, Tamaroa, Tapouaro, and Chinkoa.	
1671	The Wampanoag Nation enters into a treaty with the British colony of Plymouth Plantation which provides for allegiance to the English. The Wampanoag enter into a separate treaty with the British colony of Plymouth Plantation providing for allegiance and surrender of arms. The Sakonnet enter into a treaty with the British colony of Plymouth Plantation. The terms provide for allegiance.	

HEROES/LEADERS/ VICTIMS	ELDER WISDOM/PHILOSOPHY/ SONGS	
Cheeshatemauck (Wampanoag), the first known person from a sovereign nation to attend Harvard College, completes his studies and graduates.	I am afraid that the white men are not speaking straight; that their children will not do what is right by our children; that they will not do what you have promised. . . . *Kamiaken (Yakima)*	**1665**
Cheeshatemauck (Wampanoag), who graduated from Harvard the year before, dies of consumption (tuberculosis). Garakontie, or Moving Sun (Onondaga), principal leader, proposes peace between the Iroquois and French at a conference in Québec.		**1666**
		1667–1668
Garakontie, or Moving Sun (Onondaga), principal leader, the leading negotiator with the French, is baptized a Roman Catholic at the cathedral in Québec and takes the name of Daniel. Until he dies, he uses his authority to protect the French who live in the territory of the Onondaga.		**1669**
		1670
Metacomet, or "King" Philip (Wampanoag), Grand Sachem of the Wampanoag Confederacy, is summoned by the English authorities, who demand new peace measures, including surrender of guns owned by the Wampanoag. Awashonks, squaw sachem of Sagkonate, or Sacconet (Narraganset), before becoming principal leader, is the wife of Tolony. Later, she is an active participant in Metacomet's ("King" Philip's) war with the English, along with Wetamoo, the Wampanoag squaw sachem of Pocasset. On July 24, Awashonks signs articles of agreement with the Plymouth colony and leads the people to a settlement at what is now Sandwich, Massachusetts.	I hope my work adds something to our collective political knowledge—about relations between those with power and the powerless, between organized resistance and grass roots people. If I have a motivating conviction, it is encapsulated in Milan Kundera's remark, "The struggle of people against power is the struggle of memory against forgetting." I want to help remember. *Patricia Penn Hilden (Nez Percé)*	**1671**

73

	HISTORY/LAW/ POLITICS	LITERATURE/ART/ LEGENDS AND STORIES
1672	English and Dutch authorities at Albany compel the Mahican to keep peace with Mohawk. Haw:kuh, the largest Ashiwi, or Zuñi, village, is raided by a band of White Mountain Apache on October 7. The Apache kill the Franciscan priest, Friar Pedro de Abila y Ayala.	
1673	The Odawa, or Ottawa, and Iroquois enter into peace negotiations despite interference from the governor general of New France, Louis de Buade, Comte de Frontenac et Palluau. The Quapaw people encounter French Jesuit missionary and explorer Père Jacques Marquette, who stays in their village at the mouth of the Arkansas River in what is now Mississippi.	
1674	Coahuiltec peoples living in what is now Texas die of smallpox. The Seneca and the British colony of Maryland enter into a peace treaty. Leaders of the Iroquois League are not consulted during or after the signing of the Treaty of Westminster in February between the English and Dutch. The treaty requires the colony of New York to be returned to the English.	
1675	The Iroquois and the Odawa, or Ottawa, enter into a treaty on the border of what is now Lake Ontario. The Five Nations, or Iroquois League, bestow the title of "Corlaer" on Sir Edmund Andros, newly installed governor of New York. The league later bestows the title on subsequent governors. The Narraganset and the British colony of Massachusetts enter into a treaty of alliance. The Susquehanna Nation and Great Britain enter into a treaty which provides for land cession by the Susquehanna. The Delaware enter into a peace treaty with the British colony of New Jersey. The Kiawah Nation enters into a treaty with the British colony of South Carolina which provides for land cession by the Kiawah.	

HEROES/LEADERS/ VICTIMS	ELDER WISDOM/PHILOSOPHY/ SONGS	
	You see, I am Apache—living around wonderful rivers, grass and cactus. I will long remember the times I had with my mother when we walked across fields among the dancing flowers. With a mother around every joy is here. *Lenora Palmer (White Mountain Apache)*	**1672**
Nikinapi (Illinois), principal leader, welcomes Père Jacques Marquette and explorer Louis Jolliet at a settlement of the Peoria.		**1673**
	But, you know, Coyote he was mainly bragging when he said (I think), "My brothers, the Twins then said, 'Let's lead these poor creatures and save them.'" *Simon J. Ortiz (Acoma)*	**1674**
Metacomet, or "King" Philip (Wampanoag), principal leader of the Powhatan Confederacy, declares war in January against the English in retaliation for the mistreatment he has suffered at the hands of the English. Non-Natives refer to the war as "King" Philip's War. In the two-year war, the Wampanoag, Narraganset, and allies are nearly exterminated. Kancamagus (Pennacook) is principal leader of the Pennacook and the grandson of Passaconaway. Kancamagus wants to continue peaceful relations with the British, but after their treachery in 1675, he becomes their staunch enemy. Nauntenoo, or Canonchet (Narraganset), principal leader and son of Miantonomo, is the first signer of the treaty with the British concluded in October. Cockacoeske, or "Queen" Anne (Pamunkey), succeeds her husband, Totopotomoi, as principal leader. She leads the Pamunkey from 1675 to 1718, and receives from King Charles II of England a crown inscribed to the "Queene of Pamunkey." The Pamunkey are part of the Powhatan Confederacy. Bomazeen (Abenaki), who will become a prominent leader of the People, is born at Norridgewock, on what is known now as the Kennebec River, in Maine.	A long time ago this land belonged to our fathers, but when I go up to the river I see camps of soldiers. . . . These soldiers cut down my timber, they kill my buffalo. When I see that, my heart feels like bursting. I feel sorry. *Satanta (Kiowa)*	**1675**

1676

The Wampanoag surrender to English forces on August 28, ending the disastrous "King" Philip's War against the English colonists of the southern New England area.

The English kill or burn to death more than two thousand Narraganset on a swampy battlefield at what is now South Kingstown, Rhode Island.

The English capture four hundred Narraganset and sell them into slavery.

The Chickahominy, Powhatan, Pamunkey, Mattaponi, and other sovereign nations and tribes of what is now the Middle Atlantic seaboard enter into a peace and friendship treaty with representatives of the United Colonies.

Nathaniel Bacon, leader of what became known as Bacon's Rebellion, instigates the massacre of the Chickahominy who had taken refuge at the fort near what is now Richmond, Virginia.

D. L. (Don) Birchfield (Choctaw)
COURTESY OF D. L. BIRCHFIELD

Magnus (Narraganset), the squaw sachem of the People, becomes involved deeply in the war initiated by Metacomet against the English. Magnus is captured, along with ninety other Narraganset. All are put to death by English Major Talcot.

Cockacoeske, or "Queen" Anne of the Pamunkey (Pamunkey), is presented with a silver badge inscribed "To the Queene of Pamunkey" by English King Charles II for providing Pamunkey warriors to suppress Bacon's Rebellion.

Nauntenoo, or Canonchet (Narraganset), Grand Sachem who becomes the most important "general" during "King" Philip's War, gives refuge to Metacomet. In retaliation, Captain Benjamin Church sets fire to Nauntenoo's village, in which women and children burn to death. Captured in December, Nauntenoo is taken to Providence, Rhode Island, and sentenced to die. The English decide that his executioner should be Oneko, the son of Uncas.

Metacomet, or "King" Philip (Wampanoag), principal leader of the Powhatan Confederacy, after winning many victories, loses a major battle at South Kingstown, Rhode Island, on August 12. The English capture and behead him. His wife and son are sold into slavery in the West Indies.

Wetamoo, squaw sachem of Pocasset (Wampanoag), wife of Wamsutta, joins her brother-in-law, Metacomet, in his war against the English after her husband's death. Her sister, Wootonekauske, is Metacomet's wife. Wetamoo dies in August by drowning while swimming the Mattapoisett River to escape from the English.

How come there are no sitcoms about life on the reservation?
Lee Francis IV (Laguna Pueblo/Chippewa)

1676

1677

The Iroquois, Susquehanna, and Lenape, or Delaware, at Shackamaxon, now known as Philadelphia, enter into a treaty with the English magistrates of what is now Chester, Pennsylvania (February).

The First Covenant Chain treaty is concluded, involving the Iroquois Five Nations and the Lenape, or "River," people of what is now called the Hudson valley with the colonies of New York, Massachusetts, and Connecticut in multilateral negotiations (May).

The Iroquois Five Nations, Lenape, or Delaware, and Susquehanna conclude the Second Covenant Chain treaty with the colonies of New York, Maryland, and Virginia. The treaty ends war between the southern colonies and the united forces of the Iroquois, Lenape, and Susquehanna (August).

The Westbo and Cusabo Nations enter into a peace treaty with the representatives of the British colony of South Carolina.

People of the sovereign nations and tribes along the upper East Coast ("Eastern Indians") and representatives of the British colony of Massachusetts conclude a peace treaty.

The Pamunkey, Roanoke, Nottaway, and Nanesmond enter into a peace and allegiance treaty with Great Britain.

Patricia Penn Hilden (Nez Percé)
COURTESY OF TIMOTHY REISS

1678

The Chippewa of what is now Sault Sainte Marie, the Sioux of what is now northern Minnesota, and the Assiniboin of what is now Canada establish trade relations with French explorer Daniel Greysolon, Sieur Dulhut, or Duluth.

1679

The Five Nations and the colonies of New York, Maryland, and Virginia enter into a friendship treaty at what is now Albany, New York.

HEROES/LEADERS/ VICTIMS	ELDER WISDOM/PHILOSOPHY/ SONGS	
Garakontie (Onondaga), principal leader of the Onondaga, dies.		**1677**
		1678
	They are talking about me saying, "come with us." Is there anyone who would weep for me? My wife would weep for me. *Ojibwa battle song*	**1679**

COMBAT TIME

1680–1777

A POX UPON
THEIR HOUSES

You still sit among us, brother, your person retains its usual resemblance and continues similar to ours, without any visible deficiency except that it has lost the power of action. . . . We will not, however, bemoan thee as if thou wast forever lost to us, or that thy name would be buried in oblivion; thy soul yet lives in the great country of Spirits, with those of thy nation that are gone before thee; and though we are left behind to perpetuate thy fame, we shall one day join thee.[8]

For at least two hundred years before 1680, the People of the sovereign nations and tribes had endured the ever growing hordes of immigrant colonists, conquerors, and con artists who committed unending violence in the name of their Christian God and their respective monarchs. At long last, the patience and goodwill of the People came to an end.

All across Turtle Island, the People began to resist the continued violation of their spirits, minds, hearts, and bodies by the immigrant Europeans. The resistance began with the Zuñi, who killed a Roman Catholic friar. From east to west and north to south, the People entered into combat with a grim determination to survive. Equally determined were the immigrant colonizers, who were steadfast in their aspirations to be rid of the pagan "savages" infesting the New World.

The killing of human beings took its toll on all participants. The sacred spirit of the People weakened with every bloody battle. But the blood lust was not satiated, and the People died by the thousands while their European relations seemed to multiply.

Peace treaties were made between the People and their European conquerors, only to be broken again and again. The People all across Turtle Island learned to distrust all words and promises made by their non-Native relations. In the minds of all the People, "white man speaks with forked tongue." It is a lesson that the People ingrained into the hearts and minds of their children and their children's children, and their children's children's children.

	HISTORY/LAW/ POLITICS	LITERATURE/ART/ LEGENDS AND STORIES
1680	The Zuñi kill a Roman Catholic friar living in one of the villages and burn the mission at Halona:wa. For the next twelve years, the Zuñi keep the fortress atop Dowa Yah-llan:e in readiness to repel the Spanish army. The Great Pueblo Revolt, or "Popé's Rebellion," begins August 10 in what is now New Mexico. More than four hundred Spanish colonizers are killed, and the remaining three thousand flee south to Mexico. The Pueblo people burn and destroy all traces of Spanish Christian culture and keep the Spaniards out for more than a decade.	
1681	Peoples of the sovereign nations and tribes residing in what is now Pennsylvania travel through the area under the new colony's protection.	
1682	The Five Nations, or Iroquois League, conclude a treaty with the colonies of New York, Maryland, and Virginia at what is now Albany, New York, in August. The Five Nations, or Iroquois League, enter into treaty negotiations with the French at what is now Montréal, Québec, Canada, in September.	
1683	The Delaware, or Lenape, and the British colony of Pennsylvania enter into four treaties during the year, all of which provide for land cession by the Delaware. The Iroquois League thwarts William Penn's attempt to purchase the Susquehanna valley by entrusting the area to Thomas Dongan, governor of New York. The Wimbee and representatives of the British colony of South Carolina enter into a treaty which provides for land cession by the Wimbee.	

84

An Iroquois-initiated siege at Fort Saint Louis at Starved Rock, near what is now Utica, Illinois, falters and eventually fails.

The Onondaga, Cayuga, and Oneida of the Iroquois Confederacy sign a treaty with the English at what is now Albany, New York. The treaty ends warfare between the sovereign nations and the English colonies of Maryland and Virginia.

The Cusabo enter into a treaty with the British colony of South Carolina. The terms provide for land cession by the Cusabo.

The Delaware agree to two treaties with the British colony of Pennsylvania which provide for land cession by the Delaware.

Maurice Kenny (Mohawk)
COURTESY OF
PAUL RUSADO

The Delaware and the British colony of Pennsylvania enter into two treaties, both of which provide for land cession by the Delaware.

The Five Nations enter into a treaty with Thomas Dongan, governor of the colony of New York, and Colonel Byrd, of the colony of Virginia. The treaty regulates the passage of Iroquois war parties traveling southward.

Piscataway people living in what is now Maryland travel to Albany to make peace with the Five Nations and to ally themselves with the Covenant Chain.

The Five Nations, or Iroquois League, renew the Covenant Chain treaties with New York Governor Thomas Dongan at what is now Albany, New York, in May.

Dongan informs the Iroquois League in September that the king of England has claimed the People of the league as his "children and subjects." The People of the Five Nations are rightfully indignant.

Among the Cheyenne, it is said that Sweet Medicine was the great hero from the time of long ago. It is said that Sweet Medicine selected the first principal leaders of the Cheyenne.

The Iroquois massacre the Miami, or Illinois, near what is now Chicago, Illinois.

Seneca villages between what is now known as Seneca Lake and the Genesee River in New York are attacked and destroyed by the French and their allies of the sovereign nations and tribes.

The Five Nations enter into the Treaty at Albany in September with Thomas Dongan, governor of the British colony of New York. The terms provide for alliance between the two parties.

HEROES/LEADERS/VICTIMS	ELDER WISDOM/PHILOSOPHY/SONGS

Lorenzo Tupatu (Picuris) is one of the leaders of the Picuris during the Pueblo Revolt of August 10.

Popé (San Juan Pueblo), prophet, medicine man, dreamer, is identified as one of the leaders of the Pueblo Rebellion of August 10.

Spanish authorities capture Nicholas Catua (Tesuque), warrior messenger, and his co–warrior messenger, Pedro Omtua, two days before the start of the Pueblo Revolt.

Kateri Tekakwitha, or Lily of the Mohawks (Kahnawake Mohawk), holy woman among Roman Catholics in the present United States, dies at age twenty-four. Her parents and a brother had died in a smallpox epidemic when she was a young girl.

> The god of the Christians is dead. He was made of rotten wood.
>
> *Popé (San Juan Pueblo)*

Catiti (Santo Domingo Pueblo), war leader, is one of the principal leaders in the Pueblo Revolt of 1680. In December 1681, pretending to be filled with remorse, he surrenders to the Spaniard Dominguez Mendoza, maestro de campo, at Cochiti Pueblo. It is soon discovered that the surrender is a trick to lull the Spaniards into relaxing their guard. The plan is for the surrendering Pueblo warriors to steal the Spaniards' horses to prevent their escape from the armed warriors assembling to the north. Mendoza and his troops flee, and the reconquest of the Pueblos by the Spaniards fails.

> The white man does not obey the Great Spirit—that is why the Indians could never agree with him.
>
> *Flying Hawk (Oglala Lakota)*

Lee Francis IV (Laguna Pueblo/Chippewa)

COURTESY OF S. BLANTON COMPANY

> Brothers! I have listened to a great many talks from our Great Father. But they always began and ended in this: "Get a little farther; you are too near me."
>
> *Speckled Snake (Muscogee, or Creek)*

Tamanend III, or Tammany (Lenape), Great Sachem, signs agreements to grant extensive parcels of land in what is now southeastern Pennsylvania to the English Quaker William Penn and his followers. The immigrant English settlers begin to call Tamanend "Saint Tammany," and his name is placed on church calendars as the patron saint of America whose "feast" is celebrated on May 1. Later, a social-political club named after him and known as the Tammany Society is important in the history of New York.

> I, therefore, exhort you to peaceable councils; and, above all, I insist that the guns and swords, the cause of all our jealousy and uneasiness, be removed and sent away.
>
> *Wahunsenacawh, or Powhatan (Powhatan Confederacy)*

Garangula, or Otreouati (Onondaga), principal leader of the People, signs the Treaty at La Famine with French Governor LaBarre, who is forced to agree to a humiliating peace on behalf of the French. Garangula co-opts New France into the Covenant Chain, but the French Crown rejects the offer.	When the missionary arrived in our country with a small troop, our captain and also the others were astonished, seeing them from afar, but they did not run away or seize arms to kill them, but having sat down, they watched them. *Pablo Tac (Luiseño)*	**1684**
	It is a little surprising that when we entered into treaties with our brothers, the whites, their whole cry is more land! *Corn Tassel (Cherokee)*	**1685**
	You [principal leaders] are peacemakers. Though your son might be killed in front of your [home], you should take a peace pipe and smoke. Then you would be called an honest [leader of the people]. *Sweet Medicine, Cheyenne legendary hero*	**1686**
	Let us see, is this real, Let us see, is this real, This life I am living? You, Great Mystery who dwells everywhere, Let us see, is this real, This life I am living? *Pawnee prayer song*	**1687**

	HISTORY/LAW/ POLITICS	LITERATURE/ART/ LEGENDS AND STORIES
1688	The Iroquois Confederacy of Five Nations (Oneida, Mohawk, Onondaga, Cayuga, and Seneca) attacks Montréal, Québec, Canada, on July 26 because of continued abuse of the Iroquois people by the French. The Iroquois kill about one thousand French colonists and burn their plantations. The Onondaga, Cayuga, and Oneida enter into a treaty with Governor Denonville of what is now Montréal. The People declare their sovereignty and their commitment to remaining neutral in the conflicts between France and England. The Five Nations negotiate a treaty with Edmund Andros, governor of the Dominion of New England, at what is now Albany, New York. Andros addresses the great leaders of the Iroquois as "children," against their strenuous objections, instead of "brethren," and insists that the great leaders call him "father."	
1689	The Spanish Crown issues land grants to the pueblos of Acoma, Jemez, San Felipe, Santo Domingo, and Zia on September 20. Five days later, land grants are issued to the pueblos of Cochiti, Pecos, Picuris, San Juan, and Zuñi. The Spanish land grants continue to be recognized by the government of Mexico after its independence from Spain, and by the United States under the Treaty of Guadalupe Hidalgo. The Iroquois attack the Lachine at what is now Lachine, Québec, Canada. The Five Nations and the British colony of New York enter into a treaty which provides for alliance and allegiance.	 *Lela Northcross Wakely (Potawatomi/Kickapoo)* COURTESY OF RANDALL DAVID WAKELY
1690	The Iroquois League of the Five Nations meets in council, and the Mohawk, Onondaga, and Seneca agree to support the English against the French in King William's War, or the War of the Grand Alliance. The Oneida and Cayuga do not join in the agreement. Sovereign nations and tribes known as "Eastern Indians" and the British colony of Massachusetts conclude a peace treaty.	
1691	Caddo people living in what is now Texas die in a smallpox epidemic. The Five Nations and the British colony of New York conclude a treaty which provides for peace and delivery of captives. The Five Nations agree to an alliance treaty with the British colony of New York.	

HEROES/LEADERS/ VICTIMS	ELDER WISDOM/PHILOSOPHY/ SONGS	
	It is the will of the Great Spirit that we should meet together on this day. . . . He has taken his garment from before the sun and has caused the bright orb to shine with brightness upon us. . . . For all these favors we thank the Great Spirit. *Sagoyewatha, or Red Jacket (Seneca)*	**1688**
Kancamagus (Pennacook), principal leader, leads the attack on the English settlement at Dover, in what is now Delaware. He then escapes to Québec.		**1689**
Santa Adiva (Caddo), principal leader, greets Padre Gaspar José de Solís when he arrives in her town of the Nabedache, in what is now Texas. Noted for her beauty, she enjoys the strong support of the Caddo.	On the winter March of Death my Great Grandmother was born and lived . . . to see her people die, her future determined by something called the BIA. She told my mother of the last buffalo hunt by her people before coming to Indian Territory. *Lela Northcross Wakely (Potawatomi/Kickapoo)*	**1690**
	The white men of the east, whose numbers are like the sands of the sea, will overrun and take possession of this country. They will build wigwams and villages all over the land, and their domain will extend from sea to sea. *Senachwine (Potawatomi)*	**1691**

1692   Native People of the Southwest are slaughtered and finally defeated in the Spanish conquistadores' successful efforts to reconquer New Mexico.

The Delaware and the British colony of Pennsylvania agree to a treaty which provides for land cession by the Delaware.

1693   The Five Nations conclude treaty negotiations with the representatives of the British colony of New York, providing for peace between the two parties.

1694   At the Jemez Pueblo Massacre, on July 24, Spanish soldiers under the command of Governor Diego de Vargas attack the pueblo. At least 84 Jemez are killed, and 361 women and children are captured and held prisoner at Santa Fe. The remaining Jemez leaders, as a condition for release of the captives, help the Spanish conquerors in battle against the Tewa and Tano. After the Tano are conquered, the Jemez women and children prisoners are released on September 11.

The Five Nations and the British colonies of New York and New Jersey negotiate a treaty which provides for peace and alliance.

1695   The Onondaga receive peace emissaries in January from Louis de Buade, Comte de Frontenac, who invites the Five Nations to enter into treaty negotiations in Canada. They reject the offer.

The Iroquois League engages in war against the western tribes.

Records of transactions between the People of the sovereign nations and the English colonists continue to be kept, by the newly appointed English secretary of Indian affairs, Robert Livingston. He follows the practice established by the Dutch in New Amsterdam, which was taken over by the English and renamed New York.

Kanakuk–The Kikapoo Prophet (Kickapoo)
COURTESY OF SMITHSONIAN

HEROES/LEADERS/ VICTIMS	ELDER WISDOM/PHILOSOPHY/ SONGS	
Mateo becomes principal leader, or governor, of the Acoma people and refuses to permit the Spanish conquerors, led by Diego de Vargas, to enter the Acoma mesa. The Spanish soldiers climb to the top of the mesa, and the Acoma people cease to resist.		**1692**
	The Great Spirit has placed us all on this earth; he has given to our nation a piece of land. Why do you want to take it away and give us so much trouble? *Kanakuk, or the Kickapoo Prophet (Kickapoo)*	**1693**
Bomazeen (Abenaki) is the sachem who travels to the fort at Pemaquid, Maine, under a flag of truce, where he is seized treacherously. He is imprisoned at Boston.	At the time of death, when I found there was to be death, I was very much surprised. All was failing. My home, I was sad to leave it. I have been looking far, sending my spirit north, south, east, and west, trying to escape from death. But I could find nothing. No way of escape. *Luiseño death song*	**1694**
	Listen, that the peace may continue unto future days! Always listen to the words of the Great Creator, for he has spoken. *The Peacemaker*	**1695**

	HISTORY/LAW/ POLITICS	LITERATURE/ART/ LEGENDS AND STORIES
1696	Lorenzo Tupatu (Picuris), leader among the Picuris during the Pueblo Revolt of August 10, 1680, leads the fight against the conquerors from Spain in a renewed revolt, on June 4. Onondaga and Oneida fortifications near what is now Manlius, New York, are burned to the ground by the French in a massive invasion against the People. French soldiers also destroy cornfields surrounding the settlements. The Missisauga, Odawa, or Ottawa, and Ojibwa defeat the Iroquois at what is now the mouth of the Saugeen River, Blue Mountains, and Rice Lake, in Ontario, Canada. The Five Nations and the British colony of New York negotiate a treaty which provides for peace and alliance.	
1697	The Delaware, or Lenape, conclude a land-cession treaty with the British colony of Pennsylvania.	
1698	Laguna Pueblo, established on July 2, is composed of Keres people from Cochiti, Khe-wa, or Santo Domingo, and La Cieneguilla de Cochiti. Laguna is about sixty miles west of what is now Albuquerque, New Mexico. The Five Nations and the British colony of New York conclude a peace treaty.	
1699	The Bear River people and the British colony of North Carolina conclude a land-cession treaty.	

HEROES/LEADERS/ VICTIMS	ELDER WISDOM/PHILOSOPHY/ SONGS	
Aroniateka, or Hendrick (Mahican/Mohawk), who will become a noted sachem among the People, is born. Assacumbuit (Abenaki), principal leader, joins the French in an attack against the English at Fort Saint John, in what is now New Brunswick, Canada.	There has been very little attempt to understand or try to understand our love of the Earth our Mother and our relation to all living things. We believe we are partners in creation and so are responsible for every living thing about us . . . and to us, all we are surrounded with is alive. *Tdu-u-eh-t'sah (Laguna/Chippewa)*	**1696**
	It is only crying about myself that comes to me in song. *Tlingit prayer song*	**1697**
	We are but a few people in the Pueblos. We have inherited and kept pure from many ages ago a religion which we are told is full of beauty even to White persons. *All Indian Pueblo Council*	**1698**
Kuckeno, or Cockenoe (Montauk), who assisted John Eliot in translating the Christian Bible from English into Algonkian, dies.	Sometimes I, I go about pitying myself while I am carried by the wind across the sky. *Ojibwa prayer song*	**1699**

PERSPECTIVE

1700–1740

In the years from 1700 to 1740, the People of the sovereign nations and tribes entered into more than forty treaties with the immigrant colonists. The encroachments on the ancient homelands of the People on the East Coast, from Maine to South Carolina, continued as the land-hungry Europeans broke treaty agreement after treaty agreement.

During this time, the mothers of the sovereign nations and tribes throughout Turtle Island gave birth to those who grew to adulthood and became great leaders of the People. The names of the few of those leaders are Teedyuscung (Delaware); Coosaponakeesa, or Creek Mary, or Mary Mathews Musgrove Bosomworth (Muscogee/white); Wabasha, or Red Leaf (Mdewakanton Sioux/Chippewa); Cornstalk (Shawnee); Gelelemend, or Killbuck (Delaware); Samson Occum (Mohegan); Guyashuta (Seneca); Shateronhia, or Leatherlips (Wyandot Huron); Ganadaio, or Handsome Lake (Seneca); and the Ghigau, or Nancy Ward (Beloved Woman of the Cherokee). Their deeds reverberate through the centuries.

	HISTORY/LAW/ POLITICS	LITERATURE/ART/ LEGENDS AND STORIES
1700	The Hopi destroy Awatopi, one of their villages in what is now Arizona. They kill or capture all of the inhabitants who are under the influence and control of the Spanish missionaries. The Susquehanna and the British colony of Pennsylvania negotiate a treaty which provides for land cession by the Susquehanna. The Five Nations and the British colony of New York conclude a treaty providing for friendship, religious freedom, and trade.	
1701	The Five Nations and Great Britain conclude treaty negotiations which provide for land cession by the Five Nations and alliance between the parties. The Susquehanna, Conestoga, Shawnee, and Onondaga enter into a treaty with William Penn, representative of the British colony of Pennsylvania. The treaty provides for land cession by the People of the sovereign nations and tribes to the Pennsylvania colony, as well as for friendship, alliance, and trade.	
1702	The Chickasaw kill or capture more than twenty-three hundred Choctaw. The captives are sold to slave traders.	
1703	White settlers kill more than two hundred Apalachee and sell more than fourteen hundred into slavery. A year later, a white raiding party drives the remaining survivors out of the area of what is now Florida, where the panhandle meets the central part of Florida.	
1704	The Onondaga enter into treaty negotiations concerning trade with representatives of the colony of Pennsylvania, at Philadelphia.	*Rayna Green (Cherokee)* COURTESY OF RICHARD STRAUSS—SMITHSONIAN INSTITUTION
1705	The Muscogee and representatives of the British colony of South Carolina conclude a treaty which provides for alliance and allegiance.	

96

HEROES/LEADERS/ VICTIMS	ELDER WISDOM/PHILOSOPHY/ SONGS	
Teedyuscung (Delaware), who will become a principal leader of the People, is born in about 1700. Coosaponakeesa, or Creek Mary (Muscogee/white), Beloved Woman about whom much is written, is born in about 1700 at Coweta, in Alabama. Her American name is Mary Mathews Musgrove Bosomsworth. The surnames are of each of her three husbands, whom she outlives.	The Creeks say Mary came back as Sherman just to see what they'd taken away burned to the ground and returned to her once more. *Rayna Green (Cherokee)*	**1700**
Adario, or Kondiaronk (Huron), noted for his diplomacy and speaking skills, who converted to Christianity, dies at Montréal, Québec, Canada. The French bury him at a cemetery in Montréal. Ahookasoongh (Onondaga) signs the treaty between the Susquehanna, Conestoga, Shawnee, and Onondaga Nations and William Penn, of the British colony of Pennsylvania.	Take my advice and turn Huron—for I see plainly a vast difference between thy condition and mine. I am master of my own body. I have absolute disposal of myself. I do what I please. I am the first and last of my Nation. I fear no man and I depend only upon the Great Spirit. *Adario (Huron)*	**1701**
	clear the way in a sacred manner I come the earth is mine *Lakota war song*	**1702**
	. . . I am getting old and have witnessed for many years your increase in wealth and power while the steady consuming decline of my tribe admonishes me that [its] extinction is inevitable. *Waun-na-con, or John Quinney (Stockbridge Mahican)*	**1703**
	He wanted to make a treaty with us, and to give us presents, blankets, and guns, and flint, and steel and knives. . . We do not want your presents, and do not want you to come into our country. *Curly Chief (Pawnee)*	**1704**
Assacumbuit (Abenaki), principal leader of the People, travels to France, where King Louis XIV receives and knights him, and presents him with a sword.	I will tell you what I have felt and I ought not to have felt that way. I have said that I was conscious that I was compelled under the advance of civilization to sign the papers now that I know [that I now know] took the lifeblood of my people. *Isparhechar (Muscogee, or Creek)*	**1705**

	HISTORY/LAW/ POLITICS	LITERATURE/ART/ LEGENDS AND STORIES
1706	The Shawnee Nation enters into treaty negotiations with the British colony of Pennslyvania. The terms provide for trade regulation and friendship. The Five Nations and the British colony of New York conclude two alliance treaties.	
1707	Iroquois leaders of the Five Nations meet in September with Henry Hyde, Viscount Cornbury, at what is now Albany, New York, to emphasize their suspicions that the colonies of Virginia, Maryland, and Pennsylvania had withdrawn from the Covenant Chain, since they had not renewed their alliance in it. The Iroquois engage in war with the Catawba in what is now North Carolina and South Carolina.	*Isparhecher (Muscogee, or Creek)* COURTESY OF SMITHSONIAN
1708	A census in what is now South Carolina records the ownership of fourteen hundred "Indian" slaves by white plantation owners.	
1709	The Five Nations and the British colony of New York enter into an alliance treaty.	
1710	Principal leaders of the Iroquois League of Nations are received at the court of Queen Anne of England, in London. The Tuscarora request the provincial government of Pennsylvania for permission to move there from North Carolina. They request relocation to escape from the possibility of becoming slaves of white settlers, and because of the loss of Tuscarora lands. The Five Nations, Shawnee, and Delaware and the British colony of Pennsylvania conclude a treaty which provides for peace and land cession by the sovereign nations and tribes. The Five Nations and the Odawa, or Ottawa, negotiate a treaty with the British colony of New York which provides for alliance among the three parties. The Mohawk Nation and the British colony of New York agree to a treaty which provides for land cession by the Mohawk.	

HEROES/LEADERS/ VICTIMS	ELDER WISDOM/PHILOSOPHY/ SONGS	
Bomazeen (Abenaki) leads the attack on the colonial settlements of Chelmsford and Sudbury, in Massachusetts.	You told our younger brothers, when we first assembled, that peace was your object. *Michikinikwa, or Little Turtle (Miami/Mahican)*	**1706**
	If a nation, part of a nation, or more than one nation within the Five Nations should in any way endeavor to destroy the Great Peace by neglect or violating its laws and resolve to dissolve the League, such a nation or such nations shall be deemed guilty of treason and called enemies of the League and the Great Peace. *The Peacemaker*	**1707**

	Here once walked my ancestors,
	  I was told by the old ones,
	One can dig at the very spot,
	  And find forgotten implements.
	Emerson Blackhorse Mitchell (Navajo)
		1708

	All of the historic policies that forced, pressured, and exploited Indians did not succeed in ending the separateness of Indians. *Carter Blue Clark (Muscogee, or Creek)*	**1709**
Aroniateka, or Hendrick (Mahican/Mohawk), is among those who visit Queen Anne's court in London. 	Whenever a foreign nation enters the League or accepts the Great Peace, the Five Nations and the foreign nation shall enter into an agreement and compact by which the foreign nation shall endeavor to persuade the other nations to accept the Great Peace. *The Peacemaker*	**1710**

Carter Blue Clark
(Muscogee, or Creek)
COURTESY OF C. B. CLARK

1711

The Tuscarora revolt against the English colonists of North Carolina because of the kidnapping and enslavement of Tuscarora people and the invasion of their lands. With the assistance of the Machapunga, Pamlico, Coree, and other sovereign tribal nations, the Tuscarora attack the white settlement at the Pamlico River and kill about 130 colonists. In retaliation, the English destroy a town of the Tuscarora, who then are forced to agree to a short-lived peace.

The Coree Nation, with assistance from the Tuscarora, retaliates against the harsh treatment by white settlers of what is now North Carolina and raid a town, killing about seventy settlers.

Russell L. Bates (Kiowa)
COURTESY OF DAVID GORDON

1712

The Tuscarora Nation declares a second war against the settlers of North Carolina in retaliation for the continued kidnapping and selling of Tuscarora people into slavery. The English of North Carolina respond to the raids on their colony and launch a massive assault on Neoheroka, the palisaded town of the Tuscarora. More than 950 Tuscarora die, and the colonists take the town.

The Mohawk Nation establishes schools for its children.

The Delaware Nation and the British colony of Pennsylvania conclude a friendship treaty.

1713

The Tuscarora migrate north from what is now North Carolina and are welcomed by the Iroquois Confederacy in what is now the New York area.

The Tuscarora who were captured by Colonel John Barnwell, English commander of the South Carolina forces, are offered for sale in an advertisement in the *Boston News-Letter.*

The Tuscarora and the British colony of North Carolina negotiate a peace treaty.

HEROES/LEADERS/ VICTIMS	ELDER WISDOM/PHILOSOPHY/ SONGS	
Hancock (Tuscarora) is principal leader of the Tuscarora in North Carolina during the war of 1711–18. In response to the kidnapping and selling of the Tuscarora people into slavery by the colonists of North Carolina, Hancock, in alliance with other tribes in the region, goes to war. Eventually defeated, the Tuscarora move closer to the Five Nations, which give them protection and bring them into the Iroquois Confederacy as the Sixth Fire, or Nation.	. . . hereafter only Earthmaker shall I regard as holy. I will make no more offerings of tobacco. I will not use any more tobacco. I will not smoke and I will not chew tobacco. I have no further interest in these. *Mountain Wolf Woman (Winnebago)*	**1711**
	Contrary to popular belief, education—the transmission and acquisition of knowledge and skills—did not come to the North American continent on the *Niña, Pinta,* and *Santa Maria.* Education is as native to this continent as its Native People. *Henrietta V. Whiteman (Cheyenne)*	**1712**
Bomazeen (Abenaki), sachem of the People, signs a treaty at Portsmouth, New Hampshire, on July 13.	Have we, the first holders of this prosperous region, no longer a share in your history? Glad were your fathers to sit upon the threshold of the Longhouse; rich did they then hold themselves in getting the mere sweeping from its door. *Peter Wilson (Cayuga)*	**1713**

HISTORY/LAW/ POLITICS	LITERATURE/ART/ LEGENDS AND STORIES
1714	

The principal leaders of the Iroquois Confederacy, or the League of the Five Nations, petition the English governor of New York to recognize the peaceful intentions of the Tuscarora who had fled from North Carolina and had been given the league's protection.

The Abenaki and the British colony of Massachusetts conclude a peace treaty.

The Iroquois Confederacy (composed of the Onondaga, Oneida, Seneca, Mohawk, and Cayuga) is declared subject to the English Crown under the Treaty of Utrecht, which ends Queen Anne's War, or the War of Spanish Succession, 1702–13). Under the treaty, the French acknowledge the English claim of sovereignty over the Iroquois, who are not consulted.

1715

The Yamasee of what is now South Carolina organize a revolt among the coastal tribes against the English colonists for land theft by settlers and cheating by fur traders. More than two hundred settlers and fur traders are killed before the revolt is suppressed. The Yamasee flee to what is now Florida and settle among the Spanish at St. Augustine, where they assist the Spanish in raids against the English.

The Chickasaw and Cherokee form an alliance to drive the Shawnee from the Cumberland valley of Maryland and Pennsylvania into what is now Kentucky and Tennessee. The land of the Cherokee encompasses an area from the Ohio River south to what is now Atlanta, Georgia, and from Virginia, North Carolina, and South Carolina across Tennessee, Kentucky, and Alabama.

The Delaware, Shawnee, Conestoga, and Potomac Nations conclude a peace treaty with the British colony of Pennsylvania.

The Susquehanna and the British colony of Pennsylvania enter into a treaty which provides for friendship and trade.

The Coree and the British colony of North Carolina agree to a treaty which provides for peace and land cession by the Coree.

1714

You cannot harm me,
  you cannot harm one
    who has dreamed a dream
      like mine.

Dakota prayer song

1715

. . . We have come to the edge of the woods,
out of brown grass where we slept, unseen,
out of leaves creaked shut, out of our hiding.
We have come here too long.
        Louise Erdrich (Turtle Mountain Chippewa/German)

Low Dog (Dakota)
COURTESY OF SMITHSONIAN

	HISTORY/LAW/ POLITICS	LITERATURE/ART/ LEGENDS AND STORIES
1716	Oneida leaders vehemently complain to the colony of New York's commissioners of Indian affairs about the high prices for goods and about having been cheated by traders.	
1717	The Muscogee and representatives of the British colony of South Carolina conclude a peace treaty.	
1718	The Delaware, or Lenape, and the British colony of Pennsylvania conclude a treaty which provides for land cession by the Delaware. The Shawnee, Conestoga, and Delaware negotiate a friendship treaty with the British colony of Pennsylvania.	
1719	The Wichita tribe of what is now the Canadian River area in Oklahoma establishes trade relations with the French.	
1720	The Conestoga, Shawnee, Conoy, and Delaware meet at what is now Conestoga, Pennsylvania, with James Logan, secretary of the Pennsylvania colony. He urges them to end their raids to the south.	*Parra-Wa-Samen, or Ten Bears (Comanche)* COURTESY OF SMITHSONIAN
1721	The Five Nations conclude a friendship treaty with the British colony of New York. The Cherokee Nation agrees to a treaty with the British colony of South Carolina. The terms provide for land cession by the Cherokee.	

HEROES/LEADERS/ VICTIMS	ELDER WISDOM/PHILOSOPHY/ SONGS	
	A man ought to desire that which is genuine instead of that which is artificial. *Okute, or Shooter (Teton Sioux)*	**1716**
	When we were created we were given our ground to live on and from this time these were our rights. This is all true. *Weninock (Yakima)*	**1717**
	Alice has three heritages—African, Cherokee, European. . . . We talked about family and heritage, about race and the future . . . about tears and "trudging along" and questing for an upward path. *Awiakta (Cherokee)*	**1718**
	My people have never first drawn a bow or fired a gun against the whites. . . . It was you who sent the first soldier and we who sent out the second. *Parra-Wa-Samen, or Ten Bears (Comanche)*	**1719**
Pontiac, or Ponteach (Odawa, or Ottawa), dreamer and principal leader who organizes one of the greatest alliances among Native People in the history of Turtle Island, is born in about 1720 in what is now Ohio.		**1720**
	We . . . are living a sacred life. You must not be afraid of anything. Whatever white men may tell you, do not listen to them, my relations. *Tatanka Ptecila, or Short Bull (Brulé Sioux)*	**1721**

	HISTORY/LAW/ POLITICS	LITERATURE/ART/ LEGENDS AND STORIES
1722	The Abenaki establish peaceful relations with the French in the New England area by inviting French missionaries to live among them. English colonists destroy the Norridgewock settlement of the Abenaki, who are dispersed. Many of the Abenaki migrate to what is now the St. Francis River region of eastern Canada. The English formally recognize the Tuscarora as members of the Iroquois Five Nation Confederacy, which becomes known as the Iroquois League of the Six Nations. The Five Nations and the British colony of New York conclude a peace treaty which also provides for settlement of boundaries.	A French Roman Catholic priest, Father Sebastian Rale, writes the first dictionary of the Abenaki language.
1723	William and Mary College in Williamsburg, Virginia, opens the first permanent school for students from the sovereign nations, tribes, villages, bands, and communities. The Six Nations and representatives of the British colony of Massachusetts enter into an alliance treaty.	
1724	Principal leaders of the Six Nations visit Montréal and Caughnawaga to mediate peace between the sovereign nations and tribes of the Northeast and the colonies of New England.	
1725	Eastern peoples of the sovereign nations living in Massachusetts conclude a peace treaty with the British colony of Massachusetts.	
1726	The Seneca, Cayuga, and Onondaga enter into a treaty with Great Britain which provides for land cession by the sovereign nations.	

Mitchell L. Bush Jr. (Onondaga)
COURTESY OF STEPHEN GAMBARO

HEROES/LEADERS/ VICTIMS	ELDER WISDOM/PHILOSOPHY/ SONGS	
	My children. You complain that the animals of the forest are few and scattered. How should it be otherwise? You destroy them yourselves for their skin only, and leave their bodies to rot. . . . *The Trout (Odawa, or Ottawa)*	**1722**
Crispus Attucks (Narraganset/Negro), who later becomes known as a patriotic hero of the American Revolutionary War, is born in about 1723.	The Indian is said to be the ward of the white man, and the Negro his slave. Has it ever occurred to you . . . that while the Negro is increasing and increased by every appliance, the Indian is left to rot and die before the inhumanities of this model republic? *Waun-na-con, or John Quinney (Stockbridge Mahican)*	**1723**
Captain Moulton's soldiers kill Bomazeen (Abenaki) near Taconnet, Maine.	When the vessels approached the shore, men with light-colored skin landed. . . . As the strangers came toward the People, the latter believed the leader to be a great manido [spirit], with his companions. *Waioskasit (Menominee)*	**1724**
Cockacoeske, or "Queen" Anne of the Pamunkey (Pamunkey), principal leader of the Pamunkey, dies. Tah-gah-jute, or James Logan, or Tachnechdorus (Cayuga), who will become principal leader of the Mingo, is born at Shamokin, Pennsylvania, in about 1725. He is known by the name of James Logan, which he took from a Quaker who later became acting governor of Pennsylvania. Chicago (Illinois tribe), principal leader of the Illinois in about 1725, is known widely and respected. The present Chicago, Illinois, is named for him.	My grandfather told me that the Indians didn't fight among themselves any more. He told me to be friendly to people and never to steal or lie about anything. *Jim Whitewolf (Kiowa/Apache)*	**1725**
	The soldiers are very drunken and come to our place—they have arms and guns; they run after our women and fire into our houses and lodges; one soldier came along and wanted one of our young men to drink, but he would not, and turned to go away, and the soldier shot him. *Struck by the Ree (Yankton Sioux)*	**1726**

1727

The Mesquakie, or Fox, Nation, with the support of the Sioux, Abenaki, and several Iroquois Nations, resumes its war with the French.

Eastern peoples of the sovereign nations and tribes conclude a peace treaty with the British colony of Massachusetts.

The Mattamuskeet conclude a treaty with the British colony of North Carolina. The terms provide for land cession by the Mattamuskeet.

Eastern peoples of the sovereign nations and tribes in New York and Massachusetts negotiate a peace and alliance treaty with the two colonies.

Souligny (Menominee)
COURTESY OF SMITHSONIAN

1728

The Sioux, Chippewa, and Menominee Nations support the French, who kill twelve hundred Mesquakie, or Fox, between 1728 and 1730.

The Delaware, Shawnee, Conestoga, and Potomac and the British colony of Pennsylvania conclude a peace and friendship treaty.

The Six Nations and the British colony of New York negotiate a treaty which provides for land cession by the Six Nations and alliance with the colony.

1729

The Natchez Nation attacks Fort Rosalie, a French fort on the Mississippi River, on November 28. The attack is in retaliation for the French governor's attempt to occupy White Apple, principal village of the Natchez, and turn it into a plantation. The French, with the help of the Choctaw, destroy several villages of the Natchez, and the Natchez scatter in several groups. The French capture 450 Natchez, who are sold into slavery on the island of Santo Domingo.

Assacumbuit (Abenaki), principal leader of the Abenaki, dies. Throughout his life, he was a strong supporter of the French against the English.

Now I am greatly surprised
and therefore I shall use it,
the power of my War Song.

War song of the Five Nations

1727

*Darrell E. Drapeau
(Yankton Sioux)*
COURTESY OF
DARRELL E. DRAPEAU

The yellow-hide, the white-skin [man]
I have now put him aside
I have now put him aside
I have no more sympathy with him,
I have no more sympathy with him.

Arapaho song

1728

Stung Arm (Natchez), mother of the young Chief Sun, speaks to the Natchez people against the political intrigue among the Natchez which was harmful to the nation.

"Queen" Hopoekaw Dekaury (Winnebago), principal leader who succeeds her father, Daykauray, when he dies, marries Sabrevior De Carrie, by whom she has a son, Choukeka. Later, some well-known families in Wisconsin and Minnesota are descended from Choukeka. The family name has been written as DeKaury, Daykauray, Day Korah, Dacorah, Decori, and Decorrah.

To the red man the Great Spirit gave a different character. He gave him love of the woods, of a free life of hunting and fishing. . . . The white man does not like to live like the Indian—it is not in his nature. Neither does the Indian love to live like the white man. . . .

Daykauray (Winnebago)

1729

	HISTORY/LAW/ POLITICS	LITERATURE/ART/ LEGENDS AND STORIES
1730	The Cherokee Nation and Great Britain conclude a treaty which provides for allegiance of the Cherokee to the English king, the return of slaves, and peace.	
1731	Principal leaders of the Five Nations, with the exception of the Oneida, meet with Governor Montgomerie of the colony of New York, who renews the Covenant Chain. The governor agrees to prohibit immigrant colonizers from settling south of Lake Ontario.	
1732	The Delaware enter into a treaty with the British colony of Pennsylvania which requires land cession by the Delaware. The Six Nations and representatives of the British colony of Pennsylvania enter into a friendship treaty.	
1733	Zuñi people in what is now western New Mexico experience a smallpox epidemic in which two hundred die. The Lower Muscogee, or Creek, the Yuchi, and the Yamacraw enter into a treaty which provides for land cession, amity, and trade with the British colony of Georgia.	
1734	Onondaga principal leaders meet with Governor Beauharnais of what is now Canada, who agrees to act as mediator in a dispute between the Onondaga and Seneca.	
1735	The Iroquois of Canada and the British colony of Massachusetts conclude a peace treaty. The Muscogee conclude a treaty providing for an alliance and settlement of boundaries between them and the British colony of Georgia. The Caughnawaga, Mohawk, Western Abenaki, Housatonic, Scaghticoke, and Mohegan Nations and the British colony of New York negotiate a treaty which provides for boundary settlement, alliance, commerce, and amity.	

Tomochichi (Muscogee, or Creek) with "nephew" (adopted son, Tooanakowhi) (Muscogee, or Creek)
COURTESY OF SMITHSONIAN

HEROES/LEADERS/VICTIMS	ELDER WISDOM/PHILOSOPHY/SONGS	
The Englishman Sir Alexander Cuming crowns Ama Edohi, or Moytoy, "emperor of the Cherokee." Afterward, seven Cherokee, including Attakullakulla, or Onacona, or Little Carpenter, are taken to England for an audience with King George II, who receives them with great ceremony. Attakullakulla is the father of Tsiyugunsini, or Dragging Canoe, and probably an uncle of the Ghigau, Nancy Ward.	Canoe, and probably an uncle of the Ghigau, Nancy Ward. We have our unique religious beliefs as we have our unique philosophical concepts. We account for the constellations in the universe as we have our own accounts of history. *Henrietta V. Whiteman (Cheyenne/Arapaho)*	1730
	Let us avoid like the plague the pitfall of attempting to arrive at a composite of Native American cultural values. *Dillon Platero (Navajo)*	1731
Kiantwa'ka, or Cornplanter, or John O'Bail (Seneca/Irish), who will become a noted principal leader of the Seneca, is born in about 1732 at Conewaugus, along what is now the Genesee River in New York.	The traditional Indian culture . . . has as its ultimate good the survival of the tribe. *Arthur L. McDonald (Oglala Lakota)*	1732
Chekilli (Muscogee), principal leader of the Muscogee Confederacy who succeeds "Emperor" Bream when he dies, assumes the title of "emperor" of the Upper and Lower Muscogee. He visits England with Tomochichi and James Edward Oglethorpe, founder of the colony of Georgia.	Many have died of diseases we have no name for. *Little Wolf (Cheyenne)*	1733
	We used to stand there and look at the stars and cry to the Thunders. . . . We used to sing and scatter tobacco, standing there and watching the stars and moon. *Mountain Wolf Woman (Winnebago)*	1734
Gonwatzijyanni, or Molly Brant (Mohawk), who will become clan mother of the People, is born.	. . . will you, friend, explain to me that which I cannot understand? Why do the white people want to stop our dances and our songs? Why do they trouble us? Why do they interfere with what can harm them not? What ill did we do to any white man when we dance? *Lololomai (Hopi)*	1735

	HISTORY/LAW/ POLITICS	LITERATURE/ART/ LEGENDS AND STORIES
1736	The Chickasaw successfully defeat French attempts to capture their towns in what is now the lower Mississippi valley region.	
1737	The Mesquakie, or Fox, and the French make peace. After the disastrous war, the Mesquakie return to their ancestral homelands near what is now Green Bay, Wisconsin. The Delaware and the British colony of Pennsylvania conclude a treaty which confirms land cession by the Deleware.	Among the People of the sovereign nations and tribes are stories of visions and dreams which spread across Turtle Island during the next forty years, as the People strive to regenerate the sacred power that had enabled them to survive and prosper before the coming of the Europeans.
1738	The Cherokee in Georgia contract smallpox brought by white slave traders to Charlestown, South Carolina, through goods sold to them. The epidemic kills eleven thousand—almost half of the Cherokee. The Penobscot and Norridgewock conclude a friendship treaty with the British colony of Massachusetts.	
1739	The Shawnee and the British colony of Pennsylvania negotiate a treaty which provides for friendship and confirmation of land cession. The Muscogee, or Creek, Nation concludes a treaty with the British colony of Georgia. The terms provide for land cession and alliance.	 *Angela A. Gonzales (Hopi)* <small>COURTESY OF ANGELA A. GONZALES</small>

HEROES / LEADERS / VICTIMS	ELDER WISDOM / PHILOSOPHY / SONGS	
Kanickhungo (Iroquois) speaks at the treaty negotiations held in Philadelphia in October between the Iroquois and the British.	I hear everything, I hear everything. I am the crow, I am the crow. *Ghost Dance prayer song*	**1736**
	We have been called a nation of tourists. But I suspect, deep down, some of us know where home is—and what it has become. *Jim Barnes (Choctaw/Welsh)*	**1737**
Attakullaculla, or Onacona, or Little Carpenter (Cherokee), becomes peace leader of the Cherokee.	We watched the moon, swimming in a sea of stars. We did not suspect how swiftly our brief respite from reality would pass. *Mary Tall Mountain (Koyukon Athabascan)*	**1738**
Tomochichi (Muscogee) dies and is buried in Savannah, Georgia.	. . . it is widely believed that we "speak for our tribes." The frank truth is that I don't know very many . . . who say, "I speak for my people." It is not only unwise; it is probably impossible, and it is very surely arrogant, for We Are Self-Appointed and the self-appointedness of what we do indicates that the responsibility is ours and ours alone. *Elizabeth Cook-Lynn (Crow Creek Sioux)*	**1739**

PERSPECTIVE
1740–1780

During the first half of this forty-year period, the People of the sovereign nations and tribes entered into more and more treaties with the English colonies. The treaties were sent to the king (George II, until his death in 1760) for ratification. His successor, George III, became more and more distressed with the increasing high-handedness of his subjects toward the People.

By mid-1760, the king issued summary judgments against his lords of the New World, commanding that they encroach no more on the ancient homelands of the People. The enterprising colonists became disenchanted with their monarch, and treaties were negotiated directly between the People of the sovereign nations and the English Crown.

As more and more of the colonists were bent on severing all ties with their mother country, they engaged in civil disobedience which grew into violence. The English colonists were plunged into a civil war. The antiroyalists did all they could to persuade the People to enter into combat against the Crown. The English Crown did all it could to cajole the People to enter the fray on the side of the king. Many of the People of the sovereign nations chose to support the English monarch. Their strategy failed, and the Treaty of Paris ended the American Revolutionary War. The People were on the losing side and suffered the consequences at the hands of the new government of the United States of America.

The People of the sovereign nations and tribes who supported the American colonists in their war against the British were astounded when they too were punished by their former compatriots and forced to cede ancient homelands to the new government. With the signing of the Treaty of Paris, the entire eastern seaboard, with the exception of what is now Florida, became the new "country" of the United States of America.

The campaign to obliterate the People of the sovereign nations began in earnest with the coerced signing by the Delaware Nation in 1778 and the Six Nations (Treaty of Fort Stanwix) in 1784 of treaties with the government of the United States.

	HISTORY/LAW/ POLITICS	LITERATURE/ART/ LEGENDS AND STORIES
1740	The Chickasaw successfully defeat a second attempt by the French to capture towns in the lower Mississippi valley region. The Six Nations and Great Britain conclude a treaty which provides for peace and covenant with the People of the sovereign nations and tribes of the South. The Delaware and Mingo enter into a treaty with the British colony of Pennsylvania. The terms provide for peace, friendship, and trade regulation.	 *Diane Glancy (Cherokee)* COURTESY OF MIKE LONG
1741	The Seneca agree to a land-cession treaty with the British colony of New York.	
1742	The Penobscot, Norridgewock, Pigwacket, Malecite, Saint Francis, and Passamaquoddy conclude a treaty with the British colony of Massachusetts. The terms concern trade problems. The Six Nations, Shawnee, Delaware, and Nanticoke negotiate a treaty with the British colonies of Maryland and Pennsylvania. The terms provide for trade, land cession, and removal of white squatters. The Six Nations and the British colony of New York enter into a friendship treaty which also provides for land cession by the Six Nations.	
1743	The Six Nations and the British colony of Virginia conclude a peace and friendship treaty.	
1744	The Six Nations enter into a treaty with the British colony of Pennsylvania. The terms provide for land cession and boundary revision. The Six Nations and the British colony of New York conclude a treaty which provides for friendship and alliance.	

HEROES/LEADERS/ VICTIMS	ELDER WISDOM/PHILOSOPHY/ SONGS	
Catahecasasa, or Black Hoof (Shawnee), who will become principal leader of the Shawnee, is born in about 1740.	. . . I respect this earth, all the universe, all that is known, and that which is unknown. I respect all who acknowledge this interrelationship and pity those who squander their lives attempting to destroy it or steal its power. *Barney Bush (Shawnee)*	**1740**
	We are neither here nor there but in the midst of the journey. Part of one, part the other, revealing neither fully but indicating a struggle for reconciliation on the part of both. *Diane Glancy (Cherokee)*	**1741**
Canassatego (Onondaga), principal leader, participates in a treaty-making council at Philadelphia at which he gives a memorable speech. Thayendanegea, or Joseph Brant (Mohawk), who will become a famous warrior leader, is born.	. . . you . . . must know that different Nations have different conceptions of things and you will therefore not take it amiss, if our Ideas of this kind of Education happen not to be the same as yours. . . . Several of our young people were formerly brought up at the Colleges of the Northern Provinces: they were instructed in all your Sciences—but when they came back to us they were . . . neither fit for Hunters, Warriors, nor Counsellors, they were totally good for nothing. *Canassatego (Onondaga)*	**1742**
	Into a star, the old singer sang as he moved toward the House of mystery where the child he would give its name was waiting among the assembled representatives of the clans, arranged to repeat the starry order: Into a star you have cast yourself. *Nompehwahthe, or Carter Revard (Osage)*	**1743**
Canassatego (Onondaga), principal leader, proposes at the Indian-British gathering in July a union of all the colonies because of the Iroquois' difficulty in dealing with so many British colonial administrators. He strongly urges that the colonists form a union like the Iroquois Confederacy, which has been in existence for more than sixteen hundred years under a constitution known among the Iroquois as Kaianerekowa (the Great Law of Peace), promulgated by the Peacemaker.	We are a powerful Confederacy . . . and, by your observing the same methods our wise forefathers have taken, you will acquire fresh strength and power. Therefore, whatever befalls you, never fall out with one another. *Canassatego (Onondaga)*	**1744**

	HISTORY/LAW/ POLITICS	LITERATURE/ART/ LEGENDS AND STORIES
1745	Russian traders overwhelm the Aleut after the arrival of Russian explorer Mikhail Nerodchikov in September. The original Aleut population of twenty-five thousand declines to twenty-two hundred because of war and disease brought by the Russians. The Six Nations and the British colonies of New York and Massachusetts conclude a friendship treaty.	 *Joseph Bruchac III (St. Francis Sokoki Abenaki)* COURTESY OF MARTIN BENJAMIN
1746	The Six Nations and the Missisauga enter into a treaty with the British colonies of New York and Massachusetts. The terms provide for alliance among the parties.	
1747	The Wichita and Comanche Nations in southwestern North America conclude a permanent alliance. The Six Nations, Shawnee, and Miami and the British colony of Pennsylvania agree to an alliance treaty.	
1748	The Six Nations, Miami, and Shawnee conclude an alliance treaty with the British colony of Pennsylvania. The Six Nations and the British colonies of New York and Massachusetts enter into a friendship treaty.	
1749	The Cherokee and Muscogee, or Creek, and the British colony of South Carolina conclude a treaty to regulate trade. The Penobscot and Norridgewock conclude a peace treaty with the British colony of Massachusetts. The terms also provide for return of prisoners. The Six Nations, Delaware, and Shamokin and the British colony of Pennsylvania enter into a treaty which provides for land cession by the People.	

HEROES/LEADERS/ VICTIMS	ELDER WISDOM/PHILOSOPHY/ SONGS	
Konkapot (Stockbridge Mahican), sachem in about 1744, receives the Christian name of John. Colonists at Albany and Boston recognize him as principal leader of the Mahican. A descendant, Levi Konkapot, will serve in the American Civil War, in 1864.	There are many people who could claim and learn from their Indian ancestry, but because of the fear their parents and grandparents knew, because of past and present prejudice against Indian people, that part of their heritage is clouded or denied. *Joseph Bruchac III (Abenaki)*	1745
	I protect my Klallam tribe and the Coast Salish path because my good name is a measure of its language and its arts. *Duane Niatum (Klallam)*	1746
Catahecasasa, or Black Hoof (Shawnee), principal leader, uses his influence to maintain peace between the Shawnee and white settlers after it becomes clear that it is futile to struggle against continued encroachment on land of the Shawnee Nation.		1747
"Indian John," a slave of Richard Randolph of Virginia, is willed to his son Ryland Randolph. The English give Haiglar (Catawba), principal leader, the title "King" Haiglar.	What sort of Men must Europeans be? What Species of Creatures do they retain to? The Europeans, who must be forc'd to do Good, and have no other Prompter for the avoiding of Evil than the fear of Punishment. *Adario, or Kondiaronk (Huron)*	1748
	These wicked whisky sellers, when they have once got the Indians in liquor, make them sell their very clothes from their backs. In short, if this practice be continued we must inevitably be ruined. *Scarouady (Oneida)*	1749

	HISTORY/LAW/ POLITICS	LITERATURE/ART/ LEGENDS AND STORIES
1750	The Onondaga refuse the request of Conrad Weiser, a representative from the colony of Virginia, to enter into negotiations for peace between the Catawba and Onondaga.	
1751	Akmul Au-authm, or Pima, people rebel against the Spaniards and the Franciscan priests in November. Governor Parrilla of Sonora, in Mexico, reacts by establishing a presidio in Tubac, three miles north of what is now Tumacacori, Arizona. The garrison of fifty soldiers at the presidio is told to "maintain order." The Cherokee Nation and the British colony of South Carolina conclude a treaty to regulate trade. The Six Nations and the Catawba conclude a peace and union treaty with the British colony of New York.	
1752	The Chickasaw successfully resist a third attempt by the French to capture towns in the lower Mississippi valley region. The Six Nations and the British colonies of Virginia and Pennsylvania enter into a friendship treaty.	
1753	The Chickasaw successfully resist a fourth attempt by the French to capture towns in the lower Mississippi valley. The Penobscot agree to a treaty with the British colony of Massachusetts which provides for return of captives. The Norridgewock conclude a treaty with the British colony of Massachusetts which provides for the Norridgewock to return captives.	

HEROES/LEADERS/ VICTIMS	ELDER WISDOM/PHILOSOPHY/ SONGS	
Teedyuscung (Delaware) becomes principal leader of the Delaware when he is about fifty years old. He is a powerful statesman known for his craftiness and diplomatic skill. Canassatego (Onondaga), principal leader of the People, dies on September 6. Conrad Weiser hints that the death of Cannasatego was a political assassination.	. . . as for me, I assure you I will press on, and the contrary winds may blow strong in my face, yet I will go forward and never turn back, and continue to press forward until I have finished, and I would have you do the same. . . Though you may hear birds singing on this side and that side, you must not take notice of that, but hear me when I speak to you, and take it to heart, for you may always depend that what I say shall be true. *Teedyuscung (Delaware)*	**1750**
Luis Oacpicagigua (Pima), leader among the Pima, first serves the Spanish conquerors as captain-general against other Indian tribes but soon becomes disillusioned and plots a rebellion against the Spaniards. He leads warriors in an attack on the settlement at Saric, in what is now Arizona, where he kills eighteen Spanish soldiers on November 21.	The reason Wakan tanka does not make two birds, or animals, or human beings exactly alike is because each is placed here by Wakan tanka to be an independent individuality and to rely on itself. *Okute, or Shooter (Teton Sioux)*	**1751**
Wagomend, or the Assinsink Prophet (Assinsink Munsee), experiences his first vision and afterward exhorts the People to abandon English ways and denounce the drinking of rum. He creates a "quarterly meeting"—which lasts all day and all night—that involves walking, singing, and dancing, and concludes with cathartic weeping. He flees the Susquehanna to Ohio at the end of the Seven Years' War. He lives longer than Neolin, or the Delaware Prophet, who is his contemporary. Papoonan (Unami Delaware), a prophet who had been a drunkard, goes alone into the forest when he is about forty-five years old because of the death of his father. While in the woods, Papoonan becomes sober and shortly thereafter receives a vision. In about 1752, he begins to exhort his followers with his message of peace and reformation, urging them to adhere to their ancient traditions.	[The Master of Life] . . . has created [whites and Indians] for different purposes. Therefore, let us cling to our old customs and not depart from them. *Wagomend, the Assinsink Prophet (Assinsink Munsee)*	**1752**
Scarouady (Oneida) is principal leader at the first Indian council at Carlisle, Pennsylvania, held from September 28 through October 4, to oppose white traders who continue to sell rum to the People.	Hear what the Great Spirit has ordered me to tell you: Put off entirely from yourselves the customs which you have adopted since the white people came among us. *Neolin, or the Delaware Prophet (Delaware, or Lenape)*	**1753**

HISTORY/LAW/ POLITICS	LITERATURE/ART/ LEGENDS AND STORIES
1754 The sovereign nations and tribes join their English allies in a fight against the French and their allies of other sovereign nations and tribes in the French and Indian War, which more accurately should be called the French and English War. Major battles in which the warriors of the respective nations fight against each other include Fort Duquesne (1755), Fort William Henry (1757), Lake George (1755), and German Flats (1757). The Six Nations and the British colony of Pennsylvania conclude a treaty which provides for land cession by the Six Nations. The Norridgewock negotiate a peace treaty with the British colony of Massachusetts. The Six Nations and Great Britain enter into a treaty that provides for land cession by the Six Nations. The Penobscot agree to a peace treaty with the British colony of Massachusetts. The Catawba and the British colony of North Carolina conclude a treaty which provides for friendship and land cession.	
1755 The Cherokee Nation and Great Britain conclude a treaty which provides for land cession by the Cherokee. The Muscogee, or Creek, Nation and the British colony of Georgia enter into a friendship treaty.	
1756 The Delaware and Shawnee Nations and Great Britain conclude a peace treaty. The Muscogee, or Creek, Nation and the British colony of South Carolina negotiate a treaty which provides for trade regulation and location of a British fort on Muscogee land. The Delaware and the British colony of New Jersey agree to a treaty related to trade restrictions. The Catawba Nation and the British colony of Virginia conclude a treaty which provides for alliance and fort construction. The Cherokee Nation enters into a treaty with the British colony of Virginia. The terms provide for alliance and Indian education.	

HEROES/LEADERS/ VICTIMS	ELDER WISDOM/PHILOSOPHY/ SONGS	
Scruniyatha, or Half-King (Seneca), principal leader of the Mingo, helps George Washington, a twenty-two-year-old major, to fight the French at Great Meadows, Pennsylvania, during the so-called French and Indian War. Scruniyatha becomes a close friend and adviser of Washington's and accompanies him on an expedition. Lieutenant Governor Robert Dinwiddie of Virginia decorates Scruniyatha and gives him the white name of Dinwiddie. He dies at the home of John Harris, founder of Harrisburg, Pennsylvania, on October 1. Aroniateka, or Hendrick (Mahican/Mohawk), principal leader, speaks to the Albany Congress on July 2 and chastises the English for failing to defend the frontier against the French. His father, the Wolf, was Mahican. Aroniateka often is called "King" Hendrick.	Brothers, here is one thing you yourselves are to blame very much in; that is you rot your grain in tubs, out of which you take and make strong spirits. You sell it to our young men and give it [to] them, many times; they get very drunk with it [and] this is the very cause that they oftentimes commit those crimes that is offensive to you and us and all through the effect of that drink. It is also very bad for our people, for it rots their guts and causes our men to get very sick and many of our people has lately died by the effects of that strong drink, and I heartily wish you would do something to prevent your people from daring to sell or give them any of that strong drink, upon any consideration whatever, for that will be a great means of being free from being accused of those crimes that is committed by our young men and will prevent many of the abuses that is done by them through the effects of that strong drink. *Haiglar, or Aratswa (Catawba)* *in a speech to the authorities* *of North Carolina, on August 29*	**1754**
Neolin (Delaware), the Delaware Prophet, resides at Cayuga, near Lake Erie. Neolin's teachings call for the People to abandon the customs of the English and to avoid trading or depending on European goods. Aroniateka, or Hendrick (Mahican/Mohawk), principal leader who actively participated in the campaign against the French, is ambushed at Crown Point on Lake George, New York, where he and many of his followers are killed on September 8. He is sixty-eight years old. Teyarhasere, or Abraham, or Little Abraham (Mohawk), leader noted for considerable oratory skills, succeeds Aroniateka, or Hendrick, after the Battle of Lake George in 1755.	If they are to fight they are too few—if they are to die, they are too many. *Aroniateka, or Hendrick (Mahican/Mohawk)*	**1755**
Diwali, or the Bowl (Cherokee/Scotch-Irish), whose father was Scotch-Irish and mother was Cherokee, is born in about 1756. Sagoyewatha, or Red Jacket (Seneca), who will become a great leader of the Seneca, is born in about 1756.	We wake; we wake the day, the light rising in us like sun— our breath a prayer brushing against the feathers in our hands. *Gail Tremblay (Onondaga/Micmac/French/English)*	**1756**

	HISTORY/LAW/ POLITICS	LITERATURE/ART/ LEGENDS AND STORIES
1757	Russian fur traders and hunters plunder Aleut villages on Kanaga Island and burn them to the ground. The Six Nations, Delaware, Nanticoke, and Susquehanna enter into a treaty of alliance with the British colony of Pennsylvania. The Six Nations, Delaware, Shawnee, Nanticoke, and Mahican Nations conclude a peace treaty with Great Britain. The Muscogee, or Creek, Nation negotiates a treaty with the British colony of Georgia which provides for land cession, friendship, and peace. The Mahican, Shawnee, and Nanticoke Nations conclude a friendship treaty with Great Britain.	
1758	The first state reservation, called Brotherton, is established on August 29 by the New Jersey legislature for the Lenape, or Delaware, and the Unami Lenape. About two hundred Lenape live on the reservation. The Minisink Nation and the British colony of New Jersey conclude a peace treaty. The Muscogee, or Creek, Nation agrees to a treaty with Great Britain which provides for land cession by the Muscogee. The Six Nations, Delaware, Mahican, Nanticoke, and Minisink and the British colonies of New Jersey and Pennsylvania enter into a treaty which provides for peace and land cession. The Muscogee and Great Britain negotiate a treaty which provides for land settlement by whites. The Cherokee Nation concludes a treaty with the British colony of North Carolina. The terms provide for peace and resumption of trade.	
1759	The Iroquois League of the Six Nations (the original Five Nations—the Oneida, Onondaga, Seneca, Cayuga, Mohawk—and the sixth nation, the Tuscarora), along with the Shawnee, Delaware, Twightwee, and Wyandot meet at what is now Pittsburgh with General Stanwix to formalize by treaty the inclusion of the Wyandot in the Chain of Friendship. Orignially called the Covenant Chain, which was an alliance between the Dutch and Iroquois, it later became the Chain of Friendship, and was used to formalize alliances between the Iroquois and non-Iroquois.	
1760	The Six Nations and Great Britain enter into a friendship treaty.	

HEROES/LEADERS/ VICTIMS	ELDER WISDOM/PHILOSOPHY/ SONGS	
	. . . as a light-skinned Indian person, I am seen as a person of betweens, as a person of divided directions. *Linda Hogan (Chickasaw/white)*	**1757**
 Carol Lee Sanchez (Lugna Pueblo/Chippewa) COURTESY OF LEE FRANCIS III	yo soy india pero no soy nacio mi abuelo on the reservation, a Laguna Indian—but her daddy was a Scotsman. *Carol Lee Sanchez (Laguna/Chippewa/Scottish/Lebanese)*	**1758**
	We talk to Wakan tanka and are sure he hears us, and yet it is hard to explain what we believe about this. *Mato-kuwapi, or Chased-by-Bears (Santee/Yanktonai Sioux)*	**1759**
	I circle around— I circle around The boundaries of the earth, The boundaries of the earth— Wearing the long wing feathers as I fly, Wearing the long wing feathers as I fly. *Ghost Dance prayer song*	**1760**

1761

The Mahican, Tutelo, Nanticoke, Delaware, Conoy, Oneida, Onondaga, and Cayuga Nations negotiate a treaty with the British colony of Pennsylvania. The terms provide for land cession and the return of prisoners by both parties.

The Cherokee Nation and Great Britain enter into a treaty which provides for peace, boundary lines, and the return of prisoners by both parties.

Babeshikit (Kickapoo)
COURTESY OF SMITHSONIAN

1762

Russians participating in the Pushkareff expedition take Alaskan native women prisoner to be slaves. On the voyage to Russia, all but two of the slaves are murdered.

The Six Nations, Delaware, Shawnee, Miami, Conoy, and Kickapoo enter into a treaty with the British colony of Pennsylvania. The terms provide for land cession and the return of captives.

HEROES / LEADERS / VICTIMS	ELDER WISDOM / PHILOSOPHY / SONGS	

Neolin (Delaware), the Delaware Prophet, gains a large following with his exhortations for the People of the sovereign nations and tribes to reject the white man's culture and return to their traditional practices. The movement spreads throughout the Ohio valley and the eastern Great Lakes area. Pontiac, chief of the Odawa, or Ottawa, focuses the force of the movement into a plan to drive the immigrant English colonists from the region.

Attakullakulla, or Onacona, or Little Carpenter (Cherokee), is the principal leader who exerts his influence with the People, resulting in the signing of the Treaty of Charleston in 1761.

from heart through mind into image:
the pulse of the four directions
the voice of our blood
the spirit of breath and words.

William Oandasan (Yuki)

1761

The Shawnee kill Haiglar, or Aratswa (Catawba), principal leader. His grandson is Colonel Samuel Scott, who becomes principal leader of the Catawba and will sign a treaty with South Carolina in 1840.

You [white people] talk of the law of nature and the law of nations, and they are both against you.

Corn Tassel (Cherokee)

1762

127

1763

More than three hundred Calusa who had resisted English encroachment of land in Florida are forced to migrate to Cuba.

In April, a Great Council of all the northwestern sovereign nations and tribes is held near Detroit. Pontiac, or Ponteach, calls for the People to unite to recover their ancient lands and preserve their respective sovereign nations' ways of life. His proposal is approved unanimously, and messengers are sent to gain the assent of the more remote sovereign nations. Within weeks, a majority of the tribes of the Algonkian Confederacy and the Wyandot, Seneca, and Winnebago nations combine forces. Under Pontiac's leadership, they attack English forts in May. They capture all forts west of Fort Niagara except Fort Detroit and Fort Pitt (now known as Pittsburgh).

Two huge teams play lacrosse, the traditional sport of the People of the sovereign nations, outside Fort Michilimackinac, Michigan, on June 4.

English military leader Jeffrey Amherst, later Baron Amherst, first suggests the idea of biological warfare by infecting the People of the sovereign nations with smallpox after Pontiac's attacks on the English forts. This idea is later implemented unofficially by the United States government, which deliberately sends smallpox-infected blankets to Indians forced to live on reservations, resulting in the deaths of thousands. This atrocity instigated by a government is to have no equal until Chancellor Adolf Hitler of Nazi Germany creates his infamous death camps for Jews and other "undesirables."

The Conestoga tribe becomes almost extinct after the massacre of the last twenty men, women, and children by white frontier terrorists known as the Paxton boys on December 27 near what is now Lancaster, Pennsylvania.

Treaties between the Cherokee, Creek, Choctaw, and Chickasaw Nations and Great Britain provide for boundary definition, peace, and land cession.

1764

The Seneca Nation and Great Britain enter into a peace treaty which also provides for land cession by the Seneca.

The Huron conclude a peace and alliance treaty with Great Britain.

Teedyuscung (Delaware) is burned to death when his house is set on fire on April 19.

Pontiac, or Ponteach (Odawa, or Ottawa), dreamer and principal leader, begins his assault May 7 on Fort Detroit, a prime target.

Wawatam (Ojibwa) appeals on behalf of his captive adopted white "brother" Alexander Henry at a council lodge meeting in June. The council considers the request carefully, and later accepts Wawatam's assurances and releases the captive.

Coosaponakeesa, or Creek Mary (Muscogee/white), Beloved Woman, dies at Saint Catherine's Island, off Georgia.

... the Great Spirit and giver of light, who has made the Earth and everything therein, has brought us all together this day for our mutual good to promote the good works of peace.

Pontiac, or Ponteach (Odawa, or Ottawa)

1763

Clara Nomee (Crow)
Chairman of the
Crow Nation
COURTESY OF TONY SMITH

Neolin (Delaware), the Delaware Prophet, takes refuge at Wakatomica when the British threaten to invade his town on the Tuscarawas River. His exhortations to begin armed resistance to English expansion greatly influence Pontiac, the Great Leader of the Odawa, as well as the Seneca, Miami, Chippewa, Wyandot, Shawnee, and Potawatomi.

Papoonan (Unami Delaware) is forced to flee to the safety of barracks in Philadelphia under Quaker protection from British colonial lynch mobs in about 1764.

[Indians] ... have grown proud and covetous, which causes God to be angry and to send dry and hot summers and hard winters and also sickness among the people. ... [They must] return to the ancient customs and manners of their forefathers.

Papoonan (Unami Delaware)

1764

1765

British officers at Fort Pitt deliberately supply hospital blankets infected with smallpox to cold and starving Peoples of sovereign nations living in the Ohio valley after the defeat of Pontiac. The ensuing smallpox epidemic kills hundreds.

The Choctaw and Chickasaw Nations and Great Britain negotiate a treaty which centers on boundaries and land cession.

The Muscogee, or Creek, Nation and Great Britain conclude a treaty concerning boundary lines.

The Shawnee and Mingo Nations negotiate a peace treaty with Great Britain.

The Muscogee, or Creek, Nation and Great Britain negotiate a treaty which details boundary lines of the Muscogee Nation.

The Delaware Nation and Great Britain conclude a peace treaty.

1766

The Six Nations, Odawa, Potawatomi, Ojibwa, and Huron Nations join together and conclude a peace treaty with Great Britain.

Pushmataha (Choctaw)
COURTESY OF SMITHSONIAN

1767

The Cherokee Nation negotiates a treaty with Great Britain which relates to boundary lines.

The Muscogee, or Creek, Nation and Great Britain conclude a treaty concerning trade regulations.

1768

The Cherokee Nation's claims to land west of the Blue Ridge Mountains, in Virginia, to the Ohio River are recognized by the Treaty of Hard Harbor between the Cherokee and the English.

The Nanticoke Nation and the British colony of Maryland conclude a treaty which provides for land cession to the colonists.

The Six Nations, Shawnee, Delaware, Ohio Seneca, and "other dependent tribes" enter into a treaty at Fort Stanwix (now Rome, New York) with representatives of the British colonies of New Jersey, Virginia, and Pennsylvania, among others. Boundary lines between colonies and the lands of the People of the sovereign nations and tribes are negotiated. Because the People of the sovereign nations and tribes cede an excessive area, King George III instructs the colonies to recede some of the land.

HEROES/LEADERS/VICTIMS	ELDER WISDOM/PHILOSOPHY/SONGS	
Arpeika, or Sam Jones (Miccosukee Seminole), who will become a great war leader of the Seminole, is born. Comcomly (Chinook), who will become principal leader of the People, is born. Pushmataha (Choctaw), who will become principal leader of the Choctaw Nation, is born in about 1765 in what is now Noxubee County, Mississippi.	Down by the river you told me you were going to be a medicine woman. I wanted to believe you brewing against the background of flickering lights and fireworks. *Gloria Bird (Spokane)*	**1765**
Pontiac (Odawa, or Ottawa), dreamer and principal leader, admits defeat in April and helps his former enemies, the British, subdue remaining bands. This wins the admiration and respect of the British. Pontiac signs a peace treaty with the English at Detroit on August 17 after his unsuccessful five-month attempt to capture the fort. Chocorua (Wamesit) is the last survivor of the small tribe that lived near what is now Benton, New Hampshire. Chocorua is pursued by a white hunter and is driven over a cliff which bears Chocorua's name today. Jane King (Odawa, or Ottawa), who will become an honored medicine woman, is born on the Maumee River in what is now Ohio.	Wakan Tanka is at every direction and is everywhere in the world. *Hehaka Sapa, or Black Elk (Oglala Lakota)*	**1766**
Makatai-meshe-kiakiak, or Black Hawk (Sauk), who will become a noted principal leader, is born.	The path to glory is rough, and many gloomy hours obscure it. May the Great Spirit shed light on yours. . . . *Makatai-meshe-kiakiak, or Black Hawk (Sauk)*	**1767**
Tecumtha, or Tecumseh, (Shawnee/Muscogee), prophet and principal leader of the Shawnee, is born at Old Piqua, Ohio. "King" Johnny (Cheraw), last principal leader of the Cheraw, is killed when the Cheraw are being absorbed by the Catawba. The Cheraw no longer exist.	Time rolls on without ceasing. The winter passes quickly away, and the summer is here again. You shall soon glory in the strength of your manhood, and your enemies afar shall hear your name and tremble. *Methoataske (Muscogee), mother of Tecumtha*	**1768**

	HISTORY / LAW / POLITICS	LITERATURE / ART / LEGENDS AND STORIES
1769	The population of the sovereign nations and tribes in what is now California is estimated conservatively at one million. The Odawa, Chippewa, Potawatomi, Sac, and Fox Peoples unite against the Peoria, or Illinois, and defeat them in retaliation for the murder of Pontiac (Odawa, or Ottawa) by Black Dog (Peoria).	
1770	The Micmac gradually exterminate the Beothuk people of Newfoundland. The French reward the Micmac for every Beothuk killed. More than twenty-three hundred People of the sovereign nations and tribes—including the Six Nations, Shawnee, Nanticoke, Conloy, Tutelo, Caughnawaga, Saint Regis, Algonkian, Saint Francis Abenaki, Loretto Huron, Nipissing, and Missisauga—gather at the Shawnee village of Germantown Flats, in the colony of New York, and agree to make peace with the Cherokee and other sovereign nations of the South. Cherokee land claims recognized under the Treaty of Hard Harbor in 1768 are changed in the new Treaty of Lochaber. The boundary with the whites is moved six miles west.	
1771	The Six Nations gather in November at Onondaga, in New York colony, and accept the invitation from the sovereign nations and tribes to the south and west to meet at Scioto, near what is now Portsmouth, Ohio.	*Aleek-chea-ahoosh, or Plenty Coup (Crow) [right] and Grandmothers Knife (Crow) [left]* COURTESY OF SMITHSONIAN
1772	The Canajoharie Mohawk and Oneida, having complained bitterly about being deprived of all their land, are mollified when King George III severely reprimands William Tryon, governor of the colony of New York, for permitting the sale of the lands of the People of the sovereign nations and tribes to individual colonists. The king states that such sales are "unjustifiable collusion" and "It is the King's pleasure and positive command that you do not, upon any pretence whatever, sign any Grant or Patent for those Lands." It is doubtful that the land was returned prior to the American Revolutionary War, however.	*A Sermon Preached at the Execution of Moses Paul, An Indian Who Was Executed at New Haven, on the 2d of September 1772.* Samson Occum (Mohegan).
1773	The Muscogee, or Creek, and the Cherokee conclude a treaty with Great Britain. The terms provide for land cession by the Muscogee and Cherokee.	Among the Kiowa, it is said that a long time ago a person's name was his own and he could keep the name or give it away. It is also said that the Kiowa would not say the name of a dead person because it would be disrespectful, since the dead take their names with them when they pass over.

HEROES/LEADERS/ VICTIMS	ELDER WISDOM/PHILOSOPHY/ SONGS	
Nonhelema, or the Grenadier Squaw (Shawnee), is leader of her own village near what is now Ross County, Ohio. She is regarded highly among the Shawnee and immigrant English colonists because of her proved skill in fighting and her strength and size. Pontiac, or Ponteach (Odawa, or Ottawa), principal leader, is murdered in April by Black Dog (Peoria, or Illinois). It is thought that the British paid him for the deed.	Cherokee mothers do not wish to go to an unknown country. . . . We have understood that some of our children wish to go over the Mississippi, but this act . . . would be like destroying your mothers. *The Ghigau, or Nancy Ward (Cherokee Beloved Woman)*	**1769**
Crispus Attucks (Narraganset/Negro) is the first person killed in the Boston Massacre, which signals the start of the American Revolutionary War. His father was Negro and his mother was Narraganset. His last name was that of his mother, Ahtuk, meaning "a small deer." Tah-gah-jute, or James Logan, or Tachnechdorus (Cayuga), moves from Shamokin, or what is now Sunbury, Pennsylvania, to what is now Chillicothe, Ohio.	There was a warrior, who died the death of a warrior. There was joy in his voice! *Dakota warrior song*	**1770**
Finhioven (Kadohadacho), principal leader, facilitates the attendance of Athanase DeMézières, lieutenant governor of Spanish Louisiana, at a peace-treaty conference between the Wichita and the Spanish governors of Louisiana and Texas, on October 27. The governors commission Finhioven to plunder English towns.	The ground on which we stand is sacred ground. It is the dust and blood of our ancestors. . . . We are like birds with a broken wing. My heart is cold within me. My eyes are growing dim—I am old. . . . *Aleek-chea-ahoosh, or Plenty Coups (Crow)*	**1771**
Onpahtonga, or Big Elk (Omaha), who will become principal leader of the People, is born. Scattameck (Delaware, or Lenape), prophet to the Shawnee and Miami in about 1772, like the prophets before him, exhorts his followers to turn away from the ways of the European immigrant colonists and return to the ancient practices of their ancestors.		**1772**
Tah-gah-jute, or James Logan, or Tachnechdorus (Cayuga), principal leader of the Mingo whose Shawnee wife and children had been slaughtered by English colonists, leads the battle against John Murray, earl of Dunmore, and his forces.	I appeal to any white man to say, if he ever entered Logan's cabin hungry, and he gave him no meat; if ever he came cold and naked, and he clothed him not. . . . I had even thought to have lived with you, but for the injuries of one man, Colonel Cressap, who last spring, in cold blood, and unprovoked, murdered all the relatives of Logan, not even sparing my women and children. There runs not a drop of my blood in the veins of any living creature. . . . Who is there to mourn for Logan? Not one! *Tah-gah-jute, or James Logan, or Tachnechdorus (Cayuga)*	**1773**

	HISTORY/LAW/ POLITICS	LITERATURE/ART/ LEGENDS AND STORIES
1774	Shawnee forces respond to attack by Virginians who occupy Fort Pitt. The battle, known as Lord Dunmore's War, rages from January through October. The Shawnee, Odawa, or Ottawa, and their allies are defeated on October 10 in Lord Dunmore's War. Under the treaty at Fort Stanwix, the sovereign nations are forced to cede what is now Kentucky to the English and to permit colonists to have access to and navigation rights on the Ohio River. The Muscogee, or Creek, conclude a treaty with the British colony of Georgia. The terms provide for peace, friendship, and commerce. The Iroquois League of the Six Nations meets at Onondaga, in New York colony, and the Shawnee also attend. The clan mothers censure the Cayuga for having permitted their young soldiers to help the Shawnee without permission of the council. The young soldiers are recalled from the battle. Yellow Creek Massacre at Baker's Bottom, near what is now Steubenville, Ohio, takes place in April. Among the People of the sovereign nations who die during the massacre by English settlers are the Shawnee wife and children of Tah-gah-jute, or James Logan (Cayuga).	*A Choice Collection of Hyms* [sic] *and Spiritual Songs Intented* [sic] *for the Edification of Sincere Christians of All Denominations.* Samson Occum (Mohegan).
1775	The Northern, Southern, and Middle Departments of Indian Affairs are created by an act of the Continental Congress on July 12. Benjamin Franklin, Patrick Henry, and James Wilson are named to head the departments as commissioners. The Continental Congress funds the education of students from the sovereign nations and tribes at Dartmouth College with $500,000. Twenty million acres belonging to the Cherokee Nation is transferred under the Treaty of Sycamore Shoals to the Transylvania Company of North Carolina on March 17. The Six Nations accept the invitation of the Indian affairs commissioners of the Continental Congress to meet at Albany to enter treaty negotiations. Participating in the negotiations are the Six Nations, the Shawnee, and the Delaware. The last treaty to be negotiated at Albany provides for peace, return of hostages, and establishment of hunting boundaries. The commissioners urge the principal leaders of the Six Nations to be neutral in the war between the colonists and Great Britain. Laguna Pueblo, in what is now New Mexico, is "ministered" to by Francisco Silvestre Vélez de Escalante, who travels from Laguna to Ashiwi, or Zuñi, in June. Escalante strongly recommends to the authorities in Mexico City that force be used to convert the Hopi people to Roman Catholicism.	Among the Siksika, or Blackfeet, it is said that in the earliest times, all the People of the sovereign nations and tribes lived in peace. Then in later times, it is said, Na'pi, or Old Man, marked a piece of ground and told the People that the land was for them. The People were told that if others came and crossed the line which Na'pi had made, the People were to take up arms against the strangers. It is said that the Siksika did not obey the laws of Na'pi. They did not keep the white people from crossing the line, which is why the Siksika have suffered so much.

Wynepuechsika, or Cornstalk (Shawnee), principal leader, heads the confederation of Ohio people of the sovereign nations and tribes to prevent white settlers from planting corn north of the Ohio River. Defeated in battle at Point Pleasant, in what is now Ohio, he participates in treaty negotiations at what is now Chillicothe, Ohio, in November.

Mother Corn has fed you, as she has fed all . . . people, since the long, long ago when she was no longer than my thumb. Mother Corn is the promise of food and life.

Sevenka (Hopi)

1774

Mushulatubbee, or Muchalatubbee (Choctaw), who is to become principal leader, is born.

Tamaha, or One Eye (Mdewakanton Sioux), who will become principal leader, is born at what is now Winona, Minnesota.

Teyarhasere, or Abraham, or Little Abraham (Mohawk), principal leader, is present at the signing of the last treaty with the English at Albany in September. Thayendanegea, or Joseph Brant (Mohawk), succeeds him as principal leader of the Mohawk.

Blackfish (Shawnee), principal leader, captures frontiersman Daniel Boone outside Boonesboro, Kentucky, and adopts him into the Shawnee Nation at Detroit in the spring.

Shabonee, or Shabonna (Potawatomi), who will become a noted peace leader and speaker, is born.

My son, you are now flesh of our flesh and bone of our bone. By the ceremony which was performed this day every drop of white blood was washed from your veins. . . You are now one of us by an old strong law and custom.

Blackfish (Shawnee)
At the adoption ceremony of Daniel Boone

1775

HISTORY/LAW/ POLITICS	LITERATURE/ART/ LEGENDS AND STORIES

1776

Principal leaders of the Six Nations meet with representatives of the British Crown at what is now Niagara Falls, New York. The British strongly urge that the People of the Six Nations remain neutral in the conflict between the colonists and England.

Apache soldiers sack the mission station at Tumacacori, in present Arizona, while the garrison of Mexican soldiers stationed at the presidio in Tubac is away. The Apache take horses and cattle.

The Hidatsa living along the Missouri River in the Dakota region are plunged into internal strife between two factions with an equal number of people involved. One group migrates to the Rocky Mountain region and becomes known as the Crow Nation.

People of the sovereign nations and tribes along the East Coast of Turtle Island begin to factionalize, with some supporting the colonists and others supporting the British, after the declaration of American independence by the Congress of the United States in July.

Colonists during the American Revolutionary War against the English adopt military fighting methods of the People of the sovereign nations and tribes, including fighting from cover, camouflage, ambush, harassment, and other tactics.

Among the Athabascan of the Upper Yukon, it is said that a long time ago, water flowed all over the world. Because there was no land, the People wanted to make a world, so a muskrat was found and a long string was tied to it. It is said that the muskrat was sent down into the water and drowned, but reached the bottom and got a little mud on its hands. It is said that the muskrat was pulled up to the surface by the long string and that the mud was taken out of its hands. After the mud dried, it was crumbled into dust. The dust was blown out all over the waters, and this is how, it is said, the world was made.

1777

The Onondaga are devastated by an epidemic which results in the death of most of the principal leaders. The surviving Onondaga "cover" the great council fire.

The Mohawk and Seneca unite in support of British Colonel Barry St. Leger's forces. They fight the rebel army of farmers, Oneida, and Tuscarora under American General Nicholas Herkimer at the Battle of Oriskany, in New York, on August 6.

The Cherokee Nation enters into a treaty with the colonies of Virginia and North Carolina which specifically prohibits immigrant colonists from settling on lands of the Cherokee, including those at the fork of the French Broad and Holston Rivers.

The Oglala Lakota holy man Hehaka Sapa, or Black Elk, tells of a time long ago when a Lakota holy man called Drinks Water had a dream about the future. In his dream, Drinks Water saw that the four-leggeds were going back into the earth and that a strange race had woven a spider's web around all the Lakota people. According to Hehaka Sapa, Drinks Water said that "when this happens, you shall live in square grey houses, in a barren land, and beside those square grey houses you shall starve."

1776

Attakullakulla, or Onacona, or Little Carpenter (Cherokee), principal leader, raises a force of soldiers to assist colonists in their Revolutionary War against the English.

Tsiyu-gunsini, or Ciu Canacina, or Dragging Canoe (Cherokee), a leader among the People and son of Attakullakulla, or Little Carpenter, leads many of the Cherokee against the colonists during the Revolutionary War. He speaks at the Council of Chota in May, where he vows armed resistance against the colonists' expansion into Cherokee lands.

Cheshahadakhi, or Lean Wolf (Hidatsa)
COURTESY OF SMITHSONIAN

It may appear to those whom I have the honor to address a singular distaste for me, an Indian, to take an interest in the triumphal days for a people who occupy, by conquest or have usurped, the possessions of my fathers and have laid and carefully preserved a train of terrible miseries to end when my race [ceases] to exist.

Waun-na-con, or John Quinney (Stockbridge Mahican)

1777

Wynepuechsika, or Cornstalk (Shawnee), principal leader, travels to Point Pleasant, in what is now Ohio, under a flag of truce, but is taken hostage, along with his son Elinipsico. Enraged soldiers murder them in jail. The murderers are acquitted later in a "trial."

Honyery Doxtator (Oneida) is principal leader of the village of Oriska, which the Mohawks burn, resulting in civil war in the Iroquois League.

Francis Joseph Neptune (Passamaquoddy) is principal leader who leads the People in support of the colonists' effort against the English during the American Revolutionary War. Under his leadership, the Passamaquoddy successfully repel a British naval expedition attempting to land at Machias, Maine.

Thayendanegea, or Joseph Brant (Mohawk), principal war leader, leads Mohawk forces at the Battle of Oriskany.

Kiantwa'ka, or Cornplanter, or John O'Bail (Seneca/ Irish), principal leader of the Seneca, leads Seneca forces at the Battle of Oriskany.

. . . we shall make our laws and when all are made we shall call the organization we have formed The Great Peace. It shall be the power to abolish war and robbery between brothers and bring peace and quietness.

The Peacemaker

In the life of the Indian there is only one inevitable duty,—the duty of prayer—the daily recognition of the Unseen and Eternal.

*Ohiyesa, or Charles A. Eastman, M.D.
(Santee Dakota)*

CEREMONY TIME

Our non-Native relations have tried to melt the People of the sovereign nations and tribes into some sort of pot for centuries. When that attempt failed, our non-Native relations decided that the beliefs that the People of the sovereign nations and tribes hold in common clearly demonstrate that we are Pan-Indians. Although it may come as a shock to many non-Natives, the People of the sovereign nations and tribes are neither *pots* nor *pan* anything. What we believe is what we believe, each in our own way.

To be sure, there are beliefs and experiences which Native People hold in common. There are tragedies such as smallpox-infected blankets, Sand Creek, and Chief Big Foot that have become interwoven in the cultural practices of all the People to a greater or lesser degree. The perfidy of the United States government in its relationship with the sovereign nations and tribes is also a shared experience.

Most important are the beliefs pertaining to the Great Spirit—an aspect, if you will, of the Great Mystery—held in common by the People of the sovereign nations and tribes on Turtle Island. For the People, it isn't about belonging to a religious sect, be it Jewish, Muslim, Buddhist, Baha'i, Christian, or Native. These sects are a way to "practice" or "demonstrate" the belief that everything—both seen and unseen—is connected.

The **Ceremony Time** section is presented to give a sense of the beliefs and experiences that form a ceremonial part of every Native person's everyday life. Gaining a sense or perspective of the beliefs and experiences does not mean that the proceeding is how or what the People of the sovereign nations and tribes do in actual practice. Having a sense is like smelling a newly squeezed orange. Smelling the tangy-sweet odor of the orange is not actually eating the orange.

Above all, this segment does not reflect a Pan-Indian version of the Native Americans' spiritual practices. The sacred practices of the People are private. They belong to the People of the sovereign nations and tribes, and a person or group not of that sovereign nation or tribe does not have any right to disclose those particular sacred practices overtly or covertly.

At the same time, many people are seeking to reorganize their lives in this technologically abundant age. They desperately seek answers that will bring order to the chaotic world in which they live. The central theme of **Ceremony Time** is about order and relationships. It is about living in harmony and balance with all of creation.

Ceremony Time is based on the circle. For all Native People, the circle is the essence of understanding the prime principle: everything—both seen and unseen—is connected. The People of the sovereign nations and tribes have been telling our non-Native relations this for centuries. It is only recently, however, that our non-Native relations finally have begun to understand this principle.

The "scientists" among our non-Native relations are now able to "prove" that there is a direct cause-and-effect relationship between technologically caused pollution (cars, factories, and so forth) and depletion of the ozone layer. They have gathered "proof" that the thinning ozone layer is a primary cause of the increasing incidence of skin cancer among people. This "proof" comes as no surprise to the People of the sovereign nations and tribes. Human beings invented cars that pollute, which results in depletion of the ozone layer, which results in human beings dying of cancer. It is all very circular.

The point is, **Ceremony Time** needs to be imagined as a circle and not as a linear "calendar" with an arbitrary beginning, middle, and end. Again, in keeping with the order of the universe as perceived by human beings on Mother Earth, **Ceremony Time** consists of the four seasons—spring, summer, autumn, and winter. Each period begins with a festival celebrating that season.

Because everything is connected, **Ceremony Time** is divided further into the twelve months of the year. The first four days of each month focus on an area which always has been important to the People of the sovereign nations and tribes. In March, for example, the focus during the first four days is on the family.

MARCH

Prayer
Great Spirit, we celebrate the coming of new life and give thanks for all creation. Give us the strength of purpose to walk in harmony and balance as we honor

the good red Earth our Mother with the planting of crops. Give special strength to the elders and leaders of the People and guide them in their work so that the People may live and prosper.

Focus—Family (March 1–4)

For the People of the sovereign nations and tribes, the family includes blood relatives, those related through their respective clans, and those of the same nation. The family is important in the ceremonial and secular life of the People because it is the source of our strength and our future.

Council Fires

We honor those who have been chosen to lead and serve their respective sovereign nations and tribes. We celebrate the hard work and dedication of the elders and council members of the Akiak (Akiak, Alaska), Anvik (Anvik, Alaska), Tlingit and Haida (Juneau, Alaska), Cristochina (Gakona, Alaska), Douglas (Douglas, Alaska), Fort Yukon (Fort Yukon, Alaska), Hughes (Hughes, Alaska), Kasaan (Kasaan, Alaska), Kobuk (Kobuk, Alaska), Larsen Bay (Larsen Bay, Alaska), Naknek (Naknek, Alaska), Nikolski (Nikolski, Alaska), Oscarville (Oscarville, Alaska), Port Graham (Homer, Alaska), Scammon Bay (Scammon Bay, Alaska), Saint Michael (Saint Michael, Alaska), Tetlin (Tetlin, Alaska), Venetie (Arctic Village, Alaska), Chicken Ranch Rancheria (Jamestown, California), Jackson Rancheria (Jackson, California), Round Valley (Covelo, California), Yurok (Eureka, California), Agua Caliente (Palm Springs, California), Rohnerville Rancheria (Eureka, California), San Pasqual (Valley Center, California), Santa Ynez Mission (Santa Ynez, California), Kootenai (Bonners Ferry, Idaho), Apache (Anadarko, Oklahoma), Peoria of Oklahoma (Miami, Oklahoma), Burns Paiute (Burns, Oregon), Nooksack (Deming, Washington), Quinault (Taholah, Washington), Shoalwater Bay (Tokeland, Washington), Suquamish (Suquamish, Washington), Tulalip (Marysville, Washington).

Events

- Indian dance festival, Saint John's Mission, Gila River Reservation, Arizona, early March.
- Mul-Chu-Tha fair and rodeo, Sacaton, Arizona, second weekend of March.
- Celebration of openings of irrigation ditches, most pueblos in New Mexico, week of spring equinox.
- Spring equinox ceremonies and footraces, most pueblos in New Mexico.
- Yaqui dances and pageant, Pascua Yaqui, Tucson, Arizona.
- Festival of Saint Francis, Yaqui, Yaqui village in Tucson, Arizona.
- Spring ceremonies, most pueblos in New Mexico, after spring equinox.
- Feast day, Laguna Pueblo, Laguna, New Mexico, March 19.
- Indian fair, Wapato, Washington, midmonth.
- Yuma Quechan tribal powwow, Quechan, Fort Yuma, California, last week of the month.
- Bear dance and spring welcome, Ignacio and Towoac, Colorado, late in the month.
- Trade fair and dances, Pima, or Akmul Au-authm, Salt River, Arizona, last week of the month.
- Keresan dances, Cochiti Pueblo, Cochiti, New Mexico, March 27.

Festival of Crop Planting (March 18–25)

Corn, wild rice, squash, and beans always have been and continue to be of central importance to most of the People of the sovereign nations and tribes living on Turtle Island. The crops we plant are life-giving food which we believe are gifts given to us by the Earth our Mother.

Because corn represents our connection to earth, it is very important in sacred ceremonies and social activities among many of the People of the sovereign nations and tribes. In all instances, ceremonial activities are followed by social events centered around planting of crops which are sacred to the People of the respective sovereign nations and tribes.

The crops planted by the People of the sovereign nations and tribes signify abundance and fertility. When a kernel or seed is planted, we remember our connection with Mother Earth and to all that lives.

During this eight-day festival, let us focus our good thoughts and energies with all of creation—both seen and unseen—and celebrate our rebirth and renewal so that all creation may live and prosper.

Honoring of Infants and Children (March 26–April 2)

We especially honor the infants and children of the sovereign nations and tribes, for without them the council fires would be no more. The children are the future and the hope of the sovereign nations and tribes. It is important that the mothers of the sovereign nations and tribes who bear the children be free of alcohol and drugs throughout their pregnancies if the sovereign nations and tribes are to grow and prosper to the tenth generation. A nation of children affected by fetal alcohol syndrome and fetal alcohol effect cannot survive; such children will be unable to lead the people when they become adults.

During this eight-day honoring time, let us remember that it is the responsibility of all the People of the sovereign nations and tribes to care for the present and future mothers of the People, and to help them understand that they are directly responsible for the survival and growth of the People.

APRIL

Prayer

Great Spirit, we are grateful for our many blessings, and as we celebrate the traditional ways of the People, help us to remember always that through the power of the sacred drum we will be united forever with all of creation in the circle of the Great Mystery.

Focus—Environment (April 1–4)

During the first four days of this month, let us focus all our attention on restoring the environment. Our special relationship with the Earth our Mother has not changed for thousands of years. Long before our non-Native relations came across the sea to this place we call Turtle Island, the People of the sovereign nations and tribes took special care to live in harmony with the Earth our Mother. Few people would think of defacing or destroying such works of art as the *Mona Lisa* or Michelangelo's *David,* yet they think nothing of defacing and destroying the most magnificent of all works of art—the Earth our Mother. And although many people believe that by using the resources provided by the Earth our Mother, such as coal and other minerals, so that we all may enjoy the benefits of civilization, careful conservation of nonrenewable resources is absolutely necessary.

The same is true with renewable resources such as timber. It is interesting that governmental policy makers are, more often than not, the first to argue for balance between the need for employment in the timber industry and protecting the environment. To the People of the sovereign nations and tribes, the argument is foolish. Common sense tells us that once the resources are gone, the problem of jobs won't matter because everyone will be dead. Common sense tells us that for every tree that is cut, three must be planted—one to replace the one that was cut, the second to rebuild the forests of the earth, the third to restore the air we breathe. It is an easy solution which our non-Native relatives continue to ignore.

Council Fires

We honor those who have been chosen to lead and serve their respective sovereign nations and tribes. We celebrate the hard work and dedication of the elders and council members of the Akutan (Akutan, Alaska), Arctic Village (Arctic Village, Alaska), Chalkyitsik (Chalkyitsik, Alaska), Chitina (Chitina, Alaska), Eagle Village (Eagle, Alaska), Gakona (Gakona, Alaska), Huslia (Huslia, Alaska), Kasigluk (Kasigluk, Alaska), Kodiak (Kodiak, Alaska), Levelock (Levelock, Alaska), Nanwalek (English Bay, Alaska), Noatak (Noatak, Alaska), Ouzinkie (Ouzinkie, Alaska), Port Heiden (Port Heiden, Alaska), Selawik (Selawik, Alaska), Aleut (Saint Paul Island, Alaska), Togiak (Wainwright, Alaska), White Mountain Apache (Whiteriver, Arizona), Blue Lake Rancheria (Blue Lake, California), Campo Mission (Campo, California), Cedarville Rancheria (Cedarville, California), Cloverdale Rancheria (Cloverdale, California), Laytonville Rancheria (Laytonville, California), Rumsey Rancheria (Brooks, California), Santa Rosa Rancheria (Lemoore, California), Soboba Mission (San Jacinto, California), Table Bluff (Loleta, California), Northwestern Band of Shoshoni Nation (Fort Hall, Idaho), Tunica-Biloxi (Mansura, Louisiana), Wampanoag (Gay Head, Massachusetts), Houlton Maliseet (Houlton, Maine), Shoshone Paiute (Owyhee, Nevada), Tonkawa (Tonkawa, Oklahoma), Coos, Lower Umpqua, and Siuslaw (Coos Bay, Oregon), Oglala Sioux (Pine Ridge, South Dakota), Paiute of Utah (Cedar City, Utah), Muckleshoot (Auburn, Washington).

Events

- Spring corn dances, all pueblos in New Mexico and Arizona, April 1–4.
- Bear dance, Northern Ute, Fort Duchesne, Utah, early in the month.
- Spring powwow, Warm Springs tribe, Warm Springs, Oregon, early in the month.
- Root festival, Warm Springs tribe, Warm Springs, Oregon, midmonth.
- Gathering of Nations, intertribal powwow, University of New Mexico, Albuquerque, New Mexico, late in the month.
- Powwow, San Xavier Reservation, Tucson, Arizona, late in the month.
- Root festival, Umatilla tribe, Umatilla, Oregon, late in the month.

Celebration of Our Languages (April 3–18)

Over the past two centuries, the People of the sovereign nations and tribes firmly resisted the efforts by their non-Native immigrant relations to abolish their respective languages. Because of this adamant resistance by the People the United States military engagements during World War I and World War II were dramatically helped by the Cherokee Code Talkers, Choctaw Code Talkers, and the Navajo Code Talkers. The Code Talkers were able to communicate information between military outposts that were critically important in the winning of the two World Wars by the United States and its allies.

During the sixteen-day celebration, let us remember the courage of all the People of the sovereign Nations and tribes who continued to speak and teach their respective languages to their children. Let us also celebrate the bravery of the Code Talkers who were instrumental in bringing about victory in two World Wars.

Honoring the Red Earth Our Mother (April 19–26)

For more than five centuries, the People of the sovereign nations and tribes have urged our non-Native relations to honor and respect the red Earth our Mother. It is with glad hearts that we commend many of our non-Native relations for finally coming to understand that all is connected and that if we fail to care for the earth, all that lives will die.

During this honoring, let us focus our efforts and energies on the good red Earth our Mother by taking personal responsibility and action to protect her from further abuse. Let us do this together so that the red Earth our Mother will heal and all life will flower and thrive.

Season of Broken Treaties (April 27–May 28)

The People of the sovereign nations and tribes all across Turtle Island always have understood and acknowledged the importance of law. For the People, the most fundamental of all law is treaty law. The treaties are promises between sovereign nations that bind the citizens of those nations to honor their agreements. Sadly, the government and citizens of the United States of America continue to ignore, dismiss, discount, and break the promises made in treaties with the sovereign nations and tribes all across Turtle Island.

More than 450 solemn treaties have been made between the sovereign nations and tribes and the government of the United States. These documents are formal agreements between nations, relating to peace, trade, friendship, education, hunting and fishing rights, religious practices, and land. All treaties have been broken by the government of the United States, especially those concerning land. The rights, privileges, and prerogatives guaranteed by the treaties between the People of the sovereign nations and tribes and representatives of the United States government still are being challenged in the courts.

During this thirty-two-day season, the People of the sovereign nations and tribes must make sure their children know and understand the treaties that were made between their respective sovereign nations and the government of the United States. It is also time for the children in all public schools throughout the United States to learn about the treaties pertaining to the sovereign nations and tribes within particular school districts and states. The leaders of the sovereign nations and tribes need to prepare and distribute information about the treaties to all public schools in their areas. The citizens of the United States must join with the citizens of the sovereign nations and tribes and redouble their efforts to insist that the government of the United States honors and observes both the spirit and letter of all treaties, so that the People may live and prosper.

MAY

Prayer

Great Spirit, give strength to the mothers of the sovereign nations and tribes so that the children may continue to take pride in their heritage as they grow in harmony and balance with all of creation. We ask for the courage to endure as we walk the path of the brave despite the broken treaties and broken promises, so that the People may live and prosper.

Focus—Heritage (May 1–4)

The People of the sovereign nations and tribes have learned many lessons, and for that reason we are especially proud of our heritage and connection to this land we call Turtle Island. We greeted and welcomed our relations from across the sea and helped them survive. While their numbers grew, ours declined. They brought relations from other places to be their slaves. We also welcomed these new people to our land. Many adopted the ways of the People of the sovereign nations and tribes. We celebrate our rich and vibrant heritage because it has enabled us to endure and to grow. Our continued existence is proof of our strength and will—a heritage in which the People of the sovereign nations and tribes may take special pride.

Council Fires

We honor those who have been chosen to lead and serve their respective sovereign nations and tribes. We celebrate the hard work and dedication of the elders and members of the Alakanuk (Alakanuk, Alaska), Atka (Atka, Alaska), Chenega (Chenega Bay, Alaska), Chuathbaluk (Chuathbaluk, Alaska), Eek (Eek, Alaska), Galena (Galena, Alaska), Hydaburg (Hydaburg, Alaska), Kenai Village (Kenai, Alaska), Kokhanok (Illiamna, Alaska), Lime (Lime Village, Alaska), Napakiak (Napakiak, Alaska), Nome Eskimo (Nome, Alaska), Pedro Bay (Pedro Bay, Alaska), Port Lions (Port Lions, Alaska), Seldovia (Seldovia, Alaska), Stebbins (Stebbins, Alaska), Toksook Bay (Toksook Bay, Alaska), Wales (Wales, Alaska), Tohono O'odham (Sells, Arizona), Chemehuevi (Chemehuevi Valley, California), Benton Paiute (Benton, California), Cold Springs Rancheria (Tollhouse, California), Jamul (Escondido, California), Karok (Happy Camp, California), La Jolla Mission (Valley Center, California), Manchester/Point Arena Rancheria (Point Arena, California), Santa Rosa (Hemet, California), Smith River Rancheria (Smith River, California), Coeur d'Alene (Plummer, Idaho), Nez Percé (Lapwai, Idaho), Prairie Band Potawatomi (Mayetta, Kansas), Grand Traverse (Suttons Bay, Michigan), Hannahville (Wilson, Michigan), Lac Vieux Desert Band (Watersmeet, Michigan), Red Lake (Red Lake, Minnesota), Upper Sioux (Granite Falls, Minnesota), Devil's Lake Sioux (Fort Totten, North Dakota), Summit Lake Paiute (Winnemucca, Nevada), Comanche (Lawton, Oklahoma), Pawnee (Pawnee, Oklahoma), Alabama-Quassarte (Eufaula, Oklahoma), Modoc of Oklahoma (Miami, Oklahoma), Ottawa of Oklahoma (Miami, Oklahoma), Warm Springs (Warm Springs, Oregon), Crow Creek Sioux (Fort Thompson, South Dakota), Uintah and Ouray Ute (Fort Duchesne, Utah), Lower Elwah (Port Angeles, Washington), Stillaquamish (Arlington, Washington).

Events

- Feast day, San Felipe Pueblo, San Felipe, New Mexico, May 1.
- Festival, Nez Percé, Lapwai, Idaho.
- Feast day and corn dance, San Felipe Pueblo, San Felipe, New Mexico.
- Corn dance, Cochiti Pueblo, Cochiti, New Mexico, May 3.
- Corn dance and ceremonial dances, Taos Pueblo, Taos, New Mexico, May 3.
- Calf roping, Lower Brulé Sioux, Lower Brulé, South Dakota, May 6–August 6 (Saturdays).
- Powwow and dances, encampments at Wounded Knee, Kyle, Oglala, Allen, Porcupine, and Manderson, South Dakota, May 7.
- San Ysidro fiesta, Taos Pueblo, Taos, New Mexico, May 14–16.
- Tygh celebration, Warm Springs tribe, Tygh Valley, Warm Springs, Oregon, midmonth.
- Living Indian Village, Eastern Cherokee, Cherokee, North Carolina, May 16–Labor Day.
- Smoo-ke-shin powwow, Spokane, Spokane Reservation, Washington, May 16–18.
- Spring dances, Tesuque Pueblo, Tesuque, New Mexico, late in the month.
- Corpus Christi festival, Pala Band, Pala, California, late in the month.

- Bear dance, Southern Ute, Southern Ute Reservation, Colorado, late in the month.
- Powwow, Winnebago, Black River Falls, Wisconsin, Memorial Day weekend.
- Powwow and dances, Devil's Lake Sioux, Fort Totten, North Dakota.
- Indian dances, Havasupai Tribe, Supai, Arizona.
- Malki spring festival, Morongo Band Mission, Morongo Reservation, California.
- Festival, Swinomish tribe, La Conner, Washington.
- Tribal days, Quinault tribe, Taholah, Washington.
- Tribal days, Chehalis tribe, Chehalis Reservation, Washington.

Solemn Time of the Sacred Heyoka/Koshari (May 29–June 13)

Teaching the People of the sovereign nations and tribes through laughter and contrariness, the Heyoka, or Koshari, reminds the People that they must think for themselves. Called Koshari by the People of the southwestern region of Turtle Island and Heyoka by the Plains People, the Trickster, or Clown, teaches important truths to the People while reminding them not to take themselves or their situations so seriously. Through the power of the Heyoka, the People learn to transcend the boundaries of beliefs that prevent them from growing and, consequently, restore the balance and harmony in their lives. True self-understanding comes to the People by applying Coyote strategies in the willingness to laugh at oneself without being cruel or domineering toward others.

During this solemn time, let us remember and reflect on the lessons which Heyoka/Koshari/Coyote/Trickster teaches to all the People of the sovereign nations and tribes.

JUNE

Prayer

Great Spirit, we honor and celebrate the time of growing corn, and ask for help in teaching and educating our children in the ways of the People of the sovereign nations and tribes. We ask for wisdom as we teach our non-Native relations the ways of the People so that all may walk the good Red road of peace in harmony and balance.

Focus—Education (June 1–4)

For thousands of years, education has been important to the People of the sovereign nations and tribes. Although knowledge from books is important, the knowledge that comes from the practical experience of the elders and leaders of the sovereign nations and tribes is also important. The elders and leaders always have been and continue to be the major providers of the collective wisdom that they have learned during their lifetimes. Deep respect and honor are given to the elders because the People know the wisdom they have gained through daily living is essential to our continued growth and prosperity.

In today's world, it is the task of the elders and leaders of the sovereign nations and tribes to continue to urge the People to attend formal schools to learn the skills so necessary for the People to live and prosper. Students must learn ways to integrate what they have learned in classrooms with the cultural values and beliefs of their respective sovereign nations. For that reason, today's students need to make a special effort to learn from the elders and leaders when they are not in formal classrooms.

It is also important that the students of the sovereign nations and tribes help their non-Native relations learn how to live in harmony and balance with all of creation so that all may prosper and thrive.

Council Fires

We honor those who have been chosen to lead and serve their respective sovereign nations and tribes. We celebrate the hard work and dedication of the elders and council members of the Alatna (Alatna, Alaska), Atquasuk (Atkasuk, Alaska), Chefornak (Chefornak, Alaska), Egegik (Egegik, Alaska), Gambell (Gambell, Alaska), Igiugig (Igiugig, Alaska), Ketchikan (Ketchikan, Alaska), Lower Kalskag (Lower Kalskag, Alaska), Napaskiak (Napaskiak, Alaska), Nodalton (Nodalton, Alaska), Perryville (Perryville, Alaska), Portage Creek (Portage Creek, Alaska), Shageluk (Shageluk, Alaska), Stevens Village (Stevens Village, Alaska), Tuluksak (Tuluksak, Alaska), White Mountain (White Mountain, Alaska), Poarch Band Creek (Atmore, Alabama), Hualapai (Peach Springs, Arizona), Pascua Yaqui (Tucson, Arizona), San Juan Paiute (Tuba City, Arizona), Tonto

Apache (Payson, Arizona), Fort Mojave (Needles, California), Big Pine (Big Pine, California), Bishop (Bishop, California), Colusa Rancheria (Colusa, California), Greenville Rancheria (Greenville, California), Lone Pine (Lone Pine, California), Middletown Rancheria (Middletown, California), Morongo (Banning, California), Robinson Rancheria (Nice, California), San Manuel Mission (Highland, California), Sherwood Valley Rancheria (Ukiah, California), Seminole (Hollywood, Florida), Fort Hall (Fort Hall, Idaho), Coushatta (Elton, Louisiana), Sault Sainte Marie Chippewa (Sault Sainte Marie, Minnesota), Lower Sioux (Morton, Minnesota), Minnesota Chippewa (Cass Lake, Minnesota), Nett Lake Chippewa (Nett Lake, Minnesota), Fond du Lac Chippewa (Cloquet, Minnesota), Grand Portage Chippewa (Grand Portage, Minnesota), Leech Lake Chippewa (Cass Lake, Minnesota), Mille Lacs Chippewa (Onamia, Minnesota), White Earth Chippewa (White Earth, Minnesota), Mississippi Choctaw (Philadelphia, Mississippi), Blackfeet (Browning, Montana), Crow (Crow Agency, Montana), Lovelock (Lovelock, Nevada), Yomba (Austin, Nevada), Absentee Shawnee (Shawnee, Oklahoma), Citizen Band Potawatomi (Shawnee, Oklahoma), Delaware (Anadarko, Oklahoma), Iowa of Oklahoma (Perkins, Oklahoma), Kickapoo of Oklahoma (McLoud, Oklahoma), Kiowa (Carnegie, Oklahoma), Kialegee (Okemah, Oklahoma), Osage (Pawhuska, Oklahoma), Seneca-Cayuga of Oklahoma (Miami, Oklahoma), Alabama-Coushatta of Texas (Livingston, Texas), Kalispel (Usk, Washington), Puyallup (Tacoma, Washington), Skokomish (Shelton, Washington), Spokane (Wellpinit, Washington), Upper Skagit (Sedro Woolley, Washington), Lac Courte Oreilles Chippewa (Hayward, Wisconsin), Saint Croix (Hertel, Wisconsin), Wisconsin Winnebago (Tomah, Wisconsin).

Events
- Ancient Village and Adams Corner Rural Village, Cherokee Heritage Center, near Tahlequah, Oklahoma, through August.
- Intertribal ceremonies, Chicago Indian Center, Chicago, Illinois, evenings throughout the summer.
- Sun dance, Turtle Mountain Chippewa, Belcourt, North Dakota, all month.
- Centennial celebration and occupancy, White Earth

Chippewa, White Earth, Minnesota, all month.
- Powwow and fish fry, Red Lake Chippewa, Red Lake, Minnesota, June–August (evenings).
- Powwow, Crow Creek Sioux, Fort Thompson, South Dakota, June–Labor Day (Saturdays).
- Yaqui pageant, Gila River Indian community, Sacaton, Arizona, early in the month.
- Powwow, Chippewa, Wisconsin Dells, Wisconsin, June–Labor Day (daily).
- Stand Rock Indian powwow, Lac du Flambeau Chippewa, Lac du Flambeau, Wisconsin, June–Labor Day (Tuesdays and Thursdays).
- Horse event, Colville, Nespelem, Washington, first weekend.
- Bear dance, Ute Mountain Ute, Towaoc, Colorado, early in the month.
- Grass dance, Turtle Mountain Chippewa, Belcourt, North Dakota, early in the month.
- Games and salmon bake, Yakima, Toppenish, Washington, June 6–8.
- Buffalo dance, Santa Clara Pueblo, New Mexico, June 8.
- Ceremonials, San Carlos Apache, San Carlos, Arizona, midmonth.
- Powwow, Iowa, White Cloud, Kansas, midmonth.
- Powwow, Standing Rock Sioux, Fort Yates, North Dakota, midmonth.
- San Antonio Day, New Mexico pueblos—Cochiti, San Ildefonso, San Juan, Santa Clara, Taos, June 13.
- Feast day and corn dance, Sandia Pueblo, Sandia, New Mexico, June 13.
- Intertribal powwow, Clinton, Oklahoma, June 18–21.
- Waa-laa days, Coeur d'Alene, Plummer, Idaho, June 19–21.
- Sac and Fox All Indian Pro Rodeo, Stroud, Oklahoma, June 21.
- Will Rogers powwow, Marshfield, Missouri.
- Tinowit international powwow, Yakima, Washington.
- First Peoples powwow, Camp Rotary, Michigan.
- Wollomonuppoag, La Sallette Fairgrounds, Attleboro, Massachusetts.
- Stomish water carnival, Lummi, Bellingham, Washington, June 22–23.
- San Juan's Day, Acoma Pueblo, Acoma, New Mexico, June 23, Isleta, Laguna, San Juan, and Taos Pueblos, New Mexico; Tohono O'odham, Sells, Ari-

zona; Tule River, Porterville, California.

- Feast day, Cochiti Pueblo, Cochiti, New Mexico, June 24.
- Rooster pull, Jemez Pueblo, Jemez, New Mexico.
- Osage ceremonial dances, Osage tribe, Hominy, Grayhorse, and Pawhuska, Oklahoma.
- Games, Nez Percé, Craigmont, Idaho, last Friday of the month.
- *Unto These Hills: A Cherokee Drama,* Eastern Cherokee, Cherokee, North Carolina, late June–September 1.
- Sinte Gleska memorial celebration, Rosebud Sioux, Rosebud, South Dakota, late in the month.
- Powwow, Kickapoo, Horton, Kansas, last weekend of the month.
- Feast day, Seama Village of Laguna Pueblo, Seama, New Mexico, June 26.
- Intertribal exposition, El Reno, Oklahoma, June 26–28.
- Caddo tribal dance, Caddo, Murrow dance grounds, Binger, Oklahoma, last of the month.
- Indian days, Wind River Shoshone, Fort Washakie, Wyoming.
- Sun dance, Chippewa-Cree, Rocky Boy's Reservation, Box Elder, Montana.
- *Trail of Tears* outdoor drama, Cherokee Heritage Center, near Tahlequah, Oklahoma, through August.
- Festival, Umatilla, LaGrande, Oregon, June 27–30.
- San Pedro's day, Acoma Pueblo, Acoma, New Mexico, June 30, Isleta, Laguna, Santa Ana, and Taos Pueblos, New Mexico.

Festival of Crops Growing (June 18–25)
The People of the sovereign nations and tribes on Turtle Island join together and celebrate the growing of crops which nourish the People. From the root of corn, which is connected to the Earth our Mother, grows the stalk. The stalk is the ladder between the Earth our Mother and the Sky our Father/Grandfather. For the People of the sovereign nations and tribes, the stalk reminds us of the courage and skill we must possess to walk the path to understanding in harmony and balance.

During this eight-day festival, as we celebrate the growing of our crops, it is important that we remember to attend carefully to our duties in caring for the Earth our Mother and the Sky our Father/Grandfather. These duties are necessary so that with all of creation—both seen and unseen—the People may continue to grow and prosper in harmony and balance.

Honoring of Scholars and Learners (June 6–July 3)
Thousands of years before our non-Native relatives journeyed across the great water from the East, the People of the sovereign nations and tribes understood the importance of learning. Children learned from their parents and elders. Parents learned from the elders and leaders. All of the People, including elders and leaders, learned from nature. Today, the People of the sovereign nations and tribes continue to learn from nature, from the elders, and from one another. They also attend schools, where they learn the ways and beliefs of their non-Native relations.

During this eight-day honoring time, we celebrate the accomplishments of the scholars and learners among the People of the sovereign nations and tribes. We are glad for the knowledge and skills they bring to the sovereign nations and tribes so that the People may continue to grow and prosper.

JULY

Prayer
Great Spirit, we are especially thankful for the Great Law of Peace as we celebrate our sovereignty as nations and tribes during this time. Help us to be without anger and to be peaceful in our hearts as we gather for the Season of Powwows and Sacred Dances. We ask for special blessings for all the traditional spiritual leaders of our sovereign nations and tribes as they perform their sacred duties so that all the People may live and prosper.

Focus—Government (July 1–4)
The People of the sovereign nations and tribes have long practice at the art of government. We have organized our respective societies in forms that ranged from theocracy and autocracy to true democracy. Long before our non-Native relations came across the sea from Europe, the sovereign People of the Iroquois Confederacy were organized and governed by the

Great Law of Peace, which is the basis for the Constitution of the United States of America.

It is important that the People of the sovereign nations and tribes help our non-Native relations understand that there were no rulers or kings on Turtle Island as there were in Europe. The People are urged to help our non-Native relations understand that the person who spoke for the People of a particular sovereign nation did so because that person had been empowered to speak by the heads of the respective clans, spiritual leaders, and an overwhelming majority of all the People—including the women.

The People of the sovereign nations need to inform our non-Native relatives that women and men made decisions, and that women "voted" not only for themselves but for their minor children as well.

Council Fires

We honor those who have been chosen to lead and serve their respective sovereign nations and tribes. We celebrate the hard work and dedication of the elders and council members of the Algaaciq (Saint Mary's, Alaska), Atmautluak (Atmautluak, Alaska), Chevak (Chevak, Alaska), Circle Village (Circle, Alaska), Eklutna (Chugiak, Alaska), Goodnews Bay (Goodnews Bay, Alaska), Iliamna (Iliamna, Alaska), Kiana (Kiana, Alaska), Kongiganak Traditional (Kongiganak, Alaska), Manley (Manley Hot Springs, Alaska), Nelson Lagoon (Cold Bay, Alaska), Noorvik (Noorvik, Alaska), Petersburg (Petersburg, Alaska), Rampart (Rampart, Alaska), Shaktoolik (Shaktoolik, Alaska), Stony River (Stony River, Alaska), Tuntutuliak (Tuntutuliak, Alaska), Wrangell (Wrangell, Alaska), Cocopah (Somerton, Arizona), Yavapai-Apache (Camp Verde, Arizona), Prescott Yavapai (Prescott, Arizona), Cortina Rancheria (Citrus Heights, California), Hoopa Valley Rancheria (Hoopa, California), Mooretown Rancheria (Oroville, California), Pechunga Mission (Temecula, California), Pinolville Rancheria (Ukiah, California), Redwood Valley Rancheria (Redwood Valley, California), Stewarts Point Rancheria (Stewarts Point, California), Chitimacha (Charenton, Louisiana), Eastern Shawnee of Oklahoma (Seneca, Missouri), Las Vegas Colony (Las Vegas, Nevada), Oneida Nation of New York (Oneida, New York), Saint Regis Mohawk (Hogansburg, New York), Caddo (Binger, Oklahoma), Wichita (Anadarko, Oklahoma), Quapaw (Quapaw, Oklahoma), Klamath (Chiloquin, Oregon), Colville (Nespelem, Washington), Port Gamble (Kingston, Washington), Oneida tribe (Oneida, Wisconsin), Red Cliff (Bayfield, Wisconsin).

Events
- Indian ceremonials, Anadarko, Oklahoma, every Saturday.
- Powwow, Oneida Indian Club, Indian centers, Milwaukee, Wisconsin, summer season.
- Mohawk Indian village, Mohawk Nation, Hogansburg, New York, July 1–Labor Day.
- Indian dance, Hayward, Wisconsin.
- Indian rodeo, Navajo Nation, Window Rock, Arizona, July 1–4.
- Ceremonial, Sisseton Sioux, Sisseton, South Dakota.
- Tribal games, Nez Percé, Wolf Point, Montana, early in the month.
- All-Indian powwow, Cannon Ball, North Dakota, July 2–5.
- Sun dance, Rosebud Sioux, Rosebud, South Dakota, July 2–5.
- Feast and games, Shoshone Paiute, Duck Valley Reservation, Owyhee, Nevada, first week.
- Indian ceremonials, Fort Cobb, Oklahoma, first weekend.
- Indian dances, Fort Kipp, Montana, July 3–4.
- Mountain spirits ceremony, Mescalero Apache, Mescalero Apache Reservation, New Mexico, July 3–6.
- Sioux powwow, Rosebud Sioux, Spring Creek, South Dakota, July 3–5.
- Gourd clan dance, Kiowa, Carnegie, Oklahoma.
- Powwow dances, Crow Creek Sioux, Fort Thompson, South Dakota
- Stuck-by-the-Ree powwow, Greenwood, South Dakota.
- Feasts, games, races, most pueblos in New Mexico and Arizona, July 4.
- Waterfall ceremony, Nambe Pueblo, Nambe, New Mexico.
- Fiesta, Walker River Paiute, Walker River Reservation, Schurz, Nevada.

- Gathering of tribes, Hayward, Wisconsin.
- Indian dance contest, Red Lake Chippewa, Red Lake, Minnesota.
- Indian dance, Caddo, Binger, Oklahoma, July 4–5.
- Omaha dances, Omaha, Craigmont, Idaho.
- Festival, Swinomish, La Conner, Washington.
- Powwow, Arlee, Montana.
- Indian celebration, Colville, Nespelem, Washington.
- Trout derby, Quinault, Taholah, Washington.
- Powwow, Cannon Ball, North Dakota, July 4–5.
- Indian days, Blackfeet, Browning, Montana, second weekend of the month.
- Powwow, Sac and Fox, Jim Thorpe Park, Stroud, Oklahoma, July 9–11.
- Powwow, Lewiston, New York, second weekend of the month.
- Whaa-laa days, Worley, Idaho.
- Reenactment of "Custer's last stand," Crow Agency, Montana, July 10–12.
- Sun dance, Arapaho, Ethete, Wyoming, second week of the month.
- Indian crafts fair, Asheville, North Carolina, July 14–18.
- Green corn dance and feast, Cochiti Pueblo, Cochiti, New Mexico, July 14.
- Antelope powwow, Mission, South Dakota, July 14–16.
- Powwow, Arapaho, Ethete, Wyoming, third week of the month.
- Powwow, Santee Sioux, Flandreau, South Dakota, July 15–16.
- Iron ring celebration, Fort Peck, Poplar, Montana, third week of the month.
- All-Indian celebration, Fallon, Nevada.
- Powwow, Northern Cheyenne, Lame Deer, Montana, midmonth.
- Powwow, Mandan, New Town, North Dakota, July 17–19.
- Festival of bells, Mission San Diego de Alcala, San Diego, California, July 18.
- Redbird Smith birthday celebration, Redbird Smith grounds, near Vian, Oklahoma, July 19.
- Indian fair, Choctaw Nation, Philadelphia, Mississippi, July 22–25.
- Fort Totten days festival, Devil's Lake Sioux, Fort Totten, North Dakota, July 23–25.
- Indian pageant, Passamaquoddy Nation, Indian Township Reservation, Maine, late in the month.
- Sun dance, Southern Ute, Southern Ute Reservation, Colorado, late in the month.
- Thanks for wild rice, Chippewa Nation, Ballclub, Minnesota, third weekend of the month.
- Indian pageant, Passamaquoddy Nation, Pleasant Point Reservation, Maine, late in the month.
- Sun dance, Shoshone Nation, Fort Washakie, Wyoming, last week of the month.
- Hinmaton-yalatkit (Chief Joseph) pageant, Nez Percé, Joseph, Oregon, last week of the month.
- Rooster pull, Acoma Pueblo, Acoma, New Mexico, July 25; Santo Domingo Pueblo, Santo Domingo, New Mexico.
- Santiago's Day dances, Laguna Pueblo, Laguna, New Mexico, Santa Ana Pueblo, Santa Ana, New Mexico.
- Corn dance, Cochiti Pueblo, Cochiti, New Mexico.
- Corn dance, Taos Pueblo, Taos, New Mexico, July 25–27.
- Sun 'n' Fun festival, Colville, Nespelem, Washington, last week of the month.
- Corn dance and feast day, Acoma Pueblo, Acoma, New Mexico, July 26.
- Corn dance and feast day, Santa Ana Pueblo, Santa Ana, New Mexico.
- Powwow, Standing Rock Sioux, Little Eagle, Standing Rock Reservation, South Dakota, July 28–30.
- Sun dance, Uintah and Ouray, Uintah and Ouray Reservation, Duchesne, Utah, late in the month.
- Powwow, Otoe-Missouria, Noble County, Oklahoma.
- Sun dance, Oglala Lakota, Pine Ridge Reservation, South Dakota, July 30–August 2.
- Naman kachina, Hopi, Hopi villages, Arizona, late in the month.
- Indian pageant, Penobscot Nation, Indian Island Reservation, Maine.
- Puye ceremonial, Santa Clara Pueblo, Santa Clara, New Mexico.
- Saguaro festival, Tohono O'odham, Sells, Arizona.
- Powwow, Prairie Band Potawatomi, Mayetta, Kansas, last weekend of the month.
- Powwow, Otoe-Missouria, stomp grounds, Red Rock, Oklahoma, last of the month.

- Annual powwow, Winnebago, Nebraska, last weekend of the month.
- Powwow, Turtle Mountain Chippewa, Belcourt, North Dakota.
- Indian days, Chippewa-Cree, Rocky Boy's Reservation, Box Elder, Montana, last of the month.
- Powwow, Sac and Fox, Ed Mack farm, Shawnee, Oklahoma, July 31–August 2.

Celebration of Our Sovereignty (July 4–19)
For literally thousands and thousands of years, the People of the sovereign nations and tribes have insisted vigorously on and asserted their right of personal sovereignty. It was only when a crisis threatened the entire sovereign nation that individual sovereignty gave way to the sovereignty of the nation. When the crisis passed, the individuals immediately reclaimed their personal sovereignty.

Among the People of the sovereign nations and tribes, no one is master over another. It is a way of thinking and behaving which our non-Native relations are only now—after five hundred years—beginning to comprehend. Even when there was a war between the People of one sovereign nation and another, if a warrior decided to return home and not fight, he was not punished. Unlike our non-Native relations, a warrior of the sovereign nations was not shot or imprisoned for refusing to obey an order, or hunted down for desertion. No warrior followed a leader. Instead, the warrior joined with the leader in pursuit of a common objective.

During this eight-day celebration, it is important to remember and reflect on the concept of sovereignty as it applies to each of us. Let us remember that personal sovereignty requires each person to take responsibility for his own actions so that the People may live and prosper in peace.

Honoring of Dancers and Singers (July 20–27)
The People of the sovereign nations and tribes give special honor to the dancers and singers who continue to maintain the long traditions of their ancestors. Since the time before time, the dancers and singers have celebrated the ways of the People. Today, they proudly dance and sing at powwows and other gatherings.

During this honoring time, let us remember the dancers and singers who bring the ways of the People to our non-Native relations.

Season of Powwows and Sacred Dances (July 28–August 28)
The *powwow* (an Algonkian word for gathering) and sacred dances are important parts of the social and spiritual lives of the People of the sovereign nations and tribes. Although sacred dances are private and belong to the People of the respective sovereign nations and tribes, powwows are open to all.

At powwows, alcohol and drugs are forbidden and no one who is intoxicated or drugged is permitted to enter the circle to dance. It is also a sign of good manners for women to wear shawls when dancing. Violations of the ways of the People and powwow etiquette are handled by the arena director, but also may be attended to by the head dancers (although the head man dancer or head woman dancer usually informs the arena director of the violation). Any time an eagle feather falls to the ground, all activity must cease immediately. Only after the powwow head staff members have performed the proper observance rite may activities resume.

During this season, it is important for the People to welcome the non-Native relations into the circle and teach, by action, the ways of the People so that we all may dance in the circle together in celebration of the connectedness of all creation.

AUGUST

Prayer
Great Spirit, we give thanks for the sacred dances and powwows which bring the People together in celebration of all creation—both seen and unseen. Help us to keep our hearts free from anger and discord as we dance, and in our daily lives.

Focus—Culture (August 1–4)
The distinct and vibrant culture of the People of the sovereign nations and tribes is a model for our non-Native relations. Our myriad languages, artistic and creative endeavors, governmental and social struc-

tures, sacred ceremonies, and practices are all a reflection of the deepest beliefs, values, and attitudes of the People of the sovereign nations and tribes.

By our example, our non-Native relations have learned to bathe regularly and often—a practice they thought was primitive when they first came to Turtle Island. By our example, our non-Native relations are learning that all of creation—both seen and unseen—is connected and interwoven. Our non-Native relatives are learning that those who abuse and destroy the Earth our Mother will, in the end, bring about the destruction and death of all life. As our non-Native relations continue to learn, so do the People of the sovereign nations and tribes. We have adapted in the process of learning, and our culture today reflects the vibrancy in applying our ancient customs, beliefs, and practices to this new time and way.

Council Fires

We honor those who have been chosen to lead and serve their respective sovereign nations and tribes. We celebrate the hard work and dedication of the elders and council members of the Aleknagik (Aleknagik, Alaska), Beaver (Beaver, Alaska), Chickaloon (Chickaloon, Alaska), Clark's Point (Clark's Point, Alaska), Ekuk (Ekuk, Alaska), Holikachu (Grayling, Alaska), Inupiat (Barrow, Alaska), King Cove (King Cove, Alaska), Kotlik (Kotlik, Alaska), Manokotak (Manokotak, Alaska), Nenana (Nenana, Alaska), Northway (Northway, Alaska), Piamuit (Piamuit, Alaska), Red Devil (Red Devil, Alaska), Sheldon's Point (Sheldon's Point, Alaska), Takotna (Takotna, Alaska), Tununak (Tununak, Alaska), Yakutat (Yakutat, Alaska), Coyote Valley (Redwood Valley, California), North Fork Rancheria (North Fork, California), Susanville Rancheria (Susanville, California), Sac and Fox of the Missouri (Reserve, Kansas), Jicarilla Apache (Dulce, New Mexico), Ramah Navajo (Ramah, New Mexico), Cherokee Nation of Oklahoma (Tahlequah, Oklahoma), United Keetoowah Band Cherokee (Arkansas), Cow Creek Umpqua (Roseburg, Oregon), Flandreau Santee Sioux (Flandreau, South Dakota).

Events

- Green corn ceremony, Mohawk Nation, Saint Regis Mohawk Reservation, New York, date varies.
- Green corn dance, Onondaga Nation, Onondaga Reservation, New York.
- Indian convention, Seneca Nation, Tonawanda Reservation, New York.
- Community fair, Tuscarora Nation, Tuscarora Reservation, New York.
- Indian ceremonials, Fort Cobb, Oklahoma, first week of the month.
- Red Bottom, Assiniboin, Frazer, Montana, early in the month.
- Powwow, Ponca of Nebraska, Lake Andes, South Dakota, August 1–17 (weekends).
- Feast day, Jemez Pueblo, Jemez, New Mexico, August 2.
- Sun dance, Oglala Lakota, Pine Ridge, South Dakota, August 3–5.
- Old Pecos bull dance, Jemez Pueblo, Jemez, New Mexico, August 4.
- Ripe corn dance and fiesta, Santo Domingo Pueblo, Santo Domingo, New Mexico.
- Powwow, Standing Rock Sioux, Fort Yates, North Dakota, August 4–6.
- Choctaw fair, Choctaw Nation, Durant, Oklahoma, August 4–7.
- Shoshone-Bannock festival, Shoshone and Bannock, Fort Hall, Idaho, August 5–8.
- Powwow, Ashland, Montana, early in the month.
- All American Indian days, Sheridan, Wyoming, first weekend of the month.
- Chippewa fair, Fond du Lac Chippewa, Cloquet, Minnesota, early in the month.
- Buffalo dance, Tokio, North Dakota, first weekend of the month.
- Powwow, Fort Belknap, Harlem, Montana, early in the month.
- Games and clambake, Suquamish, Suquamish, Washington, first weekend of the month.
- Indian fair and powwow, Lower Brulé Sioux, Lower Brulé, South Dakota, August 7–9.
- Powwow, Kalispel, Usk, Washington, early in the month.
- Powwow, Arapaho, Fort Washakie, Wyoming, second week of the month.
- Huckleberry feast, Warm Springs, Warm Springs, Oregon.

- Omak stampede, Omak, Omak, Washington.
- Corn dance, Acoma Pueblo, Acoma, New Mexico, August 10; Laguna Pueblo, Laguna, New Mexico.
- Feast day, Picuris Pueblo, Picuris, New Mexico.
- Sinte Gleska powwow, Rosebud Sioux, Rosebud, South Dakota, August 11–13.
- Powwow, Barryville, New York, August 12–13.
- Feast day, Santa Clara Pueblo, Santa Clara, New Mexico, August 12.
- Powwow, Bull Head, South Dakota, August 13–15.
- Indian fair, Ponca, White Eagle, Oklahoma, mid-month.
- All-Indian fair, Shoshone-Arapaho, Fort Washakie, Wyoming.
- Crow fair, Crow Nation, Crow Agency, Montana.
- Reservation fair, Parshall, Mountrail County, North Dakota, August 14.
- Feast day, Mesita village of Laguna Pueblo, Mesita, New Mexico, August 15.
- Corn dances, Zia Pueblo, Zia, New Mexico.
- Omaha Indian homecoming, Omaha, Macy, Nebraska.
- Peach festival, Havasupai, Supai, Arizona, third week of the month.
- Games and feast, Nez Percé, Craigmont, Idaho.
- Indian fair, Colville, Nespelem, Washington, August 16–18.
- Powwow, Rosebud Sioux, Rosebud, South Dakota, August 18–20.
- Powwow, Arapaho, Canton, Oklahoma, August 19–22.
- Tribal fair and powwow, Rosebud Sioux, Rosebud, South Dakota, August 21–23.
- Oil celebration, Fort Peck, Poplar, Montana, last week of the month.
- Pi-Nee-Waus days, Nez Percé, Lapwai, Idaho.
- Powwow, Hualapai, Peach Springs, Arizona, fourth weekend of the month.
- Powwow, Crow Creek Sioux, Fort Thompson, South Dakota, August 27–29.
- Cheyenne River fair, Cheyenne River Sioux, Eagle Butte, South Dakota, August 27–29.
- Snake dance, Hopi, all Hopi villages, Arizona, late in the month.
- Crown dance and fair, White Mountain Apache, Whiteriver, Arizona, weekend before Labor Day.
- Annual powwow, Turtle Mountain Chippewa, Bel-court, North Dakota, last weekend of the month.
- Fiesta, Isleta Pueblo, Isleta, New Mexico, August 28.
- Dances and games, Makah, Neah Bay, Washington, August 29–30.
- Water pageant, Thermopolis, Washington, last of the month.

Solemn Time of the Sacred Drum
(August 29–September 13)

Among all the People of the sovereign nations and tribes, the sacred drum holds a special place in all ceremonies. It represents our connection to the rhythm or beat of the Earth our Mother. The sound of the sacred drum reminds all the people of earth of their connection to one another and to all of creation.

During this sixteen-day solemn time, let us remember that all our relations include Native and non-Native alike, and to walk in balance and harmony we all must be attentive to the beat of the sacred drum.

SEPTEMBER

Prayer

Great Spirit, we celebrate the bounty of the harvest and are grateful for the generosity of the Earth our Mother for providing us with the food which sustains the People. We ask a special blessing for the artisans, workers, dancers, and singers of the People. The People of the Thousand Fires join with all our relations and give thanks for all we have received so that the People may flower and prosper.

Focus—Health (September 1–4)

The People of the sovereign nations and tribes always have placed a high priority on health. Being healthy in spirit, mind, heart, and body is essential to the traditional ways of the People. For the People of the sovereign nations and tribes, the way to maintain health is to walk in balance and harmony with all of creation.

Now, in this time of hepatitis B, HIV, and AIDS, the People must take special care to know and understand the behaviors that will prevent and eliminate those diseases. While "scientists" work to discover formulas to fight or eradicate the diseases, it is important to practice the ways of the People by being respectful toward ourselves and others. When we are respectful of ourselves and others, we avoid alcohol and substance abuse. When we are respectful, we practice safe sex. When we are respectful, we walk in the way of the People.

Council Fires

We honor those who have been chosen to lead and serve their respective sovereign nations and tribes. We celebrate the hard work and dedication of the elders and council members of the Allakaket (Allakaket, Alaska), Belkofski (Belkofski, Alaska), Chignik (Chignik, Alaska), Craig (Craig, Alaska), Ekwok (Ekwok, Alaska), Gulkana (Gakona, Alaska), Ivanoff Bay (Ivanoff Bay, Alaska), King Island (Nome, Alaska), Kotzebue (Kotzebue, Alaska), Marshall (Fortuna Ledge, Alaska), Newhalen (Iliamna, Alaska), Nuiqsut (Nuiqsut, Alaska), Pilot Point (Pilot Point, Alaska), Ruby (Ruby, Alaska), Shishmaref (Shishmaref, Alaska), Tanacross (Tanacross, Alaska), Twin Hills (Twin Hills, Alaska), Alturas Rancheria (Alturas, California), Big Sandy Rancheria (Auberry, California), Dry Creek Rancheria (Geyserville, California), Hopland (Hopland, California), Picayune Rancheria (Coursegold, California), Timbisha Shoshone (Death Valley, California), Northern Cheyenne (Lame Deer, Montana), Eastern Cherokee (Cherokee, North Carolina), Turtle Mountain (Belcourt, North Dakota), Santee Sioux (Niobrara, Nebraska), Kaw (Kaw City, Oklahoma), Sac and Fox of Oklahoma (Stroud, Oklahoma), Choctaw Nation of Oklahoma (Durant, Oklahoma), Miami Tribe of Oklahoma (Miami, Oklahoma), Seminole Nation of Oklahoma (Wewoka, Oklahoma), Wyandotte Tribe of Oklahoma (Wyandotte, Oklahoma), Grande Ronde Confederated Tribe (Grand Ronde, Oregon), Ponca Tribe of Nebraska (Lake Andes, South Dakota), Yankton Sioux (Marty, South Dakota).

Events
- Powwow, Sisseton Sioux, Sisseton, South Dakota, Labor Day.
- Wild rice harvest, Nett Lake Chippewa, Nett Lake, Minnesota.
- Sioux fair and powwow, Devil's Lake Sioux, Fort Totten, North Dakota.

- Powwow, Cheyenne-Arapaho, Colony, Oklahoma.
- Gourd dance celebration, Comanche, Lawton, Oklahoma.
- Celebration, Ethete, Wyoming.
- One-shot antelope hunt, Lander, Wyoming.
- Powwow, Winnebago, Black River Falls, Wisconsin, September 2.
- Arapaho celebration, Wind River Arapaho, Fort Washakia, Wyoming.
- Indian ways, Warm Springs, Warm Springs, Oregon.
- Powwow, Southampton, Long Island, New York.
- Corn dance and feast day, Acoma Pueblo, Acoma, New Mexico.
- Powwow, Bull Creek, South Dakota, September 2–4.
- Powwow, Soldier Creek, South Dakota.
- Powwow, Mesquakie, Tama, Iowa, September 3–7.
- Navajo tribal fair, Navajo Nation, Window Rock, Arizona, early in the month.
- Apache fair, White Mountain Apache, Whiteriver, Arizona, September 3–6.
- Powwow, Kiowa, Carnegie, Oklahoma.
- Mopope powwow, Anadarko, Oklahoma, early in the month.
- Tribal powwow, Colony, Oklahoma, Labor Day weekend.
- Powwow, Spokane, Wellpinit, Washington.
- Cherokee national holiday, Cherokee Nation, Tahlequah, Oklahoma, Labor Day weekend.
- Feast day and dances, Isleta Pueblo, Isleta, New Mexico, first weekend in September.
- Sioux fair, Eagle Butte, South Dakota, September 5–7.
- Pinehunt festival, San Ildefonso Pueblo, San Ildefonso, New Mexico, September 8.
- Feast day, Encinal Village of Laguna Pueblo, Encinal, New Mexico.
- Tribal fair and dances, Southern Ute, Southern Ute Reservation, Colorado, September 11–13.
- Ghost dance and fiesta, Jicarilla Apache, Jicarilla Apache Reservation, New Mexico, September 14–16.
- Acorn festival, Tuolumne Me-wuk, Tuolumne, California, September 15.
- Pendleton roundup, Umatilla, Pendleton, Oregon, September 16–19.
- Tribal arts and crafts fair, Mandan-Hidatsa-

Arikara, New Town, North Dakota, September 17–19.

- Feast day and harvest dances, Laguna Pueblo, Laguna, New Mexico, September 19.
- Fiesta and harvest dance, San Juan Pueblo, San Juan, New Mexico, late in the month.
- Navajo fair, Navajo Nation, Shiprock, New Mexico.
- Annual American Indian ceremonial dance, Oklahoma City, Oklahoma, fourth weekend after Labor Day.
- Fiesta and social dances, Laguna Pueblo, Laguna, New Mexico, September 25.
- Feast day, Paguate Village of Laguna Pueblo, Paguate, New Mexico.
- Evergreen dance, Isleta Pueblo, Isleta, New Mexico, late in the month.
- Indian fair, San Juan Southern Paiute, Tuba City, Arizona.
- Tribal dances, Hominy, Oklahoma.
- Powwow, Wanblee, South Dakota, last week of the month.
- Sundown dance, Taos Pueblo, Taos, New Mexico, September 28–30.
- Feast day, Taos Pueblo, Taos, New Mexico, September 30.

Festival of Crop Harvesting (September 18–25)

As the People of the sovereign nations and tribes focus all their good thoughts on the harvest, we celebrate the results of our labors during this festival time. The gifts of the harvest give energy to our spirits, minds, hearts, and bodies.

For the People of the sovereign nations and tribes, this special time is significant because it emphasizes our connection to the Earth our Mother, who provides us with the bounty of the harvest, and to the Sky our Father/Grandfather, who enables the Cloud People and Thunder Beings to carry the Rain People to our fields. The Rain People dance upon our fields and give their essence so the fruits of the Earth our Mother will grow healthy and strong.

During this time, we honor and celebrate all of creation—both seen and unseen—as we harvest the fruits of the Earth our Mother. We are thankful for the food which nourishes us so that the People may continue to grow and prosper.

Honoring of Artisans and Workers (September 26–October 3)

For thousands of years, the People of the sovereign nations and tribes have been creative artists and diligent workers. They built magnificent earthenwork mounds which our non-Native relations still are trying to comprehend. They built and lived in five- and six-story apartment dwellings long before their non-Native relations came across the great water from the East. They built the Roman Catholic missions under pain of death from the "holy" conquerors. And throughout the hundreds of centuries from the past to the present, the People always have created exceptional beauty with their hands—beadwork, baskets, rugs, and shelters.

During this eight-day honoring time, let us celebrate and honor the works of the heart created by the artisans and workers of the People.

OCTOBER

Prayer

Great Spirit, we thank you for all the blessings we have received as we celebrate our heritage during this time, and we ask that you help us to remember always the ways of the People and keep them alive in our hearts so that the People may walk in beauty forever.

Focus—Diversity (October 1–4)

The People of the sovereign nations and tribes have honored and celebrated diversity in thought, word, and deed. The People did not regard physical differences, gender preferences, or other differences as "bad" or "evil" until the arrival of the non-Native immigrants from across the ocean. For the People, all life was sacred, and differences were considered to be blessings of the Great Mystery.

From the time our non-Native relations came to our lands, we adopted many of them into our respective nations and tribes. The Scots, French, Africans, Spaniards, Russians, Norwegians, and English were among those adopted by the sovereign nations and tribes. The People believed the strange people from across the sea were their lost relatives.

From our non-Native relations, the People learned that men are "more equal" than women, and that all life that is not human is inferior and is to be conquered, used, abused, or destroyed. We learned that the Earth our Mother can be destroyed, used, bought, and sold. All these ideas were—and continue to be—strange and frightening to the People. After five centuries, the People now applaud the fact that our non-Native relations finally have begun to learn what we always have known and believed—that everything is connected. We are glad that our non-Native relations have come to understand that the Earth our Mother is sacred and must not be destroyed in the name of progress and greed.

Council Fires
We honor those who have been chosen to lead and serve their respective sovereign nations and tribes. We celebrate the hard work and dedication of the elders and council members of the Ambler (Ambler, Alaska), Slough (Kotlik, Alaska), Chignik Lagoon (Chignik Lagoon, Alaska), Crooked Creek (Crooked Creek, Alaska), Elim (Elim, Alaska), Hamilton (Kotlik, Alaska), Kake (Kake, Alaska), Kipnuk (Kipnuk, Alaska), Koyuk (Koyuk, Alaska), McGrath (McGrath, Alaska), New Stuyahok (New Stuyahok, Alaska), Nulato (Nulato, Alaska), Pilot Station (Pilot Station, Alaska), Russian Mission (Russian Mission, Alaska), Shungnak (Shungnak, Alaska), Tanana (Tatitlek, Alaska), Tyonek (Tyonek, Alaska), Kaibab Paiute (Fredonia, Arizona), Big Valley Rancheria (Finley, California), Elk Valley Rancheria (Crescent City, California), Pit River (Burney, California), Redding Rancheria (Redding, California), Torres-Martinez Mission (Thermal, California), Woodfords Washoe of Nevada (Markleeville, California), Ute Mountain Ute (Towaoc, Colorado), Iowa of Kansas (White Cloud, Kansas), Kickapoo of Kansas (Horton, Kansas), Indian Township Passamaquoddy of Maine (Princeton, Maine), Pleasant Point Passamaquoddy of Maine (Perry, Maine), Penobscot Nation (Old Town, Maine), Fort Peck (Poplar, Montana), Standing Rock Sioux (Fort Yates, North Dakota), Winnebago (Winnebago, Nebraska), Te-Moak Western Shoshone of Nevada (Elko, Nevada), Battle Mountain (Battle Mountain, Nevada), Elko (Elko, Nevada), South Fork (Lee,

Nevada), Wells Colony (Wells, Nevada), Washoe (Gardnerville, Nevada), Carson Washoe of Nevada (Carson City, Nevada), Dresslerville Washoe of Nevada (Gardnerville, Nevada), Steward Washoe of Nevada (Carson City, Nevada), Fort Sill Apache (Apache, Oklahoma), Chickasaw Nation of Oklahoma (Ada, Oklahoma), Coquille (Coos Bay, Oregon), Cheyenne River Sioux (Eagle Butte, South Dakota), Lower Brulé Sioux (Lower Brulé, South Dakota), Rosebud Sioux (Rosebud, South Dakota), Kickapoo of Texas (Eagle Pass, Texas), Jamestown Klallam (Sequim, Washington), Lac du Flambeau (Lac du Flambeau, Wisconsin), Stockbridge-Munsee (Bowler, Wisconsin).

Events
- Powwow, Mille Lacs Chippewa, Danbury, Wisconsin, weekends.
- Chippewa dances, Chippewa, Eastlake, Wisconsin.
- Ceremonial dances, Mille Lacs Chippewa, Vineland, Minnesota.
- Coronation, Devil's Lake Sioux, Fort Totten, North Dakota, early in the month.
- Elk dance and feast day, Nambe Pueblo, Nambe, New Mexico, October 4.
- Feast, Tohono O'odham, Sells, Arizona.
- Pawnee Bill art show, Pawnee, Oklahoma, early in the month.
- Fall festival, Eastern Cherokee, Cherokee, North Carolina, October 8–11.
- Matachines dance, Jemez Pueblo, Jemez, New Mexico, October 12.
- Harvest dance celebration, Laguna Pueblo, Laguna, New Mexico, October 17.
- Feast day, Paraje Village of Laguna Pueblo, Paraje, New Mexico.
- Indian craft fair, Gatlinburg, Tennessee, October 19–24.
- Ceremonial dances, most pueblos in New Mexico and Arizona, late in the month.

Celebration of Our Heritage (October 4–19)
To the People of the sovereign nations and tribes, the Great Spirit gave the Great Law of Peace. To the People of the sovereign nations and tribes, the Great Spirit gave the task of protecting the Earth our

Mother from abuse and destruction. To the People of the sovereign nations and tribes, the Great Spirit gave the duty of learning from and teaching human beings to respect and honor all of creation—both seen and unseen. To the People of the sovereign nations and tribes, the Great Spirit gave visions and dreams of our responsibilities to ourselves and to all our relations as sovereign individuals who call no human being master. To the People of the sovereign nations and tribes, the Great Spirit gave inspiration and strength to the great leaders and heros among us. To the People of the sovereign nations and tribes, the Great Spirit shows the truth of the Great Mystery. All these blessings have been given to the People of the sovereign nations and tribes as their heritage.

During this honoring time, let us celebrate our heritage and continue to walk in beauty so that the People may live and prosper.

Honoring of the Fallen (October 20–27)
The People of the sovereign nations and tribes will remember forever in their hearts those who have fallen and died in the past five hundred years. We honor the elders, women, and children who were massacred at Acoma, Sand Creek, and Wounded Knee Creek. We honor forever the memory of those who died on the Nuna-da-ut-sun'y, or the Trail Where They Cried, and the Long Walk. We honor forever the thousands upon thousands who died from smallpox-infected blankets which the non-Native government deliberately gave to the cold and starving People of the sovereign nations and tribes. We remember forever all the innocents who have fallen because of greed and U.S. governmental policies. During this eight-day honoring time, we mourn and honor those of the People who have fallen. May the People of the sovereign nations and tribes always remember their sacrifices.

Season of Prophets, Dreamers, and Holy People (October 28–November 28)
The prophets, dreamers, and holy ones among the People of the sovereign nations and tribes foretold the hard times that were to come to the People all across Turtle Island. They foresaw in dreams and visions that thousands upon thousands of the People would die of starvation, of strange vile diseases, and in wanton massacres. In their dreams and visions,

they foresaw that uncounted numbers of the People would forget or turn away from their ancient ways and practices. They foresaw that when this happened, even more of the People would die, because of greed, drunkenness, and violence. They also foresaw that if the People of the sovereign nations and tribes survived the horrors of the dark time, they would grow strong and prosper. They foresaw that the People would teach their relations from across the ocean how to live in harmony and balance with all of creation.

The time of tears has passed. Of the estimated 30 million People of the sovereign nations and tribes who lived on Turtle Island before the arrival of our non-Native immigrant relations, only 240,000 remained by 1900. Almost a century later (1990), the number of People of the sovereign nations and tribes had grown to more than 1.9 million, with at least 6 million more claiming to be descendants of the People.

During this season, we honor the special gifts which the prophets, dreamers, and holy people have shared—and continue to share—with the People of the sovereign nations and tribes. Through their visions and dreams, the People continue to grow in numbers. We honor their visions and dreams in guiding the People along the path toward greater wisdom and understanding so that the People may grow and prosper.

NOVEMBER

Prayer
Great Spirit, we give special thanks for the prophets, dreamers, and holy people among us. Let their visions continue to inspire and guide us in our daily lives. We especially honor the great deeds of the prophets, dreamers, and holy people who gave their lives so that the People would live and prosper. We ask for help in living our lives in balance and harmony so that the visions and dreams for the People will be fulfilled.

Focus—History (November 1–4)
It is important to know the rich and vibrant history of the People of the sovereign nations and tribes. In

today's fast-paced world, it is no longer enough simply to know the history of our own respective sovereign nations. We must learn the history of all the people living on the Earth our Mother, and gain a clearer understanding of the magnitude which the Great Mystery encompasses.

The history of the People is a proud one. We have shared with our non-Native immigrant relations our values, attitudes, and beliefs. We have learned to walk in two worlds—our own and that of our non-Native relations. We have survived the most horrifying treatment and deprivations at the hands of our non-Native relations.

We have adapted our ancient traditions and practices to a world in which we became strangers in our own land. We have kept our sacred ceremonies alive despite all that has been done to obliterate them. We have refused to be mainstreamed and melted into a society that is foreign to all that we have been taught by our elders since ancient times.

We are proud of our history and it is important to tell our history—to sing our songs loudly—to our non-Native relations, and to hold on to our history as sovereign People of the nations and tribes living on Turtle Island.

Council Fires

We honor those who have been chosen to lead and serve their respective sovereign nations and tribes. We celebrate the hard work and dedication of the elders and members of the Anaktuvuk Pass (Anaktuvuk Pass, Alaska), Birch Creek (Birch Creek, Alaska), Chignik Lake (Chignik Lake, Alaska), Deering (Deering, Alaska), Emmonak (Emmonak, Alaska), Healy Lake (Delta Junction, Alaska), Kaktovik (Kaktovik, Alaska), Kivalina (Kivalina, Alaska), Koyukuk (Koyukuk, Alaska), Mekoryuk (Mekoryuk, Alaska), Metlakatla (Metlakatla, Alaska), Newtok (Newtok, Alaska), Nunapitchuk (Nunapitchuk, Alaska), Pitka's Point (Pitka's Point, Alaska), Salamatof (Kenai, Alaska), Sitka (Sitka, Alaska), Tatitlek (Tatitlek, Alaska), Ugshik (King Salmon, Alaska), Barona (Lakeside, California), Big Lagoon Rancheria (Trinidad, California), Bridgeport Colony (Bridgeport, California), Elem Pomo (Clearlake Oaks, California), Fort Bidwell (Fort Bidwell, California), Minnemucca Colony (Susanville, California), Potter Valley Rancheria (West Sacramento, California), Santa Ysabel Mission (Santa Ysabel, California), Tule River (Porterville, California), Miccosukee (Miami, Florida), Sac and Fox (Tama, Iowa), Bay Mills (Brimley, Michigan), Saginaw Chippewa (Mount Pleasant, Michigan), Chippewa-Cree (Box Elder, Montana), Three Affiliated Tribes (New Town, North Dakota), Omaha (Macy, Nebraska), Fort McDermitt (McDermitt, Nevada), Walker River Paiute (Schurz, Nevada), Seneca Nation (Salamanca, New York), Otoe-Missouria (Red Rock, Oklahoma), Chehalis (Oakville, Washington), Hoh (Forks, Washington), Bad River (Odanah, Wisconsin), Forest County Potawatomi (Crandon, Wisconsin).

Events

- All-Indian tribal fair and rodeo, Tohono O'odham, Sells, Arizona, early in the month.
- Powwow, Kiowa, Carnegie, Oklahoma, November 9–11.
- Veterans Day powwow, Indian City, Anadarko, Oklahoma.
- Umatilla Veterans Day, Umatilla, Pendleton, Oregon.
- Osage Veterans Day, Osage Nation, Pawhuska, Oklahoma, November 11.
- Struck by the Ree powwow, Greenwood, South Dakota.
- Kiowa veterans celebration, Kiowa, Carnegie, Oklahoma.
- Indian veterans celebration, Yakima, Toppenish, Washington.
- Harvest fiesta and corn dances, Jemez Pueblo, Jemez, New Mexico, November 12.
- Feast day, Pojoaque Pueblo, Pojoaque, New Mexico.
- Buffalo dances and feast day, Tesuque Pueblo, Tesuque, New Mexico.

Solemn Time of the Sacred Fire
(November 29–December 14)

The elders of the People always have taught the importance of the sacred fire. From our elders, we have learned that the sacred fire is both a reality of all that is seen and a metaphor for all that is unseen.

The People know that fire, as a reality of that which is seen, provides warmth and enables the two-leggeds to survive cold winters. The importance of fire is a central theme around which all people on the Earth our Mother agree. The fire used to cook food and to provide warmth and illumination is the same fire used to make pottery from clay.

As a metaphor for all that is unseen, the sacred fire represents Grandfather Sun as well as the eternal fire of the Great Mystery of our very life force, that burns within all, including the Stone People, the winged, the two- and four-legged, the Cloud People, and the Thunders. The power of the sacred fire manifested by Father/Grandfather Sun is also the fire which burns at the core of Earth our Mother. It is the sacred fire which forms the lava that becomes the Stone People. It is the fire of the lightning which we call the Thunder Beings. All of these manifestations of the sacred fire remind the People of the awesome power of the Great Mystery, which we honor and celebrate.

During this sixteen-day solemn time, it is important to remember the significance of the sacred fire in each of our lives so that the People may live and prosper.

DECEMBER

Prayer

Great Spirit, may the light of the Thousand Fires of the People burn bright in our hearts as we remember those who have fallen through war and disease. Help us always to remember the ways of the People, and to be generous in our hearts and compassionate in our actions as we celebrate and honor all of creation—seen and unseen—during the festival time of food and gift giving. Let your blessings rain down on the storytellers who bring the lessons of the Great Mystery to the People so that we may live and prosper.

Focus—Generosity (December 1–4)

Generosity and hospitality always have been at the heart of the People's relationships with one another and with our non-Native relations. From the earliest times, the People of the sovereign nations and tribes were generous and hospitable to our non-Native immigrant relations when they first came to Turtle Island. To help one another always has been—and continues to be—the way of the People.

Council Fires

We honor those who have been chosen to lead and serve their respective sovereign nations and tribes. We celebrate the hard work and dedication of the elders and council members of the Andreafski (Saint Mary's, Alaska), Barrow (Barrow, Alaska), Brevig Mission (Brevig Mission, Alaska), Chilkat Klukwan (Haines, Alaska), Dillingham (Dillingham, Alaska), Evansville (Bettles, Alaska), Holy Cross (Holy Cross, Alaska), Upper Kalskag (Kalskag, Alaska), Klawock (Klawock, Alaska), Kwethluk (Kwethluk, Alaska), Mentasta (Tok, Alaska), Nightmute (Nightmute, Alaska), Ohogamiut (Fortuna Ledge, Alaska), Platinum (Platinum, Alaska), Sand Point Shumagin (Sand Point, Alaska), Sleetmute (Sleetmute, Alaska), Tazlina (Glenallen, Alaska), Umkumiut (Nightmute, Alaska), Navajo Nation (Window Rock, Arizona), Colorado River (Parker, Arizona), Gila River (Sacaton, Arizona), Havasupai (Supai, Arizona), Hopi (Kykotsmovi, Arizona), Quechan (Yuma, Arizona), Salt River Pima-Maricopa (Scottsdale, Arizona), San Carlos (San Carlos, Arizona), Buena Vista Rancheria (Ione, California), Fort Independence (Independence, California), Los Coyotes Mission (Warner Springs, California), Manzanita (Boulevard, California), Pala Mission (Pala, California), Quartz Valley (Etna, California), Rincon Mission (Valley Center, California), Shingle Springs Rancheria (Shingle Springs, California), Table Mountain Rancheria (Friant, California), Tuolumne Me-wok (Tuolumne, California), Viejas (Alpine, California), Southern Ute (Ignacio, Colorado), Prairie Island Mdewakanton Sioux (Welch, Minnesota), Shakopee Sioux (Prior Lake, Minnesota), Fort Belknap (Harlem, Montana), Confederated Salish and Kootenai (Pablo, Montana), Acoma (Acoma, New Mexico), Cochiti (Cochiti, New Mexico), Jemez (Jemez, New Mexico), Laguna (Laguna, New Mexico), Nambe (Santa Fe, New Mexico), Picuris (Penasco, New Mexico), Pojoaque (Santa Fe, New Mexico), Sandia (Bernalillo, New Mexico), San Felipe (San Felipe Pueblo, New Mexico), San Ildefonso (Santa Fe, New Mexico), San Juan (San Juan Pueblo, New Mexico), Santa Ana (Bernalillo, New Mexico), Santa Clara (Española, New Mexico), Santo Domingo (Santo Domingo Pueblo, New Mexico), Taos (Taos, New Mexico), Tesuque (Santa Fe, New

Mexico), Zia (San Ysidro, New Mexico), Zuñi (Zuñi, New Mexico), Moapa (Moapa, Nevada), Pyramid Lake Paiute (Nixon, Nevada), Reno-Sparks (Reno, Nevada), Yerington Paiute (Yerington, Nevada), Cheyenne-Arapaho (Concho, Oklahoma), Ponca (Ponca City, Oklahoma), Umatilla (Pendleton, Oregon), Ysleta del Sur (El Paso, Texas), Goshute (Ibapah, Utah), Skull Valley and Uintah and Ouray (Fort Duchesne, Utah), Lummi (Bellingham, Washington), Makah (Neah Bay, Washington), Sauk-Suiattle (Darrington, Washington), Yakima (Toppenish, Washington), Arapaho (Fort Washakie, Wyoming), Shoshone (Fort Washakie, Wyoming).

Events

- Shalako kachina ceremonies, Zuñi Pueblo, Zuñi, New Mexico, early in the month.
- Celebration, Tortugas, Las Cruces, New Mexico, December 10–12.
- Indian water festival, Colorado River, Parker, Arizona, week before December 25.
- Indian festival, Umatilla, Pendleton, Oregon, December 23–28.
- Holiday dances, Arapaho-Shoshone, Fort Washakie, Wyoming.
- Holiday dances, Ethete, Wyoming.
- Night bonfires and processions, all Rio Grande pueblos, New Mexico, December 24.
- Deer and matachines dances, most pueblos in New Mexico and Arizona, December 25.
- Turtle dance, San Juan Pueblo, San Juan, New Mexico, December 26.
- Deer dance, Sandia Pueblo, Sandia, New Mexico, December 31.

Festival of Food and Gift Giving (December 18–25)

The Earth our Mother has given her children the crops of the land. The People of the sovereign nations and tribes follow that example and share with all our relations the food and good things the Earth our Mother has provided.

During this eight-day festival, it is important for the People to continue to share the abundance of food, companions, talents, ideas, love, and compassion which they have received. Let us celebrate and honor all of creation—both seen and unseen—as we share our abundance with all our relations so that the

People of the sovereign nations and tribes may live and prosper in peace.

Honoring of Storytellers and the Sacred Word Bundles (December 26–January 2)

The People of the sovereign nations and tribes honor the storytellers who are the guardians of our history and traditions. The storytellers bring the sacred word bundles to the People of the different sovereign nations and tribes. The storytellers bring the ancient teachings to the People. The storytellers enable the People to learn and apply the wisdom of the stories to their lives if they choose.

During this nine-day honoring time, we honor the storytellers and treasure the sacred word bundles of wisdom which they bring to the People so that we may continue to grow as we walk the path of the brave in balance and harmony.

JANUARY

Prayer

Great Spirit, show us the path of wisdom and give us the strength to walk it without fear. We especially honor and celebrate the gift of our sacred practices, and as we lift our voices to the four directions, let the sacred fire continue to burn brightly within each of us.

Focus—Spirituality (January 1–4)

The connection with the Great Mystery and our relationship with the Great Spirit, an aspect of the Great Mystery, which is with us always, has been—and continues to be—important to the People of the sovereign nations and tribes all across Turtle Island. For untold thousands of years, the People of the sovereign nations and tribes have understood the power of the Great Spirit, which lives in all that is unseen and seen. For the People, the Great Mystery incorporates all creation, and the Great Spirit is but one part of that creation. Although the Great Mystery is manifested in many forms, the People know and understand that all creation is eternal and continually regenerating.

It is important that our non-Native relations understand that the People of the sovereign nations and tribes believe that all that is seen and unseen has a common purpose to contribute to walking in beauty and harmony with all other aspects of creation. We know and understand that we two-leggeds are related to, and not master over, all. We know and incorporate into our daily lives our respect for our four-legged relations, our winged relations, and the thousands of other relations with whom we share creation.

In the way of the People, it is important that we remind ourselves that each of us is responsible for our actions and that all our individual actions—thoughts, words, deeds—affect all of creation, because everything that is seen and unseen is connected. It is important for us to remember that as cocreators, our duty to all of creation requires us to call upon the Great Spirit and all our relations to help us walk in harmony and balance so that the People may continue to live and prosper.

Council Fires

We honor those who have been chosen to lead and serve their respective sovereign nations and tribes. We celebrate the hard work and dedication of the elders and council members of the Akhiok (Akhiok, Alaska), Angoon (Angoon, Alaska), Buckland (Buckland, Alaska), Chilkoot (Haines, Alaska), Diomede (Diomede, Alaska), Eyak (Cordora, Alaska), Hoonah (Hoonah, Alaska), Kaltag (Kaltag, Alaska), Kluti-kaah (Copper Center, Alaska), Kwigillingok (Kwigillingok, Alaska), Minto (Minto, Alaska), Nikolai (Nikolai, Alaska), Old Harbor (Old Harbor, Alaska), Point Hope (Point Hope, Alaska), Savoonga (Savoonga, Alaska), South Naknek (South Naknek, Alaska), Kongiganak (Kongiganak, Alaska), Unalakleet (Unalakleet, Alaska), Ak Chin (Maricopa, Arizona), Mohave-Apache (Fort McDowell Reservation, Fountain Hills, Arizona), Berry Creek Rancheria (Oroville, California), Cabazon (Indio, California), Grindstone Rancheria (Elk Creek, California), Mesa Grande Mission (Santa Ysabel, California), Pauma Mission (Pauma Valley, California), Ramona Cahuilla (Anza, California), Twenty-nine Palms Mission (Twenty-nine Palms, California), Mashantucket Pequot (Ledyard, Connecticut), Keweenaw Bay (Baraga, Michigan), Mescalero Apache (Mescalero, New Mexico), Duckwater Shoshone (Duckwater, Nevada), Fallon (Fallon, Nevada), Muscogee Creek Nation of Oklahoma (Okmulgee, Oklahoma), Thlopthlocco tribal town (Okemah, Oklahoma), Narragansett (Charleston, Rhode Island), Sisseton-Wahpeton Sioux (Sisseton, South Dakota), Nisqually (Olympia, Washington), Quileute (La Push, Washington), Squaxin Island (Shelton, Washington), Sokaogon Chippewa (Crandon, Wisconsin).

Events

- Treaty day feast, Tulalip, Tulalip Reservation, Washington, date varies.
- Corn, turtle, and other dances, pueblos in New Mexico and Arizona.
- Seminole Okalee Village, Seminole Nation, Seminole Reservation, Hollywood, Florida, all year.
- Tribal New Year, White Swan, Washington, January 1.
- King's Day inauguration, pueblos of New Mexico and Arizona, January 6.
- Buffalo and Comanche dances and feast, San Ildefonso Pueblo, San Ildefonso, New Mexico, January 23.

Celebration of Our Traditions (January 3–18)

The People of the sovereign nations and tribes have held onto their respective traditions despite all attempts during five centuries by our non-Native relations to abolish them. During the centuries, our non-Native relations have imposed harsh punishment—including starvation, imprisonment, and even death—on the People of the sovereign nations and tribes who continued to celebrate their respective traditions. Even today, all across Turtle Island, there are never-ending incidents of federal, state, and local governments as well as non-Native individuals who continue to do all possible to prevent the People of the sovereign nations and tribes from celebrating their traditions.

During this eight-day celebration, let us walk in the way of our ancestors and fearlessly celebrate our traditions so that the People of the sovereign nations and tribes may continue to maintain their dignity and special relationship with all of creation.

Celebration of our Sacred Practices (January 19–26)

The People of the sovereign nations celebrate the sacred practices of the sacred pipe, the inipi/sweat lodge, kiva, sun dance, passage rites, and other ceremonies and hidden traditions. For thousands of years, the People have understood the importance of the respective sacred practices which they have passed on to generation after generation. Although many of our non-Native immigrant relations have remained ignorant and frightened and have imprisoned and/or murdered the People for continuing to conduct their sacred practices, it is important that the People continue to exercise their sovereign right to engage in their respective sacred practices as they choose.

During this six-day celebration, it is important to remember that there are many of our non-Native American relations who still are frightened and ignorant about the sacred practices of the People. Let the People remember as they conduct their sacred practices to ask that the Great Spirit calm the fears of our non-Native relations so they may respect the ways of the People.

Season of Tears and Despair (January 27–February 27)
The People of the sovereign nations and tribes mourn the loss of our ancestral homelands. We mourn the senseless deaths of our great leaders and heroes. We mourn the destruction of our societies and families. We mourn the desecration of our spiritual beliefs and sacred practices. We mourn for the thousands upon thousands who died on their forced journeys from their homelands to government reservations. We mourn for our relations addicted to alcohol and drugs.

During this season, we raise our voices and pour out our hearts to the Great Spirit and ask to be healed. We do this so the People of the sovereign nations and tribes may live.

FEBRUARY

Prayer
Great Spirit, we are thankful for all our relations and ask for help as we work in our communities to do what is proper so that the People will continue to grow and prosper.

Focus—Community (February 1–4)
For the People of the sovereign nations and tribes, the community always has been of primary importance.

Our communities help us to walk in harmony and balance. We believe that we are all interdependent and that all are responsible for their actions. When we are involved in our community, we know our harmonious place with all of creation and become empowered to reach for our highest potential.

Belonging to a community brings us closer together. Although the People do not always agree with or like everyone in the community, we put aside our differences and work together for the benefit of the community. In doing this, we learn to be patient and caring. We know and understand that when division and strife occur, it is because we have not been attentive to fulfilling our responsibilities as individual members of the community.

Council Fires
We honor those who have been chosen to lead and serve their respective sovereign nations and tribes. We celebrate the hard work and dedication of the elders and council members of the Akiachak (Akiachak, Alaska), Aniak (Aniak, Alaska), Cantwell (Cantwell, Alaska), Chinik Eskimo (Golovin, Alaska), Dot Lake (Dot Lake, Alaska), False Pass (False Pass, Alaska), Hooper Bay (Hooper Bay, Alaska), Karluk (Karluk, Alaska), Knik (Wasilla, Alaska), Kwinhagak (Quinhagak, Alaska), Mountain Village (Mountain Village, Alaska), Ninilchik (Ninilchik, Alaska), Orutsararmuit (Bethel, Alaska), Point Lay (Point Lay, Alaska), Saxman (Ketchikan, Alaska), Saint George Island (Saint George, Alaska), Teller (Teller, Alaska), Qualingin (Unalaska, Alaska), Cahuilla Mission (Anza, California), Inaja and Cosmit (Ramona, California), Resighini Coast Rancheria (Klamath, California), Upper Lake Rancheria (Sacramento, California), Isleta (Isleta, New Mexico), Ely Colony (Ely, Nevada), Siletz (Siletz, Oregon), Swinomish (La Conner, Washington), Wisconsin Menominee (Keshena, Wisconsin).

Events
• Buffalo dance and Candlemas celebration, Cochiti, Cochiti Pueblo, New Mexico, February 2; San Felipe and Santo Domingo Pueblos, New Mexico.
• Los Comanches, Taos Pueblo, Taos, New Mexico, first week of the month.
• War dances, Nez Percé, Kamiah, Idaho, February 12–13.

- Lincoln's Day, Umatilla, Pendleton, Oregon, February 12.
- Special open dances, San Juan Pueblo, San Juan, New Mexico, midmonth.
- Powwow, Seminole Nation, Seminole Reservation, Hollywood, Florida, February 20.
- George Washington celebration, Toppenish, Washington, February 22.
- Washington Day, Nez Percé, Lapwai, Idaho, February 26–28.
- Clan dances, San Juan Pueblo, San Juan, New Mexico, last of the month.
- Evergreen dances, Isleta Pueblo, Isleta, New Mexico.

Solemn Time of the Sacred Directions
(February 28–March 15)

The significance of the sacred directions is important to all the People of the sovereign nations and tribes. Each of the sacred directions teaches us about our harmonious place in the order of creation.

For the People, east is the place of all beginnings. It is the direction from which Grandfather Sun rises, signaling the start of each new day. It is the direction of our spiritual well-being from which all enter this life through the eastern doorway.

South is the place of youth and learning. It is the direction of our emotional well-being in which we focus our attention on youth, growth, and abundance.

West is where many of the People believe we depart this life through the western doorway. It is the direction of our physical well-being and of dreams and meditation. It is the direction of adulthood in which we are tested and learn perseverance.

North is the place of elder wisdom. It is the direction of mental well-being in which we focus our attention for healing, purification, and protection.

The above is the direction we look when we pray, and from it, the Great Mystery sends the People messages through the Great Spirit.

The below is the center place. It is the center of the Earth our Mother and the center within ourselves. It is the place of volition, or will.

During this sixteen-day solemn time, it is important to walk in harmony and balance as we journey through our lives so that the People may live and prosper.

TREATY TIME

1778–1871

THIS LAND WAS OURS—FIRST

> OFFICE HOURS
> 9:00 A.M.–12:00 and 1:30 P.M.–4:30 P.M.
> STUDENTS PLEASE NOTE
> Office hours operate on Treaty Time. . . .
> If we feel like honoring them we will
> if we don't—we won't.[9]

Within twenty-five years from the beginning of the republic within a democracy called the United States of America, on July 4, 1776, the People of the sovereign nations ceded by treaty more than 90 percent of their ancient homelands east of the Ohio River. By 1871, the People of the sovereign nations from "sea to shining sea" had ceded 99 percent of all their lands and were relegated to subsistence living on land unwanted by their non-Native relations. In all of human history before or since, no horror exceeds the magnitude of the one legally perpetrated on the People of the sovereign nations and tribes under the treaties they negotiated and signed in good faith—the terms of which were broken repeatedly by the U.S. government and its immigrant citizens.

It is important to remember that the Constitution of the United States declares in Article 6, Section 2:

This Constitution, and the laws of the United States which shall be made in pursuance thereof, and *all treaties made,* or which shall be made, under the authority of the United States, *shall be the supreme law of the land;*[10] and the judges in every State shall be bound thereby, anything in the Constitution or laws of any State to the contrary notwithstanding.

However, it has not been until the past twenty years that the United States' violations of treaties made with the People of the sovereign nations and tribes since 1778 have been adjudicated, more fairly than not, by the United States Supreme Court in favor of the People. Repeatedly, the courts have ruled that treaties are indeed the supreme law of the land and are superior to the laws enacted by any state, and that the treaties continue to remain in full force today as they were when they were signed by representatives of the People of the respective sovereign nations and the United States.

During a period of ninety years (1778–1868), the People of the sovereign nations and tribes all across Turtle Island negotiated and signed 414 treaties with the government of the United States. This means that an average of four treaties was signed every year for ninety years. Because of the impact of the treaties on the lives of all the People of the sovereign nations and tribes living on Turtle Island (even today), *all* known treaties are presented in the time line. Some treaties will be described at length, but the majority will be listed only by the date the treaty was concluded and the sovereign nation that signed it in good faith.

At first (1600), the treaties negotiated and signed by the People of the sovereign nations and tribes with the European immigrant colonists concerned trade relations, demarcation of lands given by the People to the colonists and land belonging to the People, and mutual "military" alliances and assistance. The treaties negotiated, beginning with the founding of the United States of America, in 1776, through 1820, centered on cessions of large tracts of land by the People and attention to the boundaries between them and the ever increasing hordes of American immigrants encroaching on the lands of the People.

From about 1816 through 1845, the treaties were the method used by the Americans to remove the People of the sovereign nations and tribes from their ancient homelands to areas that the American immigrants did not want. The treaties negotiated from 1846 through 1871 were imposed on the People by the United States, that forced the People to move and remain on small reservations. Once the treaties were agreed to, the United States broke the promises and new treaties were negotiated. The new treaties required more land cessions by the People of the sovereign nations and tribes.

The People went to war as promise after promise was broken and non-Native settlers continued to expand westward in search of gold, timber, and any natural resources that would make them rich. The killing reached new heights on both sides. In the minds of the enraged People, it would be the final war. The People were determined that they should be completely victorious or they all should die.

Sadly, the People became fragmented, and many decided that the only way to survive was to let the American rapists have their way. The People were broken in body, heart, mind, and spirit.

Two centuries later (1994), the horrors of that time are as fresh among the People as if they had occurred only yesterday. We remember Sand Creek and Wounded Knee. We remember the Trail of Tears and the Long Walk. We remember the smallpox-infected blankets sent by the U.S. Army to cold and starving People forced to live on reservations like penned animals. We remember the rapes and wanton murders of the People by pony soldiers. We remember the buffalo soldiers who were "just following orders." We remember, and our children remember, and our children's children will remember.

1778

Most Oneida and Tuscarora become allies with the United States in the American Revolutionary War, while the Seneca, Cayuga, Mohawk, and Onondaga maintain their alliance with the British.

The Assiniboin enter into a treaty of peace and friendship with the Oglala Lakota.

The Delaware, or Lenape, conclude negotiations with the newly formed government of the United States of America on September 17. It is the first known treaty between the sovereign nations and tribes and the new government.

Among the Oglala Lakota, it is said that there was a woman of the People who had visions. She would go to lonely places, and after receiving her vision would return to the People and tell them where to hunt for buffalo and when the enemy was coming. It is said that one morning she awoke but was unable to speak and "did not know anything." It is said that she soon died.

*Tenskwatawa, or The Shawnee Prophet or The Open Door
(Shawnee/Muscogee or Creek/Cherokee)*
COURTESY OF SMITHSONIAN

1779

Mohawk and Seneca forces engage in battle at Newtown, New York, on August 29 against the American army of more than four thousand troops, under the command of General John Sullivan, General James Clinton, and Colonel Daniel Brodhead.

It is said among the Iroquois that the office of Noble Peace Mother was abolished because Genetaska broke her vows to remain impartial and fell in love with an Oneida. It is said that because she broke her vows, war and tumult returned once more among the People.

Gelelemend, or Killbuck (Delaware, or Lenape) is chosen principal leader. He strongly advocates peaceful accommodation of the English immigrant colonists.

Tenskwatawa, or the Shawnee Prophet, or the Open Door (Shawnee/Muscogee), who will become the Shawnee Prophet and leader of what is known as Tecumseh's Rebellion (1809), is born in about 1778.

Such treaties may be all right for men who are too old to hunt or fight. As for me, I have my young warriors about me. We will have our lands.

Tsiyugunsini, or Dragging Canoe (Cherokee)

1778

Miguel Rashid Sanchez (Laguna Pueblo/Chippewa)
COURTESY OF
CAROL LEE SANCHEZ

Kaienkwahton, or Old Smoke (Seneca), principal leader and noted warrior, leads Seneca forces at the battle of Newtown against the American forces.

. . . Grandfather's comin back
to check us out
see if we made it
and how
and I said:
they don't even understand
the meaning of Coyote—

Carol Lee Sanchez (Laguna)

1779

PERSPECTIVE
1780–1820

During the first twenty years of the newly formed government, what is now western New York, northwestern Pennsylvania, Ohio, Tennessee, Georgia, Alabama, and Mississippi all belonged to the United States government through "legal" land theft in which the United States made great promises which were not honored completely in treaties with the People of the sovereign nations and tribes.

The People became caught in the web of conflicting alliances and ended up in battle against one another. Among the Iroquois Confederacy, for example, the Oneida allied with the United States and did battle with their relations, the Seneca, Cayuga, and Mohawk, along with the Mingo and Wyandot. Finally, the Treaty of Paris (September 3, 1783) formally ended the war between the Europeans and Americans. The Spaniards gave Florida to the English in exchange for what is now Cuba. The Seminole people, to which the land known as Florida belonged, were not consulted.

In 1786, the representatives of the United States government declared that the Ohio valley belonged to the immigrant Americans. Incensed by the outrageous declaration, the Shawnee and Miami went to war, led by Weyapiersenwah, or Blue Jacket (Shawnee), and Michikinikwa, or Little Turtle (Miami/Mahican). From 1786 through 1795, the war raged, ending with the Treaty of Greenville, which established a "permanent" boundary line between American settlers and the People of the sovereign nations and tribes. By 1803, the U.S. government's voracious appetite for land found a strong advocate in Thomas Jefferson, who decided to obtain more land west of the boundary established in the Treaty of Greenville. This provided the impetus for the call for collective resistance by new hero leaders such as Tecumtha, or Tecumseh (Shawnee/Muscogee) and his brother Tenskwatawa, or the Prophet (Shawnee/Muscogee). The call went out to the People of the sovereign nations and tribes, including the Shawnee, Potawatomi, Odawa, or Ottawa, Winnebago, Ojibwa, and Wyandot.

Fraudulent land cessions resulted in renewed attacks by the Sac Nation on Fort Madison near what is now St. Louis, led by Michikinikwa.

Tecumtha became leader of the alliance of many of the Peoples of the different sovereign nations and tribes with the British, and the War of 1812 began (1812–15). In the middle of the conflict between the Americans and British, the Muscogee, or Creek, became embroiled in civil war incited by Andrew Jackson, who led Tennessee militia, Cherokee, and White Stick Muscogee against the Red Stick Muscogee. By 1814, the Muscogee civil war had ended. The Americans and British signed the Treaty of Ghent (December 24, 1814), which ended the War of 1812.

It did not take Andrew Jackson long to continue his campaign to set the People of the sovereign nations and tribes against one another. Less than twenty months later, American troops under the command of Jackson attacked the "Negro Fort" in northwestern Florida, later called Fort Gadsden, with the idea of recapturing black fugitive slaves under the protection of the Seminole Nation. This led to raids by the Seminole. Jackson retaliated and attacked the hometown of Neamathla, principal leader of the Seminole.

This attack, on November 20, 1817, officially began the war between the People of the sovereign Seminole Nation and the forces of Andrew Jackson. By 1818, the Spanish conquerors had ceded Florida to United States forces, and the grand scheme to rid the entire eastern seaboard of the People of the sovereign nations and tribes was at last realized.

By 1820, the landholdings of the People of the sovereign nations and tribes from Maine to Florida and as far west as Lake Michigan to New Orleans were occupied by the Americans. Sadly, the violence and horror did not end with white occupation.

	HISTORY/LAW/ POLITICS	LITERATURE/ART/ LEGENDS AND STORIES
1780	The Miami engage in battle on the side of the British during the American Revolutionary War, and successfully defend their village against French forces under the command of Colonel Mottin de la Balme.	Among the Wyandot, there is a story which tells of the beginning time when the white man came to speak to a Wyandot who was sitting on the end of a log. It is said that the white man said, "Move over!" And so the Wyandot allowed the stranger to sit on the log. Again and again, the white man kept telling the Wyandot to move over. The Wyandot continued to move over as commanded. After a while, the Wyandot was at the other end of the log. Seeing this, it is said that the white man then said, "Now all of this log is mine!"
1781	The Mohawk Nation leads raiding attacks on Cherry Valley, New York, on behalf of the British.	
1782	The Gnaddenhutten Massacre is conducted by American Colonel David Williamson on March 9 at what is now Gnaddenhutten, Ohio, where peaceful Moravian, Wyandot, and Delaware people reside. The Delaware retaliate, but their towns are destroyed by American forces under the command of Colonel William Crawford. Near what is now Sandusky, the Shawnee and Delaware combine forces to rout the American troops. The Shawnee and Delaware capture Crawford, who is tortured slowly until he dies.	
1783	The People of the sovereign nations and tribes living on Turtle Island are not mentioned in the Treaty of Paris, which ends the American Revolutionary War. As a result of the treaty, the ancient homelands of the People of the sovereign nations and tribes—consisting of what is now Maine, New Hampshire, Vermont, Massachusetts, Connecticut, New York (east of Lake Ontario), the lower half of Pennsylvania, New Jersey, Delaware, Maryland, West Virginia, Kentucky, Virginia, North Carolina, South Carolina, and parts of Tennessee and Georgia—become the land "belonging" to the newly formed government of the United States of America. The People of the sovereign nations and tribes are not consulted. Chickasaw and Cherokee lands in North Carolina are confiscated by the state, which is unable to enforce its proclamation after strong resistance by the two tribes.	

HEROES/LEADERS/ VICTIMS	ELDER WISDOM/PHILOSOPHY/ SONGS	
Michikinikwa, or Little Turtle (Miami/Mahican), principal leader of the Miami, leads the People in their defense of his village against French forces. Tah-gah-jute, or James Logan, or Tachnechdorus (Cayuga), is murdered on his journey from Detroit to his home at Chillicothe, on the Scioto River in what is now Ohio. Teyarhasere, or Abraham, or Little Abraham (Mohawk), dies.	The Law is in the Corn the people of the southwest say this . . . Out here at the Eastern Door, we say it is the Original Instructions . . . This is called Democracy. This is in the land, it is in the seed. *Karoniaktatie, or Alex A. Jacobs (Mohawk)*	**1780**
Thayendanegea, or Joseph Brant (Mohawk), principal leader who is given the commission of colonel by King George III of England, leads the Mohawk, Seneca, Onondaga, Cayuga, and Tuscarora in battle on the side of the British in the American Revolutionary War.	Wherever we went the soldiers came to kill us, and it was all our own country. *Hehaka Sapa, or Black Elk (Oglala Lakota)*	**1781**
Thayendanegea, or Joseph Brant (Mohawk), principal leader of the Mohawk forces allied with the British, leads an ambush against what is now Fayette and Lincoln Counties in Kentucky, where seventy American troops are killed and more than twenty are captured.	Now I know the government is going to break the Treaty because when it was signed it was understood that it would last as long as the grass grew, the winds blew, the rivers ran, and men walked on two legs—and now they have sent us an Agent who has only one leg. *Piapot, or Flash in the Sky (Cree)*	**1782**
Cooswootna, or Juan Antonio (Cahuilla), who will become principal leader, is born at about this time in the San Jacinto Mountains of California.		**1783**

1784

Representatives of the Iroquois League are forced to sign the Treaty of Fort Stanwix with the newly formed government of the United States of America on October 22. It cedes what is now western New York and northwestern Pennsylvania. The "Commissioners Plenipotentiary from the United States" impose harsh terms on the Seneca, Mohawk, and Onondaga for having supported Great Britain during the American Revolutionary War. The Iroquois representatives who are forced to sign the treaty were not authorized to do so by the council of the Iroquois League, which later refuses to confirm the treaty.

TREATY OF FORT STANWIX
Fort Stanwix (now Rome, New York)
October 22, 1784

Made and entered between Oliver Wolcott, Richard Butler, and Arthur Lee, Commissioners Plenipotentiary from the United States, in Congress Assembled, on the one part, and the Sachems and Warriors of the Six Nations, on the other.

The United States of America give peace to the Senecas, Mohawks, Onondagas and Cayugas, and receive them into their protection upon the following conditions:

ARTICLE I

Six hostages shall be immediately delivered to the commissioners by the said nations, to remain in possession of the United States, till all the prisoners, white and black, which were taken by the said Senecas, Mohawks, Onondagas and Cayugas, or by any of them, in the late war, from among the people of the United States, shall be delivered up.

ARTICLE II

The Oneida and Tuscarora nations shall be secured in the possession of the lands on which they are settled.

ARTICLE III

A line shall be drawn, beginning at the mouth of a creek about four miles east of Niagara, called Oyonwayea, or Johnston's Landing-Place, upon the lake named by the Indians Oswego, and by us Ontario; from thence southerly in a direction always four miles east of the carrying-path, between Lake Erie and Ontario, to the mouth of Tehoseroron or Buffaloe Creek on Lake Erie; thence south to the north boundary of the state of Pennsylvania; thence west to the end of the said north boundary; thence south along the west boundary of the said state, to the river Ohio; the said line from the mouth of the Oyonwayea to the Ohio, shall be the western boundary of the lands of the Six Nations, so that the Six Nations shall and do yield to the United States, all claims to the country west of the said boundary, and then they shall be secured in the peaceful possession of the lands they inhabit east and north of the same, reserving only six miles square round the fort of Oswego, to the United States, for the support of the same.

ARTICLE IV

The Commissioners of the United States, in consideration of the present circumstances of the Six Nations, and in the execution of the humane and liberal views of the United States upon the signing of the above articles, will order goods to be delivered to the said Six Nations for their use and comfort.

Weyapiersenwah, or Blue Jacket (white/adopted Shawnee), leads the Shawnee in raids against the American colonists living in what is now Ohio.

. . . no longer powerful . . . reduced by diseases . . . thinned by civil wars . . . [Great Spirit] has shown his anger against us [for] nearly all have perished.

Coocoochee (Mohawk)

1784

1785

The Wyandot, Delaware, Chippewa, and Ottawa Nations conclude the Treaty of Fort McIntosh with the U.S. government on January 9. Two articles in the treaty are especially interesting. Article 2 provides that "The said Indian nations do acknowledge themselves and all their tribes to be under the protection of the United States and of no other sovereign whatsoever." Article 5 states, "If any citizen of the United States, or other person not being Indian, shall attempt to settle on any of the lands allotted to the Wyandot and Delaware nations in this treaty, except on the lands reserved to the United States in the preceding article, such person shall forfeit the protection of the United States, and the Indians may punish him as they please."

The Cherokee Nation, in the southeastern United States, negotiates the Treaty of Hopewell with the government of the United States on November 28. The provisions violate the treaty of 1777 between the Cherokee Nation and the former colonies of Virginia and North Carolina.

Nambe pueblo sketch by Carol Lee Sanchez
COURTESY OF CAROL LEE SANCHEZ

1786

A grand council fire is held at the Huron village near the mouth of the Detroit River on December 18. Attending are the People of the Five Nations (Seneca, Cayuga, Onondaga, Oneida, Mohawk), and the Huron, Delaware, Shawnee, Ottawa, Chippewa, Potawatomi, Twightwee, Cherokee, and Wabash Confederacy members. It is proposed and agreed that all treaty negotiations with the new United States government related to land cession by the People of the sovereign nations and tribes "should be made in the most public manner, and by the united voice of the confederacy."

The people of the Choctaw Nation conclude a treaty with the U.S. government on January 3.

The Chickasaw Nation signs a treaty with the government of the United States on January 10.

The Shawnee, or Shawano, Nation agrees to a treaty with the U.S. government on January 31.

1787

After American Colonel Benjamin Logan burns the Shawnee village at Mackachack to the ground, the Shawnee Nation goes to war against the United States.

1788

The Shawnee, Chickamauga, and Cherokee join forces to fight the American colonists in what is now the middle basin area of the Cumberland River.

HEROES/LEADERS/ VICTIMS	ELDER WISDOM/PHILOSOPHY/ SONGS	
Michikinikwa, or Little Turtle (Miami/Mahican), leads the Miami in raids throughout the Ohio valley against American colonists.	Elder Brother, you told your younger brothers, when we first assembled, that peace was your object. . . . *Michikinikwa, Little Turtle (Miami/Mahican)*	**1785**
		1786
Kekewepellethe, or Tame Hawk (Shawnee), protests that what is now Ohio is declared by U.S. government negotiator William Butler as belonging to the United States. Butler threatens to go to war with the Shawnee, and Kekewepellethe agrees to cede the entire Miami valley. The Miami and Shawnee bands repudiate the treaty of January 31. Kaienkwahton, or Old Smoke (Seneca), principal leader and noted warrior, dies at his village of Gaunudasaga, which later is called Geneva, New York.		
Hugh McGary, an American colonist soldier under the command of Colonel Benjamin Logan, murders and scalps Moluntha (Shawnee), an elder among the People.	I admit that there are good white men, but they bear no proportion to the bad; the bad must be strongest, for they rule. They do what they please. They enslave those who are not of their color, although created by the same Great Spirit who created them. *Pachgantschilias (Delaware, or Lenape)*	**1787**
Tecumtha, or Tecumseh (Shawnee/Muscogee), joins in the raids against American colonists at the Cumberland River.		**1799**

1789

The United States secretary of war is to oversee promises made in the treaties with the People of the sovereign nations and tribes across Turtle Island.

PETITION OF THE MOHEGAN

To the most Honorable Assembly of the State of Connecticut Conv'd at Hartford May 14, 1789. Your Good old Steady Friends and Bretheren the Mohegan Tribe of Indians Sendeth Greeting:

We beg Leave to lay our Concerns and Burdens at Your Excellencies Feet. The Times are Exceedingly Alter'd, Yea the Times have turn'd everything Upside down, or rather we have Chang'd the good Times, Chiefly by the help of the White People, For in Times past our Fore-Fathers lived in Peace, Love and great harmony, and had everything in Great plenty. When they Wanted meat they would run into the Bush a little ways with their weapons and would Soon bring home good venison, Racoon, Bear and Fowl. If they Choose to have Fish, they Wo'd only go to the River or along the Sea Shore and they wou'd presently fill their Cannoous With Veriety of Fish, Both Scaled and shell Fish, and they had abundance of Nuts, Wild Fruit, Ground Nuts and Ground Beans, and they planted but little corn and Beans and they kept no Cattle or Horses for they needed none—And they had no Contention about their lands, it lay in Common to them all, and they had but one large dish and they Cou'd all eat together in Peace and Love—But alas, it is not so now, all our Fishing, Hunting and Fowling is entirely gone, And we have now begun to Work on our Land, keep Cattle, Horses and Hogs And we Build Houses and fence in Lots—and now we plainly See that one Dish and one Fire will not do any longer for us—Some few are Stronger than others and they will keep off the poor, weake, the halt and the Blind, And Will take the Dish to themselves. Yea, they will rather Call White People and Molattoes to eat With them out of our Dish, and poor Widows and Orphans Must be pushed aside and there they Must Sta a Craying, Starving and die.

And so We are now Come to our Good Brethern of the Assembly With Hearts full of Sorrow and Grief for Immediate help—And therefore our most humble and Earnest Request and Petition is That our Dish of Suckuttush may be equally divided amongst us, that every one may have his own little dish by himself, that he may eat Quietly and do With his Dish as he pleases; and let every one have his own Fire.

Your Excellencies Compliance and Assistance at This Time will make our poor hearts very Glad and thankful.

This is the most humble Request and Petition of Your True Friend & Brethern Mohegan Indians. . . .

The Wyandot, Delaware, Ottawa, Chippewa, Potawatomi, and Sac Nations conclude the Treaty of Fort Harmer on January 9. The treaty seeks to address the protestations of the sovereign nations and tribes that had been forced to sign the Treaties of Fort Stanwix (1784) and Fort McIntosh (1785). Under the Treaty of Fort Harmer, the sovereign nations and tribes cede what is now Tennessee, the northwestern portion of Georgia, and the northern portion of Alabama to the United States government.

The Six Nations of the Iroquois Confederacy enter into a treaty with the U.S. government on January 9.

	HISTORY/LAW/ POLITICS	LITERATURE/ART/ LEGENDS AND STORIES
1790	The Creek Nation and the United States agree to a treaty of peace and finally sign it in New York City on August 7. The Creek Nation cedes the remainder of what is now Georgia and Alabama, except for the western portion along the border of Mississippi.	
1791	The Cherokee Nation enters into a treaty with the United States on July 2.	
1792	The Cherokee Nation concludes a treaty with the United States on February 17. The Five Nations reach an agreement with the United States on April 23.	
1793	The Shawnee Nation rejects peace offers made by the United States, and continues to battle American forces throughout the Ohio valley.	
1794	The Cherokee Nation enters into a treaty with the United States on June 26. The Six Nations negotiate and sign a treaty with the United States on November 11. The Oneida, Tuscarora, and Stockbridge Nations conclude a treaty with the United States called the Treaty with the Oneidas on December 2. President George Washington submits it to the United States Senate for ratification on January 2, 1795. At the Battle of Fallen Timbers, on August 20, Michikinikwa, or Little Turtle (Miami/Mahican), leads the Miami, Shawnee, Ojibwa, Delaware, Potawatomi, and Ottawa people against the United States at Fort Miami on the Maumee River.	

HEROES/LEADERS/ VICTIMS	ELDER WISDOM/PHILOSOPHY/ SONGS	
Cornplanter (Seneca), principal leader, travels to Philadelphia, where he meets with U.S. President George Washington to present the grievances of the Seneca. Arapoosh (Crow), who becomes military leader of the River Crow, is born at about this time. Cooweescoowee, or John Ross (Cherokee/Scottish), who will become principal chief of the Cherokee Nation, is born on October 3.		**1790**
Michikinikwa, or Little Turtle (Miami/Mahican), leader of the Miami, and Weyapiersenwah, or Blue Jacket (white/adopted Shawnee), leader of the Shawnee, head their collective forces in a successful battle against American troops in the plateau area above the upper Wabash River. More than 600 American soldiers are killed and more than 250 are wounded.		**1791**
	Cooweescoowee, or John Ross (Cherokee) COURTESY OF SMITHSONIAN	**1792**
		1793
		1794

	HISTORY/LAW/ POLITICS	LITERATURE/ART/ LEGENDS AND STORIES
1795	The Wyandot, Delaware, Shawnee, Ottawa, Chippewa, Potawatomi, Miami, Eel River, Wea, Kickapoo, Piankashaw, and Kaskaskia Nations sign the Treaty of Greenville, in which the People of the sovereign nations and tribes relinquish all their lands in what is now Ohio, southern Indiana, and southeastern and western Illinois, including Chicago.

Oshkosh (Menominee)
COURTESY OF SMITHSONIAN |
1796	The Seven Nations of Canada enter into a treaty with the United States on May 31. The Creek Nation signs a treaty with the United States on June 29.	
1797	The Mohawk Nation and the United States government sign the Treaty at Big Tree on March 29. The Seneca Nation concludes and signs a treaty with the United States on September 15.	
1798	The Cherokee Nation negotiates a treaty with the United States which is signed on October 2.	
1799	Tlingit in the region now known as Sitka, Alaska, engage in limited contact with trappers of the Russian Fur Company, which has been granted a charter by Czar Paul I.	
1800	The total population of the People of the sovereign nations and tribes living on Turtle Island is estimated to be six hundred thousand, compared with more than 30 million before the arrival of non-Native immigrants. War with non-Native invaders, disease, and destruction of ways of life among the People are the major causes for the decline in population.	

HEROES/LEADERS/ VICTIMS	ELDER WISDOM/PHILOSOPHY/ SONGS	
Halpatter Tustenugee, or Alligator (Seminole), who will become a war leader among the People, is born. Blackfoot (Crow), who will become principal leader, is born. Oshkosh (Menominee), who will become principal leader, is born at what is now Old King's Village, in Wisconsin.	Now, my friend, the Great Wind, do not deceive us in the manner that the French, the British, and Spaniards have heretofore done. The English have abused us much; they have made us promises which they never fulfilled; they have proved to us how little they have ever had our happiness at heart; and we have severely suffered for placing our dependence on so faithless a people. My friend, I am old, but I shall never die. I shall always live in my children, and children's children. *New Corn (Potawatomi)*	1795
Gonwatzijyanni, or Molly Brant (Mohawk), clan mother of the People, dies at Cataraui, or what is now Kingston, Ontario, Canada. Cornplanter (Seneca) receives from the state of Pennsylvania a personal grant of 640 acres in Pennsylvania near the border of New York.		1796
		1797
William Apes (Pequot), author, is born on January 31.		1798
		1798
Medicine Calf, or James Beckwith (Irish/African/adopted Crow), who will become a principal leader of the Crow, is born. Onpahtonga, or Big Elk (Omaha), succeeds Washinga Sakba, or Black Bird, as principal leader of the People and becomes known by whites as a fine orator. Timpooche Barnard (Yuchi/Scottish), who becomes a strong ally of the Americans, is born at about this time.	Perhaps when the wild animals are gone, the Indians will be gone too. *Hehaka Sapa, or Black Elk (Oglala Lakota)*	1800

1801

The Chickasaw Nation enters into a treaty with the United States on October 24.

The Choctaw Nation agrees to a treaty with the United States on December 17 at Fort Adams.

1802

The Tlingit capture the Russian stronghold at New Archangel, or what is now Sitka, Alaska. The Tlingit hold the settlement for two years against Russian forces under the leadership of Aleksandr Andreyevich Baranov.

The Omaha living at Large Village in what is now northeastern Nebraska are decimated by smallpox and cholera. Fewer than three hundred survive from a population of thirty-five hundred.

The Creek Nation negotiates and signs a treaty with the United States on June 16.

The Seneca Nation concludes and signs two treaties with the U.S. government on June 30.

The Choctaw Nation and the U.S. government sign a treaty on October 17 in which the Choctaw Nation cedes more land.

Payouska (Osage)
COURTESY OF SMITHSONIAN

1803

The Delaware, Shawnee, Potawatomi, Miami, Eel River, Wea, Kickapoo, Piankashaw, and Kaskaskia Nations enter into a treaty with the U.S. government on June 7.

The Eel River, Kaskaskia, Kickapoo, Piankashaw, and Wyandot enter into a treaty on August 7 with the U.S. government.

The Kaskaskia, Mitchigamia, Cahokia, and Tamaroi peoples who are consolidated into the Kaskaskia by the U.S. government agree to the treaties negotiated at Vincennes, in Indiana Territory, and signed on August 13. Under one treaty, the "chiefs and warriors of the said tribe . . . do relinquish and cede to the United States, all the lands in the Illinois country . . . reserving to themselves however the tract of about three hundred and fifty acres near the town of Kaskaskia and which was secured to them by the act of Congress of the third day of March, one thousand seven hundred and ninety-one, and also the right of locating one other tract of twelve hundred and eighty acres within the bounds of that now ceded, which two tracts of land *shall remain to them forever*."[11] The land ceded under the treaty consisted of what is now the central section of Illinois, from the north to the border of Tennessee.

The Choctaw Nation and the United States negotiate a treaty which is signed on August 31.

HEROES/LEADERS/ VICTIMS	ELDER WISDOM/PHILOSOPHY/ SONGS	
American Horse or Iron Shield (Oglala Lakota), who will become a warrior leader among the Lakota, is born. Cornplanter (Seneca), principal leader, meets with President Thomas Jefferson in Washington, D.C., to discuss the landholdings of the Seneca.		**1801**
George Bonga (Chippewa/black), who will become a multilingual interpreter, is born. Washinga Sakba, or Black Bird (Omaha), principal leader of the People, dies from smallpox.	It is said that when the enfeebled survivors saw the disfigured appearance of their children and companions they resolved to put an end to their existence, since both comeliness and vigor were gone. *Francis La Flesche (Omaha)*	**1802**
Mokatavato, or Black Kettle (Southern Cheyenne), who will become a noted peace leader, is born.	Where today is the Pequod? Where the Narraganset, the Mohawk, Pocanoket, and many other once powerful tribes of our race? They have vanished before the avarice and oppression of the white men, as snow before a summer sun. *Tecumtha, or Tecumseh (Shawnee/Muscogee)*	**1803**

1804

On August 18, the Delaware Nation signs a treaty with the United States. Under the treaty, the Delaware cede northwestern Kentucky.

The Piankashaw conclude a treaty with the United States which is signed on August 27.

The Cherokee Nation enters into a treaty on October 24 with the U.S. government. With this treaty and the subsequent one with the Sac and Fox, all land that now comprises the state of Illinois is ceded to the United States.

The Sac and Fox conclude and sign a treaty with the United States on November 3 at St. Louis, in what is now Missouri. Under the treaty, the Sac and Fox agree to cease their battles with the Great and Little Osage Nations. The Sac and Fox cede their land in the St. Louis area because, according to Thomas Jefferson, they complained that they were not connected by any treaty to the United States and he felt it was expedient to "engage their friendship." That "friendship" cost the Sac and Fox most of their ancestral homelands, consisting of what is now most of Iowa, the remainder of Illinois, northeastern Missouri (including St. Louis), and part of southwestern Wisconsin.

1805

The Wyandot, Ottawa, Chippewa, Munsee and Delaware, Shawnee, and Potawatomi Nations conclude and sign a treaty with the United States on July 4.

The Chickasaw Nation negotiates and signs a treaty on July 23 with the United States in "Chickasaw Country" which modifies previous treaties between the parties. In all instances, every new treaty and modification results in cession of land by the Chickasaw so that white Americans could travel from Natchez to Nashville freely.

The Delaware, Eel River, Miami, Potawatomi, and Wea enter into a treaty with the United States at Grouseland on August 21 by which two million acres considered to be "some of the finest land in the . . . country" is ceded to the United States.

The Sioux Nation concludes and signs a treaty with the United States on September 23. The treaty finally is ratified by the U.S. Senate on April 16, 1808.

The Cherokee Nation and the United States conclude and sign a treaty on October 25.

The Creek Nation negotiates with the United States a treaty which both parties sign on November 14.

The Choctaw Nation enters into a treaty with the United States at Mount Dexter in which the Choctaw Nation cedes five million acres.

The Piankashaw negotiate and sign a treaty with the United States on December 30 in which the Piankashaw cede the remaining area of what is now southeastern Illinois.

Secettu Mahqua, or Black Beaver (Lenape, or Delaware)
COURTESY OF SMITHSONIAN

Galagina, or Buck Watie, or Elias Boudinot (Cherokee/English), who will become a noted journalist among the Cherokee, is born in about 1804.

. . . an evil day befell us when we became a divided nation, and with that division our glory deserted us, leaving us with the hearts and heels of the rabbit in place of the courage and strength of the bear.

Makatai-meshe-kiakiak, or Black Hawk (Sauk, or Sac)

1804

Ayonwaeghs, or John Brant (Mohawk), son of Thayan-danegea, or Joseph Brant (Mohawk), and Catherine Croghan (Mohawk/white), who will become principal leader of the People, is born.

Cameahwait (Lemhi Shoshone) is principal leader who provides his sister Cogewea, or Sacagawea, and members of the Lewis and Clark expedition with supplies and guides for their journey through the Rockies.

Tenskwatawa (Shawnee/Muscogee), or the Prophet, receives his vision and begins to urge the People of the sovereign nations and tribes to stop intermarrying with white Americans, reject their religions, customs, and clothing, and return to the traditional ways of the People.

Pompey, or Jean Baptiste Charbonneau (Lemhi Shoshone/French), the son of Cogewea, or Sacagawea (Lemhi Shoshone), and Toussaint Charbonneau (French), is born.

Comcomly (Chinook), principal leader, welcomes the Lewis and Clark expedition and receives a medal and flag of the United States from the explorers. He continues to cultivate close friendships with white American pioneers until his death.

Weyapiersenwah, or Blue Jacket (white/adopted Shawnee), principal battle leader in the Battle of Fallen Timbers in 1794, dies.

We now begin to know the value of land—But when it is almost too late. . . . We the chiefs here present consider that if you, the White people, had such land to dispose of, and the Red people had to buy it of you, you, we are convinced, would not let us have it, without you got the full value for it.

William McIntosh (White Stick Creek)

1805

1806

The Cherokee Nation and the United States enter into a treaty which is signed on January 7.

1807

The Cherokee Nation accepts the conventions to previous treaties made with the United States, on September 11.

The Chippewa, Ottawa, Potawatomi, and Wyandot Nations enter into a treaty at Detroit on November 17 in which the Ottawa cede land in the Detroit area. The final article of the treaty is an example of the growing arrogance of the United States toward the People of the sovereign nations and tribes: "The said nations of Indians acknowledge to be under the protection of the United States and no other power, and will prove by their conduct that they are worthy of so great a blessing."

Keokuk (Saulk, or Sac) and his son, Mu-s-wont (Saulk, or Sac)
COURTESY OF SMITHSONIAN

1808

The Great and Little Osage Nations negotiate a treaty with the United States which the Osage adopt on November 10 and which is submitted to the United States Senate on March 14, 1810, by President James Madison. Under the treaty, more than 25 million acres of the "finest country of the Louisiana Purchase" is ceded to the United States, for which the Osage Nations are to be paid twenty-five hundred dollars with a promise of fifteen hundred dollars annual annuity. The land ceded comprises what is now all of Missouri, the northern half of Arkansas from Little Rock to Missouri, the northeastern area of Oklahoma, and the southern half of Kansas, from Topeka.

The Chippewa, Ottawa, Potawatomi, Shawnee, and Wyandot Nations enter into a treaty with the United States on November 25. Under the treaty, land in what is now southeastern Wisconsin west of Lake Michigan and in southeastern Michigan east of Lake Michigan is ceded to the United States.

HEROES/LEADERS/ VICTIMS	ELDER WISDOM/PHILOSOPHY/ SONGS	
Jesse Chisholm (Cherokee/Scottish), who will be the pathfinder of what becomes known as the Chisholm Trail, is born in about 1806. Secettu Mahqua, or Black Beaver (Delaware), who will become an interpreter and negotiator on behalf of the People, is born. Tenskwatawa (Shawnee/Muscogee), the prophet of the Shawnee, accurately predicts the eclipse of the sun on June 16. Degataga, or Stand Watie (Cherokee), is born. He will become a Confederate brigadier general.	Let us form one body, one heart, and defend to the last warrior our country, our homes, our liberty, and the graves of our fathers. *Tecumtha, or Tecumseh (Shawnee/Muscogee)*	**1806**
	We Choctaws and Chickasaws are a peaceful people, making our subsistence by honest toil; but mistake not, my Shawnee brethren, we are not afraid of war. Neither are we strangers to war, as those who have undertaken to encroach upon our rights in the past may abundantly testify. *Pushmataha (Choctaw)*	**1807**
Paddy Carr (Muscogee/Irish), who will become a U.S. Army interpreter and guide, is born. Tenskwatawa (Shawnee/Muscogee) and his brother Tecumtha, or Tecumseh (Shawnee/Muscogee), move from Indiana to Ohio, where they establish Prophetstown, known among the People as the former Miami village of Tippecanoe.	Since the treaty was made they have come upon our lands and killed our men. We did not revenge ourselves, because we had given a pledge not to go onto their land. *Keokuk (Sauk, or Sac)*	**1808**

1809	The Delaware, Eel River, Kickapoo, Miami, Potawatomi, and Wea enter into the Treaty of Fort Wayne with the United States at what is now Fort Wayne, Indiana. Separate treaties and conventions are signed on September 30 with the Delaware, Potawatomi, Miami, and Eel River; Miami and Eel River on September 30; Wea on October 26; and Kickapoo on December 9.	
1810	The Shawnee, Sac and Fox, Miami, Wyandot, Kickapoo, Menominee, and Winnebago join together at Prophetstown, at the confluence of Tippecanoe Creek and the Wabash River, in anticipation of a great battle against the white American forces.	
1811	The Battle of Tippecanoe is fought under the leadership of Tenskwatawa (Shawnee/Muscogee), who is defeated by forces under the leadership of William Henry Harrison, governor of Indiana Territory. Tenskwatawa and his forces surrender on November 7.	*Dull Knife (Cheyenne) [seated] and Little Wolf (Cheyenne) [standing]* COURTESY OF SMITHSONIAN
1812	The Potawatomi massacre a garrison of United States troops stationed at Fort Dearborn (now Chicago, Illinois). The People of the sovereign nations and tribes of the region regain complete control of what is referred to as the Old Northwest. The Shawnee Nation allies with the British in the War of 1812 between the United States and Great Britain.	

HEROES/LEADERS/ VICTIMS	ELDER WISDOM/PHILOSOPHY/ SONGS	
	. . . the contrary winds may blow strong in my face, yet I will go forward and never turn back, but continue to press forward until I have finished. . . . *Teedyuscung (Delaware)*	**1809**
Tecumtha, or Tecumseh (Shawnee/Muscogee), meets with Indiana Territory Governor William Henry Harrison at Vincennes in August. Tecumtha demands the United States' repudiation of the Fort Wayne Treaty. Halpatter Miko, or Billy Bowlegs (Seminole), who will become a noted leader in the Seminole Wars, is born. Tah-me-la-pash-me, or Dull Knife (Northern Cheyenne), who will become a war leader of the Northern Cheyenne, is born. Tuup-weets, or Colorow, or Colorado (Jicarilla Apache/adopted Mouache Ute), whose mother was captured by the Comanche and who will become a noted warrior and principal leader of the People, is born.	As the great chief [United States President James Madison] is to determine the matter, I hope the Great Spirit will put sense enough into his head to induce him to give up this land. It is sure, he is so far off he will not be injured by the war. He may sit still in his gown and drink his wine, whilst you [William Henry Harrison] and I will have to fight it out. *Tecumtha, or Tecumseh (Shawnee/Muscogee)*	**1810**
In a speech to the Choctaw people, Pushmataha (Choctaw), principal leader, strongly opposes the efforts of Tecumtha, or Tecumseh, to organize the sovereign nations and tribes against the white settlers.	Shall it be said of our race that we knew not how to extricate ourselves from the three most dreadful calamities—folly, inactivity and cowardice? *Tecumtha, or Tecumseh (Shawnee/Muscogee)*	**1811**
Cochise (Chiricahua Apache), who will become a noted principal leader of the Apache, is born in about 1812. Michikinikwa, or Little Turtle (Miami/Mahican), principal leader of the People, dies in July.	Elder Brother. Listen to me with attention. You told us you discovered on the Great Miami traces of an old fort. It was not a French fort, brother; it was a fort built by me. *Michikinikwa, or Little Turtle (Miami/Mahican)*	**1812**

1813

The Creek Nation civil war begins with the attack on the Red Stick Creek by two hundred White Stick Creek, who are joined by twenty companies of Cherokee and five thousand Tennessee militia led by Andrew Jackson.

The Red Stick Creek engage United States forces in battle at Frenchtown (now Monroe, Mississippi).

The Sioux Nation joins with the Shawnee, Miami, and others at Amherstburg, Ontario, raising the number of warrior troops committed to fight the United States forces to twenty-five hundred.

Michikinikwa, or Little Turtle (Miami/Mahican)
COURTESY OF SMITHSONIAN

1814

The Creek Nation civil war ends after the Battle of Horseshoe Bend, in which 750 of the 900 Red Stick forces are killed by Andrew Jackson and his troops.

The Wyandot, Delaware, Potawatomi, Kickapoo, Miami, Ottawa, Shawnee, and Seneca sign what is known as the Treaty with the Wyandot at Greenville, Ohio. Under the treaty, the People of the sovereign nations agree "to give their aid to the United States in prosecuting the war against Great Britain, and such of the other Indian tribes as still continue hostile."

The Creek Nation is forced to sign the peace Treaty of Fort Jackson with the United States at Fort Jackson, in Alabama, on August 9. Tustunnuggee Thulucco (Creek), the speaker for the Upper Creek, is one of the signers.

1815

The sovereign nations and tribes and the United States enter into seven treaties during three days. The Potawatomi and Piankashaw sign separate treaties on July 18; the Teton Sioux, Sioux of the Lakes, River Saint Peter's Sioux, and Yankton Sioux sign separate treaties on July 19; and the Mahi sign a treaty on July 20.

The Kickapoo Nation signs a treaty with the United States on September 2.

The Wyandot, Delaware, Seneca, Shawnee, Miami, Chippewa, Ottawa, and Potawatomi negotiate a treaty with the United States which they sign on September 8.

The Great and Little Osage Nations enter into a treaty with the United States on September 12.

The Sac Nation signs a treaty on September 13 with the United States government.

The Fox Nation enters into a treaty with the United States which is signed on September 14.

The Iowa, or Ioway, agree to a treaty with the U.S. government on September 16.

The Kansa Nation concludes a treaty on October 28 with the United States.

Little Warrior (Creek), principal leader of the Red Stick Creek and ally of the British, leads six hundred Creek forces in a successful attack against American troops at what is now Monroe, Mississippi, on January 21 and demolishes the opposition. More than four hundred American militia are killed and five hundred are captured by Creek forces. Only thirty-three Americans escape.

Tecumtha, or Tecumseh (Shawnee/Muscogee), prophet and principal leader of the Shawnee, is killed in the Battle at Thamesville, Ontario, at age forty-five. He had devoted his adult life to forming a federation of all Indian nations and tribes to stop the whites' ever-expanding encroachments on Indian land. Like his brother, Tenskwatawa, he sought to spread the call for restoration of sacred power.

Will we let ourselves be destroyed in our turn without a struggle, give up our homes, our country bequeathed to us by the Great Spirit, the graves of our dead, and everything that is dear and sacred to us? I know you will cry with me, Never! Never!

Tecumtha, or Tecumseh (Shawnee/Muscogee)

1813

We are a poor distressed people involved in ruin, which we have brought on ourselves.

Tustunnuggee Thulucco (Creek)

1814

Otoh-hastis, or Tall Bull (Southern Cheyenne), who will become a prominent leader of the Dog Soldiers, is born.

Here . . . is a pipe which I present you, as I am accustomed to present pipes to all the red skins in peace with us. It is filled with such tobacco as we were accustomed to smoke before we knew the white people.

Petalesharo (Pawnee)

1815

Selene Rilatos (Siletz confederated tribes)
Courtesy of Vicki Grayland

1816

The Cherokee Nation agrees to two treaties with the United States and signs them on March 22.

The Rock River Sac sign a treaty on May 13 with the United States.

The Sioux of the Leaf, Sioux of the Broad Leaf, and Sioux Who Shoot in the Pine Tops conclude a treaty with the United States on June 1.

The Winnebago sign a treaty on June 3 with the United States.

The Wea and Kickapoo sign a treaty on June 4 with the United States.

The Potawatomi, Ottawa, and Chippewa ("United Tribes") negotiate and sign a treaty with the United States on August 24.

The Cherokee sign a treaty with the United States on September 14.

The Choctaw Nation enters into the Treaty of Choctaw Trading House, in Mississippi, with the United States. It is signed on October 24.

Juanita (Navajo)–Manuelito's favorite wife
COURTESY OF SMITHSONIAN

1817

The Menominee enter into a treaty agreement with the United States on March 30.

The Otoe agree to a treaty with the United States and sign it on June 24.

The Ponca, or Poncarar, conclude and sign a treaty with the United States government on June 25.

The Cherokee Nation signs the Cherokee Indian Treaty of 1817 at the Cherokee agency at present Calhoun, Tennessee, on July 8. The treaty begins a sequence of events leading to the forced removal of the Cherokee from their ancestral homelands to what is now Oklahoma.

The Wyandot, Seneca, Delaware, Shawnee, Potawatomi, Ottawa, and Chippewa agree to a treaty with the United States and sign it on September 29.

1818

The Creek Nation concludes and signs a treaty with the United States on January 22.

The Grand Pawnee, Pitavirate Noisy Pawnee, Pawnee Republic, and Marhar Pawnee agree to separate treaties during five days with representatives of the United States. The Grand Pawnee sign their treaty on June 18, the Pitavirate Noisy Pawnee on June 19, the Pawnee Republic signs at St. Louis on June 20, and the Marhar Pawnee sign on June 22.

The Quapaw Nation agrees to and signs a treaty with the United States on August 24 at St. Louis in which the Quapaw cede their land south of the Arkansas River.

(continued)

HEROES/LEADERS/ VICTIMS	ELDER WISDOM/PHILOSOPHY/ SONGS	
Mushulatubbee, or Muchalatubbee (Choctaw), principal leader, signs the Treaty of Choctaw Trading House, in Mississippi, on October 24.		**1816**
	Brothers: We wish to remain on our land, and hold it fast. We appeal to our father the President of the United States to do us justice. We look to him for protection in our hour of distress. We are now distressed with the alternative proposal to remove from this country to the Arkansas, or stay and become citizens of the United States. We are not yet civilized enough to become citizens of the United States; nor do we wish to be compelled to move to a country so much against our inclination and will, where we would, in the course of a few years, return to the same savage state of life that we were in before the United States, our white brothers, extended their fostering care towards us, and brought us out of a savage state into a state similar to theirs. *Cherokee council of North Carolina*	**1817**
Chyalpinish (Yokuts), principal leader, heads the revolt that is defeated by the Spanish under the command of Don Ignacio Vallejo at what is now San Miguel, in San Luis Obispo County, California. Kahgegagahbowh, or George Copway (Ojibwa), who will become a writer and Methodist missionary, is born in Ontario, Canada. Hastin, or Manuelito (Diné, or Navajo), who will become leader of the Navajo War of 1863–66, is born in southeastern Utah, near Bear Ears Peak.		**1818**

	HISTORY/LAW/ POLITICS	LITERATURE/ART/ LEGENDS AND STORIES
1818	*(continued from page 192)* The Wyandot, Seneca, Shawnee, Ottawa, Delaware, and Miami agree to a treaty with the United States, which the Wyandot, Seneca, Shawnee, and Ottawa sign on September 17. The Wyandot alone sign an amended treaty on September 20. The Delaware sign on October 3, and the Miami on October 6 at Saint Mary's, in Michigan Territory. In this treaty, the Delaware cede all claims to land in what is now Indiana and agree to move west. The Miami cede some of their land but retain "reservations" for their use. The Wyandot refuse to move west, but exchange some of their ancestral lands for other land held by the United States. The Peoria, Kaskaskia, Mitchigamia, Cahokia, and Tamaroi of the Illinois Nation conclude a treaty with the United States which is signed on September 25. The Great and Little Osage Nations agree on September 25 to a treaty with the United States. The Potawatomi and Wea Nations conclude separate treaties with the United States which they sign on October 2. The Chickasaw Nation signs a treaty with the United States on October 19.	
1819	The Cherokee Nation negotiates and signs a treaty on February 27 with the United States. The Kickapoo conclude a treaty with the United States and sign it on July 30. The Vermillion River Kickapoo enter into a treaty on August 30 with representatives of the United States. The Chippewa Nation signs a treaty with the United States on September 24.	

Perits, or Shenakpas, or Medicine Crow (Crow)
COURTESY OF SMITHSONIAN

PERSPECTIVE
1820–1860

For the People of the sovereign nations and tribes across Turtle Island, period of 1820 to 1860 can be equated with the horrors of the Nazi death camps, where millions of Jewish people went to their deaths. It began with a mind-set espoused by Thomas Jefferson and brought into reality by Andrew Jackson, a mind-set geared toward the genocide of the People of the sovereign nations and tribes. Among the Americans, the mind-set was captured in an elusive phrase—"the Indian Problem." For Jackson, the way to solve "the Indian Problem" was to get rid of the People of the sovereign nations and tribes, and he did his best to achieve his goal.

Beginning with the cession of twenty-five million acres by the White Stick Muscogee, or Creek, with William McIntosh fraudulently claiming to represent the Seminole and Muscogee, the battles raged across Turtle Island. From 1820 through 1860, 243 treaties were made between the People of the sovereign nations and tribes and the United States. The majority of treaties from 1820 through 1830 required the People to cede their ancestral homelands to the United States.

When Andrew Jackson became president of the United States, he convinced Congress to pass the Indian Removal Act (IRA), which he signed into law. Like Hitler a century later, who declared the Jewish people nonhuman to justify his genocidal horror, the leaders of the U.S. government armed themselves with their legislation and proceeded to exterminate thousands of the People who refused to be moved from their ancient homelands. After 1830, the treaties

required not only cession of land by the People of the sovereign nations and tribes, but also that the People "remove" themselves from the East to west of the Mississippi River.

It took less than fifty years (1784–1830) for the evolution of America's policy toward the People of the sovereign nations and tribes across Turtle Island to change from that of Thomas Jefferson, who wanted only to "protect" the People from the awful settlers by moving the eastern People beyond the Mississippi River, through the time of John C. Calhoun, who wanted to educate (i.e., brainwash) the People to "accept the need for removal," to Jackson's policy of forced removal or death.

A combination of war, epidemics, and removal was too much for the People, and nation after nation was exterminated. It was a time of horror, anguish, and death for the People. By 1860, a majority of the Choctaw, Chickasaw, Creek, Sac and Fox, Cherokee, and Seminole all had been removed from their ancient homelands.

Again, all known treaties between the People of the sovereign nations and tribes and the United States are presented here as a memorial to those nations which no longer exist because of the genocidal politics of the United States, and as a reminder to all Americans that treaties are a solemn compact between sovereign nations. The obligations of the compact do not go away after a couple of decades. A century or two later, more and more of the People of the sovereign nations and tribes are "winning" legal battle after legal battle because of the treaties agreed to with the U.S. government. It would seem that the treaty negotiators for the United States believed that the "Indians" would cease to exist as a People. However, we are here, and we expect the United States to fulfill its treaty obligations.

On the West Coast, the People of northern California, the Yuma, Yakima, Tutuni, and Takelmeo, Coeur d'Alene, Navajo, Paiute, and Apache declared war against the vileness committed by the American settlers and their contemptible government. They fought losing battle after losing battle. Then the Americans became embroiled in their own Civil War. The People, especially those living west of the Rio Grande, were releived because the Americans were too busy exterminating one another to bother with exterminating the People of the sovereign nations and tribes.

	HISTORY/LAW/ POLITICS	LITERATURE/ART/ LEGENDS AND STORIES
1820	The Chippewa Nation negotiates and signs a treaty with the United States on June 16. The Ottawa and Chippewa Nations conclude a treaty with the United States which they sign on July 6. The Kickapoo Nation enters into a treaty on July 19 with the United States. The Wea agree on August 11 to a treaty with the United States government. The Vermillion Kickapoo sign a treaty with the United States on September 5. The Choctaw Nation agrees to the Treaty of Doak's Stand, signed at Treaty Ground, Mississippi, on October 18. Under the treaty, the Choctaw cede the remaining area of what is now Alabama, all of Mississippi, and the remaining portion of Tennessee, and agree to move west beyond the Mississippi River. *Hatchootucknee, or Peter Perkins Pitchlynn (Choctaw/White)* COURTESY OF SMITHSONIAN	 *Hatchootucknee, or Peter Perkins Pitchlynn (Choctaw/White)* COURTESY OF SMITHSONIAN
1821	The Creek Nation signs two treaties with the United States on January 8. The Ottawa, Chippewa, and Potawatomi Nations conclude a treaty with the United States which they sign on August 29.	Sequoyah, or George Gist, or Guess (Cherokee/white), demonstrates to tribal leaders the syllabary he has developed for the Cherokee language. Within a few years, many Cherokee can read and write in their own language.
1822	The Great and Little Osage Nations enter into a treaty on August 31 with the United States. The Sac and Fox ("United") Nations agree on September 3 to a treaty with the United States.	
1823	The Seminole Nation agrees to the Camp Moultrie Treaty (made with the "Florida Tribes of Indians," all being of the Seminole Nation) and signs it on September 18. Under the treaty, the Seminole Nation cedes all of its lands in what is now Florida to the United States.	*Poor Sarah, or Religion Exemplified in the Life and Death of an Indian Woman.* Galagina, or Elias Boudinot (Cherokee).

HEROES/LEADERS/ VICTIMS	ELDER WISDOM/PHILOSOPHY/ SONGS	
Bislahalani, or Barboncito (Diné, or Navajo), who will become a celebrated singer and war leader of the Diné, is born. George Bonga (Chippewa/black), son of a Chippewa mother and a black father, fluent in English, French, and Algonkian, serves as interpreter at the Fond du Lac peace council held at what is now Fond du Lac, Minnesota. Sagoyewatha, or Red Jacket (Seneca), dies. While he was principal leader of the Seneca, he was given a medal by U.S. President George Washington which he wore with great pride. Later, it was held in custody by the Historical Society of Buffalo, New York. Mushulatubbee, or Muchalatubbee (Choctaw), principal leader, signs the treaty of Doak's Stand at Treaty Ground, Mississippi, on October 18.	We wish to remain here, where we have grown up as the herbs of the woods; and do not wish to be transplanted into another soil. *Pushmataha (Choctaw)*	**1820**
Ayonwaeghs, or John Brant (Mohawk), travels to England and strongly advocates the land claims of the Mohawk.		**1821**
Medicine Calf, or James Beckwith (Irish/black/adopted Crow), is freed from slavery by his father, Sir Jennings Beckwith, an Irish noble. Medicine Calf moves from Fredericksburg, Virginia, to St. Louis, Missouri, where he settles for a while. He travels to the Green River region of Wyoming and eventually is adopted by Big Bowl, principal leader of the Crow, who was deceived into believing that Medicine Calf was the son of a Cheyenne principal leader. Sharitarish (Pawnee), principal leader, meets with President James Monroe and Secretary of War John C. Calhoun in Washington, D.C., in February.		**1822**
Watomika, or James Bouchard (Delaware), who will become the first Native Roman Catholic priest, is born. Pompey, or Jean Baptiste Charbonneau (Lemhi Shoshone/French), travels to Europe with German Prince Paul Wilhelm of Württemberg and stays at a castle near Stuttgart. For the next six years, Pompey studies languages and travels throughout Europe and Africa.	It is the responsibility of the tribe to teach its children about their connection with the ancestors and to establish their place of inclusion in the circle of their Nation. *E. K. (Kim) Caldwell (Cherokee/Shawnee)*	**1823**

1824

The Office of Indian Affairs (later called the Bureau of Indian Affairs) is created within the War Department of the U.S. executive branch of government. It is responsible for ensuring that the United States fulfills the promises made in treaties with the People of the sovereign nations and tribes across Turtle Island.

With the Seminole Nation's cession of what is now Florida to the United States, almost half of the ancestral homelands of thePeople of the soveriegn nations and tribes on Turtle Island are possessed by the United States.

The Sac and Fox enter into a treaty with the United States on August 4.

The Iowa, or Ioway, agree to a treaty on August 4 with the United States.

The Quapaw Nation concludes and signs a treaty on November 15 with the United States government.

E. K. (Kim) Caldwell (Cherokee/Shawnee)
COURTESY OF E. K. CALDWELL

1825

The Choctaw Nation signs a treaty with the United States on January 20 at Washington, D.C.

The Creek Nation is party to a treaty with the United States that is agreed to and signed by a small fraction of the Creek Nation on February 12 at Indian Springs, Georgia.

The Great and Little Osage Nations negotiate a treaty with the United States at St. Louis on June 2. Under the treaty, the Osage Nations cede "lands lying within the State of Missouri and Territory of Arkansas and all lands lying West of the said State of Missouri and Territory of Arkansas. . . ."

The Kansa, or Kansas, Nation enters into a treaty with the United States which is signed on June 3 at St. Louis. By this treaty, the Kansa cede "all lands lying within the State of Missouri. . . ."

The Ponca Nation agrees to a friendship treaty with the United States on June 9 at the Ponca Village, in what is now Nebraska. Article 2 provides an insight into the continued growing arrogance of the United States toward the People of the sovereign nations and tribes: "The United States agree to extend to them, from time to time, such benefits and acts of kindness as may be convenient, and seem just and proper to the President of the United States."

The Teton, Yankton, and Yanktonai bands of the Sioux Nation agree to a treaty on June 22.

The Creek Nation negotiates an agreement with the United States on June 29 which is not ratified by the U.S. Senate.

The Sioune and Oglala bands of the Sioux Nation enter into a treaty on July 5 with the United States.

The Cheyenne Nation signs a treaty on July 6 with the United States.

(continued)

HEROES/LEADERS/VICTIMS	ELDER WISDOM/PHILOSOPHY/SONGS	
Mushulatubbee, or Muchalatubbee (Choctaw), principal leader, is one of the Choctaw delegates who meets the Marquis de Lafayette in December in Washington D.C. Pushmataha (Choctaw), principal leader, dies December 24 and is buried in Congressional Cemetery, in Washington D.C.	We wish our children to be educated. We wish to derive lasting, and not transient benefits from the sales of our lands. The proceeds of those sales we are desirous should be applied for the instruction of our young countrymen. . . We are . . . anxious that our rising generation should acquire a knowledge of literature and arts, and learn to tread in those paths . . . to . . . greatness. *Mushulatubbee (Choctaw)*	**1824**
William Warren (Chippewa), author, is born on May 27. Mushulatubbee, or Muchalatubbee (Choctaw), principal leader, signs the Treaty of Washington [D.C.] on January 20. Mistahimuskwa, or Big Bear (Cree), who is to become principal leader of the Cree, is born. Big Foot, or Si Tanka, or Spotted Elk (Miniconjou Sioux), who will become a formidable principal leader, is born. William McIntosh (White Stick Creek), claiming to represent White Stick and Red Stick Creek as well as the Seminole Nation, cedes twenty-five million acres in Georgia to the United States. A majority of the Creek Nation repudiates the cession, and members of the Creek Nation later assassinate McIntosh for having signed away the land.		**1825**

HISTORY / LAW / POLITICS	LITERATURE / ART / LEGENDS AND STORIES

1825

(continued from page 200)

The Hunkpapa band of the Sioux Nation concludes a treaty with the United States which is signed on July 16.

The Arikara (Ricara) agree on July 18 to a treaty with the United States.

The Belantse-eta, or Minitaree, Nation signs a treaty with the United States on July 30.

The Mandan enter into a treaty on July 30 with the United States.

The Crow Nation signs a treaty on August 4 with the United States.

The Great and Little Osage Nations negotiate a treaty with the United States on August 10.

The Kansa agree to a treaty with the United States on August 16.

The Sioux, Chippewa, Sac and Fox, Menominee, Iowa, Winnebago, Ottawa, and Potawatomi Nations enter into a treaty on August 19 with the United States.

The Otoe and Missouria sign a treaty with the United States on September 26.

The Pawnee Nation concludes a treaty on September 30 with the United States.

The Maha sign a treaty on October 6 with the United States.

The Shawnee Nation agrees to a treaty with the United States which they sign on November 7.

1826

The Creek Nation enters into a treaty with the United States which is signed on January 24 at Washington, D.C. This treaty nullifies the treaty concluded at Indian Springs on February 12, 1825. In the new treaty, the Creek agree to cede "all the land belonging to the said Nation in the State of Georgia," for which the Creek Nation is to be paid $217,600 and a perpetual annuity of $20,000. In the 1825 treaty, the United States had agreed to pay $400,000 with no perpetual annuity.

The Creek Nation accepts on March 31 the supplementary article to the treaty of January 24 which specifically repudiates the 1825 treaty.

The Chippewa Nation enters into a treaty on August 5 with the United States.

The Potawatomi Nation signs a treaty with the United States on October 16.

The Miami Nation concludes treaty negotiations with the United States and signs the treaty on October 23.

1825

Nakui-owaisto, or Yellow Bear (Cheyenne)
COURTESY OF SMITHSONIAN

Unaduti, or Dennis Wolf Bushyhead (Cherokee/white), who will become principal chief of the Cherokee Nation in what is now Oklahoma, is born.

. . . no part of the land can be sold without a full council, and without the consent of all the nation; and, if a part of the nation choose to leave the country, they cannot sell the land they have, but it belongs to the nation.

Tuckabatchee Micco (Creek)

1826

	HISTORY/LAW/ POLITICS	LITERATURE/ART/ LEGENDS AND STORIES
1827	The Chippewa, Menominee, and Winnebago Nations enter into a treaty on August 11 with the United States. The Potawatomi Nation concludes a treaty on September 19 with the United States. The Creek Nation agrees to the treaty signed on November 15 with the United States.	*Sketches of Ancient History of the Six Nations*. David Cusick (Tuscarora).
1828	The *Cherokee Phoenix*, published in English and Cherokee, is the first Native-language newspaper among all the People of the sovereign nations and tribes living on Turtle Island. The Eel River Miami agree to a treaty with the United States on February 11. The Cherokee Nation enters into what is referred to as the Treaty with the Western Cherokee, signed at Washington, D.C., on May 6. The Western Cherokee had moved from the Southeast to the west of the Mississippi River. The Winnebago, Potawatomi, Chippewa, and Ottawa ("United Tribes") agree to a treaty on August 25 with the United States. The Potawatomi conclude and sign a treaty on September 20 with the United States.	*A Revery*. Young Beaver (Cherokee).
1829	The Chippewa, Ottawa, and Potawatomi ("United Nations") agree to a treaty with the United States on July 29. The Winnebago Nation concludes and signs a treaty with the United States on August 1. The Delaware of Sandusky River, in Ohio, negotiate a treaty with the United States which is signed on August 3. The Delaware Nation concludes and signs a treaty with the United States on September 24.	

HEROES/LEADERS/ VICTIMS	ELDER WISDOM/PHILOSOPHY/ SONGS	
		1827
		1828
	We have always the proposition to purchase some of our lands. We have decided that we have none to spare. If a man should give one-half of his garment, the remainder would be of no use—and take two fingers from the hand, the remainder would be of little use. When we had land to spare, we gave it, with very little talk. . . . *Pushmataha (Choctaw)*	1829

205

1830

The Indian Removal Act is passed by the United States Congress and signed into law by President Andrew Jackson on May 28. With Jackson's election in December 1829, the previous twelve years' policy of moderation by the United States toward the sovereign nations and tribes on Turtle Island had ended. The People of the sovereign nations understood that with Jackson as president, the People's only recourse was to try to get the most money for their land. They had no doubt that he would relish removing the People from their ancient homelands by killing every Native who defied him in any way.

The Sac and Fox, the Mdewakanton, Wahpeton, Wahpekute, and Sisseton bands of Sioux, and the Omaha, Iowa, Otoe, and Missouria sign a treaty with the United States on July 15.

The Chickasaw Nation signs a treaty on August 31 with the United States. It is not ratified by the U.S. Senate.

The Choctaw Nation negotiates and signs the Treaty of Dancing Rabbit Creek in Noxubee County, Mississippi, on September 27, and supplementary articles to the treaty on September 28. Under the treaty, the Choctaw, after thousands of years of living in the Mississippi region, reluctantly agree to move west. They know if they do not, President Andrew Jackson will order U.S. soldiers to hunt down and kill every man, woman, and child of the Choctaw Nation.

Satanta, or White Bear (Kiowa)
COURTESY OF SMITHSONIAN

1831

The Menominee Nation signs a treaty with the United States on February 17.

The Sandusky River Seneca agree on February 28 to a treaty with the United States.

The Seneca and Shawnee (mixed bands) sign a treaty on July 20 with the United States.

The Shawnee Nation concludes a treaty of August 8 with the United States.

The Ottawa of Ohio sign a treaty with the United States on August 30.

A Son of the Forest: The Experience of William Apes, a Native of the Forest, Comprising a Notice of the Pequod Tribe of Indians, Written by Himself. William Apes (Pequot).

		1830

Ayonwaeghs, or John Brant (Mohawk), is selected principal leader of the Mohawk Nation, at the Six Nations reserve in what is now Burlington, Ontario, Canada.

Comcomly (Chinook), principal leader of the Chinook, dies from smallpox. His head is taken by a trader and sold in Edinburgh, Scotland.

Mushulatubbee, or Muchalatubbee (Choctaw), principal leader of the Choctaw, signs the Treaty of Dancing Rabbit Creek, Mississippi, on September 27.

Hot'tsa-sodono, or Deerfoot, or Louis Bennett (Seneca), who will become a noted runner at track events, is born.

Zaepkoheeta, or Big Bow (Kiowa), who will become war leader of the People, is born.

Satanta, or White Bear (Kiowa), who will become known as the Orator of the Plains, is born on the northern Plains.

		1831

Charlot (Kalispel), who will become principal leader, is born.

Catahecasasa, or Black Hoof (Shawnee), principal leader, dies at Wapakoneta, Ohio.

1832

The Wyandot at Big Springs, Ohio, sign a treaty with the United States on January 19.

The Creek Nation signs the Treaty with the Creeks at Washington, D.C., on March 24, in which the Creek Nation cedes 5,200,000 acres to the United States. It will not be until 139 years later, in 1971, that the Indian Claims Commission rules that the Creek Nation "had been improperly deprived of lands ceded by the Treaty of March 24, 1832, because of a lack of fair and honorable dealings on the part of the United States."

The Seminole Nation signs the Treaty of Payne's Landing with the United States on May 9, in which the Seminole cede all claim to lands of the Territory of Florida and agree to move west of the Mississippi to "the country assigned to the Creeks." The Seminole later rescind the agreement after discovering massive fraud by the United States. A subsequent treaty is negotiated in 1833.

The Winnebago Nation signs a treaty with the United States on September 15.

The Sac and Fox sign a treaty with the United States on September 21.

The Apalachicola band signs a treaty with the United States on October 11.

The Prairie and Kankakee Potawatomi sign a treaty with the United States on October 20.

The Chickasaw Nation is forced to agree to a treaty with the United States at Pontotoc Creek, in Mississippi, on October 20 that requires them to cede their ancestral homelands and move west of the Mississippi.

The Chickasaw Nation agrees to supplementary articles in a second treaty with the United States on October 22.

The Kickapoo Nation signs a treaty with the United States on October 24.

The Potawatomi Nation signs a treaty with the United States on October 26.

The Shawnee and the Cape Girardeau Delaware sign a treaty on October 26 with the United States.

The Potawatomi living in Indiana and what is now Michigan sign a treaty with the United States on October 27.

The Kaskaskia, Peoria and Michigamea, Cahokia, and Tamarois bands of the Illinois Nation sign a treaty on October 27 with the United States.

The Menominee Nation signs a treaty with the United States on October 27.

The Brotherton and other nations sign a treaty on October 27 with the United States.

The Piankashaw and Wea Nations sign a treaty with the United States on October 29.

The Kickapoo accept on November 26 the supplemental articles to the treaty signed on October 24, 1832.

The Seneca and Shawnee ("United Nations") sign a treaty with the United States on December 29.

Ayonwaeghs, or John Brant (Mohawk), principal leader of the People, dies of cholera.

This history clearly indicates that the United States did not deal fairly and honorably with the Creek Nation. It allowed Alabama to extend its jurisdiction over the Creek Nation in a clear violation of treaty and federal law. It misrepresented to the Creeks that the United States had no legal power to stop Alabama and that Alabama had the legal right to extend its jurisdiction into the Creek Nation. It failed to protect the Creeks against white intruders on their lands. It forced the Creek Nation to enter into the 1832 treaty by representing that only this treaty would allow them to remain on their ancestral lands. It then violated nearly every provision of that treaty with the result that the Creeks were deprived not only of title to their land but also of the main consideration for which they had agreed to enter the treaty, that being the right to remain on their ancestral lands. If this record does not establish a lack of fair and honorable dealings, then I can conceive of no situation which would establish such lack.

Brantley Blue (Lumbee)

1832

HISTORY/LAW/ POLITICS	LITERATURE/ART/ LEGENDS AND STORIES
1833 The Cherokee residing west of the Mississippi sign a treaty with the United States on February 14. The Creek Nation signs a treaty with the United States on February 14. The Ottawa residing on the Miami Reservation in Ohio sign a treaty with the United States on February 15. The Seminole Nation signs the Treaty of Fort Gibson on March 28, addressing their grievances with the Treaty of Payne's Landing of May 9, 1832. The Quapaw Nation signs a treaty with the United States on May 13. The Apalachicola band signs a treaty with the United States on June 18. The Otoe and Missouria bands sign a treaty with the United States on September 21. The Chippewa, Ottawa, and Potawatomi ("United Nations") sign a treaty with the United States on September 26. The Chippewa, Ottawa, and Potawatomi agree to additional treaty articles on September 27. The Grand Pawnee, Pawnee Loups, Pawnee Republic, and Pawnee Tappaye bands agree to a treaty with the United States on October 9.	*The Experience of the Five Christian Indians of the Pequod Tribe; or the Indian's Looking-Glass for the White Man.* William Apes (Pequot). *The Autobiography of Black Hawk.* Makatai-meshe-kiakiak, or Black Hawk (Sauk), as told to Antoine LeClaire.
1834 The Chickasaw Nation signs a treaty on May 24 with the United States and agrees to supplementary articles the same day. The Miami Nation agrees to a treaty with the United States and signs it on October 23. The Potawatomi Nation signs a treaty with the United States on December 4. The Potawatomi Nation signs a treaty with the United States on December 10. The Potawatomi Nation signs a treaty with the United States on December 16. The Potawatomi Nation signs a treaty with the United States on December 17.	
1835 The Seminole successfully attack U.S. troops near what is now Tampa Bay, Florida, on the Withlacoochee River. Only three of nine hundred U.S. soldiers survive. The Cherokee Nation accepts an agreement with the United States on March 14 which is not ratified by the U.S. Senate. The Caddo Nation signs a treaty with the United States on July 1. The Comanche and Wichita Nations sign a treaty with the United States on August 24. Some Treaty Party Cherokee conclude and sign the Treaty of New Echota at New Echota, Georgia, on December 29. Under the treaty, the Cherokee are to move from the homelands they had occupied for thousands of years in the Southeast to the west of the Mississippi River. The Cherokee Nation had not authorized the signers to negotiate a treaty, and the vast majority of the Cherokee oppose it.	*Indian Nullification of the Unconstitutional Laws of Massachusetts, Relative to the Marshpee Tribe, or, The Pretended Riot Explained.* William Apes (Pequot).

HEROES / LEADERS / VICTIMS	ELDER WISDOM / PHILOSOPHY / SONGS	
Makatai-meshe-kiakiak, or Black Hawk (Sauk), principal leader, imprisoned at Fort Monroe, in Virginia, meets U.S. President Andrew Jackson. Wa-ana-tan, or Martin Charger (Sans Arc Sioux/white), who will organize the first society of peace warriors among the People, is born.	My father [President Andrew Jackson], that high sense of justice which has always marked your way and brought you to the presidency will not suffer you to let a few powerless Indians be oppressed. . . . *Levi Colbert (Chickasaw)* *Principal leader of the Chickasaw Nation*	**1833**
The Wapameepto, or Big Jim (Absentee Shawnee), who will become principal leader of the Absentee Shawnee, is born. Arapoosh (Crow), the noted war leader of the Crow against the Blackfeet, Northern Cheyenne, and Sioux, traditional enemies of the Crow, dies during a battle against the Blackfeet.	Forget not . . . that we are bound in peace . . . by a sacred treaty and the Great Spirit will punish those who break their word. *Pushmataha (Choctaw)*	**1834**
Halpatter Tustenugee, or Alligator (Seminole), one of the principal war leaders of the Second Seminole War (1835–42), leads 380 warriors against U.S. troops under the command of Major Francis Dade near what is now Tampa Bay, Florida. Kange'su-nka, or Crow Dog (Brulé Sioux), who will be known as the murderer of Sinte Gleska, or Spotted Tail (Brulé Sioux), is born.		**1835**

1836

A smallpox pandemic brought to the northern plains of the Pacific Northwest, Alaska, and Canada kills more than forty-three thousand People of the sovereign nations and tribes. Of those, seven thousand were Blackfeet, Piegan and Blood, two thousand Pawnee, twenty-five hundred Mandan, twenty-six hundred Arikara and Minnetaree, fifteen hundred Osage, twelve hundred Crow, four hundred Yanktonai Dakota, forty-five hundred Assiniboin, and an estimated twenty-five thousand of the People of the sovereign nations and tribes living in what is now north-central California.

Sovereign nations and tribes living in the Texas region enter into a treaty with the Republic of Texas which establishes homelands for the People. The republic's senate does not ratify the treaty.

The Ottawa and Chippewa Nations sign a treaty with the United States on March 28.

The Potawatomi bands sign nine treaties with the United States during the year, beginning on March 26. On March 29, the Potawatomi Nation signs another treaty with the United States. On April 22, the Okahmause, Keewawnay, Neeboashs, Matchisjaws, Naswawkee, and Quashquaw bands sign treaties. On August 5, the Pepinakaw, Notawkah, and Mackahtahmoah bands sign a treaty with the United States. The Mematway and Chequawkako bands sign a treaty on September 20, the Mosack band on September 23, and the Wabash Potawatomi on September 27.

The Ohio Wyandot sign a treaty with the United States on April 23.

The Swan Creek and Black River Chippewa sign a treaty with the United States on May 9.

The Menominee Nation signs a treaty on September 3 with the United States.

The Wahashaw, or Wausau, agree to articles of convention between their nation and the United States on September 10.

The Iowa Nation and the Missouri Sac and Fox agree to a treaty with the United States on September 17.

The Sac and Fox of Missouri sign a treaty on September 27 with the United States.

The Sac and Fox of Mississippi sign a treaty on September 28 as one of the "Confederated Tribes" of the Sac and Fox.

The Otoe, Missouria, and Omaha, and the Yankton and Santee Sioux sign a treaty with the United States on October 15.

The Wahpekute, Sisseton, and Upper Mdewakanton Sioux enter into a treaty on November 30 with the United States.

Eulogy on King Philip, as Pronounced at the Odeon, in Federal Street, Boston by the Reverend William Apes, an Indian. William Apes (Pequot).

Kiantwa'ka, or Cornplanter, or John O'Bail (Seneca/Irish), dies at Cornplantertown, New York.

Isah-pomu'xika, or Crowfoot (Blood/adopted Blackfoot), who will become principal leader of the Blackfoot Confederacy, is born in about 1836.

I have a red skin, but my grandfather was a white man. What does it matter? It is not the color of the skin that makes me good or bad.

Wopohwahts, or White Shield (Arikara)

1836

Ku-nugh-na-give-nuk, or Rushing Bear, or Son of the Star (Arikara)
COURTESY OF SMITHSONIAN

HISTORY/LAW/ POLITICS	LITERATURE/ART/ LEGENDS AND STORIES

1837

Smallpox and cholera decimate the Mandan people. Their population is reduced from more than fifteen thousand to fifteen hundred.

Seminole warriors under the leadership of Osceola, Alligator, Wild Cat, and Arpeika, or Sam Jones, are forced to retreat after the Battle of Lake Okeechobee in December, having inflicted major casualties against United States soldiers.

The Saginaw Chippewa negotiate and sign a treaty with the United States on January 14.

The Choctaw and Chickasaw Nations conclude a treaty on January 17 with the United States.

The Cheechawkose, Ashkum Weesaw, Muckkose, and Quiquito Potawatomi sign a treaty with the United States on February 11.

The Kiowa, Kataka, and Tawakaro Nations enter into a treaty on May 26 with the United States.

The Chippewa Nation concludes a treaty on July 29 with the United States.

The Sioux Nation agrees to a treaty with the United States on September 29.

The Sac and Fox ("Confederated Tribes") and Missouri Sac and Fox sign a treaty with the United States on October 21.

The Yankton Sioux negotiate and sign a treaty on October 21 with the United States.

The Winnebago Nation signs a treaty with the United States on November 1.

The Iowa Nation agrees to a treaty with the United States which is signed on November 23.

The Saginaw Chippewa sign a treaty on December 20 with the United States.

Hatikainye, or Elaine Murphy Schroeter (Ioway, or Iowa, of Kansas and Nebraska)
COURTESY OF ELAINE SCHROETER

1838

Smallpox carried by white American traders kills more than five hundred Choctaw as well as Chickasaw, Kiowa, Apache, Gros Ventre, Winnebago, Comanche, and Cayuse.

The People of the sovereign nations and tribes in New York conclude a treaty with the United States on January 15.

The Saginaw Chippewa conclude a treaty with the United States on January 23.

The First Christian and Orchard Oneida bands enter into a treaty on February 3 with the United States.

The People of the sovereign nations and tribes in New York sign a treaty with the United States on February 13.

The Iowa Nation agrees to a treaty with the United States on October 19.

The Miami Nation signs a treaty with the United States on November 6.

The Creek Nation enters into a treaty with the United States on November 23.

The U.S. government forces about seventeen thousand Cherokee to leave their homes in the Southeast for Indian Territory. Their horrendous journey was referred to popularly as Nuna-da-ut-sun'y, "The Trail Where They Cried," or the Trail of Tears.

1839

Weather Smokey (Mandan) dies on July 14, the first person known to have died of smallpox brought by traders of the American Fur Company at Fort Clark on the steamboat *Saint Peter's*.

Máh-to-toh-pa, Mato-tope, or Four Bears (Mandan), principal leader of the People, dies of smallpox on July 30.

Arpeika, or Sam Jones (Miccosukee Seminole), is one of the leaders in the Second Seminole War, in the battle of Lake Okeechobee in December.

My Friends one and all, Listen to what I have to say—Ever since I can remember, I have loved the whites. I have lived with them since I was a boy, and to the best of my knowledge, I have never wronged a white man. On the contrary, I have always protected them from the insults of others, which they cannot deny. . . . I do not fear death my friends. You know it. But to die with my face rotten, that even the wolves will shrink with horror at seeing me, and say to themselves, that is the Four Bears, the friend of the whites. Listen well what I have to say, as it will be the last time you will hear from me. Think of your wives, children, brothers, sisters, friends, and in fact all that you hold dear, are all dead, or dying, with their faces all rotten, caused by those dogs the whites. Think of all that my friends, and rise all together and not leave one of them alive.

Mahtotohpa, or Four Bears (Mandan)

1838

Quatie, or Elizabeth Brown Henley Ross (Cherokee), wife of Cherokee chief John Ross, dies during the vile removal of the Cherokee from their homelands.

Mushulatubbe, or Muchalatubbee (Choctaw), principal leader, dies of smallpox in the Choctaw Nation in Indian Territory.

Makatai-meshe-kiakiak, or Black Hawk (Sauk), principal leader, dies at what is now Iowaville, in Iowa.

Wahcheehahska, or Man Who Puts All out of Doors (Winnebago), principal leader of the People, dies of smallpox.

In the great night my heart will go out.
Toward me the darkness comes rattling
In the great night my heart will go out.
Tohono O'odham death song

	HISTORY/LAW/ POLITICS	LITERATURE/ART/ LEGENDS AND STORIES
1839	Smallpox decimates the Sioux.	*Narrative of the Life and Adventures of Paul Cuffe, a Pequot Indian, During Thirty Years Spent at Sea, and in Traveling in Foreign Lands*. Paul Cuffe (Pequot).
	The Delaware, Kickapoo, Shawnee, and Texas Cherokee unsuccessfully resist forces of the Republic of Texas and are defeated in battle along the Angelina River.	
	The Seminole warriors under the leadership of Halpatter Miko, or Billy Bowlegs (Seminole), successfully attack the Harney trading post, in Florida, and kill most of the garrison.	
	The Great and Little Osage Nations enter into a treaty with the United States on January 11.	
	The Saginaw Chippewa negotiate two treaties with the United States on February 7.	
	The Stockbridge and Munsee agree to a treaty on September 3 with the United States.	
	The Cherokee complete their forced removal to Indian Territory in March. About four thousand of the seventeen thousand die during or shortly after the journey.	
1840	The Miami Nation concludes and signs a treaty with the United States on November 28.	
1841	After an intense period of treaty making (1814–40), no treaties are entered into in 1841 between the People of the sovereign nations and tribes on Turtle Island and the United States. It would seem that a large majority of influential white citizens of the United States are suffering pangs of conscience because of the horrors committed by the United States on the People of the sovereign Cherokee Nation in forcing them on the Trail of Tears (1838–39), during which thousands of the People died.	
1842	The Wyandot Nation signs a treaty with the United States on March 17.	
	The Seneca Nation agrees on May 20 to a treaty with the United States.	
	The Mississippi and Lake Superior Chippewa enter into a treaty on October 4 with the United States.	
	The Sac and Fox of Iowa sign a treaty with the United States on October 11.	

HEROES/LEADERS/ VICTIMS	ELDER WISDOM/PHILOSOPHY/ SONGS	

1839

O-wapa-shaw (Sioux), principal leader, and half his band die of smallpox.

Juaquin Seloso becomes governor of the Acoma people.

Diwali, or the Bowl (Cherokee), dies in battle against troops of the Republic of Texas.

Major Ridge, John Ridge, and Galagina, or Elias Boudinot, are assassinated by Cherokee tribal members for having signed the fraudulent Treaty of New Echota, which forced the Cherokee removal.

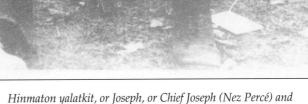

1840

Wasechun-tashunka, or American Horse (Oglala Lakota), possibly the nephew of American Horse (Iron Shield), who will become a noted warrior and orator of the People, is born.

Kintpuash, or Kintpoos, or Captain Jack (Modoc), who will become principal leader, is born.

Hinmaton-yalatkit, or Chief Joseph (Nez Percé), who will become principal leader of the Nez Percé, is born in about 1840 in what is now Oregon, in the Wallowa valley. His father is Teukakas, principal leader of the Wallam-watkin, and his mother is Khapkhaponimi.

1841

1842

Marie L. McLaughlin (Standing Rock Sioux), author, is born on December 8.

Tashunka Witco, or Crazy Horse (Oglala/Brulé Sioux), who will become a noted warrior and principal leader, is born in about 1842 east of Pa'ha Sap'a (the Black Hills), near what is now Rapid City, South Dakota.

Hinmaton yalatkit, or Joseph, or Chief Joseph (Nez Percé) and General Gibbon

COURTESY OF SMITHSONIAN

217

	HISTORY/LAW/ POLITICS	LITERATURE/ART/ LEGENDS AND STORIES
1843	The Delaware and Wyandot Nations sign an agreement with the United States on December 14.	
1844		
1845	The Creek and Seminole Nations enter into a treaty on January 4 with the United States.	
1846	Captain John C. Frémont attacks Yana people peacefully gathered on what is now known as Bloody Island at the mouth of Battle Creek, tributary of the Sacramento River. The Kansa, or Kansas, Nation negotiates and signs a treaty with the United States on January 14. The Comanche, Ioni, Anadaca, Caddo, Lipan Apache, Longwha, Keechy, Tahwacarro, Wichita, and Waco Nations and tribes sign a treaty on May 15 with the United States. The Chippewa, Ottawa, Prairie Potawatomi, Wabash Potawatomi, and Indiana Potawatomi Nations sign two treaties with the United States, the first on June 5 and the second on June 17. The Cherokee Nation, the Treaty Party Cherokee, and the Western Cherokee ("Old Settlers") enter into a treaty on August 6 with the United States. The Winnebago Nation signs a treaty with the United States on October 13.	*Quanah, or Quanah Parker (Kwahadie Comanche/White)* COURTESY OF SMITHSONIAN
1847	Taos people living in what is now northern New Mexico rise in revolt against white interlopers. The Mississippi and Lake Superior Chippewa sign a treaty with the United States on August 2. The Pillager Chippewa sign a separate treaty on August 21.	*The Life, History, and Travels of Kah-ge-ga-gah-bowh (George Copway), a Young Indian Chief of the Ojebwa Nation, with a Sketch of the Present State of the Ojebwa Nation, in Regard to Christianity and Their Future Prospects.* Kahgegagah-bowh, or George Copway (Ojibwa).

HEROES/LEADERS/ VICTIMS	ELDER WISDOM/PHILOSOPHY/ SONGS	
George Bent (Southern Cheyenne/white), who will become an interpreter and writer and an important warrior among the People, is born.		**1843**
Unaduti, or Dennis Wolf Bushyhead (Cherokee/white), who will become principal chief of the Cherokee Nation in what is now Oklahoma, enrolls at Princeton University. He leaves before completing his course of study and returns to Indian Territory, or what is now Oklahoma.		**1844**
Quanah, or Quanah Parker (Kwahadie Comanche/white), who will become a principal leader and religious leader of the Comanche, is born in about 1845.		**1845**
Chitto Harjo, or Wilson Jones (Muscogee), who will become principal leader among the Snake Muscogee, is born near what is now Boley, Oklahoma. Onpahtonga, or Big Elk (Omaha), principal leader, dies. He is succeeded by his son, also named Big Elk. *Nah-ah-sa-na, or Warloupe, or Gualoupe (Caddo)* COURTESY OF SMITHSONIAN		**1846**
Ahdoltay, or Big Tree (Kiowa), who will become one of the youngest war leaders among the People, is born.		**1847**

	HISTORY/LAW/ POLITICS	LITERATURE/ART/ LEGENDS AND STORIES
1848	The Grand Pawnee, Pawnee Loups, Pawnee Republic, and Pawnee Tappage ("Confederated Bands of Pawnee") sign a treaty with the United States on August 6. The Menominee Nation signs a treaty on October 18 with the United States. The Stockbridge Nation enters into a treaty on November 24 with the United States.	
1849	The United States Congress creates a Department of the Interior in the executive branch and transfers the duties and responsibilities of the Office of Indian Affairs to it. The Navajo Nation enters into a treaty with the United States on September 9. The Utah Nation signs a treaty with the United States on December 30.	
1850	The Wyandot Nation enters into a treaty on April 1 with the United States.	
1851	The Apangassa, Awalache, Coconoon, Potoyunte, and Siyante tribes agree to a treaty with the United States on March 19. The Chowchilla, Pohoneechees, Nookchoos, Cassons, Toomnas, Howechees, Chookchanees, Tallinchees, Poskesas, Itachees, Wachaets, Choenemnees, Notonotos, Wemalchees, and Pitcachees agree to a treaty with the United States on April 29. The Yokuts, Cahwais, Tolumnes, Wicchumnes, Holcumas, Torneches, Intimpeaches, Tuhucmaches, Choinues, Wemilches, Taches, and Notontors sign a treaty with the United States on May 13. The Wechillas, Succaahs, Iouolumnes, Cotoplanemis, and Chappahsims enter into a treaty on May 28 with the United States. *(continued)*	

HEROES/LEADERS/ VICTIMS	ELDER WISDOM/PHILOSOPHY/ SONGS	
		1848
Pochanawkwoip, or Buffalo Hump (Penateka Comanche), war leader during what is referred to as the Comanche Wars of 1830–50, becomes principal leader of the Penateka Comanche. Marpeya Wicas'ta, or Cloudman (Mdewakanton/Santee Sioux), leader of the Sisseton Sioux, founds the town of Lake Calhoun at what is now Minneapolis, later relocated to the south side of the Minnesota River.		**1849**
Kootah-wecoot-soole-lehoola-shar, or Big Hawk Chief (Pawnee), who will become a noted athlete, is born.	*Eddie Webb (Cherokee)* Courtesy of Eddie Webb	**1850**
Nockoist, or James Bear's Heart (Southern Cheyenne), who will become a noted warrior of the People, is born.		**1851**

1851

(continued from page 220)

The Koyate, Nuchowwe, Wolassi, Wacksache, Palwisha, Pokowwe, and Yawilchine tribes agree to a treaty with the United States on May 30.

The Chunute, Kayete, Wowol, and Yalumne tribes sign a treaty with the United States on June 3.

The Castake, Buena Vista, Texon, San Imirio Uvas, Carisis, Senahuow, Holoclame, Sohonuts, and Tocia sign a treaty with the United States on June 10.

The Yamado, Yolamir, Wannuck, Sacumna, Onopoma, Nemshaw, Moneda, Daspia, and Benpi tribes sign a treaty on July 18 with the United States.

The Sisseton and Wahpeton Sioux enter into a treaty with the United States on July 23.

The Batsi, Cheno, Eskuin, Hololupi, Michopda, Simsawa, Sunus, and Toto tribes sign a treaty with the United States on August 1.

The Mdewakanton and Wahpekute Sioux enter into a treaty on August 5 with the United States.

The Noima, Noema, Nome, Noime, Oylacca, and Ylacca tribes sign a treaty with the United States on August 16.

The Calanapo, Chankai, Checom, Danohab, Habinapo, Howkuma, Medamadec, and Moalkai tribes conclude a treaty on August 20 with the United States.

The Pomo, Sainell, Massutakaya, and Yuki negotiate and sign a treaty with the United States on August 22.

The Cha, Chammetco, Cohena, Collus, Docduc, Tatnah, and Tocde tribes sign a treaty with the United States on September 9.

Ten thousand Arapaho, Arikara, Assiniboin, Cheyenne, Crow, Gros Ventre, Mandan, and Teton Dakota (Sioux) gather for a great council at Fort Laramie, in what is now Wyoming, and agree to a treaty on September 17. The Treaty of Fort Laramie, although never ratified by the United States Senate, is recognized as being in force in subsequent agreements. What is significant about the treaty is that for the first time in their thousand-year history, the sovereign nations of the Plains are restricted by an outside authority to specific areas beyond which they are forbidden to travel or live.

The Yassi, Loclumne, Wopumnes, and Culu agree to a treaty with the United States on September 18.

Lower Klamath (Pohlik), Wetchpeck, Whusi, Cappel, Morriahs, Seragoines, Pakwan, Utchapa, Uppagoines, Savonra, Chammakonee, Cockoman, Cneenah, Hoopa, Siwah, Oppeo, Hekoneck, and Inneck tribes enter into a treaty on October 6 with the United States.

Eeh, Idakariwakaha, Ikaruck, Kosetah, Odellah, and Watsahewa tribes sign a treaty with the United States on November 4.

Running Sketches of Men and Places, in England, France, Germany, Belgium, and Scotland and *The Traditional History and Characteristic Sketches of the Ojibway Nation.* Kahgegagahbowh, or George Copway (Ojibwa).

Me-ra-pa-ra-pa, or Lance (Mandan)
COURTESY OF SMITHSONIAN

	HISTORY/LAW/ POLITICS	LITERATURE/ART/ LEGENDS AND STORIES
1852	The San Luis Rey, Kahweas, Toova, and Cocomcahras tribes enter into a treaty with the United States on January 5. The Diegueño tribe signs a treaty with the United States on January 7. The Chickasaw Nation concludes a treaty on June 22 with the United States. The Apache Nation signs a treaty on July 1 with the United States.	
1853	The Comanche, Kiowa, and Apache Nations enter into a treaty with the United States on July 27. The Rogue River tribe signs a treaty with the United States on September 10. The Cow Creek Umpqua agree to a treaty with the United States on September 19.	*Journal of the Reverend Peter Jacobs, Indian Wesleyan Missionary, from Rice Lake to the Hudson's Bay Territory and Returning Commencing May 1852.* Pahtahsega, or Peter Jacobs (Ojibwa).
1854	The Cahuilla, under the leadership of Cooswootna, or Juan Antonio, attack white settlers in southern California in retaliation for the state senate's nonratification of the 1852 treaty. The treaty would have provided for Cahuilla control of ancestral lands. The Otoe and Missouria Nations agree to a treaty with the United States on March 15. The Otoe Nation cedes three million acres. In a contemporary newspaper, an article notes: Half of all Indian country is now ceded and were the negotiations intrusted to the gallant [Charles] Gatewood it would not be many "moons" until the WHOLE OF IT were thrown open to the Anglo-Saxon plough! The Omaha Nation concludes and signs what is referred to as the Treaty with the Omahas with the United States at Washington, D.C., on March 16. Under the treaty, the Omaha Nation cedes ten million acres of its ancestral homeland to the United States. The Delaware Nation agrees to a treaty with the United States on May 6. The Shawnee Nation signs a treaty on May 10 with the United States. The Menominee Nation negotiates and signs a treaty with the United States on May 12. The Iowa, or Ioway, Nation signs a treaty with the United States on May 17. The Sac and Fox of Missouri sign a treaty on May 18 with the United States. The Kickapoo Nation signs a treaty with the United States on May 18. The Kaskaskia, Peoria, Piankashaw, and Wea ("United Tribes") agree to a treaty with the United States on May 30. *(continued)*	*The Life and Adventures of Joaquín Murieta, Celebrated California Bandit, by Yellow Bird.* Yellow Bird, or John Rollin Ridge (Cherokee).

HEROES/LEADERS/ VICTIMS	ELDER WISDOM/PHILOSOPHY/ SONGS	
Walking Hail (Yankton Sioux) agrees to marry Wa-ana-tan, or Martin Charger (Sans Arc Sioux/white).		**1852**
		1853
Marpeya Wicas'ta, or Cloudman (Mdewakanton/Santee Sioux), leader of the Sisseton Sioux, founds the Hazelwood Republic, in Dakota Territory, a constitutional government of Christian Native People. Mohe, or Cahoe, or William Cohe (Southern Cheyenne), who will become a warrior and afterward a noted artist, is born in what is now Colorado. Mah-toio-wah, or Whirling Bear, or Conquering Bear (Brulé Sioux), principal leader of the Brulé, is killed during what became known as the Grattan fight, on August 29.	Daddy was an Aleutian, and the people there have Russian names from the early days when Russia colonized some of the islands and hunted sea otter and seal skins. *Harriet Godfrey (Siuslaw/Coos/Umpqua/Siletz-Aleut)*	**1854**

1854

(continued from page 224)

The Miami Nation signs a treaty on June 5 with the United States.

The Creek Nation agrees on June 13 to a treaty with the United States.

The Lake Superior and Mississippi Chippewa enter into a treaty with the United States on September 30.

The Choctaw and Chickasaw Nations agree to a treaty with the United States on November 5.

The Rogue River tribe signs a treaty on November 15 with the United States.

The Cownanatico, Sacheriton, and Naalye Scoton, the Quilsieton and Nahelta Chasta, or Shasta, and the Grave Creek Umpqua tribes sign a treaty with the United States on November 18.

The Umpqua and Calapooia Nations sign a treaty with the United States on November 29.

The Otoe and Missouria ("Confederated Tribes") sign a treaty with the United States on December 9.

The Nisqually, Puyallup, Steilacoom, Squawskin, S'Homamish, Stehchass, T'Peeksin, Squiaitl, and Sahehwamish tribes sign what is referred to as the Treaty with the Nisqually at Medicine Creek in the Territory of Washington on December 26. More than six hundred of the People attend the treaty negotiations. "The right of taking fish, at all usual and accustomed grounds and stations, is further secured to said Indians" is an important article in the treaty because it is the first time the United States has agreed to guarantee fishing rights in a treaty. It provides the basis for court decisions in later times.

1855

Gold-lusting white miners attack and burn Native rancherias (villages) at Weitschpeck, in what is now Oregon.

People of the sovereign nations and tribes living in the region of what is now Klamath Falls, Oregon, are forced to move to a reservation on the Klamath River.

The Calapooias, Molala, Tumwater, and Clackamas tribes sign a treaty with the United States on January 22.

The Duwamish, Suquamish, Sktahimish, Samahmish, Smalhkamish, Skopeahmish, Stkahmish, Snoqualmoo, Skaiwhamish, N'Quentlmamish, Sktahlejum, Stoluckwhamish, Snohomish, Skagit, Kikiallus, Swinamish, Squinahmish, Sahkumehu, Moowhaha, Nookwachahmish, Meeseequagulich, and Chobahahbish Nations enter into a treaty with the United States which is signed on January 22 at Point Elliott, in what is now Washington. The S'Klallam, Skokomish, Toanhooch, and Chemakum sign on January 26 at Point no Point, in what is now Washington. In add-

(continued)

1854

1855

Watomika, or James Bouchard (Delaware/French) is the first among all the People of the sovereign nations and tribes living on Turtle Island to be ordained a Roman Catholic priest in the Jesuit order.

1855

(continued from page 226)

ition to ceding ancestral lands (as is the case with all previous and subsequent treaties with the Peoples of the sovereign nations and tribes across Turtle Island), the treaty follows the format of the Treaty with the Nisqually and guarantees fishing rights to the People of the sovereign nations.

The Wyandot Nation signs a treaty with the United States on January 31.

The Makah Nation signs a treaty with the United States on January 31.

The Mississippi, Pillager, and Lake Winnibigoshish Chippewa enter into a treaty on February 22 with the United States.

The Winnebago Nation signs a treaty with the United States on February 27.

The Walla Walla, Cayuse, and Umatilla Nations agree to a treaty with the United States on June 9.

The Yakima, Palouse, Pisquouse, Wanatshapam, Klikatat, Klinquit, Kowwassayee, Liaywas, Skinpah, Wisham, Shyiks, Ochechotes, Kahmiltpah, and Seapocat bands of the Yakima Nation sign a treaty with the United States on June 9.

The Nez Percé Nation agrees to a treaty with the United States on June 11.

The Choctaw and Chickasaw Nations sign a treaty with the United States on June 22.

The People of the sovereign nations and tribes in what is now middle Oregon sign a treaty with the United States on June 25.

The Quinault and Quileute Nations enter into a treaty on July 1 with the United States.

The Flathead, Kootenai, and Upper Pend d'Oreilles ("Confederated Tribes") sign what is referred to as the Treaty of Hell Gate on July 31 at Hell Gate in the Bitterroot valley of the Territory of Washington. A significant point about the treaty is that it was the basis of a successful lawsuit brought to the United States Court of Claims in 1971, almost 120 years later, by the Confederated Salish and Kootenai Tribes of the Flathead Reservation *(Montana v. United States)*.

The Sault Sainte Marie, Grand River, Grand Traverse, Little Traverse, and Mackinac bands of the Ottawa and Chippewa Nations negotiate what is referred to as the Treaty with the Ottawas and Chippewas at Detroit, Michigan, on July 31. With Andrew Jackson long gone from the presidency of the United States, this treaty is important because it modifies the harsh social policy of absolute removal of the People of the sovereign nations and tribes from their ancestral homelands as given in the treaty of

(continued)

The Two Companions. Icy (Cherokee).

Paul Showeway (Cayuse)
COURTESY OF SMITHSONIAN

	HISTORY/LAW/ POLITICS	LITERATURE/ART/ LEGENDS AND STORIES

1855	*(continued from page 228)*
	
	March 28, 1836, and opens the possibility of Native and non-Native people living side by side. Tragically, this treaty also requires the dissolution and abolition of the ancient governmental and organizational structure and practices of the Ottawa and Chippewa, except as necessary to carry out the provisions of the treaty.
	    The Sault Sainte Marie, Saginaw, Swan Creek, and Black River bands of Chippewa agree to a treaty with the United States on August 2.
	    The Blackfoot, Flathead, and Nez Percé Nations enter into a treaty on October 17 with the United States.
	    The Molala Nation signs a treaty with the United States on December 21.	

1856	The Stockbridge and Munsee Nations enter into a treaty with the United States on February 5.
	    The Menominee Nation signs a treaty with the United States on February 11.
	    The Creek and Seminole Nations agree to a treaty with the United States on August 7.	

1857	Klamath warriors in what is now Oregon engage in raiding expeditions against the Pit River people. The Klamath capture women and children whom they take back to Oregon and sell as slaves.
	    The Pawnee Nation ("Four Confederated Bands") enters into a treaty with the United States on September 24.
	    The Tonawanda Seneca agree to a treaty with the United States on November 5.	

1858	The Ponca Nation enters into a treaty on March 12 with the United States.
	    The On April 19, the Yankton Sioux sign a treaty with the United States.
	    The Mdewakanton, Wahpekute, Sisseton, and Wahpeton Sioux sign two treaties with the United States on June 19.	

1859	The Winnebago Nation signs a treaty with the United States on April 15.
	    The Swan Creek and Black River Chippewa and Munsee Nation agree on July 16 to a treaty with the United States.
	    The Mississippi Sac and Fox sign a treaty with the United States on October 1.
	    The Kansa, or Kansas, Nation signs a treaty with the United States on October 5.	

HEROES / LEADERS / VICTIMS	ELDER WISDOM / PHILOSOPHY / SONGS	
		1855
Robert Latham Owen (Cherokee), who will become one of the first two senators from Oklahoma, is born in Lynchburg, Virginia.		**1856**
Wovoka, or Jack Wilson (Northern Paiute), who will become the founder of the second Ghost Dance movement, is born in about 1857 in what is now Nevada, along the Walker River in Mason Valley. Laylake (Klamath) leads an expedition against the Pit River people. José Lovato becomes governor of the Acoma people. Francis La Flesche (Omaha), noted ethnologist and author, is born on December 25.		**1857**
Ohiyesa, or Charles A. Eastman, M.D. (Santee Sioux), noted author and lecturer, is born on February 19.		**1858**
John N. B. Hewitt (Tuscarora), author, is born on December 16.		**1859**

PERSPECTIVE
1860–1900

With the advent of the Civil War in 1861, the People of the sovereign nations and tribes began to regain some hope that they would prevail against the violence of the American government.

The first confrontation occurred when thousands of Native People attacked Fort Defiance, in what is now Arizona. The wars between the People and their American oppressors escalated with the rapes of two Southern Paiute women by traders, and the Paiute retaliated. Then the Apache people revolted against the tyranny of the American government.

In 1862, starving Santee Sioux were refused money and food guaranteed by treaty. It was little wonder that the men of the sovereign nations and tribes were enraged at the sight of their starving infants, children, mothers, daughters, sisters, and old people. It was little wonder that hate burned white-hot when they were told that if the People are hungry, "let them eat grass."[12] It was little wonder that the Santee Sioux went to war.

The wars continued to multiply. In 1863, the Shoshone revolted, as did the Navajo. In 1864, the Cheyenne, Arapaho, and Sioux attacked white settlers in Colorado and Kansas. Unfortunately for the People of the sovereign nations and tribes, the American Civil War ended in 1865.

The next twenty-five years witnessed the decimation and extinction of many sovereign nations and tribes. In all the annals of history, such mass murder committed by one race against another will have no equal. In the end, the People were balanced precariously on the edge of extinction.

In response to the devastation and disintegration of their way of life due to war and removal, epidemic disease, and starvation, many of the People of the sovereign nations and tribes decided that they must regain balance and harmony. The People heard the voices of the Northern Paiute, or Paviotso, prophets—Wodziwob and, later, Wovoka—who originated the Ghost Dance movements. Through the power of the Ghost Dances, the People of the sovereign nations and tribes came to believe that their dead relatives would return. The dream of a better world was reborn.

The first Ghost Dance movement, led by Wodziwob, began in the late 1860s near the Walker River Reservation in what is now the westernmost part of Nevada. It spread east as far as central Nevada, south to San Diego, California, west to the Pacific coast, and as far north as central Oregon. Among the sovereign nations and tribes that embraced the first Ghost Dance were the Achumawi, Bannock, Coos, Gosiute, Kalapuya, Karok, Klamath, Miwok, Modoc, Paiute, Pomo, Shoshone, Siuslaw, Tolowa, Tutuni, Ute, Wappo, Washo, Wintun, Yana, Yuki, Yokuts, and Yurok.

By the mid-1870s, the first Ghost Dance movement had declined in favor among the People of the sovereign nations and tribes. Although its impact was limited to the People of the sovereign nations and tribes in the West, the movement was significant because one of its strong disciples was Tavaibo, or Numataivo (Northern Paiute). He passed on his deeply held beliefs to his son, Wovoka.

The Paviotso Prophet, Wovoka, or Jack Wilson, instituted the second, more powerful, Ghost Dance in 1887. As a result of his vision, Wovoka prescribed certain dance movements and promised that if the People performed them as directed, they would be reunited with their loved ones, who would return from the dead.

Wovoka's message exploded in all four directions from the Walker River Reservation. The People of the sovereign nations and tribes in North Dakota, South Dakota, Nebraska, Kansas, central and western Oklahoma, northeastern New Mexico, Colorado, Wyoming, central to southern Montana, central to southern Idaho, Utah, northwestern Arizona, Nevada, lower inland to far northern inland California, and southeastern Oregon all became active participants of the second Ghost Dance. As the People danced, many began to wear "ghost shirts" which they believed would protect them from the bullets of the hated U.S. Army soldiers. At the Chief Big Foot Massacre (Wounded Knee Creek, South Dakota) on December 29, 1890, the Ghost Dance dream of the People finally died.[13]

	HISTORY/LAW/ POLITICS	LITERATURE/ART/ LEGENDS AND STORIES
1860	The Delaware Nation signs a treaty with the United States on May 30. The Minnesota Reservation Sioux agree on June 27 to a treaty with the United States.	*Life and Journals of Kahkewaquonaby (Rev. Peter Jones), Wesleyan Missionary.* Kahkewaquonaby, or Peter Jones (Ojibwa).

1861	The Arapaho and Cheyenne of the Upper Arkansas enter into a treaty on February 18 with the United States.
	
	    The Missouri Sac and Fox and Iowa Nations agree to a treaty with the United States on March 6.
	
	    The Delaware Nation signs a treaty with the United States on July 2.
	
	    The Kansas Potawatomi sign a treaty with the United States on November 15.
	
	    The People of the sovereign nations and tribes are drawn into the American Civil War on both sides, especially in Indian Territory, or what is now Oklahoma.
		History of the Ojebway Indians, with Especial Reference to Their Conversion to Christianity. Kahkewaquonaby, or Peter Jones (Ojibwa).

1862	The Kansa, or Kansas, Nation enters into a treaty with the United States on March 13.
	
	    The Blanchard's Fork and Roche de Boeuf Ottawa sign a treaty with the United States on June 24.
	
	    The Kickapoo Nation agrees to a treaty with the United States on June 28
	
	    Thirty-eight Dakota are publicly hanged in Mankato, Minnesota, and more than 250 Dakota are captured at the conclusion of the "Minnesota Uprising."	

Gaynwah, or Thomas Wildcat Alford (Absentee Shawnee), who will become a leader among the Shawnee, is born.

Batsinas, or Jason Betzinez (Mimbreño Apache), cousin of Goyathlay, or Geronimo, is born. Batsinas will become a writer.

Chato (Chiricahua Apache), who will become a war leader of the Apache, is born.

Hot'tsa-sodono, or Deerfoot, or Louis Bennett (Seneca), travels to England, successfully competes in track meets, and wins substantial prize money.

Arpeika, or Sam Jones (Miccosukee Seminole), dreamer, prophet, and war leader of the Seminole, dies.

Charles Curtis (Kansa), who becomes thirty-first vice-president of the United States, is born in North Topeka, Kansas.

Everything changes, and yet nothing changes but the holders of life. In Great Mystery, it is unending. Grandma and Grandpa would say that this is the way of Great Mystery. It knows not time.
Anna L. Walters (Pawnee/Otoe-Missouria)

1860

Chato (Chiricahua Apache)
COURTESY OF SMITHSONIAN

1861

Tekahionwake, or Emily Pauline Johnson (Mohawk), noted author, is born on March 10.

Marpeya Wicas'ta, or Cloudman (Mdewakanton/Santee Sioux), leader of the Sisseton Sioux and great-grandfather of Ohiyesa, or Charles A. Eastman, M.D., dies.

Tayateduta, or Little Crow (Mdewakanton Sioux), leads the Santee in what is known as the "Minnesota Uprising" on December 26.

It is not necessary for crows to become eagles.
Tatanka Iyotake, or Sitting Bull (Hunkpapa Lakota)

1862

235

1863

The Massacre of the Northwestern Shoshone occurs during the Bear River Campaign. The Shoshone people fight a losing battle against Third California Infantry volunteers under the command of Patrick Connor. In the battle, which lasts less than five hours, about 250 Shoshone men, women, and children are killed. The remaining 150 women and children are taken prisoner.

Union forces under the command of Colonel James Blunt defeat Choctaw, Chickasaw, Creek, Seminole, and Cherokee volunteers under the command of Confederate Colonel Douglas H. Cooper at the Battle of Honey Springs, Indian Territory, on July 17.

Much of the Great Basin is ceded to the United States under treaties signed by the People of the sovereign nations and tribes.

The Mississippi, Pillager, and Lake Winnibigoshish Chippewa sign a treaty with the United States on March 11.

The Nez Percé Nation enters into a treaty on June 9 with the United States.

The Eastern Shoshone agree to a treaty on July 2 with the United States.

The Northwestern Shoshone sign a treaty with the United States on July 30.

The Western Shoshone sign a treaty with the United States on October 1.

The Red Lake and Pembina Chippewa enter into a treaty on October 2 with the United States.

The Tabegauche Utah Nation signs a treaty on October 7 with the United States.

The Shoshone-Goship sign a treaty with the United States on October 13

Car-io-scuse, or Curly Bear (Blackfoot)
COURTESY OF SMITHSONIAN

1864

The Long Walk of the Navajo begins in March. U.S. Army soldiers under the command of Christopher "Kit" Carson force more than twenty-four hundred Navajo to march three hundred miles east of their ancient homelands to Bosque Redondo, in what is now eastern New Mexico. More than two hundred Navajo die on the march.

The Red Lake and Pembina Chippewa sign a treaty with the United States on April 12.

The Mississippi, Pillager, and Lake Winnibigoshish Chippewa enter into a treaty on May 7 with the United States.

The Klamath, Modoc, and Yahooskin Snake Nations agree to a treaty with the United States on October 14.

The Saginaw, Swan Creek, and Black River Chippewa sign a treaty with the United States on October 18.

| | | **1863** |

Hehaka Sapa, or Black Elk (Oglala Lakota), who will become a visionary and holy man of the Lakota, is born.

Cooswootna, or Juan Antonio (Cahuilla), principal leader of the People in southern California, dies from smallpox.

Wirasuap, or Bear Hunter (Northwestern Shoshone), principal leader of the People, is killed by California infantry volunteers at the Massacre of the Northwestern Shoshone.

Kahgegagahbowh, or George Copway (Ojibwa), noted author and Methodist missionary, dies.

| | | **1864** |

Bislahalani, or Barboncito (Diné, or Navajo), is captured at Cañon de Chelly in September by U.S. soldiers under the command of Colonel Christopher "Kit" Carson, and forcibly removed to Bosque Redondo in what is now eastern New Mexico.

Halpatter Miko, or Billy Bowlegs (Seminole), noted leader of the People, dies.

Official bounties had been placed on the scalps of Indians—any Indians—in places as diverse as Georgia, Kentucky, Texas, the Dakotas, Oregon, and California. They remained in effect until resident Indian populations were decimated or disappeared.

Ward Churchill (Creek/Cherokee métis)

1865

White settlers Robert A. Anderson and Hiram Good lead the Massacre of the Yana at Three Knolls on Mill Creek, in California.

Oglala, Hunkpapa, and Brulé Lakota, Northern Cheyenne, and Northern Arapaho engage in battle against immigrant American settlers who are trespassing on a major buffalo range by traveling on the Bozeman and Oregon Trails.

The Arapaho are defeated at the Battle of Tongue River, in what is now Wyoming, on August 29 by U.S. Army cavalry troops under the command of General Patrick Connor.

The Omaha Nation signs a treaty with the United States on March 6.

The Winnebago Nation signs a treaty on March 8 with the United States.

The Ponca Nation signs a treaty with the United States on March 10.

The Wollpahpe Snake tribe signs a treaty with the United States on August 12.

The Great and Little Osage Nations sign a treaty with the United States on September 29.

On October 10, the Miniconjou Sioux sign a treaty with the United States.

The Lower Brulé Sioux sign a treaty with the United States on October 14.

The Arapaho and Cheyenne of the upper Arkansas River enter into a treaty on October 14 with the United States.

The Apache, Cheyenne, and Arapaho Nations sign a treaty with the United States on October 17.

The Comanche and Kiowa Nations agree to a treaty with the United States on October 18.

The Two Kettle Sioux and Blackfeet Sioux sign separate treaties with the United States on October 19.

The Sans Arc, Hunkpapa, and Yanktonai bands of Sioux sign separate treaties on October 20 with the United States.

The Upper Yanktonai and Oglala Sioux sign separate treaties with the United States on October 28.

The People of the sovereign nations and tribes in middle Oregon enter into a treaty on November 15 with the United States.

The American Civil War ends. It is said that the five "Civilized" tribes of Indian Territory (Cherokee, Creek, Choctaw, Chickasaw, and Seminole) lost a higher proportion of lives than any state.

Bislahalani, or Barboncito (Diné, or Navajo), escapes with five hundred of the People from Bosque Redondo, in what is now eastern New Mexico, where he had been held forcibly by U.S. soldiers.

Black Bear (Arapaho), principal leader, and his warriors are defeated at the Battle of Tongue River in what is now Wyoming. His son is killed in the fighting.

Weeping, I, the singer, weave my song of flowers of sadness. I call to memory the youths, the shards, the fragments, gone to the land of the dead; once noble and powerful here on earth, the youths were dried up like feathers, were split into fragments like an emerald, before the face and in the sight of those who saw them on earth, and with the knowledge of the Cause of All.

Aztec prayer song

1865

Minnesota Chippewa Civil War veterans
COURTESY OF PAULETTE FAIRBANKS MOLIN

1866

The Seminole Nation signs a treaty with the United States on March 21.

The Potawatomi Nation enters into a treaty on March 29 with the United States.

The Bois Fort Chippewa agree on April 7 to a treaty with the United States.

The Choctaw and Chickasaw Nations sign a treaty with the United States on April 28.

The Creek Nation enters into a treaty on June 14 with the United States.

On July 4, the Delaware Nation signs a treaty with the United States.

The Cherokee Nation agrees to a treaty with the United States on July 19 in Washington, D.C.

Vee F. Browne (Navajo)
COURTESY OF DELILAH BROWNE

1867

The Yahi Yana people are murdered and scalped by white settlers led by Normal Kingsley at a cave north of Mill Creek, in California.

The Mississippi Sac and Fox Nation agrees to a treaty with the United States on February 18.

The Sisseton and Wahpeton Sioux sign a treaty with the United States on February 19.

The Seneca, "Mixed" Seneca, Shawnee, Quapaw, "Confederated" Peoria, Kaskaskia, Wea, and Piankashaw, Miami, Blanchard's Fork and Roche de Boeuf Ottawa, and Wyandot agree to a treaty with the United States on February 23.

The Kansas Potawatomi sign a treaty on February 27 with the United States.

The Mississippi Chippewa agree on March 19 to a treaty with the United States.

The Kiowa and Comanche Nations sign a treaty with the United States on October 21. A separate treaty is agreed to on that day by the Kiowa, Comanche, and Apache Nations.

The Cheyenne and Arapaho Nations agree to a treaty with the United States on October 28.

HEROES/LEADERS/ VICTIMS	ELDER WISDOM/PHILOSOPHY/ SONGS	
Cooweescoowee, or John Ross (Cherokee/Scottish), principal chief of the Cherokee Nation since 1828, dies on August 1 in Washington, D.C. Hastin, or Manuelito (Diné, or Navajo), surrenders with twenty-three followers to the U.S. Army at Fort Wingate, in what is now Arizona, in November. Bislahalani, or Barboncito (Diné, or Navajo), with twenty-five followers, surrenders in November to U.S. soldiers at Fort Wingate, in what is now Arizona.	In the end, non-Indians will have complete power to define what is and what is not Indian, even for Indians. We are talking here about a complete ideological/conceptual subordination of Indian people in addition to the total physical subordination they already experience. *Pam Colorado (Oneida)*	**1866**
Medicine Calf, or James Beckwith (Irish/African/ adopted Crow), principal leader of the Crow, dies.	The fact that [the U.S. Congress] called those treaties "agreements" does not change the fact that . . . they both have the same legal effect. *Vine Deloria Jr. (Standing Rock Sioux)*	**1867**

	HISTORY/LAW/ POLITICS	LITERATURE/ART/ LEGENDS AND STORIES
1868	The Massacre at Sand Creek occurs in what is now Colorado, on November 27. More than one hundred Cheyenne are killed brutally by troops under the command of Colonel John M. Chivington. Of those killed, ten were warriors and the rest were women and children. The Ute Nation negotiates and signs a treaty on March 2 with the United States. The Cherokee Nation and the United States agree to a treaty which is signed on April 27. The Sioux Nation and the Arapaho people sign a treaty on April 29 with representatives of the U.S. government. The Crow negotiate a treaty with the U.S. government and sign the document on May 7. The Northern Cheyenne and Northern Arapaho sign a treaty on May 10 with the United States. On June 1, the Navajo Nation signs a treaty with the United States which establishes the Navajo Reservation. The Eastern Band of Shoshone and the Bannock sign a treaty on July 3 with the U.S. government. The Nez Percé sign the last document known as a "treaty" between the United States and a sovereign nation, on August 13. Afterward, all such documents are called "agreements" between the sovereign nations and the government of the United States.	
1869	The Battle at Summit Springs, a Cheyenne encampment near what is now Atwood, Colorado, occurs on July 11 in what is known as the Republican River Expedition. Under the command of General Eugene Carr and led by William F. Cody, or "Buffalo Bill," the cavalry batallions kill more than fifty warriors, capture twenty women and children, and obliterate the Cheyenne camp.	
1870		*Origin and Traditional History of the Wyandotts,* and *Sketches of Other Indian Tribes of North America: True Traditional Stories of Tecumseh and His League, in the Years 1811 and 1812.* Peter Dooyentate Clarke (Wyandot).

Sophia Alice Callahan (Muscogee), author, is born on January 1.

Mokatavato, or Black Kettle (Southern Cheyenne), peace leader, peacefully tries to stop the forces under the command of Colonel John M. Chivington from attacking the People at Sand Creek. Mokatavato and his wife are shot and killed by the advancing troops on November 27.

Jesse Chisholm (Cherokee/Scottish), pathfinder who, because of his fluency in more than twelve languages of the People, worked diligently as an interpreter between the People and their non-Native relations, dies at Left Hand Spring near what is now Oklahoma City, Oklahoma.

Tah-me-la-pash-me, or Dull Knife (Northern Cheyenne), is one of the signers of the Fort Laramie Treaty of 1868.

There at Sand Creek, is one chief, Nawat (or Left Hand); White Antelope and many other chiefs lie there; our women and children lie there. Our lodges were destroyed there, and our horses were taken from us there. . . .

Hose, or Little Raven (Southern Arapaho)

1868

Ely Samuel Parker (Seneca) is the first from among the People of the sovereign nations and tribes to be appointed commissioner of Indian affairs in the United States Department of the Interior. He serves until 1871. It will be ninety-seven years (1966) before another from among the People is appointed commissioner.

Otoh-hastis, or Tall Bull (Southern Cheyenne), prominent leader of the Dog Soldiers, is killed at the Battle of Summit Springs.

Hose, or Little Raven (Arapaho) holding youngest child, Grass Woman. At right is Colonel Bent and next are the sons of Little Raven
COURTESY OF SMITHSONIAN

1869

Emmet Starr, M.D. (Cherokee), historian and genealogist, is born on December 12.

Hastin, or Manuelito (Diné, or Navajo), becomes principal leader of the Diné, or Navajo.

I am very sad. I want peace quick, or else let the soldiers come and make haste and fight. . . . I don't want to shoot or be shot. . . . I want to live in peace.

Kintpuash, or Captain Jack (Modoc)

1870

1871

The United States Congress enacts legislation on March
3 declaring that:

Hereafter no Indian Nation or Tribe within the Territory
of the United States shall be acknowledged or recog
nized as an independent nation, tribe, or power with
whom the United States may contract by treaty.

Set-angya, or Satank, or Sitting Bear (Kiowa)
COURTESY OF SMITHSONIAN

Ahdoltay, or Big Tree (Kiowa), noted war leader, is arrested and sentenced to death at Fort Sill, in what is now Oklahoma, for the deaths of at least five non-Natives in Texas. His death sentence is commuted and he is imprisoned along with Satank (Kiowa) at Huntsville, Texas.

Bislahalani, or Barboncito (Diné, or Navajo), dies in the Chuska Mountains on the Navajo Reservation, in what is now Arizona.

Degataga, or Stand Watie (Cherokee), the last Confederate general to surrender in the Civil War, dies.

Hastin, or Manuelito (Diné, or Navajo), becomes chief of the Navajo police in addition to being principal leader of the Diné, or Navajo.

The guns you gave us we do not point at the whites. We do not shoot our white friends. We are true when we look you in the face. On our hands is no white man's blood.
Blackfoot (Mountain Crow)

1871

245

BUREAU TIME

1872–1994

THE EARTH IS OUR RESERVATION

> Several hundred years of history and a substantial body of law (5,000 statutes, 2,000 regulations, 389 treaties, 2,000 federal court decisions, and 500 opinions of the Attorney General) have defined the unique status of Indians and Indian tribes in this society.[14]
>
> *Jerome Buckanaga (Minnesota Chippewa)*

Take all the atrocities committed by people and governments from the beginning of time until 1900, and it will not equal the madness willfully committed against the People of the sovereign nations and tribes during two centuries (1700 to 1900).

What is comforting is that from East Coast to West Coast and from the Canadian border to the Mexican border, the People of the sovereign nations and tribes survived the holocaust instituted by so-called civilized people. What is comforting is that a majority of the People of the sovereign nations and tribes still maintain their dignity of spirit.

The year 1872 begins this final segment because of a signal event—the declaration by the Congress of the United States that it no longer would ratify treaties between the People of the sovereign nations and tribes and the U.S. government. It is understandable that the government should take this step, because the People of the sovereign nations and tribes, willingly or not, had ceded 99 percent of their ancient homelands to the U.S. government in treaties from 1778 through 1871. The government did not need to "play" at making treaties with the Indians anymore, and it said so.

Immediately before this declaration, the first Ghost Dance movement gained adherents among the Peo-

ple of the sovereign nations and tribes living in a limited area. Some years after the declaration, the second Ghost Dance movement gained so many adherents that the U.S. government and many Christian Americans became extremely frightened. The People learned their lesson. They learned that they did not have the rights guaranteed to Americans in the U.S. Constitution. They did not have the freedom to practice their religion. They did not have the freedom to do anything unless specifically directed by the Great White (racist) Father. And so the People of the sovereign nations and tribes played the role assigned to them by "civilized" Americans. The People of the sovereign nations and tribes dutifully followed directions. They went to school, went to work, went wherever they were told to go. But the People of the sovereign nations and tribes told their children stories.

They told the children to be silent and listen. They told the children about the smallpox-infected blankets. They told the children about the broken treaties. They told the children about the fraudulent land deals, the starvation, the wanton massacres of the People. They told the children about the rapes, the degradation, the enslavement of the People. And the children remembered and they told their children.

"Of the People am I born" was the phrase I was

taught as a child and committed to memory. As a child, I also was instructed carefully about my clan and lineage: "Of Oak Clan am I; of Meta, the mother of Agnes who was the mother of Ethel who is my mother am I descended." I was told many stories about the People, and I have told my own child the stories, and I have no doubt he will tell the stories to the next generation. It is the way of the People.

Listen, then, to the story about the People. Hear their voices. Experience their sorrow and anger. Delight in the strength and determination of the human spirit to go beyond survival. See how the People of the sovereign nations and tribes rise from the ashes of destruction to become internationally acclaimed writers, poets, cultural and political leaders, dancers, musicians, artists, doctors, scholars, attorneys, actors, inventors, engineers, scientists, caretakers, and caregivers. Understand that the People of the sovereign nations and tribes have been through the crucible of fire and have emerged to lead our non-Native relations on the long walk back to sanity.

	HISTORY/LAW/ POLITICS	LITERATURE/ART/ LEGENDS AND STORIES
1872	The Modoc under the leadership of Kintpuash, or Kint-poos, or Captain Jack (Modoc), engage in battle with United States soldiers in California and Oregon. The Yavapi of what is now Arizona and the Apache of what is know New Mexico and Arizona battle against General George Crook in the Tonto Basin campaign.	
1873	The International Indian Fair is held in Indian Territory, or what is now Oklahoma. As the first such event, it is a precursor of today's social powwows held throughout the United States.	
1874	The Chiricahua Apache Reservation is established at Apache Pass in what is now Arizona. Treaties with the Great Sioux Nation are ignored by non-Native immigrant miners when gold is discovered in the Black Hills of what is now South Dakota. The Comanche, Kiowa, and Cheyenne engage in what becomes known as the Red River War on the southern Plains.	
1875		

HEROES/LEADERS/ VICTIMS	ELDER WISDOM/PHILOSOPHY/ SONGS	
Wapameepto, or Big Jim (Absentee Shawnee), becomes principal leader of the people. Charlot (Kalispel), principal leader of the People, refuses to move from his ancestral homelands in the Bitterroot Mountains of what is now Montana and Idaho.		1872
Ahdoltay, or Big Tree (Kiowa), noted war leader of the People, is released from prison in Huntsville, Texas, along with Satank. Black Jim (Modoc), a loyal warrior in what is referred to as the Modoc War (1872–73), is executed. Kintpuash, or Kintpoos, or Captain Jack (Modoc), principal leader who leads the fight against the U.S. Army in the Modoc War, is captured on June 1 and executed by hanging on October 3. Alexander Lawrence Posey (Muscogee), noted author and journalist, is born on August 3.	 *Terri C. Hansen (Nebraska Winnebago)* COURTESY OF LEE FRANCIS III	1873
John M. Oskison (Cherokee), noted author, is born on September 1. Pi'ta Le-shar (Pawnee), principal leader, is murdered by a white settler. Zaepkoheeta, or Big Bow (Kiowa), a principal war leader of the Kiowa, is the last to surrender and take his followers onto the Kiowa-Comanche lands in Indian Territory, now known as Oklahoma. Cochise (Chiricahua Apache), noted principal leader of the Chiricahua Apache, dies on the reservation at Apache Pass. Taza (Chiricahua Apache), son of Cochise, succeeds his father as principal leader of the Chiricahua Apache.		1874
Mohe, or Cahoe, or William Cohe (Southern Cheyenne), surrenders at the Cheyenne Agency in Indian Territory, or what is now Oklahoma, and is convicted of killing whites. He is sent to prison at Fort Marion near St. Augustine, Florida.		1875

1876	The People of the Plains tribes are victorious in a battle with the U.S. Seventh Cavalry at the Little Bighorn in what is now Montana. The battle becomes known as "Custer's Last Stand." The People of the sovereign nations referred to as Pueblos, residing in what is now New Mexico and Arizona, are declared by the United States Supreme Court not to be considered wards of the United States government as are other Native nations and tribes across Turtle Island. The Chiricahua Apache Reservation at Apache Pass, in what is now Arizona, is terminated.	
1877	The Blackfoot, Blood, Piegan, and Sarcee sign "Treaty Number 7," in which they agree to cede fifty thousand acres to Canada. The land is now part of southern Alberta. The Mimbreño Apache forced to live on the San Carlos Reservation, on the Gila River in what is now Arizona, are led by Victorio (Mimbreño Apache) in an uprising against United States soldiers. Hundreds of Kiowa, Kiowa-Apache, Comanche, and Wichita people die from a measles and fever epidemic that rages across their lands in Texas. At what is referred to as the Battle of Wolf Mountain, Tashunka Witco, or Crazy Horse (Oglala Lakota), and his forces are defeated by more than four hundred United States soldiers under the command of General Nelson A. Miles. The Miniconjou Teton Sioux are defeated at the Battle of Lame Deer, in what is know Montana, by United States Army troops under the command of General A. Nelson Miles, in May.	

Looking Glass (Nez Percé)
COURTESY OF SMITHSONIAN

1878	Hampton Normal and Agricultural Institute, at Hampton, Virginia, enrolls the first group of Native American students who were prisoners of war at Fort Marion, Florida. The Bannock, Northern Paiute, and Cayuse of Idaho and Oregon go to war against United States soldiers in what is referred to as the Bannock War.	
1879	The Ute living in Colorado engage in battle with United States forces in what is known as the Ute War. People of the sovereign nations and tribes, in a landmark decision, are guaranteed the right to sue by the federal court at Omaha, Nebraska, as a result of the trial of Standing Bear (Ponca).	

HEROES/LEADERS/ VICTIMS	ELDER WISDOM/PHILOSOPHY/ SONGS	
American Horse, or Iron Shield (Oglala Lakota), son of Smoke, principal leader of the Oglala, is wounded fatally in the Battle of Slim Buttes, in what is now South Dakota, on September 9. After he dies, U.S. soldiers scalp him. Zitkala-Sa, or Gertrude Simmons Bonnin (Yankton Sioux), noted author, is born on February 22. Kootah-wecoot-soole-lehoola-shar, or Big Hawk Chief (Pawnee), becomes a scout for the United States Army and fights against the Sioux and their allies in Wyoming and Nebraska. Also in 1876, he runs the first recorded mile in less than four minutes. It will not be until 1954 that Roger Bannister runs the first "official" four-minute mile.		**1876**
José Berrendo becomes governor of the Acoma people. Blackfoot (Crow), principal leader, dies of pneumonia near what is now Meeteetse, Wyoming. On September 5, Tashunka Witco, or Crazy Horse (Oglala/Brulé Sioux), principal leader of the People, is bayoneted in the stomach by a soldier while in custody at Fort Robinson on the Red Cloud agency, in what is now northwestern Nebraska. Isah-pomu'xika, or Crowfoot (Blood/adopted Blackfoot), principal leader of the Blackfoot Confederacy, signs "Treaty Number 7" at Blackfoot Crossing, one hundred miles north of what is now Fort Macleod, in Canada. Hinmaton-yalatkit, or Chief Joseph (Nez Percé), surrenders to General Nelson A. Miles on October 5.	I am tired of fighting. Our chiefs are killed. Looking Glass is dead. Toohoolhoolzote is dead. All the old men are dead. . . . My people, some of them, have run away to the hills and have no blankets, no food; no one knows where they are—perhaps freezing to death. I want to have time to look for my children and see how many I can find. Maybe I shall find them among the dead. Hear me, my chiefs. I am tired. My heart is sick and sad. From where the sun now stands, I will fight no more forever. *Hinmaton-yalatkit, or Chief Joseph (Nez Percé)*	**1877**
Mohe, or Cahoe, or William Cohe (Southern Cheyenne), a prisoner of war at Fort Marion near St. Augustine, Florida, is sent to Hampton Institute, in Hampton, Virginia. Buffalo Horn (Bannock), principal leader, is killed during the first battle of the Bannock War at what is now Silver City, Idaho, in June.		**1878**
Will Rogers (Cherokee), noted social critic, movie star, and humorist, is born on November 4 in Cooweescoowee District of the Cherokee Nation, in Indian Territory. Knud Rasmussen (Inuit), author, is born on June 8. Mohe, or Cahoe, or William Cohe (Southern Cheyenne), is permitted to leave Hampton Institute and attend Carlisle Indian School in Pennsylvania, founded by Richard H. Pratt. At Carlisle, he continues to excel in art and becomes noted for his paintings of life among the Plains people.	My friend, you and I have the same skin, and what I tell you is for your good. I speak to you as a friend, and what I say to you now is so that you may save your women and children. It is of no use for you to try to fight the white people. I have been among them, and I know how many they are. They are like the grass. . . . If you try to fight them they will hunt you like a ghost. Wherever you go they will follow after you, and you will get no rest. *Little Warrior (Pawnee)*	**1879**

	HISTORY/LAW/ POLITICS	LITERATURE/ART/ LEGENDS AND STORIES
1880		*The Indian Question.* Unakuh (Cherokee).
1881	The Hunkpapa Lakota, led by Tatanka Iyotake, or Sitting Bull (Hunkpapa Lakota), surrender to authorities at Fort Buford, in what is now North Dakota. The Choctaw Nation is the first of the sovereign Native nations and tribes to be granted access to the United States Court of Claims.	*Legends, Traditions and Laws of the Iroquois or Six Nations and History of the Tuscarora Indians.* Elias Johnson (Tuscarora).
1882	The Indian Rights Association is founded in Philadelphia, Pennsylvania.	
1883	*Ex Parte Crow Dog*, the landmark case ruled on by the United States Supreme Court, determines that federal courts have no jurisdiction over crimes committed on reservation treaty lands by the People of the sovereign nations and tribes. As a result, Kange'su-nka, or Crow Dog (Brulé Sioux), the convicted murderer of Sinte Gleska, or Spotted Tail (Brulé Sioux), is pardoned and freed from prison.	*Yoo Pescha Pallaguianna.* Santiago Quintano (Pueblo). *Life Among the Piutes: Their Wrongs and Claims.* Sarah Winnemucca Hopkins (Paiute).
1884	The right of Eskimo Alaska Natives to Alaskan territorial lands is acknowledged by the United States Congress.	
1885	The last of the great buffalo herds are exterminated by non-Native buffalo-hunters. The Cree forces of Canada engage in battle in what becomes known as the Second Riel Rebellion, along the Saskatchewan River of the Canadian provinces of Alberta and Saskatchewan. The Major Crimes Act, passed by the United States Congress and signed into law by President Grover Cleveland, provides that a person of the sovereign nations and tribes committing a major crime against another Native, such as burglary or murder, is subject to the laws of the territory or state where the crime is committed.	*History of the Ojibways, Based on Traditions and Oral Statements.* William Whipple Warren (Ojibwa).

HEROES/LEADERS/ VICTIMS	ELDER WISDOM/PHILOSOPHY/ SONGS	
Martín del Vallo (Acoma) is selected as governor of Acoma Pueblo. Secettu Mahqua, or Black Beaver (Delaware), guide, Union scout, and distinguished speaker on behalf of the Delaware tribe, dies at Anadarko in what is now Oklahoma.	*Carlisle Indian School–1994* COURTESY OF MARY A. FRANCIS	**1880**
Arthur C. Parker (Seneca), author, is born on April 5. Kange'su-nka, or Crow Dog (Brulé Sioux), shoots and kills Sinte Gleska, or Spotted Tail (Brulé Sioux). Ma-tih-eh-loge-go, or Hollow Horn Bear (Brulé Sioux), arrests Kange'su-nka, or Crow Dog (Brulé Sioux), for the murder of Sinte Gleska, or Spotted Tail (Brulé Sioux.)		**1881**
	The Great Spirit made us all–he made my skin red, and yours white; he placed us on this earth, and intended that we should live differently from each other. *Sharitarish (Pawnee)*	**1882**
Paulette Fairbanks Molin (White Earth Chippewa) COURTESY OF LEE FRANCIS III		**1883**
Martín del Vallo (Acoma) is reselected as governor of Acoma Pueblo.		**1884**
Martín del Vallo (Acoma) is reselected as governor of Acoma Pueblo. Mistahimuskwa, or Big Bear (Cree), principal leader of the Plains Cree, joins the métis in their battle against the Canadian government for lands along the North and South Saskatchewan Rivers. Mistahimuskwa, with his warriors, surrenders on July 2 at Fort Carlton.	God said he was the father and earth was the mother of mankind; that nature was the law; that the animals, and fish, and plants obeyed nature, and that man only was sinful. You ask me to plow the ground! Shall I take a knife and tear my mother's bosom? Then when I die she will not take me to her bosom to rest. You ask me to dig for stone! Shall I dig under her skin for her bones? Then when I die I cannot enter her body to be born again. You ask me to cut grass and make hay and sell it, and be rich like white men! But how dare I cut off my mother's hair? *Smohalla (Wanapun)*	**1885**

	HISTORY/LAW/ POLITICS	LITERATURE/ART/ LEGENDS AND STORIES
1886	The People of the sovereign nations and tribes attending missionary and government schools are forbidden to speak in their ancient languages. The U.S. Department of the Interior's commissioner of Indian affairs orders all Indian agents to enforce the order requiring that only English is permitted to be spoken. The Mohawk living on what is now the Caughnawaga Reserve in Québec, Canada, are employed as high-steel construction workers on a bridge crossing the Saint Lawrence River.	 *Meta Atsye (Laguna Pueblo)* COURTESY OF LEE FRANCIS III
1887	The General Allotment Act, often referred to as the Dawes Severalty Act, is passed by the United States Congress. This legislation enables the non-Native government of the United States of America to divide Native People's lands into 160-acre parcels which are assigned to individual members of the sovereign nations and tribes. Many of the People of Turtle Island oppose the abolition of tribal landholding. Ute warriors engage in battle to leave their reservation, in Colorado. In their unsuccessful attempt, several non-Natives are killed.	*History of the Ottawa and Chippewa Indians of Michigan; a Grammar of Theirr [sic] Language and Personal and Family History of the Author.* Mackawdebenessy, or Andrew J. Blackbird (Odawa, or Ottawa). *Story of Polly's Life.* Bertha Nason (Chippewa).
1888	The name of the newspaper at Carlisle Industrial Indian School at Carlisle, Pennsylvania, originally *Eadle Keatoah Toh*, or *Big Morning Star*, is changed to the *Red Man*, which reflected nineteenth-century views concerning Native American education.	*A Fairy Tale.* Clyde Bow (Sioux).
1889	The U.S. government opens "unassigned lands" in Oklahoma Territory (formed from western Indian Territory) to white settlers. It is the first of five land runs eventually held in what is now Oklahoma, as the United States opens more and more of the Native People's lands to whites.	

HEROES/LEADERS/ VICTIMS	ELDER WISDOM/PHILOSOPHY/ SONGS	
Solomon Bibo (Acoma) is selected as governor of Acoma Pueblo. "Aunt Jane" (Odawa, or Ottawa), the honored medicine woman who also was known as Jane King, dies at age 120 on the Odawa, or Ottawa, Reservation east of what is now Miami, Oklahoma. James Francis (Jim) Thorpe (Sac and Fox/Potawatomi), famous athlete, is born near what is now Prague, Oklahoma.	. . . I have to compare my generation with the old generation. We are not as good as they were—we are not as healthy as they were. *Flaming Arrow, or James Paytiamo (Acoma)*	**1886**
Maria Montoya Martinez (San Ildefonso), famous potter, is born at San Ildefonso Pueblo in what is now New Mexico.		**1887**
Mistahimuskwa, or Big Bear (Cree), principal leader of the Plains Cree, dies shortly after his release from imprisonment by the government of Canada. Tuup-weets, or Colorow, or Colorado (Jicarilla Apache/adopted Mouache Ute), dies on the Southern Ute Reservation near Ignacio, Colorado.		**1888**
Wovoka, or Jack Wilson (Northern Paiute), holy man and prophet, has a vision that signals the start of the second Ghost Dance movement which spreads among the People. Watomika, or James Bouchard (Delaware), the first Native to become a Roman Catholic priest, dies.	We shall live again We shall live again. *Ghost Dance song (Comanche)*	**1889**

| 1890 | The population of the People of the sovereign Native nations and tribes reaches its lowest point to date, fewer than 250,000.

The Ghost Dance is banned in the Sioux reservations at Pine Ridge and Rosebud, in South Dakota, by United States military officials, in November.

The Chief Big Foot Massacre at Wounded Knee Creek, in South Dakota, occurs on December 29 shortly after eight o'clock in the morning. In less than ten minutes, more than three hundred old men, women, and children are massacred by U.S. Army troops of the Seventh Cavalry, under the command of Colonel George Alexander Forsyth. | *A Trip to the Moon.* Nellie Robertson (Sioux). |

Nawat, or Left Hand (Arapaho)
COURTESY OF SMITHSONIAN

| 1891 | Lands allotted to the People of the sovereign Native nations and tribes by the United States are permitted to be leased by non-Native settlers under the amendment to the Dawes Severalty Act, or General Allotment Act, of 1887. | |

| 1893 | The Dawes Commission is created by the United States Congress.

Under the Indian Appropriations Act, passed by the United States Congress, responsibility for Indian education on reservations is transferred to superintendents of schools. The act also eliminates the positions of Indian agents. | |

| 1894 | | *Big Eagle's Story of the Sioux Outbreaks of 1862.* Wamditonka, or Jerome Big Eagle (Mdewakanton Sioux). |

| 1895 | | *The White Wampum.* Tehakionwake, or Emily Pauline Johnson (Mohawk). |

HEROES/LEADERS/ VICTIMS	ELDER WISDOM/PHILOSOPHY/ SONGS	
Nawat, or Left Hand (Southern Arapaho), principal leader of the Southern Arapaho, visits Washington, D.C., where he signs an "agreement" with the U.S. government for "allotment lands" in Indian Territory, or what is now Oklahoma. Buffalo Child Long Lance, or Sylvester Long (Lumbee), author, is born on December 1. Ted Couro (Diegueño), author, is born on April 2. Big Foot, or Si Tanka, or Spotted Elk (Miniconjou Sioux), principal leader, dies at Chankpe Opi Wakpala, or Wounded Knee Creek. The photograph of his frozen, contorted body lying in the snow is a horrifying image of the massacre, similar to photographs of the bodies in Nazi Germany's death camps for Jews. Isah-pomu'xika, or Crowfoot (Blood/adopted Blackfoot), principal leader of the Blackfoot Confederacy, dies.	Fully three miles from the scene of the massacre we found the body of a woman completely covered with a blanket of snow, and from this point on we found them scattered along as they had been relentlessly hunted down and slaughtered while fleeing for their lives. Some of our people discovered relatives or friends among the dead, and there was much wailing and mourning. When we reached the spot where the Indian camp had stood, among the fragments of burned tents and other belongings we saw the frozen bodies lying close together or piled one upon another. *Ohiyesa, or Charles A. Eastman, M.D. (Sioux)* *At the Chief Big Foot Massacre at Wounded Knee Creek*	**1890**
	Although I have adapted to my environment, like immigrants have done, I am still a native of the wilderness. *Red Fox (Sioux)*	**1891**
James LaPointe (Pine Ridge Sioux), author, is born on April 6.		**1893**
Te Ata (Chickasaw), author, is born on December 4. Hastin, or Manuelito (Diné, or Navajo), dies.		**1894**
John C. Adams (Stockbridge-Munsee/white), a delegate and lobbyist on behalf of the Stockbridge-Munsee's efforts to gain United States citizenship and end the protected status of their tribe, dies. Leftwich Taliaferro (Chickasaw), author, is born on March 2. James McCarthy (Tohono O'odham, or Papago), author, is born on October 16. John Joseph Mathews (Osage), author, is born on November 16.		**1895**

	HISTORY/LAW/ POLITICS	LITERATURE/ART/ LEGENDS AND STORIES
1896	The People of the sovereign Native Alaska nations residing in Alaska and the Yukon Territory of Canada are overwhelmed by the arrival of non-Natives prospecting for gold in what is known as the Klondike gold rush of 1896–1898.	
1897		*Complete Both Early and Late History of the Ottawa and Chippewa Indians.* Mackawdebenessy, or Andrew J. Blackbird (Odawa, or Ottawa).
1898	Governments of the People of the sovereign Native nations and tribes in what is now Oklahoma are dissolved with the passage of the Curtis Act by the United States Congress. The act requires the sovereign nations that were abolished to submit to having their lands allotted.	
1899		*An Episode of the Spring Roundup '77, Anoska Nimiwina,* and *In the Name of His Ancestor.* William Jones (Sac and Fox). *A Returned Prodigal* and *Aunt Mary's Christmas Dinner.* Ora V. Eddelman Reed (Cherokee). *O-gî-mäw-kwè Mit-i-gwä-kî (Queen of the Woods).* Simon Pokagon (Potawatomi).

HEROES/LEADERS/ VICTIMS	ELDER WISDOM/PHILOSOPHY/ SONGS	
Agnes Atsye Gunn (Laguna Pueblo/Scottish), grandmother of the author, is born on March 15. William Oquillak (Inuit), author, is born on March 27. Rosalio Moises (Yaqui), author, is born on September 4. Florence E. Davidson (Haida), author, is born on September 15. George Barker (Salteaux), author, is born on November 20. Hot'tsa-sodono, or Deerfoot, or Louis Bennett (Seneca), famous track star, dies on the Cattaraugus Reservation near Buffalo, New York.		**1896**
Chitto Harjo, or Wilson Jones (Muscogee), establishes the Snake "government" as an alternative to the Muscogee, or Creek, Nation in Indian Territory, or what is now Oklahoma.	*Na-tu-ka, or Two Medicine (Piegan, or Blackfoot) and her son, Nat-tai-ya, or Blessed (Piegan, or Blackfoot/White)* COURTESY OF SMITHSONIAN	**1897**
Edwin Simon (Koyukon), author, is born on October 1. W. S. Folson-Dickerson (Choctaw), author, is born on December 16. Unaduti, or Dennis Wolf Bushyhead (Cherokee/white), former treasurer and principal chief of the Cherokee Nation in what is now Oklahoma, dies.		**1898**
Tomochichi (Muscogee) is honored posthumously with a monument erected by the Colonial Dames of America in Savannah, Georgia. Gladys Tantaquidgeon (Mohegan), author, is born on June 15. Dan George (Coast Salish), principal leader and noted actor, is born on June 24. Lynn Riggs (Cherokee), poet and playwright, is born on August 31 at Lone Elm, Cooweescoowee District, Cherokee Nation, Indian Territory (now Rogers County, Oklahoma). Elsie Allen (Pomo), author, is born on September 22. James Redsky (Ojibwa), author, is born on October 31.		**1899**

PERSPECTIVE
1900–1940

The total population of the People of the sovereign nations and tribes reached its lowest point in 1900. From the millions who inhabited Turtle Island in 1500, the number of People of the sovereign nations and tribes had declined to a recorded 237,196 in 1900. It was forty years before the population grew to 343,252. In that same period, the population of the United States was 62.9 million in 1900 and 131.7 million by 1940.

The remaining great leaders among the People of the sovereign nations and tribes who had not been killed in the pogroms of the previous forty years died of old age and broken hearts. At the same time, a new cadre of future leaders among the People was being born. With each birth, the embers of hope became stronger among the People. New warriors joined the military and fought in World War I, serving the government whose soldiers had raped and wantonly murdered their grandparents.

They returned from battle to the desolation, hopelessness, and poverty of the reservations. Many of the new warriors moved to cities in the vain hope that they would be accepted. They discovered that even black African-Americans were granted higher status by the white majority. And so, many of the People drank themselves into oblivion. Those who remained on the reservations struggled to feed themselves and their families. Many were filled with despair and, like their Native relations in the cities, drank themselves into oblivion. The few in the cities and on the reservations who were able to function took on leadership responsibilities, and the People of the sovereign nations and tribes survived. The children were in their late teens and early twenties, and they joined the military to fight in World War II.

	HISTORY/LAW/ POLITICS	LITERATURE/ART/ LEGENDS AND STORIES

1900	The population of the People of the sovereign Native nations and tribes decreases from 248,000, in 1890, to 237,000.	*The Usurper of the Range* and *The Lone Star Ranger*. William Jones (Sac and Fox).
		  Only an Indian Girl and *Lucy and I as Missionaries*. Ora V. Eddelman Reed (Cherokee).
		  The Middle Five: Indian School Boys of the Omaha Tribe. Francis La Flesche (Omaha).

1901	Chitto Harjo, or Wilson Jones (Muscogee), leads the Crazy Snake uprising against white settlers and against Native People who had accepted allotted land in Indian Territory under the Dawes Severalty Act of 1887.	*The Indian and the Devil*. Charles Gibson (Muscogee). *The Story of a Vision*. Francis La Flesche (Omaha). *When the Grass Grew Long*. John Milton Oskison (Cherokee). *Old Indian Legends, Retold by Zitkala-Sa*. Zitkala-Sa, or Gertrude Simmons Bonnin (Sioux).
1902	Eskimo Alaska Native people living on Southampton Island, in Hudson Bay, are decimated by typhus.	*Indian Boyhood*. Ohiyesa, or Charles A. Eastman, M.D. (Lakota). *The Colored Man's Story of Providence and David and Jonathan*. Charles Gibson (Muscogee).
1903		*Canadian Born*. Tehakionwake, or Emily Pauline Johnson (Mohawk).
1904		*Red Hunters and the Animal People*. Ohiyesa, or Charles A. Eastman, M.D. (Lakota). *Iroquoian Cosmology*. John H. B. Hewitt (Tuscarora).

HEROES/LEADERS/VICTIMS	ELDER WISDOM/PHILOSOPHY/SONGS	
Maggie Culver Fry (Cherokee), author and, later, poet laureate of Oklahoma, is born on July 28. Wapameepto, or Big Jim (Absentee Shawnee), principal leader of the People, dies of smallpox after moving from the Sabine Reservation, in Texas, to Mexico. Zaepkoheeta, or Big Bow (Kiowa), militant war leader who became a scout for the U.S. Army, dies. Charlot (Kalispel), principal leader who, with his followers, had been forced to move onto a reservation by U.S. Army troops, dies. Wa-ana-tan, or Martin Charger (Sans Arc Sioux/white), peace advocate, dies.	Since 1492, the ways that American Indians have organized have undergone considerable change, to be sure. Yet the term tribe is still used to refer to American Indian groups, typically by both Indians and non-Indians. . . . Indian peoples, it seems to me, are free to term themselves as they desire. *Russell Thornton (Cherokee)*	**1900**
Federal marshals and United States cavalry arrest Chitto Harjo, or Wilson Jones (Muscogee), after the Snake, or Crazy Snake uprising. He is brought to trial in February and found guilty, but permitted to return to his home at Hickory Hills in what is now Oklahoma.	Everyone laughed at the impossibility of it, but also the truth. Because who would believe the fantastic and terrible story of all our survival, those who were never meant to survive. *Joy Harjo (Muscogee, or Creek)*	**1901**
Todd Downing (Choctaw), author, is born on March 29.		**1902**
		1903
Hinmaton-yalatkit, or Chief Joseph (Nez Percé), principal chief of the Nez Percé, dies on the Colville Reservation at Nespelem, Washington. D'Arcy McNickle (Cree métis/adopted Salish-Kootenai), noted author, is born on January 18. Ticasuk, or Emily Ivanoff Brown (Inuit), noted author, is born on February 21. Sahgandeoh, or Lucille Winnie (Seneca/Cayuga), author, is born on March 27. Iron Eyes Cody (Cherokee), noted actor and author, is born on April 3. Littlecoon, or Louis Oliver (Yuchi/Muscogee), noted author, is born on April 9.	 *Joy Harjo (Muscogee, or Creek)* COURTESY OF PAUL ABDOO	**1904**

265

	HISTORY/LAW/ POLITICS	LITERATURE/ART/ LEGENDS AND STORIES
1905	Access to fishing sites is reserved under treaty rights for the People of the sovereign Native nations and tribes in a decision of the United States Supreme Court, in *United States v. Winans*.	
1906	Taos Pueblo people are enraged by the United States government's seizure of more than forty thousand acres of their sacred land, known as Blue Lake Wilderness Area, in what is now New Mexico. It will take more than sixty years of legal maneuvering and lobbying the United States Congress before the land will be returned, in 1970. The Burk Act, which amends the Dawes Severalty Act, or General Allotment Act, of 1887, is passed by the United States Congress. Under the act, the secretary of the interior is granted the authority to eliminate restrictions on the sale of allotted lands.	*Geronimo: His Own Story*. S. M. Barrett, editor. Goyathlay, or One Who Yawns, or Geronimo (Apache). *The Grave of Goingsnake*. Cha-lahgee (Cherokee). *We Are All Fullbloods*. Charles Gibson (Muscogee).
1907	On November 16, Oklahoma Territory and Indian Territory enter the Union as the state of Oklahoma, superseding the tribal governments.	*Old Indian Days*. Ohiyesa, or Charles A. Eastman, M.D. (Lakota). *A Stolen Girl*. Clara Bussell (Klamath). *The Problem of Old Harjo and Making an Individual of the Indian*. John M. Oskison (Cherokee). *Tah-se-tih's Sacrifice*. Bertrand Walker (Wyandot).
1908	The Gros Ventre and Assiniboin seek help from the United States Department of Justice, which brings a suit against Henry Winters that is heard by the United States Supreme Court. In a landmark eight-to-one decision, the Court rules that the People of the sovereign nations and tribes (specifically the Gros Ventre and Assiniboin) had "a prior and paramount right" to water as needed. The Court proclaimed that the water rights which were not specifically ceded in treaties with the Unites States belonged to the People of the sovereign nations and tribes. This decision is referred to now as the "Winters doctrine."	
1909	Two-and-a-half million acres of timbered land on trust lands of the sovereign Native nations and tribes all across Turtle Island is transferred to the United States under executive orders issued by United States President Theodore Roosevelt, several days before he leaves office.	
1910	The Sun dance, a spiritual ceremony practiced among sovereign Native nations and tribes of the Plains, is prohibited by the United States government because it is viewed as self-torture.	*The Flying Canoe Legend*. Carlysle Greenbrier (Menominee). *The Poems of Alexander Lawrence Posey*. Alexander Lawrence Posey (Muscogee, or Creek).

HEROES/LEADERS/ VICTIMS	ELDER WISDOM/PHILOSOPHY/ SONGS	
Eleanor Brass (Cree/Salteaux), author, is born on May 1. Madeline Solomon (Koyukon), author, is born on December 22.		1905
Anne Anderson (métis Cree/Iroquois), author, is born on February 3. Rupert Costo (Cahuilla), author, is born on May 10. Anahareo, or Gertrude Bernard Mottke (Iroquois/Cree), author, is born on June 18.	When Usen created the Apaches He also gave them their homes in the west. He gave them such grain, fruits, and game as they needed to eat. . . . He gave them a pleasant climate and all they needed for clothing and shelter was at hand. *Goyathlay, or Geronimo (Chiricahua Apache)*	1906
Rosebud Yellow Robe (Rosebud Sioux), author, is born on February 26.		1907
Jeannette Henry (Cherokee), author, is born on June 27. James Shoulderblade (Northern Cheyenne), author, is born on November 10. Wasechun-tashunka, or American Horse (Oglala Lakota), noted warrior, treaty negotiator, and actor who toured with "Buffalo Bill" Cody's Wild West Show, dies.		1908
Verna Patronella Johnston (Ojibwa), author, is born on February 15.		1909
	Goyathlay, or Geronimo (Chiracahua Apache) and wife Marionetta (Chiracahua Apache) COURTESY OF SMITHSONIAN	
Aren Akweks, or Ray Fadden (Mohawk), author, is born on August 23.		1910

	HISTORY/LAW/ POLITICS	LITERATURE/ART/ LEGENDS AND STORIES
1911	The Society of American Indians is founded. It strongly advocates the conferring of U.S. citizenship on the People of the sovereign nations and tribes across Turtle Island.	*The Soul of the Indian: An Interpretation.* Ohiyesa, or Charles A. Eastman, M.D. (Lakota). *Legends of Vancouver.* Tehakionwake, or Emily Pauline Johnson (Mohawk). *The Story of Deerskin.* Emma LaVatta (Bannock). *The Morning and Evening Star.* Moses Friday (Arapaho). *Sheldrake Duck.* John McInnis (Washo).
1912	The Four Mothers Society is founded by members of the Cherokee, Muscogee, or Creek, Choctaw, and Chickasaw tribes who are opposed to the allotment of lands of the People to individuals. The Society of American Indians holds its second conference, in Columbus, Ohio. The *Quarterly Journal of the Society of American Indians* begins publication. The journal stresses the development of a "pan-Indian spirit" as well as American patriotism.	
1913	Reversing its decision of 1876, the United States Supreme Court declares in the Sandoval case that "Pueblo Indians" are indeed wards of the U.S. government, and are not permitted to dispose of any land or other assets without permission of the federal government. The International Olympic Committee (IOC) takes back the two gold medals won by Jim Thorpe and strikes his name from the record books of Olympic medalists for having accepted expense money when he played in minorleague baseball in 1909 and 1910. It will be 1973 before his amateur status will be restored by the Amateur Athletic Union (AAU), and 1982 before the IOC acknowledges his amateur status.	*Indian Child Life.* Ohiyesa, or Charles A. Eastman, M.D. (Lakota). *The Moccasin Maker and The Shagganappi.* Tehakionwake, or Emily Pauline Johnson (Mohawk).
1914	The Muscogee, or Creek, Indian Memorial Association is founded at Okmulgee, Oklahoma.	*Flint and Feather.* Tehakionwake, or Emily Pauline Johnson (Mohawk).
1915	The Bureau of Indian Affairs is authorized to purchase land for landless People of the sovereign Native nations and tribes in California, in an appropriations act passed by the United States Congress.	*The Indian To-day: The Past and Future of the First Americans.* Ohiyesa, or Charles A. Eastman, M.D. (Lakota).

HEROES/LEADERS/ VICTIMS	ELDER WISDOM/PHILOSOPHY/ SONGS	
Howard Rock (Inuit), author, is born on August 10. Charles R. Penoi (Cherokee/Laguna), author, is born on William Harjo, or Thomas E. Moore (Muscogee), author, is born on October 1. Peter Kalifornsky (Denaina), author, is born on October 12. Will Rogers Jr. (Cherokee), publisher, journalist, and son of "cowboy philosopher" Will Rogers, is born on October 20. Quanah, or Quanah Parker (Kwahadie Comanche/ white), principal leader of the Comanche, dies.		**1911**
James Francis (Jim) Thorpe (Sac and Fox/Potawatomi) wins a gold medal for the decathlon and another for the pentathlon at the Olympic Games, held in Sweden. Adelphina Logan (Onondaga), author, is born on June 9. Twylah Hurd Nitsch (Seneca), author, is born on December 5. Chitto Harjo, or Wilson Jones (Muscogee), principal leader of the Snake Muscogee, dies while hiding from lawmen.	Thanks, King. *Jim Thorpe (Sac and Fox/Potawatomi)* *Response to congratulations by the king of Sweden*	**1912**
Natachee Scott Momaday (Eastern Cherokee), author, is born on February 13. Hector Coutu (métis), author, is born on August 27. David Illasenor (Otomi), author, is born on September 25. James Sewid (Kwakiutl), author, is born on December 31.	 *Robert M. Owens (Lakota)* COURTESY OF ROBERT M. OWENS	**1913**
Robert E. Lewis (Zuñi/Cherokee), future governor of the Zuñi, is born on August 24. Tom Whitecloud (Chippewa), author, is born on October 8.		**1914**
Jack Frederick Kilpatrick (Cherokee), author and composer, is born on September 23 in Oklahoma. Lela Kiana Oman (Yupiat), author, is born on December 15.		**1915**

	HISTORY/LAW/ POLITICS	LITERATURE/ART/ LEGENDS AND STORIES
1916	*Wassaja: Freedom's Signal for the Indians*, a monthly publication edited by Wassaja, or Carlos Montezuma, M.D. (Yavapai), is first published in April. It will continue to be published until November 1922.	*From the Deep Woods to Civilization: Chapters in the Autobiography of an Indian.* Ohiyesa, or Charles A. Eastman, M.D. (Lakota). *Indian Story.* Martha Smith (Oneida).
1917	Births among the People of the sovereign Native nations and tribes across Turtle Island exceed deaths for the first time since 1867. Nearly twelve thousand People of the sovereign nations and tribes across Turtle Island join the military forces of the United States and fight in Europe during World War I.	*The Century Clock: Story of a 49'er.* Charles E. Waterman (Seneca).
1918	The Native American Church is incorporated in Oklahoma by members of the Apache, Cheyenne, Comanche, Kiowa, Otoe, and Ponca Nations. "Code talkers" of the Choctaw Nation play a pivotal role in helping American forces win several key battles in the Meuse-Argonne Campaign in France, during World War I.	*Indian Heroes and Great Chieftains.* Ohiyesa, or Charles A. Eastman, M.D. (Lakota).
1919		*Rogersisms: The Cowboy Philosopher on the Peace Conference* and *Rogersisms: The Cowboy Philosopher on Prohibition.* Will Rogers (Cherokee).
1920		*The Autobiography of a Winnebago.* Paul Radin, editor. Crashing Thunder, or Big Winnebago, or Sam Blowsnake (Winnebago).
1921	Education, medical, and social services for the People of the sovereign Native nations and tribes become the responsibility of the United States Department of the Interior under the Snyder Act, which was passed by the United States Congress.	*An Indian Girl's Story.* Waheenee, or Buffalo Bird Woman (Hidatsa). *American Indian Stories.* Zitkala-Sa, or Gertrude Simmons Bonnin (Sioux).

HEROES/LEADERS/VICTIMS	ELDER WISDOM/PHILOSOPHY/SONGS	
Edward P. Dozier (Santa Clara), author, is born on April 23. He will become the first of the Santa Clara people to receive a Ph.D. degree. Richard M. Courchene (Assiniboin), author, is born on May 23. Tdu-u-eh-t'sah, or Ethel Gunn Haynes Gottlieb Francis (Laguna/Scottish/Chippewa), philosopher, is born on July 26.		**1916**
Anna Gritts Kilpatrick (Cherokee), author, is born on March 7. Glenn J. Twist (Cherokee/Creek), storyteller and author, is born on July 20. Vynola Beaver Newkumet (Caddo), author, is born on September 15.	I am a storyteller. . . . I am the last generation of my family to be born in the Boston Mountains of Arkansas and Oklahoma, as well as on a Cherokee allotment. If I don't preserve the stories I've heard they will be lost forever. *Glenn J. Twist, Cherokee/Creek elder*	**1917**
Mary Tall Mountain (Koyukon), poet and author, is born on June 19. Vi Hilbert (Upper Skagit), author, is born on July 24. Kenneth Jacob Jump (Osage), author, is born on July 12. Pablita Velarde (Santa Clara), artist and potter, is born on September 19. George Bent (Southern Cheyenne/white) dies. His book *Forty Years with the Cheyennes* is an important piece of writing about the late 1800s and early 1900s.		**1918**
Frederick J. Dockstader (Oneida), author, is born on February 3. Daphne Odjig Beavon (Odawa/Potawatomi), author, is born on September 11.		**1919**
Bill Reid (Haida), author, is born on January 12. Katherine Siva Saubel (Cahuilla), author, is born on March 7.	*Glenn J. Twist (Cherokee/Creek, or Muscogee)* COURTESY OF GLENN J. TWIST	**1920**
Raven Hail (Cherokee), author, is born on January 27. Norman Russell (Cherokee), author, is born on November 28.		**1921**

	HISTORY/LAW/ POLITICS	LITERATURE/ART/ LEGENDS AND STORIES
1922	The All Indian Pueblo Council (AIPC) unites the Pueblo people of New Mexico and Arizona in a common cause against proposed legislation known as the Bursum Bill that would grant rights to non-Native squatters on land belonging to the People. The proposed legislation is defeated. The Inter-Tribal Indian Ceremonial Association is founded at Church Rock, New Mexico.	*Indian Christmas Story.* Jennie Pratt (Pawnee).
1923	The Committee of One Hundred is formed by the United States Department of Interior to review federal policy concerning People of the sovereign Native nations and tribes.	*Seneca Myths and Folktales.* Arthur C. Parker (Seneca).
1924	An Act of Congress imposes United States citizenship on the People of the sovereign nations and tribes, even though a large number do not want to be citizens. Although designated as citizens, most of the People of the sovereign nations and tribes are not permitted to vote for federal officeholders (U.S. Senate and House of Representatives) or state officers.	*The Illiterate Digest.* Will Rogers (Cherokee). *The Magic Mirror.* Eunah J. Tiger (Muscogee).
1925	The Indian Defense League is organized. Its efforts reestablish the right of the People of the sovereign Native nations and tribes to cross the border between the United States and Canada, as given under the Jay Treaty of 1794.	*Wild Harvest: A Novel of the Transition Days in Oklahoma.* John Milton Oskison (Cherokee).
1926		*Black Jack Davy.* John Milton Oskison (Cherokee). *Letters of a Self-Made Diplomat to His President.* Will Rogers (Cherokee).

HEROES/LEADERS/VICTIMS	ELDER WISDOM/PHILOSOPHY/SONGS	
Allen P. Slickpoo (Nez Percé), author, is born on May 5. Kay C. Bennett (Diné, or Navajo), author, is born on July 15. Ugidali, or Lee Piper (Cherokee), author, is born on October 4. Adolph L. Dial (Lumbee), author, is born on December 12.		1922
Helen Attaquin (Wampanoag), author, is born on February 6. Popovi Da (San Ildefonso), noted potter and artist, is born on April 10. Grey Eagle, or Kenneth Jackson, Ph.D. (Anishinabe/Ojibwa), noted author and poet, is born on April 27. Joe S. Sando (Jemez), noted author, is born on August 1. Ira Hamilton Hayes (Pima) is born. He will serve in the United States Marine Corps and be one of the Marines to raise the United States flag on Iwo Jima in World War II.		1923
Mohe, or Cahoe, or William Cohe (Southern Cheyenne), warrior and noted artist, dies.		1924
		1925
Eleanor Sioui (Huron), author, is born on May 20. Dallas Chief Eagle (Sioux), author, is born on August 14.		
Ralph Salisbury (Cherokee), noted author and university professor, is born on January 24. Robert Burnett (Rosebud Sioux), author, is born on January 26. Louise Abeita (Isleta/Laguna), author, is born on September 9. Wilfrid Pelletier (Odawa), author, is born on October 16. Dillon Platero (Diné, or Navajo), author and educator, is born on November 17.		1926

Agnes Gunn Haynes (Laguna Pueblo/Scot) and husband Robert B. Haynes (Chippewa/Métis)
COURTESY OF LEE FRANCIS

273

	HISTORY/LAW/ POLITICS	LITERATURE/ART/ LEGENDS AND STORIES
1927		*Cogewea, the Half-Blood: A Depiction of the Great Montana Cattle Range,* by Hum-ishu-ma, "Mourning Dove," *Given through Sho-pow-tan.* Humishuma, or Mourning Dove, or Cristal McLeod Galler (Okanogan). *There's Not a Bathing Suit in Russia and Other Bare Facts.* Will Rogers (Cherokee).
1928	*The Merriam Report* is released, unequivocally documenting abuses in the Bureau of Indian Affairs and citing the General Allotment Act as the major cause of starvation and poverty among the People of the sovereign Native nations and tribes.	
1929	 <div align="center">*W. S. (Bill) Penn (Nez Percé)* COURTESY OF JENNIFER PENN</div>	*A Texas Titan: The Story of Sam Houston.* John Milton Oskison (Cherokee). *Esther and Me, or "Just Relax."* Will Rogers (Cherokee).
1930	The United States Senate Investigating Committee on Indian Affairs conducts an investigation of federal policy and practices applied to the People of the sovereign Navajo Nation. The investigation reveals the practice of BIA school officials kidnapping Navajo children to "educate" them.	

274

HEROES/LEADERS/ VICTIMS	ELDER WISDOM/PHILOSOPHY/ SONGS	
George Manuel (Shuswap), author, is born on February 17. Nora Marks Dauenhauer (Tlingit), author, is born on May 8. Gogisgi, or Carroll Arnett (Cherokee), poet, author, and university faculty member, is born on November 9.		**1927**
Howard Adams (métis/Cree), author, is born on September 8. John C. Rouillard (Santee Sioux), noted educator and author, is born on December 31.	Never again would I want to hear the story of Gibbon's men sneaking up on the Nez Percé encampment and slaughtering women and babies in a surprise dawn raid. I lost twenty pounds of sleepless fat over the next few months, realizing that I was worse than Gibbon's Bannock scouts. *Bill Penn (Nez Percé)*	**1928**
Russell M. Peters (Wampanoag), author, is born on January 5. Robert Chute (Skoki Abenaki), author, is born on February 13. D. Bruce Sealey (métis/Cree), author, is born on May 11. Basil H. Johnston (Cape Croker Ojibwa), author, is born on July 13. Maurice Kenny (Mohawk), noted poet, author, and editor of Contact II, is born on August 16. Sun Bear, or Vincent LaDuke (Chippewa), author, is born on August 31 in Minnesota. Orville Keon (Iroquois), author, is born on November 20. Ahdoltay, or Big Tree (Kiowa), the youngest war leader among the Kiowa, who had married Omboke (Kiowa), dies on Kiowa land in Oklahoma. Charles Curtis (Kansa) is elected vice president of the United States as the running mate of President Herbert Hoover.		**1929**
Oren Lyons (Onondaga), noted author, is born March 5. Nompehwathe, or Carter Revard (Osage), noted poet, author, and university professor, is born on March 25. Ted C. Williams (Tuscarora), noted author, is born on April 6. Charles G. Ballard (Quapaw/Cherokee), noted author, is born on June 4. Alice French (Inuit), author, is born on June 29. Elizabeth Cook-Lynn (Crow Creek Sioux), noted author, is born on November 17. Charles Brashear (Cherokee), noted author, poet, and university professor, is born on December 11.		**1930**

	HISTORY/LAW/ POLITICS	LITERATURE/ART/ LEGENDS AND STORIES
1931		*My Indian Boyhood, by Chief Luther Standing Bear, Who Was the Boy Ota K'te (Plenty Kill).* Ota K'te, or Luther Standing Bear (Sioux). *Wooden Leg, a Warrior Who Fought Custer.* Wooden Leg (Cheyenne).
1932	The Leavitt Act, passed by the United States Congress, releases liens totaling more than $5 million against lands of the People of the sovereign Native nations and tribes.	*Black Elk Speaks: Being the Life Story of a Holy Man of the Oglala Sioux.* John G. Neihardt, editor. Hehaka Sapa, or Black Elk (Oglala Lakota). *The Sacred Pipe: Black Elk's Account of the Seven Rites of the Oglala Sioux.* Joseph Epes Brown, editor. Hehaka Sapa, or Black Elk (Oglala Lakota). *Flaming Arrow's People, by an Acoma Indian.* Flaming Arrow, or James Paytiamo (Acoma). *Red Mother.* Pretty-Shield Medicine Woman (Crow).
1933	 *Wovoka, or The Cutter, or Jack Wilson (Northern Paiute) [seated]* COURTESY OF SMITHSONIAN	*Coyote Stories.* Humishuma, or Mourning Dove, or Cristal McLeod Galler (Okanogan). *Land of the Spotted Eagle.* Ota K'te, or Plenty Kill, or Luther Standing Bear (Sioux).

HEROES/LEADERS/ VICTIMS	ELDER WISDOM/PHILOSOPHY/ SONGS	

1931

Sin-a-paw, or Don Whiteside (Muscogee), author, is born on May 9 in Brooklyn, New York.

June Bullshoe Tatsey (Blackfoot), author, is born on June 10.

Honganozhe, or Louis Wayne Ballard (Quapaw/Cherokee), composer and educator, is born on July 8 at Miami, Oklahoma.

Jack Gregory (Cherokee), author, is born on June 25.

Max Gross-Louis (Huron), author, is born on August 6.

Robert Lewis (Zuñi/Cherokee)
COURTESY OF ROBERTA M. LEWIS

1932

Wovoka, or Jack Wilson (Northern Paiute), prophet and holy man who founded the second Ghost Dance movement, dies on the Walker River Reservation near Schurz, Nevada.

Rita Joe (Micmac), author, is born on March 15.

Dawn Richardson (Iroquois/Cree), author, is born on August 23.

Alanis Obomsawin (Abenaki), author, is born on August 31.

We were sent up here [Rapid City, South Dakota] to be open-minded and we have tried our best to be, although some things are not clear. I am praying that tomorrow I will have a clear vision of all things. . . . I believe Adam and Eve were Winnebago. . . . We have learned a lot and will learn some more.

Felix White (Winnebago)

1933

Henry Roe Cloud, Ph.D. (Winnebago), is the first Native person to become president of Haskell Institute, in Lawrence, Kansas.

John Snow (Assiniboin), principal leader and author, is born on January 31.

Virginia Driving Hawk Sneve (Rosebud Sioux), author, is born on February 21.

Joan Bullshoe Kennerly (Blackfoot), author, is born on March 5.

Vine Deloria Jr. (Standing Rock Sioux), noted author, social commentator, and university professor, is born on March 26.

Jim Barnes (Choctaw), noted poet, author, and university professor, is born on December 22.

In this bill [Wheeler-Howard Act], it gives the Commissioner of Indian Affairs power to take away from one Indian and give to another Indian, if he so desires. Now everybody knows this is not right. This is the United States, and according to this Bill if it were passed we could not exercise our own rights and we might just as well live in Russia.

Joe Irving (Crow Creek)

	HISTORY/LAW/ POLITICS	LITERATURE/ART/ LEGENDS AND STORIES
1934	The United States Congress passes the Indian Reorganization Act, or Wheeler-Howard Act, ending the allotment policy as mandated under the Indian General Allotment Act of 1887 (Dawes Severalty Act). The IRA supposedly is to reestablish the sovereign nations and tribes as political entities with some restoration of internal sovereignty. The act enables the People of the sovereign nations and tribes to eject non-Natives from their lands and to assert rights over the natural resources of their lands.	*Nez Percé Texts.* Archie Phinney (Nez Percé). *Stories of the Sioux.* Ota K'te, or Plenty Kill, or Luther Standing Bear (Sioux).  *Ada E. Deer (Menominee)* COURTESY OF ADA E. DEER
1935	A Navajo syllabary is devised, using what is referred to as the Harrington-La Farge alphabet. It enables the Navajo language to be written. The Indian Arts and Crafts Board (IACB) is established as an independent agency in the Bureau of Indian Affairs of the United States Department of the Interior.	*Brothers Three.* John Milton Oskison (Cherokee).

1934

Jack D. Forbes (Powhatan/Delaware), noted author and university professor, is born on January 7.

Carol Lee Sanchez, (Laguna Pueblo/Scottish/Chippewa/ métis Lebanese), noted visual artist, poet, and author, is born on January 13.

Navarre Scott Momaday (Kiowa/Cherokee), recipient of the Pulitzer Prize in fiction (*House Made of Dawn*), noted author, poet, and university professor, is born on February 27.

Edward Benton Banai (Chippewa), author, is born on March 4.

Douglas Cardinal (métis/Cree), author, is born on March 7.

Ruth Roessel (Diné, or Navajo), author, is born on April 14.

Shirley Hill Witt (Mohawk), author, is born on April 17.

Tim Giago (Oglala Lakota), publisher of *Indian Country Today* (formerly *Lakota Times*), is born on July 12.

Will Antell (Chippewa), author, is born on October 2.

Gerald Vizenor (White Earth Chippewa), noted author and university professor, is born on October 22.

Beryl Blue Spruce (Laguna/San Juan), noted physician born on November 24, will be the first among the Pueblo people to receive an M.D. degree.

Chato (Chiricahua Apache), war leader of the People during the so-called Apache Wars from 1881 through 1886 and afterward a U.S. Army scout, dies in an automobile accident on the Mescalero Apache Reservation in southeastern New Mexico, near Ruidoso.

Since this Wheeler-Howard bill has been interpreted to me, I never can get heads nor tails to the thing. I just imagine that it does not amount to anything to me. It seems as though if this bill were passed it would be no protection really for my children and that is the reason I want to protect myself and give my reasons for not wanting this bill passed.

James Saluskin (Yakima)

1935

Carmen Bullshoe Marceau (Blackfoot), author, is born on January 28.

Charles Trimbel (Pine Ridge Sioux), author, is born on March 12.

Minerva Allen (Assiniboin), author, is born on April 24.

Jean Starr (Cherokee), noted poet, author, and classroom teacher, is born on July 6.

Bernard Assiniwi (Cree/Algonkian), author, is born on July 31.

Ada E. Deer (Menominee), author, social worker, assistant secretary of the U.S. Department of the Interior, and university professor, is born on August 7.

Lynn Moroney (Chickasaw), author, is born on October 28.

Oklahoma's "favorite son" Will Rogers (Cherokee) and famous aviator Wiley Post are killed when their plane crashes near Point Barrow, Alaska, on August 15.

	HISTORY/LAW/ POLITICS	LITERATURE/ART/ LEGENDS AND STORIES
1936	The United States Congress passes the Alaska Reorganization Act, which permits Native Alaskans to establish constitutions or tribal corporations, and to create reservations on land occupied by them. The United States Department of the Interior establishes the Indian Arts and Crafts Board in Washington, D.C. The Oklahoma Indian Welfare Act, passed by the United States Congress, provides for reorganization of the sovereign Native nations and tribes which were without land and whose governments had been dissolved by the Curtis Act of 1898.	*The Autobiography of a Papago Woman.* Ruth M. Underhill, editor. Maria Chona (Tohono O'odham, or Papago). *The Surrounded.* D'Arcy McNickle (Salish).
1937		
1938		*Left Handed, Son of Old Man Hat: A Navaho Autobiography.* Left Handed (Diné, or Navajo). *Tecumseh and His Times: The Story of a Great Indian.* John Milton Oskison (Cherokee).
1939	The People of the sovereign Tonawanda Seneca band, of New York, declare their independence from the state of New York in a modern version of the United States Declaration of Independence.	*I Am a Pueblo Indian Girl.* Louise Abeita (Isleta/Laguna).

HEROES/LEADERS/ VICTIMS	ELDER WISDOM/PHILOSOPHY/ SONGS	
Awiakta, or Marilou Awiakta (Cherokee), noted poet and author, is born on January 24. D. C. Cole (Chiricuaha Apache), author, is born on March 28. Eagle Man, or Ed McGaa (Pine Ridge Sioux), author, is born on April 16. Doris Seale (Santee Sioux/Cree), author, is born on July 10. Danny Lopez (Tohono O'odham, or Papago), author, is born on December 24. Charles Curtis (Kansa), former vice president, dies.		**1936**
Moses Nelson Big Crow (Rosebud Sioux), author, is born on February 17. Bernelda Wheeler (métis Cree/Ojibwa/Salteaux), author, is born on April 8. Peter Blue Cloud (Mohawk), noted poet, author, and publisher, is born on June 10. Sylvester J. Brito (Comanche/Tarascan), author and university professor, is born on September 26. Frank LaPeña (Wintun/Nomtipom), author, is born on October 5. Fritz Scholder (Luiseño), noted author and artist, is born on October 6.		**1937**
Gaynwah, or Thomas Wildcat Alford (Absentee Shawnee), a leader among the People who was employed by the Bureau of Indian Affairs (BIA), dies. Duane McGinnis Niatum (Klallam), noted author, is born on February 13. Benjamin Abel (Okanagan), author, is born on July 20. Martin F. Dunn (métis), author, is born on August 12. Albert White Hat (Rosebud Sioux), author, is born on November 18. Kahionhes, or John Fadden (Mohawk), author, is born on December 26.		**1938**
Ohiyesa, or Charles Alexander Eastman, M.D. (Lakota), dies. Duke Redbird (métis/Ojibwa), author, is born on March 18. Alfonso Ortiz (San Juan), noted author and university professor, is born on April 30. Kateri Tekakwitha, or Lily of the Mohawks (Kahnawake Mohawk), 1656–1680, the holy woman among Roman Catholics in the United States, is declared "venerable" by Pope Pius XII on May 19. Howard L. Meredith (Cherokee/Akokisa), author, is born on May 25. Russel Means, American Indian activist, actor, producer, is born on November 10.		**1939**

PERSPECTIVE
1940–1980

From 1940 to 1980, the People did not melt into an allegorical pot as so ardently desired by some of their non-Native relations. Instead, the number of the People of the sovereign Native nations and tribes grew from 345,000 in 1940 to 1.4 million by 1980.

The 1940s began with the onset of World War II, in which more than twenty thousand of the People from the sovereign Native nations and tribes across Turtle Island served in the military forces of the United States. Of special importance to the war effort was the work of the Choctaw, Comanche, and Navajo "code talkers." What is especially significant is that in 1883, the language, culture, and religion of the People had been "outlawed" by the United States government. Ironically, the government, which had done all in its power to obliterate the culture, traditional practices, spiritual ways, and particularly the languages of the People during the previous two centuries, dramatically benefited in its war effort because of the stubborn determination of the People to keep their respective languages despite the violence imposed on them for "clinging to their savage ways."

Parenthetically, those who favor making English the official national language of the United States would do well to remember that were it not for the languages of the People, the U.S. flag might never have been raised at Iwo Jima on Mount Suribachi.

The spirit of the People continued to heal as they returned from World War II and, with renewed vigor, established organizations such as the National Congress of American Indians (NCAI), in 1944, to address the economic and social injustices endured by the

People for centuries. Slowly, quietly, the embers of hope and courage among the People continued to be fanned gently throughout the 1950s and early 1960s.

In the undeclared war in Vietnam, from 1965 through 1975, more than forty-two thousand Native People served in the armed forces of the United States. Many of them, like their non-Native relations, gave their lives during a sad period for the world.

By 1968, the People had become swept up in the movement to demand equality and justice for all. "Red Power" became the call of the young among the People of the sovereign Native nations and tribes as they marched and demonstrated all across Turtle Island. During this tumultuous time, Alcatraz Island (across from San Francisco, California) became a focal point for the airing of long-held grievances of the People to the media throughout the world. The headquarters of the hated U.S. Department of the Interior's Bureau of Indian Affairs also was occupied by the young among the People.

Political activism among the younger People continued to escalate, culminating in the tragedy at Wounded Knee on the Pine Ridge Reservation of South Dakota. The young activists among the People during the 1960s and 1970s gained important experience from Wounded Knee, and they became the outstanding leaders of the mid-1980s and 1990s. The new leaders are committed to ensuring that the values, practices, and traditions of the People of the sovereign Native nations and tribes all across Turtle Island are respected and honored by our non-Native relations.

	HISTORY/LAW/ POLITICS	LITERATURE/ART/ LEGENDS AND STORIES
1940		*Land of Good Shadows: The Life Story of Anauta, an Eskimo Woman.* Heluis Chandler Washburne, editor. Anauta (Eskimo). *Uses of Plants Among the Indians of Southern New England.* Gladys Tantaquidgeon (Mohegan).
1941	Twenty-five thousand People of the sovereign Native nations and tribes across Turtle Island serve on active duty in the United States armed forces during World War II, and thousands more work in war-related industries. However, some of the People of the sovereign nations and tribes are imprisoned as war resisters. Many of the resisters cite the verbal promise made by George Washington that no member of a sovereign Native nation or tribe ever would be forced to fight in a war conducted by the United States.	

HEROES/LEADERS/VICTIMS	ELDER WISDOM/PHILOSOPHY/SONGS	
Richard G. Green (Mohawk), author, is born on March 21. Joseph Senungetuk (Inuit), author, is born on March 29. Robert F. Gish (Cherokee), author, is born on April 1. Maria Campbell (métis/Cree), author, is born on April 6. Rennard J. Strickland (Cherokee/Osage), noted author, is born on September 26 in St. Louis, Missouri. A. C. (Allan "Chuck") Ross (Santee Dakota), noted author, is born on October 25. James Welch (Blackfoot/Gros Ventre), acclaimed author, is born on November 18. Robert J. Conley (United Keetoowah Band Cherokee), highly acclaimed author, is born on December 29. He later writes twenty-four books published in seven years, and is a board member of the Western Writers Association of America and Wordcraft Circle of Native Writers and Storytellers.		**1940**
Dean Chavers (Lumbee), noted author, is born on February 4. Gilbert Honanie Jr. (Hopi), nationally recognized architect, is born on April 11 at Tuba City, Arizona. Nasnaga, or Richard Rogers (Shawnee), author, is born on April 13. Simon J. Ortiz (Acoma), noted poet and author, is born on May 27. Beth Brant (Bay of Quinte Mohawk), noted poet, author, and *Gathering of Spirit* book editor, is born on May 6. Russell Bates (Kiowa/Wichita), noted poet, author, screenwriter, and winner of an Emmy Award for a "Star Trek" segment, is born on June 6. Ssipsis (Penobscot), author, is born on June 10. Geary Hobson (Cherokee/Quapaw/Chickasaw), noted author, poet, and university professor, is born on June 12. Clara Sue Kidwell (Choctaw/Chippewa), noted historian, author, and university professor, is born on July 8 in Tahlequah, Oklahoma. She becomes Native American Studies Department chairman at the University of California, Berkeley, and deputy director for cultural resources at the National Museum of the American Indian (NMAI). Fred Bigjim (Kiowa), author, is born on July 20. Vickie Sears (Cherokee), poet, is born on August 2. David Lester (Muscogee), noted community leader, is born on September 25 at Claremore, Oklahoma. Ethel Constance Krepps (Kiowa/Miami), attorney, registered nurse, and author, is born on October 31.		**1941**

1942

Seventeen Comanche "code talkers" devise innovative phrases in the Comanche language to communicate important military information that baffles the enemy, during World War II.

Of the first twenty-nine Navajo "code talkers" serving in the U.S. Marine Corps, twenty-six are sent to Guadalcanal. They worked in teams of two, conversing by walkie-talkie and field telephone to transmit significant military information, including the reporting of the enemy's location and the directing of American troop movements.

Navajo Creation Myth: The Story of the Emergence. Hosteen Klah (Diné, or Navajo).

Sun Chief: The Autobiography of a Hopi Indian. Don C. Talayesva (Hopi).

1943

Maria Proctor Dadgar (Piscataway Conoy)
COURTESY OF MARIA P. DADGAR

Will Rogers Jr. (Cherokee) is elected to the U.S. House of Representatives from the Sixteenth District in California.		**1942**

Will Rogers Jr. (Cherokee) is elected to the U.S. House of Representatives from the Sixteenth District in California.

Alice Neundorf (Diné, or Navajo), author, is born on February 2.

Terry Lusty (métis), author, is born on February 9.

Buffy Sainte-Marie (Cree), noted folksinger, poet, and actress, is born on February 20.

Russell Thornton (Cherokee), author, is born on February 20.

Markoosie (Inuit), author, is born on June 19.

Rayna Green (Cherokee), noted poet, author, folklorist, documentary film producer, and director of the American Indian Program at the Smithsonian Institution's Museum of American History, is born on July 18 in Dallas, Texas.

Duane K. Hale (Muscogee), author, is born on August 4.

Michael Kabotie (Hopi), author, is born on September 3.

Joseph Bruchac III (Abenaki), noted storyteller, poet, author, director of the Greenfield Literary Review Center, and publisher, is born on October 16.

Annharte, or Marie Baker (Salteaux), author, is born on November 14.

Rokwaho, or Daniel Thompson (Salteaux), author, is born on November 14.

Gladys Cardiff (Eastern Cherokee), noted poet and author, is born on November 23.

Lana Grant (Sac and Fox), author, is born on November 25.

Walter J. Hillabrant (Citizen Band Potawatomi), psychologist and author, is born on December 17.

1943

John Tebbel (Ojibwa) becomes associate editor at E. P. Dutton publishing company in New York.

Byron Mallot (Tlingit), renowned business executive, is born on April 6.

Crying Wind, or Linda Stafford (Kickapoo), author, is born on April 23.

Thomas King (Cherokee), noted author, is born on April 24.

Marcia Keegan (Cherokee), photographer and author, is born on May 23.

Ted Palmanteer (Colville), author, is born on June 28.

Gus Palmer (Kiowa), author, is born on September 19.

Ross O. Swimmer (Cherokee), who will become assistant secretary of the U.S. Department of the Interior and director of the Bureau of Indian Affairs, is born on October 26 in Oklahoma.

HISTORY/LAW/ POLITICS	LITERATURE/ART/ LEGENDS AND STORIES
1944 The National Congress of American Indians (NCAI) is founded in Denver by Native employees of the Bureau of Indian Affairs. NCAI acts as a forum for the People of the sovereign nations and tribes across Turtle Island. Membership is composed of delegates from the sovereign nations and tribes as well as individuals. Six reservations are established in Alaska by the United States Department of the Interior. Forty-nine Native Alaska villages establish constitutions and incorporate as corporations. Comanche "code talkers" of the U.S. Army's Fourth Signal Division are commended by the commanding general for outstanding service in World War II.	
1945	 *Lee Francis III (Laguna Pueblo/Scotch/Chippewa/Lebanese)* *Courtesy of Lee Francis III*

1944

Gordon L. Pullar (Koniag Alaska Native), journalist, publisher, and tribal leader, is born on January 22.

Ron Welburn (Cherokee/Conoy), author, is born on April 30.

Richard Lucero Jr. (Mescalero Apache/Seminole), noted health-care advocate, is born on September 24.

Lance Henson (Southern Cheyenne), author, is born on September 20.

Van T. Barfoot (Choctaw) is awarded the Medal of Honor on October 4 for valor in the U.S. military above and beyond the call of duty on May 23.

Ernest Childers (Muscogee, or Creek) is awarded the Medal of Honor on April 8 for valor in the U.S. military above and beyond the call of duty on September 22, 1943.

Paulette Fairbanks Molin (White Earth Chippewa), author and educator, is born on November 16.

Ron Welburn (Southeastern Cherokee Confederacy)
COURTESY OF BEN BARNHART/UMASS PHOTO SERVICES

1945

Harold Cardinal (Cree), author, is born on January 27.

Michael Dorris (Modoc), noted author, is born on January 30.

Emerson Blackhorse Mitchell (Diné, or Navajo), author, is born on March 3.

Roxy Gordon (Choctaw), poet and author, is born on March 7.

Gail Bear (Cree), author, is born on May 6.

Lee Francis (Laguna Pueblo), poet, author, and national director of Wordcraft Circle of Native Writers, is born on May 21.

Hanay Geoigamah (Kiowa/Delaware), noted author, playwright, and screenwriter, is born on June 22.

John E. Echohawk (Pawnee), attorney, is born on August 11.

John Mohawk (Seneca), journalist, is born on August 30.

Joseph McLellan (métis/Ojibwa–Nez Percé), author, is born on September 27.

Cora Weber-Pillwas (métis/Cree), author, is born on November 2.

Wilma P. Mankiller (Cherokee), principal chief of the Cherokee Nation of Oklahoma, poet, and author, is born on November 18. She will become the first woman chief of a major tribe.

Gail Tremblay (Onondaga/Micmac), noted poet, is born on December 15.

	HISTORY/LAW/ POLITICS	LITERATURE/ART/ LEGENDS AND STORIES
1946	Legislation enacted by the United States Congress establishes the Indian Claims Commission. The commission enables the sovereign nations and tribes across Turtle Island to avoid having to have an act of Congress passed to sue the United States in the U.S. Court of Claims for land and money losses in violations of treaties.	
1947		*Old Mexican, Navaho Indian: A Navaho Autobiography.* Old Mexican (Diné, or Navajo).

HEROES/LEADERS/ VICTIMS	ELDER WISDOM/PHILOSOPHY/ SONGS	
Robert L. Perea (Pine Ridge Sioux), author, is born January 5. Carter Blue Clark (Muscogee, or Creek), author and educator, is born on January 11. Ed Edmo (Shoshone/Bannock), noted author, is born on March 16. Durbin Feeling (Cherokee), author, is born on April 2. Adrian C. Louis (Paiute), noted author, is born on April 24. Mimi Valenzuela (Yaqui), author, is born on May 17. Duane Big Eagle (Osage), noted poet, is born on May 20. Duwayne Leslie Bowen (Seneca), author, is born on July 7. John Red House (Diné, or Navajo), author, is born on July 25. Barney Bush (Shawnee/Cayuga), noted poet and author, is born on August 27. Lorenzo Baca (Mescalero Apache/Isleta), author, is born on September 9. Anna Lee Walters (Pawnee/Otoe-Missouria), noted poet, author, and educator, is born on September 9. Annette Jaimes (Juaneño/Yaqui), noted author and university faculty member, is born on September 10. Regina Hadley-Lynch (Diné, or Navajo), author, is born on September 17. Noel V. Starblanket (Saskatchewan), great-great-grandson of White Calf, is born on September 27. Raymond D. Apodaca (Ysleta del Sur), author, is born on October 15. crystos (Menominee), noted poet and author, is born on November 7. R. A. Swanson (Nett Lake Chippewa), author, is born on November 24. Wayne Keon (Ojibwa), author, is born on December 12.		**1946**
President Harry Truman presents Cayoni, or Joseph F. Johns (Muscogee), with the Silver Life Saving Medal for his service in the U.S. Coast Guard. Robert Latham Owen (Cherokee), former U.S. senator from Oklahoma, dies. Janet Campbell Hale (Coeur d'Alene), noted author and educator, is born on January 11. William Oandasan (Yuki), noted author and educator, is born on January 17. Roberta Hill Whiteman (Oneida), noted author and educator, is born on February 17. Linda Hogan (Chickasaw), author, is born on July 16. Lorna Williams (Lillooet), author, is born on September 27. Ward Churchill (Muscogee/Cherokee), noted author, social critic, and university faculty member, is born on October 2.		**1947**

1948

In a court decree by the Supreme Court of Arizona after the trial of a man from the sovereign Tewa tribe of Arizona, the state is forced to permit the People of the sovereign Native nations and tribes to vote in state elections.

The Assimilative Crimes Act, passed by the United States Congress, requires that crimes committed on reservations of the People of the sovereign Native nations and tribes punishable under state law must be tried in federal court.

Under legislation passed by the United States Congress, power to grant right-of-way on lands of the People of the sovereign Native nations and tribes with their consent is given to the secretary of the United States Department of the Interior.

The People of the sovereign Sioux Nation at Standing Rock and Cheyenne River Reservations, in South Dakota, are forced to relinquish more than 160,000 acres to the U.S. Army Corps of Engineers for the construction of Oahe Dam, near Pierre, South Dakota.

Denial of the right to vote for the People of the sovereign Native pueblos and tribes of New Mexico is found to be in violation of the Fifteenth Amendment of the United States Constitution, and the New Mexico constitutional provision for such denial is overturned in federal court.

Beth Brant (Bay of Quinte Mohawk)
COURTESY OF TEE CORINNE

1949

Termination of the trust relationship of the United States government toward the People of the sovereign Native nations and tribes is recommended strongly by the Hoover Commission on the Reorganization of Government. Forty-six years later, the 104th Congress of the United States, in the name of reorganization, drafts legislation that will, in the end, result in termination of the federal government's trust responsibility that had been agreed to in treaties between the People and the United States.

They Came Here First: The Epic of the American Indian. D'Arcy McNickle (Salish).
Peyote Music. David P. McAllester (Narraganset).

HEROES/LEADERS/ VICTIMS	ELDER WISDOM/PHILOSOPHY/ SONGS	
Jeannette C. Armstrong (Okanagan), noted author, is born on February 5. Linda Skinner (Choctaw), author, is born on March 5. Leslie Marmon Silko (Laguna), noted author, is born on March 5. Wendy Rose (Hopi/Miwok), poet, is born on May 7. Kenneth H. York (Mississippi Choctaw), educator and author, is born on May 15. Charles W. Murphy (Standing Rock Sioux), noted tribal leader, is born on May 24. Janie Leask (Haida/Tsimshian), Alaskan Native leader, is born on September 17. Veronica Velarde Tiller (Jicarilla Apache), author, is born on November 5. Ronald Rogers (Cherokee), author, is born on November 20.	There is no doubt that we see the universe through a different set of values and beliefs. It is impossible for non-Natives to feel the sorts of emotions that are called upon when Indigenous peoples speak about ancestors, about Earth, about the symbiosis that exists between human and animal. *Beth Brant (Bay of Quinte Mohawk)*	**1948**
Betty Mae Jumper (Seminole) is the first of the Seminole Nation to receive a high school diploma from Cherokee (North Carolina) Indian School. Emma Laroque (métis), author, is born on January 2. Cheryl May (Cherokee), noted science journalist, is born on February 22. Beth Cuthand (Cree), author, is born on March 1. Clifford E. Trafzer (Wyandot), noted author and university professor, is born on March 1. Janice Gould (Maidu), noted poet and author, is born on April 1. John C. Francis (Laguna/Chippewa), entrepreneur and producer of The Crystal Skull documentary film, is born on May 5. Jon R. Penoi (Cherokee/Laguna), author, is born on June 29. Beatrice Culleton Mosionier (métis), author, is born on August 27. Patricia Tatsey Newman (Blackfoot), author, is born on December 17. Andrew Hope III (Tlingit), author, is born on December 23.		**1949**

HISTORY/LAW/ POLITICS	LITERATURE/ART/ LEGENDS AND STORIES
1950	
The sovereign Navajo Nation is the recipient of funds appropriated by the United States Congress, under the Navaho Rehabilitation Act.	*The Shinnecock Indians.* Lois Marie Hunter (Shinnecock). *Delaware Indian Art Designs.* Gladys Tantaquidgeon (Mohegan).
1951	
The sovereign nations and tribes across Turtle Island file more than eight hundred claims with the Indian Claims Commission.	*Life and Death of an Oilman: The Career of E. W. Marland.* John Joseph Mathews (Osage).

1950

Hehaka Sapa, or Black Elk (Oglala Lakota), visionary and holy man of the Lakota, dies.

Frank Clarke (Hualapai) receives his M.D. degree from the St. Louis University School of Medicine.

Moses Jumper Jr. (Seminole), author, is born on January 4.

Earle Thompson (Yakima), author, is born on March 13.

Beverly Hungry Wolf (Blood), author, is born on April 1.

Cheryl Savageau (Abenaki), noted author and university faculty member, is born on April 14.

Lee Maracle (métis Cree/Salish), noted author, is born on July 2.

Richard Hill (Tuscarora), author, is born on August 7.

Lenore Keeshig-Tobias (Cape Croker Ojibwa), author, is born on October 7.

Judith Mountain Leaf Volborth (Comanche), noted poet, author, and university faculty member, is born on October 23.

Francis A. Levier (Citizen Band Potawatomi), educator and business executive, is born on November 13.

Bruce King (Oneida), author, is born on November 2.

Mitchell Red Cloud (Ho'Chunk) is awarded the Medal of Honor for valor in the U.S. military above and beyond the call of duty on November 5, 1950.

Quentin Saludes (Coquelle)
COURTESY OF QUENTIN SALUDES

1951

Annie Dodge Wauneka (Navajo) is elected as a council member of the Navajo Nation.

Donald L. Fixico (Shawnee/Sac and Fox/Muscogee/Seminole), noted author, is born on January 22.

Ted Jojola (Isleta), noted author, educator, and administrator, is born on November 19.

nila northsun (Shoshone/Chippewa), noted poet and author, is born on February 1.

LeAnne Howe (Choctaw), noted poet and author, is born on April 29.

Joy Harjo (Muscogee, or Creek), saxophonist, poet, and author, is born on May 9.

Harold Littlebird (Laguna/Khe-wa, or Santo Domingo), poet, is born on May 28.

Alootook Ipellie (Inuit), author, is born on August 11.

David Yeagley (Comanche), author, is born on September 5.

Georges Sioui (Huron), author, is born on November 3.

Thomson Highway (Brochet Cree), author, is born on December 6.

I am glad we are going to this cocktail party. I think I'm going to get some parrot feathers. I hear the people in California have many kinds of birds and the feathers are pretty.
Alcario Montoya (Cochiti)

	HISTORY/LAW/ POLITICS	LITERATURE/ART/ LEGENDS AND STORIES
1952	The Voluntary Relocation Program is implemented by the Bureau of Indian Affairs (BIA). Under the program, more than seventeen thousand People of the sovereign Native nations and tribes are moved to large urban areas, including Oakland, San Francisco, Los Angeles, Denver, and Chicago.	
1953	The United States terminates its relationship with the sovereign nations and tribes in California and New York, the Florida Seminole, Texas Alabama-Coushatta, Wisconsin Menominee, Montana Flathead, Oregon Klamath, Kansas and Nebraska Potawatomi, and North Dakota Turtle Mountain Chippewa, as mandated by the U.S. Congress under House Concurrent Resolution 108. This permits state governments to assume jurisdiction in criminal and civil matters over the People of the sovereign nations and tribes residing on reservations. Prohibition laws pertaining to the People of the sovereign Native nations and tribes across Turtle Island are repealed by an act of the United States Congress. A resolution to terminate its special trust responsibilities with the sovereign Native nations and tribes across Turtle Island is passed by the United States Congress.	
1954	The People of the sovereign Native nations and tribes of Maine are granted the right to vote in state elections. The trust status of more than sixty sovereign Native nations, tribes, bands, and communities is revoked by the United States Congress, and the People of those nations and tribes are stripped of federal services and protection. Under Public Law 280, passed by the United States Congress, legislatures are empowered to assume criminal and civil jurisdiction on lands of the People without their consent.	*Nevada Indians Speak.* Jack D. Forbes (Rappahannock/Delaware), editor. *Runner in the Sun: A Story of Indian Maize.* D'Arcy McNickle (Salish). *Hopi Customs, Folklore and Ceremonies.* Edmund Nequatewa (Hopi). *Enemy Way Music.* David P. McAllester (Narraganset). *George Washington's America.* John Tebbel (Ojibwa)

HEROES/LEADERS/VICTIMS	ELDER WISDOM/PHILOSOPHY/SONGS	
Felipe Molina (Yaqui), author, is born on January 1. Greg Sarris (Pomo/Coast Miwok), noted poet and author, is born on February 12. Daniel Davis Moses (Delaware), author, is born on February 18. Terry Tafoya (Warm Springs/Taos), author, is born on March 25. Laura Tohe (Diné, or Navajo), noted poet and educator, is born on October 5. Victor Montejo (Maya), author, is born on October 9. Ruby Slipperjack (Ojibwa), author, is born on December 24.	 *Laura Tohe (Navajo)* COURTESY OF JEROME TILLMAN	**1952**
Jim Thorpe (Sac and Fox/Potawatomi), Olympic Games hero, dies. Doug Allard (Flathead/Salish/Kootenai), Korean War veteran, is awarded the Korean War Ribbon, U.N. Medal, and two Battle Stars for service in the United States Marine Corps from 1950 to 1953. Robert Johnston (Comanche), attorney and author, is born on January 28. Karoniaktatie, or Alex A. Jacobs (Mohawk), poet, is born on February 28. Ronald Keon (Ojibwa/Iroquois), author, is born on September 24. Ramson Lomatewama (Hopi), author, is born on October 20. Rokwaho, or Dan Thompson (Mohawk), graphic artist, editor, and author, is born on November 7. Lucy Tapahonso (Diné, or Navajo), author and educator, is born on November 8.	It is important to note that in our Indian language the only translation for termination is to "wipe out" or "kill off" . . . how can we plan our future when the Indian Bureau threatens to wipe us out as a race? It is like trying to cook a meal in your tipi when someone is standing outside trying to burn the tipi down. *Earl Old Person (Blackfoot)*	**1953**
Charles George (Eastern Cherokee) is awarded the Medal of Honor on March 18 for valor in the U.S. military above and beyond the call of duty on November 30, 1952. John Tebbel (Ojibwa) is appointed chairman of the Department of Journalism at New York University, Manhattan. Salli M. K. Benedict (Mohawk), author, is born on January 5. Ofelia Zepeda (Tohono O'odham, or Papago), author, is born on March 24. Louise Erdrich (Turtle Mountain Chippewa), noted poet, author, and educator, is born on July 6. Joseph L. Concha (Taos), author, is born on October 8. Edgar Heap of Birds (Southern Cheyenne), author, is born on November 22.		**1954**

	HISTORY/LAW/ POLITICS	LITERATURE/ART/ LEGENDS AND STORIES
1955	Responsibility for health and medical care of the People of the sovereign Native nations and tribes is shifted from the Bureau of Indian Affairs (BIA) to the Public Health Service of the United States Department of Health, Education and Welfare, later called the Department of Health and Human Services.	*Black Hawk: An Autobiography.* Donald Jackson, editor. Black Hawk (Sioux). *Heap Big Laugh.* Dan C. Madrano (Caddo).
1956	The *Tribal Tribune*, a monthly publication of the Confederated Colville of Nespelem, Washington, is first published and remains in publication by the tribe. The Adult Vocational Training program for the People of the sovereign Native nations and tribes is established in the Bureau of Indian Affairs (BIA). The program emphasizes clerical, trade, and service jobs.	*Myth and Prayers of the Great Star Chant.* David P. McAllester (Narraganset). *The Magic of Balanced Living.* John Tebbel (Ojibwa).
1957	People of the sovereign Mohawk Nation of New York reoccupy lands expropriated by non-Native squatters. People of the sovereign Seneca nation of New York actively oppose construction of Kinzua Dam on the Allegheny Reservation, in New York.	*The American Indian in Graduate Study: A Bibliography of Theses and Dissertations.* Frederick J. Dockstader (Oneida).
1958	More than three thousand Lumbee gather in Robeson County, North Carolina, and break up a Ku Klux Klan rally.	
1959	Provision of essential sanitation facilities by the surgeon general of the United States for the People of the sovereign Native nations and tribes is authorized by the United States Congress. The Catawba tribal council approves federal termination by a vote of forty to seventeen. The U.S. Congress revokes the Catawba's constitution after giving 340 of the People title to five acres of land and giving three hundred dollars in cash to 290. The *Navajo Times Today* first is published by the sovereign Navajo Nation. The name is shortened later to the *Navajo Times*.	*I Fought with Geronimo.* Wilbur Sturtevant Nye, editor. Batsinas, or Jason Betzinez (Mimbreño Apache). *A Pima Remembers.* George E. Webb (Pima).

HEROES/LEADERS/ VICTIMS	ELDER WISDOM/PHILOSOPHY/ SONGS	
Gordon D. Henry Jr. (White Earth Chippewa), noted author and university faculty member, is born on October 19. Michael Lacapa (White Mountain Apache), author, is born on November 25. Ira Hamilton Hayes (Pima), a World War II hero of the People, dies and is buried at Arlington National Cemetery, Arlington, Virginia.	This is our own, our very own, and I speak this not for the Hopi but for all Indian people who were here first. . . . We are not going to . . . give this life and land to anyone but will continue this life that our forefathers have followed. . . . *Don Monongye (Hopi)*	**1955**
Everett Ronald Rhoades (Kiowa) receives his M.D. degree from the University of Oklahoma College of Medicine, Norman. Bernice Armstrong (Diné, or Navajo), author, is born on March 8. Vee F. Browne (Diné, or Navajo), noted children's author and educator, is born on September 4. Julie Moss (Cherokee), author, is born on September 22.		**1956**
Diane Burns (Chippewa/Chemehuevi), poet and author, is born on January 11. Linda Noel (Concow/Maidu), author, is born on March 9.		**1957**
Walter L. Moffett (Nez Percé) becomes pastor of the Kamiah-Kooshia United Presbyterian Churches in Kamiah, Idaho. Annette Arkeketa (Otoe-Missouria/Muscogee), author, is born on May 27.	*Elizabeth Woody (Warm Springs/ Yakima/Wasco/ Navajo)* COURTESY OF JOE CANTRELL	**1958**
Phillip Martin (Mississippi Choctaw) is elected chairman of the Mississippi Choctaw Nation. Herbert W. Pencille (Chemehuevi) becomes president of Pest Control Operators of California. Alyce Sadongei (Tohono O'odham, or Papago/Kiowa), author, is born on August 11. Winona LaDuke (Chippewa), author, is born on August 18.	Elizabeth Woody (Warm Springs/Yakima/Wasco/Diné, or Navajo), noted poet and author, is born on December 26. I can't go around and tell people who's right and who's wrong, but there's always going to be people who are opportunistic, Indian, non-Indian or whatever race or culture—that's the choice they make. *Elizabeth Woody (Warm Springs/Yakima/Wasco/Navajo)*	**1959**

	HISTORY/LAW/ POLITICS	LITERATURE/ART/ LEGENDS AND STORIES
1960	Kinzua Dam, built by the U.S. Army Corps of Engineers, floods 10,500 acres on the Allegheny Reservation, in New York. The grave of the principal leader of the Seneca, Kiantwa'ka, or Cornplanter, or John O'Bail (Seneca/Irish), a sacred site for the People, is submerged.	*Old Father, the Story Teller.* Pablita Velarde (Santa Clara). *The American Indian Wars.* John Tebbel (Ojibwa).
1961	Federal funds for economic development are granted to the sovereign Native nations and tribes on reservations, under the Area Redevelopment Act. The National Indian Youth Council (NIYC) is founded in Gallup, New Mexico, under the leadership of Melvin Thom (Paiute) and Clyde Warrior (Ponca).	*The Assiniboines: From the Accounts of the Old Ones Told to First Boy.* First Boy, or James Larpenteur Long (Assiniboin). *Mountain Wolf Woman, Sister of Crashing Thunder: The Autobiography of a Winnebago Indian.* Mountain Wolf Woman (Winnebago). *Indian Music of the Southwest.* David P. McAllester (Narraganset).
1962	Three Native newspapers begin publication—the *Fort Apache Scout*, a biweekly which still is being published by the White Mountain Apache in Whiteriver, Arizona; the *Jicarilla Chieftain*, a biweekly published by the Jicarilla Apache in Dulce, New Mexico; and the *Tundra Times*, in Anchorage, Alaska. Native People of federally recognized tribes are offered vocational training under the Manpower Development and Training Act. The Institute of American Indian Arts (IAIA) is opened in Santa Fe, New Mexico.	*The Indian Tribes of the United States: Ethnic and Cultural Survival.* D'Arcy McNickle (Salish). *The Inheritors.* John Tebbel (Ojibwa).
1963	*Americans Before Columbus*, a bimonthly publication, is first published by the National Indian Youth Council of Albuquerque, New Mexico. It continues to be published.	*The Dancing Horses of Acoma.* Wolf Robe Hunt (Acoma).
1964	The Survival of American Indians Association is founded to bring attention to fishing rights of the sovereign nations and tribes as provided by treaties with the United States. Rough Rock Demonstration School, at Chinle, Arizona, is the first school to be under the complete control of a sovereign nation. The all-Navajo school board and board of directors determine policy and curriculum. The American Indian Historical Society is organized in San Francisco, California. It publishes the *Indian Historian*.	*Kaibah: Recollections of a Navajo Girlhood.* Kay Bennett (Diné, or Navajo). *Strange Journey: The Vision Life of a Psychic Indian Woman.* Louise Lone Dog (Mohawk/Delaware). *No Turning Back: A True Account of a Hopi Indian Girl's Struggle to Bridge the Gap Between the World of Her People and the World of the White Man.* Polingaysi Qoyawayma, or Elizabeth Q. White (Hopi). *Friends of Thunder.* Jack Frederick Kilpatrick (Cherokee) and Anna Gritts Kilpatrick (Cherokee). *Raising the Moon Vines.* Gerald R. Vizenor (Chippewa).

HEROES/LEADERS/ VICTIMS	ELDER WISDOM/PHILOSOPHY/ SONGS	
William S. Yellow Robe (Assiniboin), author, is born on February 4. Batsinas, or Jason Betzinez (Mimbreño Apache), dies.		**1960**
Greg Young-Ing (Cree), noted author, is born on March 18. Connie Fife (Cree), author, is born on August 27. Louis Mofsie (Hopi/Winnebago) is elected president of the Indian League of the Americas–New York.	For generations it has been traditional that all historical literature on Indians be a recital of tribal histories from the pre-Discovery culture through the first encounter with the white man to about the year 1890. At that point the tribe seems to fade gently into history, with its famous war chief riding down the canyon into the sunset. *Vine Deloria Jr. (Standing Rock Sioux)*	**1961**
Ferguson Plain (Sarnia Ojibwa), author, is born on April 21. Drew Hayden Taylor (Ojibwa), noted author, is born on July 1. Charlotte W. Heath (Cherokee) is a Peace Corps volunteer in Ethiopia, where she teaches English as a second language.		**1962**
President John F. Kennedy presents Annie Dodge Wauneka (Navajo) with the Medal of Freedom. Overton James (Chickasaw) becomes the twenty-seventh governor of the Chickasaw Nation, the youngest person to serve in that position. Everett Ronald Rhoades, M.D. (Kiowa), is elected a fellow of the American College of Physicians.		**1963**
Beryl Blue Spruce (Laguna/San Juan) receives his M.D. degree from the University of Southern California. He is the first among the Pueblo people to receive an M.D. degree.	I am glad our children are learning to read and write English, but I'm also very glad they're learning about the Navajo culture and the Navajo way. We want our children to be proud that they are Navajos. . . . *Robert A. Roessel Jr. (Navajo)*	**1964**

	HISTORY/LAW/ POLITICS	LITERATURE/ART/ LEGENDS AND STORIES
1965	From all across Turtle Island, 42,500 People of the sovereign nations and tribes serve in the United States armed forces in Vietnam. The All Indian Pueblo Council (AIPC) adopts its first written constitution and bylaws.	*The Raven and the Redbird.* Raven Hail (Cherokee). *Anishinabe Nagamon.* Gerald Vizenor (Ojibwa). *Walk in Your Soul.* Jack Frederick Kilpatrick (Cherokee) and Anna Gritts Kilpatrick (Cherokee). *The Life of America.* Charles Brashear (Cherokee).
1966	The Alaska Federation of Natives is founded at Anchorage. Special programs for children of the sovereign Native nations and tribes across Turtle Island are provided because findings by the White House Task Force on Indian Health and the Coleman Report on Indian Education. Hunting and fishing rights, as provided by treaty, are preserved in the decision by the United States Supreme Court referred to as *Menominee Tribe of Indians v. United States.*	*Karnee: A Paiute Narrative.* Annie Lowry (Paiute). *The Arapaho Way: A Memoir of an Indian Boyhood.* Carl Sweezy (Arapaho). *Compact History of the Indian Wars.* John Tebbel (Ojibwa).
1967	The American Indian Law Center is founded in Albuquerque, New Mexico.	*Miracle Hill: The Story of a Navaho Boy.* Emerson Blackhorse Mitchell (Diné, or Navajo). *Empty Swings.* Gerald R. Vizenor (Chippewa). *Cheyenne Memories, a Folk History.* John and Liberty Stands in Timber (Cheyenne).
1968	The United States Congress passes the Indian Civil Rights Act (ICRA) and it becomes Public Law 90-284. It incorporates modified versions of the First and Fourth through Eighth Amendments of the U.S. Constitution's Bill of Rights into federal law which the governments of the sovereign nations tribes are forbidden to abridge. President Lyndon B. Johnson creates the Vice President's Council on Indian Opportunity. The American Indian Movement (AIM) is founded in Minneapolis, Minnesota, to promote civil rights for Native People.	*Winter Count.* Dallas Chief Eagle (Sioux). *Creative Writing: Fiction, Drama, Poetry, the Essay.* Charles Brashear (Cherokee). *House Made of Dawn.* Navarre Scott Momaday (Kiowa/Cherokee). *Pima Indian Legends.* Anna Moore Shaw (Pima). *The Warrior Who Killed Custer: The Personal Narrative of Chief Joseph White Bull.* Joseph White Bull (Sioux). *Starr's History of the Cherokee.* Rennard J. Strickland (Cherokee/Osage). *Escorts to White Earth.* Gerald R. Vizenor (Chippewa). *Sah-gan-de-oh, the Chief's Daughter.* Sahgandeoh, or Jerry, or Lucille Winnie (Seneca/Cayuga).

HEROES/LEADERS/ VICTIMS	ELDER WISDOM/PHILOSOPHY/ SONGS	
Robert L. Bennett (Oneida) is appointed commissioner of Indian affairs (BIA), U.S. Department of the Interior. Byron Mallott (Tlingit) is elected mayor of Yakutat, Alaska.		**1965**

Robert L. Bennett (Oneida) is the first from among the People to be appointed commissioner of Indian affairs in the U.S. Department of the Interior since 1869.
    Forest Funmaker (Salteaux), author, is born on May 26.
    Sherman J. Alexie Jr. (Spokane/Coeur d'Alene), noted author, is born on October 7.
    William L. Hensley (Inuit) is elected to the Alaska house of representatives.
	We are more than just writers. We are [Native] story-tellers. We are spokespeople. We are cultural ambassadors. We are politicians. We are activists. We are all of this simply by nature of what we do, without even wanting to be.
	Sherman Alexie (Spokane/Coeur d'Alene)
	
	Sherman Alexie
	(Spokane/Coeur d'Alene)
	<small>COURTESY OF REX RYSTEDT</small>
		1966

Tatanga Mani, or Walking Buffalo, or George McLean (Stoney Assiniboin), dies. Jeff W. Muskrat (Cherokee) retires from the United States Army with the rank of lieutenant colonel. He is awarded the Silver Star, Bronze Star with Oak Leaf Cluster, Army Commendation Medal with two Oak Leaf Clusters, and Presidential Unit Citation.		**1967**

Sekon, or Jim, Nimohoyah (Kiowa), a Vietnam War hero, is awarded two Purple Hearts, a Bronze Star for valor, a Vietnamese Service Ribbon, and a Presidential Unit Citation.
    Betty Mae Jumper (Seminole) is the first woman to be elected chairman of the Seminole Nation.
    Arthur L. McDonald (Oglala Lakota) is appointed chairman of the Department of Psychology at Montana State University.
		1968

1969

American Indian Scholarships, Inc., is founded at Albuquerque, New Mexico.

Navajo Community College at Tsaile, Arizona, is established. It is the oldest chartered community college among the sovereign nations and tribes across Turtle Island.

The final report by the U.S. Senate Subcommittee on Indian Education, titled "Indian Education: A National Tragedy—A National Challenge," is issued. Native People refer to the document as the "Kennedy Report" after U.S. Senator Edward M. Kennedy, who completed the work of his brother, Senator Robert F. Kennedy, after his death.

Native activists occupy Alcatraz Island in San Francisco Bay, California, to call attention to the vile conditions and suffering of the People of the sovereign Native nations and tribes all across Turtle Island. The occupation will last until 1971.

Custer Died for Your Sins: An Indian Manifesto. Vine Deloria Jr. (Standing Rock Sioux).

The Way to Rainy Mountain. Navarre Scott Momaday (Kiowa/Cherokee).

Cherokee Spirit Tales. Rennard J. Strickland (Cherokee/Osage).

Lonely Deer. Joseph L. Concha (Taos).

The Tewa World: Space, Time, Being, and Becoming in a Pueblo Society. Alfonso Ortiz (San Juan).

Me and Mine: The Life Story of Helen Sekaquaptewa as Told to Louise Udall. Helen Sekaquaptewa (Hopi).

Guests Never Leave Hungry: The Autobiography of James Sewid, A Kwakiutl Indian. James Sewid (Kwakiutl).

Tanaina Tales from Alaska. Bill Vaudrin (Chippewa).

Jim Whitewolf: The Life of a Kiowa Apache. Jim Whitewolf (Kiowa/Apache).

1970

Fifty-four Native People are arrested for violation of state fishing regulations on the Puyallup River. The regulations are in direct conflict with fishing rights granted under treaties of the United States with the Puyallup and other sovereign nations and tribes.

Four hundred claims of an original eight hundred to the Indian Claims Commission still are pending. Of the four hundred adjudicated, one-fourth were dismissed. Awards totaling about $350 million were made for one-fourth, and no awards were made for the remaining two hundred claims.

Blue Lake and forty-eight thousand acres of land are returned to the Taos Pueblo by an act of Congress.

The American Indian Education Policy Center is founded at University Park, Pennsylvania.

The American Indian Law Students Association is founded at Albuquerque, New Mexico.

The American Indian Tribal Court Judges Association is founded.

Americans for Indian Opportunity is founded in Washington, D.C., and later moved to Bernalillo, New Mexico.

The National Indian Education Association (NIEA) is founded in Minneapolis, Minnesota.

The North American Indian Women's Association (NAIWA) is founded in Atlanta, Georgia.

The Native American Rights Fund is founded in Boulder, Colorado.

We Talk, You Listen: New Tribes, New Turf. Vine Deloria Jr. (Standing Rock Sioux).

The Pueblo Indians of North America. Edward P. Dozier (Santa Clara).

Indian Voices. Jeannette Henry (Cherokee).

Harpoon the Hunter. Markoosie (Eskimo).

There Is My People Sleeping: The Ethnic Poem-Drawings of Serain Stump. Serain Stump (Shoshone).

Anishinabe Adioskan: Tales of the People. Gerald Vizenor (Ojibwa).

The Hopi Way. Louis Mofsie (Hopi/Ho'Chunk).

1969

Louis R. Bruce (Sioux/Mohawk) is appointed commissioner of Indian Affairs in the U.S. Department of the Interior.

Phillip Martin (Mississippi Choctaw) is selected president of the Chata Development Company, in Philadelphia, Mississippi.

1970

William L. Hensley (Inuit) is elected to the Alaska state senate.

Byron Mallott (Tlingit) becomes executive director of the Rural Alaska Community Action Program.

Phillip Martin (Mississippi Choctaw) is named president of the board of regents of Haskell Indian Junior College, Lawrence, Kansas.

A core part of tribal identity among Indian people is based on being a member of a community and having the ability to make appropriate, positive contributions to that community.

LaDonna Harris (Comanche)

LaDonna Harris (Comanche)
COURTESY OF WALTER BIGBEE (COMANCHE)

	HISTORY/LAW/ POLITICS	LITERATURE/ART/ LEGENDS AND STORIES
1971	Under the Alaska Native Claims Settlement Act, passed by the United States Congress, forty-four million acres and $1 billion are awarded to Native Alaskans in the largest single land-settlement award in two centuries. This settlement enables construction to begin on the oil pipeline from Valdez to Prudhoe Bay. The Association of American Indian Physicians is founded in Oklahoma City, Oklahoma. The Organization of North American Indian Students (ONAIS) is founded in Marquette, Michigan.	*Indian Man: A Life of Oliver La Farge.* D'Arcy McNickle (Salish). *New Voices from the People Named the Chippewa.* Gerald R. Vizenor (Chippewa). *Of Utmost Good Faith.* Vine Deloria Jr. (Standing Rock Sioux). *Creek-Seminole Spirit Tales.* Rennard J. Strickland (Cherokee/Osage). *The Tall Candle: The Personal Chronicle of a Yaqui Indian.* Rosalio Moises (Yaqui). *Riding the Earthboy.* James Welch (Blackfoot/Gros Ventre). *Navaho History.* Ethelou Yazzie (Diné, or Navajo). *Somethings I Did.* Roxy Gordon (Choctaw).
1972	The United States Congress passes the Indian Education Act and it is signed into law. The act establishes the Office of Indian Education (OIE) and the National Advisory Council on Indian Education (NACIE). The National Indian Health Board is founded in Denver, Colorado. Followers of the American Indian Movement (AIM) organize the Trail of Broken Treaties caravan. The journey ends in Washington, D.C., where demonstrators occupy and destroy offices of the Bureau of Indian Affairs (BIA). People of the sovereign Native nations and tribes can receive loans under the State and Local Fiscal Assistance Act, passed by the United States Congress. The first non–commercial radio station (KTDB-FM) owned and operated by a sovereign Native nation begins operation, in Ramah, New Mexico. More than five hundred of the People protest the coroner's ruling of death by exposure in the fatal beating of Raymond Yellow Thunder by whites. In a subsequent trial, two participants in the beating are convicted of manslaughter. They serve brief prison terms. The U.S. government returns twenty-one thousand acres to the Yakima Nation in Washington state.	*The First Hundred Years of Nino Cochise.* Ciye N. Cochise (Apache). *The Taos Indians and Their Sacred Blue Lake.* Marcia Keegan (Cherokee). *Folk Medicine in the Delaware and Related Algonkian Indians.* Gladys Tantaquidgeon (Mohegan). *Jimmy Yellow Hawk.* Virginia Driving Hawk Sneve (Rosebud Sioux). *Cherokee Law Ways.* Rennard J. Strickland (Cherokee/Osage). *Red Man in the New World Drama.* Vine Deloria Jr. (Standing Rock Sioux). *Attica: Official Report of the New York State Special Commission on Attica.* David C. Harrison (Osage/Cherokee). *Lame Deer, Seeker of Visions.* Lame Deer, or John Fire (Lakota), and Richard Erdoes. *Alcatraz Is Not an Island.* Aroniawenate, or Peter Blue Cloud (Mohawk). *Zuñi Tales.* Robert E. Lewis (Zuñi/Cherokee). *American Indian Authors.* Natachee Scott Momaday (Eastern Cherokee). *New Perspectives on the Pueblos.* Alfonso Ortiz (San Juan), editor. *The Secret of No Face: An Ireokwa Epic.* Chief Everett Parker (Seneca) and Oledoska (Abenaki). *Pitseolak: Pictures out of My Life.* Pitseolak (Eskimo). *Sanapia, Comanche Medicine Woman.* Sanapia (Comanche). *Nu Mee Poom tit Wah Tit (Nez Percé Stories).* Allen P. Slickpoo (Nez Percé).

HEROES/LEADERS/ VICTIMS	ELDER WISDOM/PHILOSOPHY/ SONGS	
Richard Vance La Course (Yakima), noted journalist, becomes managing editor of the *Confederated Umatilla Journel.*		**1971**
Everett Ronald Rhoades, M.D. (Kiowa), is elected president of the Association of American Indian Physicians. Byron Mallott (Tlingit) is appointed commissioner of the Department of Community and Regional Affairs for the state of Alaska by the governor of Alaska. Herbert W. Pencille (Chemehuevi) is elected chairman of the Chemehuevi Indian tribal council.		**1972**

HISTORY/LAW/ POLITICS	LITERATURE/ART/ LEGENDS AND STORIES
1973 Two hundred armed members of the American Indian Movement (AIM) occupy the Pine Ridge Reservation, in South Dakota, for more than two months. The University of Oklahoma, at Norman, drops the "Little Red" mascot of its sports teams. The Menominee Restoration Act, which reestablishes the trust relationship between the sovereign Menominee Nation and the United States government, is signed into law by President Richard M. Nixon.	*American Indian Authors for Young Readers: A Selected Bibliography.* Mary G. Byler (Cherokee), editor. *Halfbreed.* Maria Campbell (Métis). *God Is Red.* Vine Deloria Jr. (Standing Rock Sioux). *The American Indian Reader: Literature.* Jeanette Henry (Cherokee), editor. *Haida Reader.* Erma G. Lawrence (Haida). *Native American Tribalism: Indian Survivals and Renewals.* D'Arcy McNickle (Salish). *Hopi Roadrunner, Dancing.* Wendy Rose (Hopi). *The Native American Factor.* Howard L. Meredith (Cherokee). *Literature of the American Indian.* Thomas E. Sanders Cherokee/Nippawanock) and Walter W. Peek (Narraganset/Wampanoag).
1974 The International Indian Treaty Council is founded at New York, New York. Activists in the sovereign Mohawk Nation claim original title to land at Eagle Bay, at Moss Lake in the Adirondacks, and occupy it. They name the place Ganienkeh, or the Land of Flintstone. The first trial resulting from the occupation of Wounded Knee, on Pine Ridge Reservation, in South Dakota, begins in Minnesota. The Navajo-Hopi Land Settlement Act, passed by the United States Congress, is a misguided attempt to resolve the dispute over land possession between the sovereign Hopi and sovereign Navajo peoples. Housing is provided to the People of the sovereign Native nations and tribes under provisions of the Housing and Community Development Act, passed by the United States Congress. Hiring preference of People of the sovereign Native nations and tribes is affirmed in a decision by the United States Supreme Court, in the case *Morton v. Mancari*.	*Anadu Iwacha; The Way It Was: Yakima Indian Legend Book.* Virginia Beavert (Yakima), et al., editors. *Histoire des Indiens du Haut et du Bas Canada.* Bernard Assiniwi (Cree/Algonkian). *Behind the Trail of Broken Treaties and The Indian Affair.* Vine Deloria Jr. (Standing Rock Sioux). *Short Haida Stories.* Erma G. Lawrence (Haida). *Mother Earth, Father Sky.* Marcia Keegan (Cherokee). *Betrayed.* Virginia Driving Hawk Sneve (Rosebud Sioux). *Psychology and Contemporary Problems.* Arthur L. McDonald (Oglala Lakota). *The Future Is Now.* Walter J. Hillabrant (Citizen Band Potawatomi). *Owl Song.* Janet Campbell Hale (Coeur d'Alene). *The Story of an American Indian.* Maria [Montoya] Martinez (San Ildefonso). *Angle of Geese and Other Poems.* Navarre Scott Momaday (Kiowa/Cherokee). *Ascending Red Cedar Moon.* Duane McGinnis Niatum (Klallam). *A Pima Past.* Anna Moore Shaw (Pima). *Laguna Woman.* Leslie Marmon Silko (Laguna). *Winter in the Blood.* James Welch (Blackfoot/Gros Ventre).
1975 Violent confrontation on Pine Ridge Reservation, in South Dakota, between American Indian Movement (AIM) activists and agents of the Federal Bureau of Investigation (FBI) results in the deaths of two FBI agents. Leonard Peltier is convicted. Eighteen sovereign Native nations are granted 346,000 acres held by the United States government since 1933, by an act of the United States Congress. *(continued)*	*Le Bras Coupe and Lexique des noms Indiens en Amerique.* Bernard Assiniwi (Cree/Algonkian). *The Judge: The Life of Robert A. Hefner.* Clifford E. Trafzer (Wyandot). *Bidato.* Duane Big Eagle (Osage). *The Last Song.* Joy Harjo (Creek). *Bright Eyes: The Story of Susette La Flesche, an Omaha Indian.* Clara Sue Kidwell (Choctaw/Chippewa).

HEROES/LEADERS/ VICTIMS	ELDER WISDOM/PHILOSOPHY/ SONGS	
Morris Thompson (Tanana) is appointed commissioner of Indian affairs in the U.S. Department of the Interior. He serves until 1976. Odrik Baker (Lac Courte Oreilles Chippewa) becomes tribal chairman. John E. Echohawk (Pawnee) becomes executive director of the Native American Rights Fund (NARF).		**1973**
Sheldon A. Chicks (Stockbridge-Munsee), a physician in private practice, becomes president of the Association of American Indian Physicians. Virginia Driving Hawk Sneve (Rosebud Sioux) receives the prestigious Western Writers of America Award for her book *Betrayed*.		**1974**
C. Lawrence Huerta (Pasqua Yaqui) becomes chancellor of Navajo Community College. Richard Vance La Course (Yakima) becomes managing editor of the *Yakima Nation Review* in Toppenish, Washington. Anna Mae Aquash (Sioux) is shot to death on the Pine Ridge Reservation, in South Dakota.	Time is more a proving factor than a controlling factor to the Indian way of living. *Herbert Blatchford (Navajo)*	**1975**

HISTORY/LAW/ POLITICS	LITERATURE/ART/ LEGENDS AND STORIES
1975 (continued from page 308) The Indian Self-Determination and Education Assistance Act is passed by the United States Congress and signed into law by President Gerald R. Ford. The act states in part: The Congress hereby recognizes the obligation of the United States to respond to the strong expression of the Indian people for self-determination by assuring maximum Indian participation in the direction of educational as well as other Federal services to Indian communities so as to render such services more responsive to the needs and desires of those communities. The Council of Energy Resource Tribes (CERT) is organized to manage energy resources on reservation lands of the People of the sovereign Native nations and tribes. Radio station KRNB-FM, owned and operated by the sovereign Makah Nation, begins broadcasting from Neah Bay, Washington.	*Bobbie Lee: Indian Rebel.* Lee Maracle, or Bobbie Lee (Métis). *Conversations from the Nightmare.* Carol Lee Sanchez (Laguna). *O-hu-kah-kan: Poetry, Songs, Legends, and Stories by American Indians.* Gilbert Walking Bull (Sioux) and Montana Walking Bull (Cherokee). *We Can Still Hear Them Clapping.* Marcia Keegan (Cherokee).
1976 	*The Dreams of Jesse Brown.* Joseph Bruchac III (Abenaki). *Tsalagi.* Carroll Arnett (Cherokee). *Songs and Dances of the Lakota.* Ben Black Bear Sr. (Sioux) and R. D. Theisz, editors. *To Frighten a Storm.* Gladys Cardiff (Eastern Cherokee). *The Tales of Okanogans.* Humishuma, or Mourning Dove, or Cristal McLeod Galler (Okanogan). *Ojibwa Heritage.* Basil H. Johnston (Ojibwa). *Memoirs of an American Indian House.* Ted Jojola (Isleta). *Gii-Ikwezensiwiyaan—When I Was a Little Girl.* Maude Kegg (Ojibwa). *The Gourd Dancer.* Navarre Scott Momaday (Kiowa/Cherokee). *Going for the Rain.* Simon J. Ortiz (Acoma). *Message Bringer Woman.* Carol Lee Sanchez (Laguna). *The Pueblo Indian.* Joe S. Sando (Jemez). *Wo Ya-ka-pi: Telling Stories of the Past and the Present.* Gilbert Walking Bull (Sioux) and Montana Walking Bull (Cherokee). *The Dilemma for Indian Woman—Wassaja.* Annie D. Wauneka (Diné, or Navajo). *Entering into the Silence—The Seneca Way.* Twylah Hurd Nitsch (Seneca). *The Reservation.* Ted Williams (Tuscarora).
1977 The position of assistant secretary for Indian affairs is created in the U.S. Department of the Interior. The International Indian Treaty Council, founded in 1974, is recognized as a non-governmental organization of the United Nations because of a resolution presented at the International Human Rights Conference in Geneva, Switzerland, by activists among the People of the sovereign Native Nations and tribes. *(continued)*	*Then Badger Said This.* Elizabeth Cook-Lynn (Sioux). *Crying Wind.* Crying Wind, or Linda Stafford (Kickapoo). *Great North American Indians: Profiles in Life and Leadership.* Frederick J. Dockstader (Oneida). *Indians of the Pacific Northwest.* Vine Deloria Jr. (Standing Rock Sioux).

HEROES/LEADERS/ VICTIMS	ELDER WISDOM/PHILOSOPHY/ SONGS	
Dennis Banks (Ogala Sioux) and Russell Means (Ogala Sioux) are convicted of assault and riot charges.		**1975**
Benjamin Reifel (Sioux) is appointed commissioner of Indian affairs, U.S. Department of the Interior, but leaves office after a year. Byron Mallott (Tlingit) becomes chairman of the board of Sealaska Corporation. John Mohawk (Seneca) becomes editor of *Akwesasne Notes*, in Rooseveltown, New York.		**1976**
Raymond Butler (Blackfoot) becomes acting commissioner of Indian affairs in the U.S. Department of the Interior and serves for one year, while the position of commissioner is "restructured" and the additional position of assistant secretary is established.	To me being indian does not mean I am red like the earth or talk in stilted English. To me being indian does not mean I have to live on the Reservation or go on my vision quest. To me being indian means to be closer to nature, closer to mother earth. It means you open your eyes to see a sunset. And open your heart to hear the rhythm. *Lee Francis IV (Laguna/Chippewa)*	**1977**

	HISTORY/LAW/ POLITICS	LITERATURE/ART/ LEGENDS AND STORIES

1977	*(continued from page 310)*
	
	     Racial bias against the People of the sovereign Native nations and tribes of Oklahoma is acknowledged in a report issued by the Oklahoma Human Rights Commission.
		"Whitehorn v. State: Peyote and Religious Freedom in Oklahoma," American Indian Law Review. Robert Johnston (Comanche).
		     The Great Sioux Nation. Roxanne Dunbar Ortiz (Southern Cheyenne).
		     I Am Nokomis, Too: The Biography of Verna Patronella Johnston. Verna Patronella Johnston (Ojibwa).
		     Dance Around the Sun: The Life of Mary Little Bear Inkanish, Cheyenne. Mary Little Bear (Cheyenne).
		     Digging Out the Roots. Duane McGinnis Niatum (Klallam).
		     A Good Journey. Simon J. Ortiz (Acoma).
		     Academic Squaw: Reports to the World from the Ivory Tower. Wendy Rose (Hopi).
		     Nine Poems. Mary Tall Mountain (Koyukon Athabascan).
		     Mi Ta-ku-ye: About My People. Gilbert Walking Bull (Sioux) and Montana Walking Bull (Cherokee).

1978	The Longest Walk, in which thousands of activists among the People of the sovereign Native nations and tribes participate, begins in San Francisco and ends in Washington, D.C. The walk is organized to commemorate the forced "walks" the People had made in the past.
	     The American Indian Science and Engineering Society (AISES) is founded in Boulder, Colorado.
	     Congress passes the Indian Child Welfare Act to provide federal assistance for child and family programs established by federally recognized and state-recognized sovereign Native nations and tribes.
	     Congress passes the American Indian Freedom of Religion Act, which declares that Native religious practices are protected under the First Amendment of the United States Constitution.
	     The Indian Youth of America is founded in Sioux City, Iowa.
		Abiding Appalachia: Where Mountain and Atom Meet. Awiakta, or Marilou Awiakta (Cherokee).
		     Entering Onondaga. Joseph Bruchac III (Abenaki).
		     White Corn Sister and Back Then Tomorrow. Aroniawenate, or Peter Blue Cloud (Mohawk).
		     Fox Texts. William Jones (Mesquakie, or Fox).
		     Wind from the Enemy Sky. D'Arcy McNickle (Salish).
		     Ceremony. Leslie Marmon Silko (Laguna).
		     Big Falling Snow. Albert Yava (Tewa/Hopi).

1979	More than forty-three thousand Native students across Turtle Island are enrolled in boarding, day, and dormitory schools operated by the U.S. Department of the Interior Bureau of Indian Affairs (BIA).
	     Off-reservation fishing rights, as provided under treaty, are addressed by the United States Supreme Court in its ruling in *Washington v. Washington State Commercial Passenger Fishing Vessel Association.* The ruling is not definitive and has spawned subsequent cases.
		A Snug Little Purchase: How Richard Henderson Bought Kaintuckee from the Cherokees in 1777. Charles Brashear (Cherokee).
		     Sevukakmet: Ways of Life on St. Lawrence Island. Helen Slwooko Carius (Eskimo).
		     White Eagle—Green Corn. Solomon McCombs (Creek).
		     Wisdom of the Senecas. Twylah Hurd Nitsch (Seneca).
		     Speaking of Indians. Agnes Picotte and Paul Pavich, editors. Ella Cara Deloria (Sioux).
		     The Metaphysics of Modern Existence. Vine Deloria Jr. (Standing Rock Sioux).
		     My Horse and a Jukebox. Barney Bush (Shawnee/Cayuga).
		     What Moon Drove Me to This. Joy Harjo (Creek).
		     The Remembered Earth: An Anthology of Contemporary Native American Literature. Geary Hobson (Quapaw/Cherokee/Chickasaw).
		     The Death of Jim Loney. James Welch (Blackfood/Gros Ventre).

Forrest Gerard (Blackfoot) is the first from among the People to be appointed to the newly created position of assistant secretary for Indian affairs in the U.S. Department of the Interior. He serves until 1981.

Byron Mallott (Tlingit) is elected president of the Alaska Federation of Natives.

President Gerald R. Ford appoints Richard Lucero Jr. (Mescalero Apache/Seminole) to the National Drug Abuse and Adolescents Task Force.

Lee Francis IV (Laguna/Chippewa), published poet, is born on April 17.

Loren Tapahe (Navajo) becomes general manager of the *Navajo Times* publishing company.

Norbert S. Hills Jr. (Oneida)
COURTESY OF LEE FRANCIS III

1977

Dean Chavers (Lumbee) becomes president of Bacone College, Muskogee, Oklahoma.

Martin Seneca Jr. (Seneca) is appointed acting commissioner of Indian affairs in the U.S. Department of the Interior.

Louis R. Headley (Arapaho) is named Outstanding Young Man of America by the Jaycees.

1978

Frances A. Levier (Citizen Band Potawatomi) is appointed to the board of regents of Haskell Indian Junior College at Lawrence, Kansas.

William Hallett (Chippewa) is appointed as commissioner of Indian Affairs in the U.S. Department of the Interior.

Winter lasts and kills and graves can't be dug by ordinary hands with ordinary shovels.
Gordon D. Henry Jr. (White Earth Chippewa)
COURTESY OF ROBERT TURNEY

1979

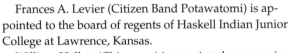

Gordon Henry, Jr. (White Earth Chippewa)
COURTESY OF ROBERT TURNEY

PERSPECTIVE
1980–1994

All across Turtle Island, the People of the sovereign nations and tribes continued to thrive. The population grew from 1.4 million in 1980 to 1.9 million by 1990. Equally important was the information gained from a new question on the 1990 census inquiring about heritage, to which more than six million people identified themselves as having had Native ancestors.

Building on the activism of the previous twenty years, Native People continued to pursue an agenda for economic and social justice. Throughout the 1980s and early 1990s, Native leaders gained prominence as storytellers, writers (including a Pulitzer Prize recipient for literature, N. Scott Momaday, *House Made of Dawn*, 1968), poets, scholars, publishers, lawyers, educators, scientists, medical doctors, engineers, musicians, athletes, military officers and soldiers, and as elected or appointed officials in tribal, federal, state, and local government.

Despite significant strides in court decisions in favor of the People and new federal laws, many issues remain to be resolved. Foremost are the twin issues of cultural appropriation of traditional practices, ceremonies, and stories by our non-Native relations and the use of blood quantum to determine who is a "real live Indian."

By the beginning of the late 1980s, the ancient practices of the People of the sovereign Native nations and tribes all across Turtle Island had become "popular" among non-Natives. Unable to take any more land, since the United States government had accomplished that task a century earlier, a growing number of non-Natives began to appropriate the cultural and spiritual practices and ceremonies of the People.

Self-proclaimed "shamans," "medicine men," and "medicine women" abounded, hawking their newfound New Age ersatz "Native spirituality" to unsuspecting buyers. Once again, the desperate and spiritually impoverished non-Natives failed to understand that true Native spirituality, like the land, is never for sale.

Would Muslims object if a Native person began to perform their sacred ceremonies without knowing anything about the Koran? Would the Jewish community be upset if Native People began to give seminars on how to be a traditional Jewish rabbi? Would Roman Catholic officials denounce as a fraud an advertisement about "authentic Roman Catholic masses" performed by a Native person who, although "not ordained," had "learned everything from an elderly Roman Catholic priest or bishop"?

The issue of blood quantum, which grew out of the aberrant "custom" pertaining to African-Americans (i.e., one drop of "Negro" blood makes you a Negro), is an equally contentious issue confronting the People of the sovereign Native nations and tribes all across Turtle Island. Blood quantum as applied by the Bureau of Indian Affairs (BIA) in the United States Department of the Interior came about as a "legally nice" way for the United States government to "deal" with what is referred to euphemistically as "the Indian Problem." Initially, after a majority of Native People had survived genocidal policies and practices and were forced onto reservations, they were identified as being "full-blooded."

If a full-blood married a full-blood, then their children would be "full-bloods" and "entitled" to the "benefits" (i.e., food, shelter, blankets, and clothing) as provided under treaty between the People of that sovereign nation or tribe and the government of the United States. If, however, a "full-blood" left the reservation and married a non-Native, then the children were "half-breeds."

The tragedy is that far too many of the People of the sovereign Native nations and tribes all across Turtle Island have accepted blood quantum of a certain degree as a criterion for tribal membership.

Despite these two divisive issues, the People of the sovereign Native nations and tribes across Turtle Island are becoming more and more united. What is especially significant is the gathering of literally thousands of the People at powwows and national Native conferences. For example, more than three thousand Native people attended the National Indian Education Association (NIEA) conferences in Albuquerque, New Mexico (1992), and St. Paul, Minnesota (1994). Likewise, more than 3,200 Native People attended the national conference of the American Indian Science and Engineering Society (AISES) at San Jose, California (1994).

In essence, a new dawn has come for the People of the sovereign Native nations and tribes on Turtle Island, and our hearts are filled with hope for the future.

HISTORY/LAW/ POLITICS	LITERATURE/ART/ LEGENDS AND STORIES
1980 The population of the People of the sovereign Native nations and tribes across Turtle Island grows from 237,000, in 1990, to more than 1,418,000, according to the United States Bureau of the Census. The United States recognizes the Southern Paiute tribe and returns five thousand acres to the tribe. The Sioux Nation is awarded $122 million by the United States Supreme Court for the 7.3 million acres in the Black Hills illegally taken from it in 1876. The Alaska National Interest Lands Conservation Act is signed into law by President Jimmy Carter. It guarantees food-gathering rights of the sovereign Alaska Native peoples from approximately 100 million acres of public land set aside in Alaska for wildlife refuges, forests, and national parks. The Houlton Maliseet, Passamaquoddy, and Penobscot Nations of Maine agree to abandon their land claims under the Maine Indian Claims Settlement Act, passed by the United States Congress, in exchange for a trust fund of approximately $27 million and a federal land-acquisition fund of approximately $54 million. Jurisdiction of the state of Washington and the issue of state sales tax as it applies to the People of the sovereign Native nations and tribes are addressed by the United States Supreme Court in its decision in *Washington v. Confederated Tribes of the Colville Indian Reservation*. The ruling states that the tax did not apply.	*Translator's Son*. Joseph Bruchac III (Abenaki). *Yuma: Frontier Crossing of the Far Southwest*. Clifford E. Trafzer (Wyandot). *The Volga Germans: Pioneers of the Pacific Northwest*. Clifford E. Trafzer (Wyandot) with Richard D. Scheuerman. *American Indian Leaders: Studies in Diversity*. David R. Edmunds (Cherokee). *Sociology of American Indians: A Critical Bibliography*. Russell Thornton (Cherokee) with Mary K. Grasmick. *New Native American Drama: Three Plays*. Hanay Gieogamah (Kiowa). *The Fish on Poteau Mountain*. Jim Barnes (Choctaw). *Calling Myself Home*. Linda Hogan (Chickasaw). *The Ways of My Grandmothers*. Beverly Hungry Wolf (Blackfoot). *Numa-Nu: The Fort Sill Indian School Experience*. Delores T. Sumner (Comanche). *Spirit Woman*. Wa Wa Calachaw, or Bonita Nuñez (Luiseño). *Fight Back: For the Sake of the People, for the Sake of the Land*. Simon J. Ortiz (Acoma). *Lost Copper*. Wendy Rose (Hopi). *The Autobiography of a Yaqui Poet*. Refugio Savila (Yaqui).
1981 The National Vietnam Era Veterans Inter-Tribal Association is founded at Oklahoma City, Oklahoma. Funding of social programs for the People of the sovereign Native nations and tribes across Turtle Island is cut radically, by almost 40 percent, under policies implemented by the administration of President Ronald Reagan. The *Lakota Times*, later called *Indian Country Today*, begins publication in July, in South Dakota.	*The Choctaws: A Critical Bibliography*. Clara Sue Kidwell (Choctaw/Chippewa). *Gorky Park*. Martin Cruz Smith (Modoc). *Native American Women: A Bibliography*. Rayna Green (Cherokee), editor. *Echoes of Our Being*. Robin Coffee (Cherokee/Muscogee/Lakota). *A Strong Medicine Wind*. Ethel Constance Krepps (Kiowa/Miami). *Cattle Management*. Cheryl May (Cherokee). *Daughters I Love You*. Linda Hogan (Chickasaw). *Songs for the Harvester of Dreams*. Duane McGinnis Niatum (Klallam). *From Sand Creek*. Simon J. Ortiz (Acoma). *Storyteller*. Leslie Marmon Silko (Laguna). *There Is No Word for Goodby*. Mary Tall Mountain (Koyukon Athabascan). *Winter of the Salamander*. Ray A. Young Bear (Mesquakie).

1980

Vivian M. Adams (Squamish/Quinault-Yakima/ Puyallup) receives the Outstanding Artistic and Academic Achievement Award from the Institute of American Indian Arts at Santa Fe, New Mexico.

William Oandasan (Yuki) becomes editor of the *American Indian Culture and Research Journal*, University of California, Los Angeles.

Maria Montoya Martinez (San Ildefonso), the famous potter of San Ildefonso Pueblo, dies.

It is important to present our cultural history and traditions from our Native American Indian point of view to promote a better understanding by other cultures.
Vivian M. Adams (Squamish/Quinault-Yakima/Puyallup)

Ernie Dog Wolf Lovato (Apache Mestizo)
COURTESY OF ERNIE DOG WOLF LOVATO

1981

Tom Fredericks (Mandan Hidatsa) is appointed assistant secretary for Indian affairs in the U.S. Department of the Interior. His appointment is temporary.

Kenneth Smith (Wasco) is appointed assistant secretary for Indian affairs in the U.S. Department of the Interior. He serves in this position until 1985.

Patricia Penn Hilden (Nez Percé) receives a Ph.D. degree from King's College of Cambridge University, in Cambridge, England.

Gordon L. Pullar (Koniag) becomes assistant editor of *Nations* magazine of Seattle, Washington.

Phillip Martin (Mississippi Choctaw) is elected president of the National Tribal Chairmen's Association.

HISTORY/LAW/ POLITICS	LITERATURE/ART/ LEGENDS AND STORIES
1982 Gay American Indians is founded at New York City. A Tohono O'odham, or Papago, water-rights suit against Arizona is responded to by an act of the United States Congress that appropriates $112 million to settle the suit. President Ronald Reagan vetoes the settlement. Later, the federal government agrees to pay $40 million to the Tohono O'odham, or Papago. The People of the sovereign Eskimo First Nation of Canada gain approval for establishment of a new territory in Canada's Northwest Territories, to be known as Nunavut. The leaders of the territory are to be Eskimo. Plans for the establishment of Nunavut are still under way. The Indian Tribal Governmental Tax Status Act, passed by the United States Congress, is aimed at ending discriminatory treatment under the Internal Revenue Code of sovereign Native nations and tribal governments. The act permits them to issue bonds under limited circumstances. The issues of severance taxes and sovereignty of Native nations and tribes are decided by the United States Supreme Court, in *Merrion v. Jicarilla Apache Tribe*, which grants limited sovereignty to the Jicarilla.	*The Urbanization of American Indians: A Critical Bibliography*. Russell Thornton (Cherokee) with Gary D. Sandefur and Harold G. Grasmick. *Language of the Trees*. Twylah Hurd Nitsch (Seneca). *The Stylistic Development of Navajo Jewelry*. Rain Parrish (Navajo). *La Salle and His Legacy: Frenchmen and Indians in the Lower Mississippi Valley*. Kenneth H. York (Mississippi Choctaw). *Enwhisteetkwa: Walk in Water*. Jeannette C. Armstrong (Okanagan). *American Book of the Dead*. Jim Barnes (Choctaw). *The Kit Carson Campaign: The Last Navajo War*. Clifford E. Trafzer (Wyandot). *Petroglyphs*. Barney Bush (Shawnee/Cayuga). *Blackrobe*. Maurice Kenny (Mohawk).
1983 Settlement by an act of the United States Congress of a land-claim suit in the amount of $900,000, brought by the sovereign Pequot Nation against Connecticut, is vetoed by President Ronald Reagan. The People of the sovereign Lac Courte Oreilles Chippewa retain their hunting, fishing, gathering, and trapping rights as provided in the Treaties of 1837, 1842, and 1852, in what is referred to as the Voight decision, rendered by the United States Seventh Circuit Court of Appeals. Sinte Gleska College, on the Rosebud Reservation in South Dakota, the first postsecondary institution of higher education controlled by a sovereign Native nation, is granted full accreditation by the North Central Association of Colleges and Schools for its baccalaureate degree programs. The issue of regulatory jurisdiction over hunting and fishing is decided by the United States Supreme Court, in *New Mexico v. Mescalero Apache Tribe*, in favor of the Mescalero people, but with several restrictions. The Inuit Circumpolar Conference, founded in 1977, is granted status as a nongovernmental organization by the United Nations. The conference is composed of Inuit people of Alaska, Canada, and Greenland. The American Indian Research and Resource Institute is founded at Gettysburg, Pennsylvania. Replicas of the two Olympic Gold Medals won by Jim Thorpe (Sac and Fox/Potawatomi) are presented to his heirs on January 18, about seventy years after the International Olympic Committee had taken them from Thorpe.	*Il n'y plus d'Indiens (a play)*. Bernard Assiniwi (Cree/Algongian). *In Search of Our Mother's Gardens*. Awiakta, or Marilou Awiakta, (Cherokee). *Native American Women: A Contectual Bibliography*. Rayna Green (Cherokee). *Eclipse*. Linda Hogan (Chickasaw). *Native American Substance Abuse*. Wayne Lee Mitchell (Santee Sioux/Mandan). *Woven Holy People*. Rain Parrish (Navajo). *American Indians, American Justice*. Vine Deloria Jr, (Standing Rock Sioux). *Legacy: Engineering at Kansas State University*. Cheryl May (Cherokee).

Janie Leask (Haida/Tsimshian) is elected president of the Alaska Federation of Natives.

Byron Mallott (Tlingit) becomes chief executive officer of Sealaska Corporation. He also is named a director of Alaska Airlines and director of the Federal Reserve Bank, Seattle.

I am a writer simply because Americans stress the written word as the primary establishment of truth. If it is not written down, then one has no "proof." I am a writer because I respect this earth, all the universe, all that is known, and that which is unknown. I respect all who acknowledge this interrelationship and pity those who squander their lives attempting to destroy it or steal its power.

Barney Bush (Shawnee)

1982

Gordon L. Pullar (Koniag) becomes publisher of the *Kodiak Times.*

Charles W. Murphy (Standing Rock Sioux) is elected chairman of the Standing Rock Sioux tribal council and chief executive officer of the tribal government.

Peterson Zah (Navajo) is elected chairman of the Navajo Nation.

Ross Swimmer (Cherokee) is reelected principal chief of the Cherokee Nation of Oklahoma, and Wilma P. Mankiller (Cherokee) is elected deputy chief.

Barney Bush (Shawnee/Cayuga)
COURTESY OF CHARLES HAMMOND

1983

	HISTORY/LAW/ POLITICS	LITERATURE/ART/ LEGENDS AND STORIES
1984	The Select Committee on Indian Affairs becomes a permanent committee of the United States Senate. The Native American Press Association is reorganized as the Native American Journalists Association (NAJA). The leaders of the sovereign Eastern Band of Cherokee Indians, of North Carolina, and the Cherokee Nation of Oklahoma meet in joint council at Red Clay, in southeastern Tennessee, for the first time since the Cherokee Nation was split and thousands of its people were removed forcibly on what is known as the Trail of Tears to Indian Territory (present Oklahoma). The Great Jim Thorpe Longest Run is held during the Summer Olympics in Los Angeles, California, in honor of Olympian Jim Thorpe (Sac and Fox/Potawatomi).	*That's What She Said: Contemporary Poetry and Fiction by Native American Women.* Rayna Green (Cherokee), editor. *Neekna and Chemai.* Jeannette C. Armstrong (Okanagan). *Love Medicine.* Louise Erdrich (Turtle Mountain Chippewa). *The Nations Within.* Vine Deloria Jr. (Standing Rock Sioux). *Nature Chants and Dances.* Twylah Hurd Nitsch (Seneca). *. . . And with the Wagon—Came God's Word.* Betty Mae Jumper (Seminole). *Round Valley Songs and Moving Island.* William Oandasan (Yuki).
1985	The sovereign Jicarilla Apache Nation, in New Mexico, becomes the first sovereign Native nation to sell tax–exempt "A"-rated municipal bonds to institutional investors. The Navajo Nation passes the Navajo Business Preference Law, which requires first preference to Navajo-owned business on all contract-letting jobs. The right of sovereign Native nations and tribes to sue to enforce ancient land rights is decided by the United States Supreme Court in *County of Oneida, New York, v. Oneida Indian Nation of New York.* The issues of sovereignty and non-IRA taxation power of sovereign Native nations and tribes are decided by the United States Supreme Court in *Kerr-McGee Corp. v. Navajo Tribe of Indians.* The ruling gives the authority to tax and grants limited sovereignty. At a meeting in Reno, Nevada, the National Tribal Chairmen's Association votes overwhelmingly to reject the proposals of U.S. President Ronald Reagan's Commission on Indian Reservation Economics.	*Inherit the Blood.* Barney Bush (Shawnee/Cayuga). *A Season of Loss.* Jim Barnes (Choctaw). *Mohawk Trail.* Beth Brant (Bay of Quinte Mohawk). *Tracking.* Joseph Bruchac III (Abenaki). *Excerpts from a Mountain Climber's Handbook.* Carol Lee Sanchez (Laguna).
1986	Native veterans of the United States military service are honored with a memorial at Arlington National Cemetery, Arlington, Virginia.  *Ben Nighthorse Campbell (Cheyenne)–United States Senator from Colorado* COURTESY OF BEN NIGHTHORSE CAMPBELL	*Red Cedar Warrior.* Sylvester J. Brito (Comanche/Tarascan). *Near the Mountains.* Joseph Bruchac III (Abenaki). *Back to Malachi.* Robert J. Conley (United Keetoowah Band Cherokee). *We Shall Live Again: The 1870 and 1890 Ghost Dance Movements as Demographic Revitalization.* Russell Thornton (Cherokee). *Indians, Superintendents and Councils: Northwestern Indian Policy, 1850–1855.* Clifford E. Trafzer (Wyandot), editor. *Northwestern Tribes in Exile: Modoc, Nez Percé, and Palouse Removal to the Indian Territory.* Clifford E. Trafzer (Wyandot), editor. *The Renegade Tribe: The Palouse Indians and the Invasion of the Inland Pacific Northwest.* Clifford E. Trafzer (Wyandot) with Richard D. Scheuerman.

HEROES/LEADERS/ VICTIMS	ELDER WISDOM/PHILOSOPHY/ SONGS	

Richard Lucero Jr. (Mescalero Apache/Seminole) becomes president of the American Indian Health Care Association.

Rokwaho, or Dan Thompson (Mohawk), is cofounder of *Akwekon*, a literary and arts quarterly.

Charles W. Murphy (Standing Rock Sioux) is elected to the school board in Bismarck, North Dakota.

William L. Engles (Oneida) is appointed commissioner of the Administration for Native Americans (ANA), U.S. Department of Health and Human Services.

Wilma Mankiller (Cherokee)
COURTESY OF SAMMY STILL

1984

John Adams Barrett (Citizen Band Potawatomi), president of Barrett Refining at Shawnee, Oklahoma, is the only Native to be awarded a $50 million jet-fuel contract from the U.S. Department of Defense.

William Oandasan (Yuki) receives the prestigious American Book Award from the Before Columbus Foundation.

Ross O. Swimmer (Cherokee) is appointed assistant secretary for Indian affairs (BIA) in the U.S. Department of the Interior. He serves until 1989. Wilma Mankiller succeeds Swimmer as principal chief of the Cherokee Nation of Oklahoma.

Ted Jojola (Isleta) Ph.D., receives the certificate of international human rights law from the University of Strasbourg in France.

Karoniaktatie, or Alex A. Jacobs (Mohawk) is selected editor of the *Akwekon Literary Journal*.

1985

1986

	HISTORY/LAW/ POLITICS	LITERATURE/ART/ LEGENDS AND STORIES
1987	Members of the sovereign Oglala Sioux Nation and authorities of the United States Postal Service commemorate the issuing of a new ten-cent stamp honoring Red Cloud, a chief of the Oglala Sioux Nation, for his role in the negotiations of the Treaty of 1868 between the People of the Sioux Nation and the United States. The National Historic Trail of Tears, established by an act of the United States Congress, commemorates the forced removal of People of the sovereign Cherokee Nation from their homelands in the Southeast to Indian Territory, an odyssey covering nine states. The "National Native News" network program of Anchorage, Alaska, begins broadcasting and is aired on more than two hundred radio stations all across Turtle Island.	*Survival This Way: Interviews with American Indian Poets.* Joseph Bruchac III (Abenaki). *The Actor.* Robert J. Conley (United Keetoowah Band Cherokee). *Harper's Anthology of 20th Century Native American Poetry.* Duane McGinnis Niatum (Klallam), editor. *Grandmother's Christmas Story: A True Quechan Indian Story.* Richard Red Hawk, or Clifford E. Trafzer (Wyandot). *American Indian Holocaust and Survival: A Population History Since 1492.* Russell Thornton (Cherokee).
1988	Destruction of sacred ancient sites of the People of the sovereign nations and tribes is found to be legal by the United States Supreme Court in its decision *Lyng v. Northwest Indian Cemetery Protective Association.* The United States Department of the Interior's Forest Service continues to bulldoze sacred spiritual sites with scant protest by non-Native Americans. At "A Celebration of Native American Life" on October 29, several hundred people gather to honor the People of the sovereign nations and tribes buried at Congressional Cemetery in Washington, D.C. Wilma P. Mankiller (Cherokee), Principal Chief of the Cherokee Nation, is the keynote speaker.	*Killing Time, The Witch of Goingsnake and Other Stories, and Wilder and Wilder.* Robert J. Conley (United Keetoowah Band Cherokee). *Grandfather's Origin Story: The Navajo Beginning.* Richard Red Hawk, or Clifford E. Trafzer (Wyandot).
1989	The French government honors Choctaw and Comanche "code talkers" with the Chevalier de L'Ordre National du Mérite. The New York State Museum, in Albany, returns twelve wampum belts to the Onondaga Nation of New York. The request to return a 150-year-old sacred bundle to a representative of the sovereign Cree First Nation of Canada is refused by the American Museum of Natural History, in New York City. A Cree man from Alberta had run more than twenty-five hundred miles to take possession of the sacred object on behalf of the People. The National Museum of the American Indian, to be built in Washington, D.C., as part of the Smithsonian Institution, is established by the U.S. Congress and signed into law by President George Bush.	*The Broken Cord.* Michael A. Dorris (Modoc). *La Plata Cantata.* Jim Barnes (Choctaw). *Elderberry Flute Song: Contemporary Coyote Tales.* Aroniawenate, or Peter Blue Cloud (Mohawk). *The Way of a Peyote Redman.* Sylvester J. Brito (Comanche/Tarascan). *Colfax and The Saga of Henry Starr.* Robert J. Conley (United Keetoowah Band Cherokee).

HEROES/LEADERS/ VICTIMS	ELDER WISDOM/PHILOSOPHY/ SONGS	
Gary Fife (Muscogee/Cherokee) is producer/host of the "National Native News" program. Wilma P. Mankiller (Cherokee) is elected to her first full term as principal chief of the Cherokee Nation of Oklahoma.		**1987**
	When white men first witnessed Indians impersonating animal spirits in costume and dance, and worshipping rocks and rainbows, they failed to see this as a deep form of religious worship. To their Christian minds, these were deplorable pagan rites. Worship of more than one deity, and sacrificial offerings directed at the natural world, stamped Indians as misguided, lesser form of mankind. Here were Christless heathens crying to be rescued from eternal damnation. *Peter Nabakov* *Native American Testimony:* *An Anthology of Indian and White Relations*	**1988**
Tom Tso (Diné, or Navajo) becomes chief justice of the Navajo Nation Supreme Court. Ed Brown (Pascua Yaqui) is appointed assistant secretary for Indian affairs (BIA) in the U.S. Department of the Interior and serves in that position until William Jefferson Clinton is elected president of the United States.	I regret that the outside world has never recognized that Navajos were functioning with sophisticated and workable legal and political concepts before the American Revolution. I regret even more that the ways in which we are different are neither known nor valued by the dominant society. Because we are viewed as having nothing to contribute, much time has been wasted. *Tom Tso (Navajo)*	**1989**

HISTORY/LAW/ POLITICS	LITERATURE/ART/ LEGENDS AND STORIES
1990 Congress passes the Native American Grave Protection and Repatriation Act, and President George Bush signs it into law. The United States Supreme Court, in *Employment Division of Oregon v. Smith*, rules that sacramental use of peyote in religious services of the People of the sovereign nations and tribes is not constitutionally protected under the United States Constitution's freedom of religion clause and that states are permitted to outlaw such use. The United States Congress passes the Native American Languages Act on October 30. One section states that "acts of suppression and extermination directed against Native American languages are in conflict with United States policy of self-determination for Native Americans." The 1886 policy finally is "against the law," but it will take a long time for the People of the sovereign nations and tribes all across Turtle Island to reclaim their ancient languages.	*The Other Side of Nowhere*. Aroniawenate, or Peter Blue Cloud (Mohawk). *A Quaker Promise Kept: Philadelphia Friends' Work with the Allegany Senecas*. Duwayne Leslie Bowen (Seneca). *Quitting Time* and *Go-Ahead Rider*. Robert J. Conley (United Keetoowah Band Cherokee). *Mean Spirit*. Linda Hogan (Chickasaw). *Contemporary Insanities, Short Fictions*. Charles Brashear (Cherokee). *To Lead and to Serve: Indian Education at Hampton Institute, 1879–1923*. Paulette Fairbanks Molin (White Earth Chippewa) and Marilou Hultgren (white), with introduction by Rayna Green (Cherokee).
1991 The Larsen Bay peoples of Kodiak Island, Alaska, receive the remains of more than seven hundred of the People from the Smithsonian Institution's National Museum of Natural History. More than three thousand People of the sovereign nations and tribes across Turtle Island serve in the United States Armed Forces in the Persian Gulf War ("Desert Storm"). A memorial to People of the sovereign nations and tribes who died in 1876 at the Little Bighorn, in what is now Montana, is authorized by legislation passed by Congress and signed by President George Bush. The legislation changes the name of the site from Custer Battlefield National Monument to Little Bighorn Battlefield National Monument. Sacred objects of the sovereign Omaha Nation that were stolen in about 1898 are returned by representatives from the National Museum of the American Indian. Leases held by non-Natives for land belonging to the sovereign Seneca Nation at Salamanca, on the Allegheny Reservation in New York expire. Leaseholders want to pay only the price agreed to in the original ninety-nine year lease—one dollar per year. The People of the sovereign Mississippi Choctaw Nation vote by an overwhelming majority to reject a proposal to permit disposal of manufacturing-waste products on land they own.	*Monster Slayer*. Vee F. Browne (Diné, or Navajo). *The State of Native America*. Annette Jaimes (Juaneño/Yaqui). *Voices of the Heart*. Robin Coffee (Cherokee/Muscogee/Lakota). *Strange Company* and *Ned Christie's War*. Robert J. Conley (United Keetoowah Band Cherokee). *The Crown of Columbus*. Louise Erdrich (Turtle Mountain Chippewa) and Michael Dorris (Modoc). *Women in American Indian Society*. Rayna Green (Cherokee).

HEROES/LEADERS/ VICTIMS	ELDER WISDOM/PHILOSOPHY/ SONGS	
Littlecoon, or Louis Oliver (Yuchi/Muscogee), noted poet and author, dies at age eighty-six.	To ourselves at least, our religion is more precious than even our lives. There is no future for the Race of the Indians if its religion is killed. We must be faithful to each other now. *Declaration of the All Indian Pueblo Council in 1924*	**1990**
Wilma P. Mankiller (Cherokee) is reelected as principal chief of the Cherokee Nation of Oklahoma with more than 82 percent of the vote.	Almost without exception, whites who married Indians took up the ways of their in-laws and their breed children took to Indian life. *Roxy Gordon (Choctaw)*	**1991**

	HISTORY/LAW/ POLITICS	LITERATURE/ART/ LEGENDS AND STORIES
1992	The Pentagon honors the Navajo "code talkers" with an exhibit which documents their history. People of the sovereign Mashantucket Pequot Nation dedicate and open Foxwoods High Stakes Bingo and Casino at Ledyard, Connecticut. It is the largest Native-owned and -operated gaming operation in Turtle Island. The Wordcraft Circle is organized after a historic gathering of Native writers and storytellers at the first Returning the Gift Festival, held July 7–10 at the University of Oklahoma, in Norman. More than two hundred Native writers and storytellers participate in the event. The Dickson Mounds Museum of Illinois, the last public museum on Turtle Island to display the remains of Native people, is closed by order of Governor Jim Edgar. More than 160 radio stations, including those owned and operated by sovereign Native nations and tribes across Turtle Island, air *National Native News*, produced by Alaska Public Radio Network.	*The Bronze Serpent*. Barney Bush (Shawnee/Cayuga). *Mountain Windsong: A Novel of the Trail of Tears* and *The Real People: The Way of the Priests*. Robert J. Conley (United Keetoowah Band Cherokee). *The Business of Fancydancing: Stories and Poems*. Sherman Alexie (Spokane/Coeur d'Alene). *Pueblo Nations: Eight Centuries of Pueblo Indian History*. Joe S. Sando (Jemez). *Talking Indian: Reflections on Survival and Writing*. Anna Lee Walters (Pawnee/Otoe-Missouria).  *Toe Ga Juke Juke Gan Hoke Sheena, or Roxy Gordon (Choctaw/Assiniboine)* COURTESY OF KENDALL McCOOK
1993	The Wordcraft Circle of Native Writers and Storytellers is incorporated in the commonwealth of Virginia as a not-for-profit organization which brings together beginning, emerging, and established Native writers and storytellers. It is the first Native organization devoted exclusively to Native writers and storytellers.	*Selu: Seeking the Corn-Mother's Wisdom*. Awiakta, or Marilou Awiakta (Cherokee). *The Real People: The Dark Way* and *The Real People: The White Path*. Robert J. Conley (United Keetoowah Band Cherokee). *Women, Work, and Politics: Belgium, 1830–1914*. Patricia Penn Hilden (Nez Percé). *Mankiller: A Chief and Her People*. Wilma Mankiller (Cherokee) and Michael Wallis.
1994		*Dawn Land*. Joseph Bruchac III (Abenaki).

HEROES/LEADERS/ VICTIMS	ELDER WISDOM/PHILOSOPHY/ SONGS	
	The women's dance, the women's circle moves on. They sing, and the song is ours. *Rayna Green (Cherokee)*	**1992**

Returning The Gift Festival Participants

Ada Deer (Menominee) is the first woman from among the People to be appointed assistant secretary for Indian affairs (BIA) in the U.S. Department of the Interior. Will Rogers Jr. (Cherokee), journalist and politician, dies.		**1993**
Lee Francis (Laguna Pueblo / Chippewa/ Scottish/ Lebanese), national director of Wordcraft Circle of Native Writers and Storytellers, is appointed director of the Washington Internships for Native Students (WINS) at the American University, Washington, D.C.	The writings by contemporary Native authors are critically important not only as a way for Native people to learn more about each other but also because such writings continue to influence the thinking of those in decision-making roles throughout the world. *Lee Francis (Laguna Pueblo)*	**1994**

PROLOGUE:
1994 AND BEYOND

Of all the astounding events since the time the Lenape People began their *return* journey to the East Coast of Turtle Island from Asia, the historic gathering of the principal leaders of the People of the sovereign nations and tribes at the White House with United States President William Jefferson Clinton is perhaps one of the more significant. For the first time since the United States of America came into existence in 1776, the principal leader of the people of the United States accepted responsibility for more than two hundred years of misery imposed on the People of the sovereign nations and tribes by non-Native Americans and their government. The People, however, remember what has gone before. Although we are filled with cautious hope, we are sharply aware of the reality that "white man speaks with forked tongue." It remains to be seen if there *is* a new reality.

The People of the sovereign nations and tribes will watch to see if indeed the actions reflect the words that William Jefferson Clinton spoke to the principal leaders of the People on April 29, 1994:

> . . . There is a yearning for us to be able to live together so that all of us can live up to our God-given potential and be respected for who and what we are.
>
> It is in that spirit and with great humility I say to the leaders of the first Americans, the American Indian and Alaska Natives, welcome to the White House. Welcome home.
>
> So much of who we are today comes from who you have been for a long time. Long before others came to these shores there were powerful and sophisticated cultures and societies here—yours. Because of your ancestors, democracy existed here long before the Constitution was drafted and ratified.
>
> Just last week, people all around the world celebrated the twenty-fourth annual Earth Day. Yet for thousands of years, you have held nature in awe, celebrating the bond between Earth and the Creator. You have reminded people that all of us should make decisions not just for our children and their grandchildren, but for generation upon generation yet to come.
>
> I believe in your rich heritage and in our common heritage. What you have done to retain your identity, your dignity and your faith in the face of often immeasurable obstacles is profoundly moving—an example of the enduring strength of the human spirit.
>
> We desperately need this lesson now. We must keep faith with you and with that spirit and with the common heritage so many of us cherish. That is what you came to talk to me about, and what I would like to respond to today.
>
> In every relationship between our people, our first principle must be to respect your right to remain who you are, and to live the way you wish to live. And I believe the best way to do that is to acknowledge the unique government-to-government relationship we have enjoyed over time. Today I reaffirm our commitment to self-determination for tribal governments.

I pledge to fulfill the trust obligations of the federal government. I vow to honor and respect tribal sovereignty based upon our unique historic relationship. And I pledge to continue my efforts to protect your right to fully exercise your faith as you wish. . . .

This then is our first principle—respecting your values, your religions, your identity and sovereignty. This brings us to the second principle that should guide our relationship. We must dramatically improve the federal government's relationships with the tribes and become full partners with the tribal nations. . . .

The Great Law of the Six Nations Iroquois Confederacy contained this advice: "In our every deliberation, we must consider the impact of our decision on the next seven generations." We are stewards, we are caretakers. That standard will keep us great if we have the vision of your forefathers.

As we look back on the American journey, the test ahead is always whether we are moving in the right direction of more tolerance, wider justice and greater opportunity for all. It is the direction that counts, always the direction. And our choices will set that direction.

Of course, as you well know, our history has not always been a proud one. But our future can be, and that is up to us. Together we can open the greatest era of cooperation, understanding and respect among our people ever. I know that we will. And when we do, the judgment of history will be that the President of the United States and the Leaders of the sovereign . . . nations met and kept faith with each other and our common heritage, and together lifted our great nations to a new and better place.

President William J. Clinton

Although the People of the sovereign Native nations and tribes strongly hope for a new era of sincere commitment, it must be said that the old truism "once burned, twice shy" has special meaning among the People.

After reading this book, some might feel that it is too political and even, in some instances, excessively harsh. My non-Native relations might feel that this book is thinly disguised "white-bashing."

Many of my non-Native relations will be quick to point out that they are not to blame for the actions of their respective non-Native ancestors toward the People. It is important to understand that every time my non-Native relations are silent about injustices committed against the People of the sovereign Native nations and tribes on Turtle Island, they are as guilty as their ancestors. My non-Native relations of today are guilty, for example, when a golf course is built by non-Native land developers on sacred land of the People and my non-Native relations do not raise a hue and cry against such desecration.

For literally centuries, the People of the sovereign Native nations and tribes have been saying that it is wrong to violate our sacred places such as gravesites. What is interesting is that although United States federal law and state laws prohibit "disturbing graves" of my non-Native relations, it would seem that such laws do not apply to the People. I submit that if the People were to unearth the remains of Abraham Lincoln to study, the entire United States military forces would be brought to bear. In short, the vileness must stop. Sacred sites and remains must be treated with the same respect and protection as are synagogues, mosques, and churches.

Finally, it must be said that although the People of the sovereign Native nations and tribes all across Turtle Island have been subjected to unbelievably contemptible treatment, the fact remains—we not only have survived, but more important, we continue to live and grow stronger in the ways of the People.

Máh-meh t'd-ou-y-eh

ENDNOTES

1. All stories in the Laguna Pueblo tradition begin with "Hu-em-eh ha-ah . . ." or "And so . . ." Not to follow the form, so to speak, would be much like failing to follow the rules for writing a classical Italian or Shakespearean sonnet.

2. The word *People* is used whenever I refer to the people of the sovereign nations, tribes, bands, villages, pueblos, rancherias, and communities. *People* with a capital *P* is how we refer to ourselves in our respective languages. For example, in my Keresan language, we call ourselves *Hano* which, loosely translated, means "the People."

3. A powwow is a recent phenomenon which has its origins in the soldier/warrior societies of the People prior to the 1800s. With the advent of the so-called Ghost Dance religion and the horror of the Chief Big Foot Massacre (known among non-Native Americans as Wounded Knee), the outward form was changed to avoid non-Native reprisal. The word *powwow* is said to have been derived from the Lenni Lenape *pawa*, which means having rich and powerful dreams, and *wapa*, the word for "east."

4. Among all the People of the sovereign nations and tribes there is a common understanding about the four directions. East is the beginning place because it is where the sun first touches Turtle Island. South is the place of change or youth. West is the place of maturity and adulthood. North is the place of wisdom and old age.

5. Storytelling always has been one of the ways among the People to respectfully point out certain truths.

6. Linda Poolaw, grand chief, Delaware Nation Grand Council of North America, Inc., Anadarko, Oklahoma, foreword in *The Red Record—The Wallam Olum: The Oldest Native North American History,* translated and annotated by David McCutchen (Garden City Park, New York: Avery Publishing Group, Inc., 1993), pp. ix–x.

7. McCutchen, p. 52.

8. *Touch the Earth: A Self-Portrait of Indian Existence,* compiled by T. C. McLuhan (New York: Pocket Book edition/ Simon & Schuster, Inc., 1972), p. 31.

9. A sign on the door of the Native American Indian Studies Department office at San Francisco State University, c. 1990.

10. Emphasis added.

11. Emphasis added.

12. Andrew Myrick, a trader with the Santee Sioux, made this statement at a council meeting with the Minnesota Santee, August 15, 1862.

13. As I sit in front of my computer recounting the history for the reader, I cry uncontrollably. The Massacre at Wounded Knee Creek occurred more than a century ago, and still it evokes incredible anguish and grief within me. I wonder if that "racial memory" always will bring tears and sadness.

14. Jerome Buckanaga, "Interracial Politics: The Pressure to Integrate an Experimental School," in *The Schooling of Native America,* edited by Thomas Thompson (Washington, D.C.: American Association of Colleges for Teacher Education and the Teacher Corps, U.S. Office of Education, 1978), p. 53.

ABOUT THE AUTHOR

Lee Francis III, son of Ethel Gunn Haynes Gottlieb Francis and E. Lee Francis, is of Laguna Pueblo, Chippewa, Scottish, and Lebanese descent. He was born in Albuquerque, New Mexico, and lived for thirteen years in Cubero, New Mexico, a Mexican land-grant village near Laguna Pueblo. He married Mary Elaine Allen (Celtic [English and Irish]/Greek) in 1972. They have one son, Lee Francis IV, born in 1977.

At San Francisco State University, Francis received a B.A. degree in 1982 and an M.A. in 1983. In March 1991, he received a Ph.D. in higher education and social change from the Western Institute for Social Research at Berkeley, California.

While caring for his mother during her final illness, Francis began work on this book.

In 1992, Francis became national director of Wordcraft Circle of Native Writers and Storytellers.

Francis lives in Fairfax, Virginia, with his wife, son, and two cats, Patches and her son Whiskey.

WORDCRAFT CIRCLE

Sherman Alexie (Spokane/
Coeur d'Alene)
Hemeh Alexis (Suquamish)
Faith Allard (Sault Sainte Marie
Chippewa)
Robert H. Annesley (Cherokee)
Awiakta or Marilou Awiakta
(Cherokee/Appalachian)
Alice Hatfield Azure (Mi'kmaq)
Carol Snow Moon Bachofner (Abenaki)
Susan Barnett (Abenaki)
Louise Barton (Cherokee/Mohawk)
Russell L. Bates (Kiowa/Wichita)
Sharon M. Begay (Navajo)
Kathryn Bell (Southern Cheyenne)
Sherrole Benton (Oneida/Ojibwa)
Charmaine M. Benz (Anishnabe-
Ojibwa/SaginawChippewa)
Duane Big Eagle (Osage)
D. L. (Don) Birchfield (Choctaw)
Kenneth P. Biron (Sault Sainte Marie
Chippewa)
Theresa A. Biron (Sault Sainte Marie
Chippewa/Ojibwa)
Kimberly Blaeser (White Earth
Chippewa)
Sonciray Bonnell (Sandia/Isleta/
Salinan)
Michelle Lynn Boursaw (Anishnabe/
Mackinaw Island Ojibwa)
Beth Brant (Bay of Quinte Mohawk)
Charles Brashear (Cherokee)
Vee F. Browne (Navajo)
Shirley Brozzo (Chippewa)
James Bruchac (Abenaki)
Jesse Bruchac (Abenaki)
Joseph Bruchac III (St. Francis
Sokoki/Abenaki)
Christina Bryant (Cherokee/
Shinnecock)
Dana R. Buckles (Fort Peck Assiniboin/
Sioux)
Melissa G. Buckles (Fort Peck Assiniboin/
Sioux)
Barney Bush (Shawnee/Cayuga)
L. Michael Butler (Lac Courte Orielles
Chippewa)
Cathy Jo Caldwell (Stockbridge-
Munsee Mahican)
E. K. (Kim) Caldwell (Cherokee/Shawnee)

Jeanetta Calhoun (Delaware)
Kimberly Calvillo (Zapotec/Waco)
Clifford W. Case Jr. (Grand
Ronde/Siletz confederated tribes)
Robin M. Caudell (Cherokee)
C. B. Clark (Muscogee, or Creek)
Brandon Clay (Choctaw/Chickasaw)
Susan Clements (Métis [Blackfoot/
Mohawk/Seneca])
Mary Jo Cole (Cherokee)
Robert J. Conley (United Keetowah
Band Cherokee)
Bonnie J. Cote (White Earth
Chippewa)
David M. Cunningham Jr. (Nez Percé)
Maria Proctor Dadgar (Piscataway
Conoy)
Donna M. Dean (Cherokee)
Charlotte DeClue (Osage)
Pamela Graham DeRensis (Lumbee)
Patricia A. Dyer-Deckrow (Grand Tra-
verse Odawa/Mississippi Choctaw)
Heid Erdich (Turtle Mountain
Chippewa)
Chris Eyre (Arapaho/Cheyenne)
Phoebe Farris (Powhatan Renape)
Tula Fitzgerald (Shawnee/Cherokee)
Chris Fleet (Akwesasne Mohawk)
Jack D. Forbes (Powhatan
Renape/Delaware)
John C. Francis (Laguna
Pueblo/Chippewa)
Lee Francis III (Laguna
Pueblo/Chippewa)
Lee Francis IV (Laguna
Pueblo/Chippewa)
Rebecca Gallen (Koyukon Athabascan)
José L. Garza or Blue Heron (Coahuil-
tec/Lipan Apache)
Gloria M. Gearhart (Mohawk)
Diane Glancy (Cherokee)
Harriet Godfrey (Siuslaw-Coos-
UmpquaSiletz/Aleut)
Angela A. Gonzales (Hopi)
Mary E. Goose (Mesquakie/Chippewa
Marcella Kay Gordon (Cherokee)
Roxy Gordon (Choctaw)
Rayna Green (Cherokee)
Norman Guardipee (Blackfoot)
Raven Hail (Cherokee)

Ruth Ann Hail (Hidatsa/Sioux)
Annie Hansen (Lenape)
Terri C. Hansen (Nebraska Winnebago)
Joy Harjo (Muscogee, or Creek)
Bea Harrell (Choctaw)
LaDonna Harris (Comanche)
Taiawagi Helton (Cherokee)
Gordon D. Henry Jr. (White Earth
Chippewa)
Lance Henson (Cheyenne)
Patricia Penn Hilden (Nez Percé)
Patricia Davis Hinrichs (Comanche)
Stuart Hoahwah (Comanche/Arapaho)
Barbara Hobson (Comanche)
Geary Hobson
(Cherokee/Quapaw/Chicksaw)
Monelle Boyett Holley (Cherokee)
Thurman Hornbuckle II (Eastern
Cherokee)
Gregg Howard (Cherokee/Powhatan)
Michelle Howe (Standing Rock Sioux)
Shari Huhndorf (Cook Inlet Yupik)
Ruth Hunsinger (Lakota)
Mary E. Hunter (Makah)
LeAnne J. Ike (Omaha/Shoshone)
Ken Jackson or Grey Eagle (Anishinabe/
Ojibwa
Alex A. Jacobs or Karoniaktatie
(Akwesasne Mohawk)
M. A. Jaimes-Guerrero
(Juaneño/Yaqui)
David M. James (Wyandot)
Tom Jenks (Northern Ute)
Donna John (Stevens Village
Athabascan)
Janet Linn Johnson (Cherokee)
Judith L. Jones (Cherokee)
Maurice Kenny (Mohawk)
Billy Keys Jr. (Cherokee)
Clara Sue Kidwell
(Choctaw/Chippewa)
Paul Michael Kinville (Sault Sainte
Marie Chippewa)
Pamela Green LaBarge (Wisconsin
Oneida)
Debbie LaCroix (Sisseton-Wahpeton
Sioux/Choctaw)
William Lang (Lenni Lenape)
Bennis Blue Lathan (Cherokee)
Jeanne LaTraille (Oneida)

Roberta M. Lewis (Zuñi/Cherokee)
Stephanie Little Wolf
  (Lakota/Shoshone)
Mary Lockwood (Inupiat)
Marlane D. Logan (Akwesasne Mohawk)
Jamison C. Mahto (Red Lake
  [Lakota/Anishnabe/Flathead])
Joyce Carletta Mandrake (White Earth
  Chippewa)
Victoria L. Manyarrows (Earstern
  Cherokee)
Brian Maracle (Mohawk)
Jacqueline Martain (Blackfoot)
Rosemary McCombs Maxey
  (Muscogee)
Yvonne McDonald (Lumbee)
Franklin McLemore (Cherokee)
Howard Meredith (Cherokee/Akokisa)
Tiffany Midge (Hunkpapa Lakota)
Paulette Fairbanks Molin (White Earth
  Chippewa)
MariJo Moore (Cherokee)
Ray Moore (Cherokee)
Gloria T. Mora (Navajo)
Albert Lee Moran (Rosebud Sioux)
Duane McGinnis Niatum (Klallam)
Josh Norris (Yurok)
Lela Northcross (Potawatomi/Kickapoo)
Yolanda Nyerges (Pascua Yaqui)
Erin Olson (Sault Sainte Marie
  Chippewa)
Penny J. Olson (Sault Sainte Marie
  Chippewa)
Robert M. Owens (Lakota)
Pahdopony (Comanche)
Dottie Pearle (Cherokee)
David Pego (Saginaw Chippewa)
W. S. (Bill) Penn (Nez Percé)
Dawn Karima Pettigrew
  (Creek/Cherokee/Chickasaw)
Gil Pettigrew
  (Creek/Cherokee/Chickasaw)
Cornel Pewewardy
  (Comanche/Kiowa)
Susan Power (Standing Rock Sioux)
Susan Power Sr. (Standing Rock Sioux)
Michael B. Price (Odawa/Ojibwa)
Katherine Quartz (Walker River Paiute)
Suzanne Rancourt (Abenaki)
Valerie Red-Horse
  (Cherokee/Cheyenne River Sioux)
Martin Reinhardt (Garden River
  Ojibwa/Sault Sainte Marie
  Chippewa)

Pamela D. Rentz (California Karuk)
Virginia Richardson (Mahican)
Selene Rilatos (Siletz confederated
  tribes)
Fredy Amilcar Roncalla (Peruvian
  Andean)
LaVera M. Rose (Rosebud Lakota)
Richard A. Rose (Cherokee)
A. Chuck Ross (Santee Dakota)
Gayle Ross (Cherokee)
Ron Rowell (Choctaw/Kaskaskia/
  Chickasaw)
Loriene Roy (White Earth Chippewa)
Carol Lee Sanchez (Laguna
  Pueblo/Chippewa)
Otilia Sanchez (Yaqui)
Cheryl Savageau (Abenaki)
Elaine Schroeter (Iowa of Kansas and
  Nebraska)
Martha Sebastian (Cherokee)
Lana Shaughnessy (Kiowa)
Edgar Silex (Tigua/Pueblo)
Harriett Skye (Standing Rock Sioux)
Carolyna Smiley-Marques (San Juan
  Pueblo)
Virginia Driving Hawk Sneve (Rose-
  bud Sioux)
Patricia Ann Snyder (Cat [Erie] Nation/
  Métis)
Renée Stock (Cherokee)
Rachael Tadgerson (Sault Stainte Marie
  Chippewa)
Candece Tarpley (Blackfoot/Cherokee)
Sacheen Tattooed (Sioux/Cowichan)
Laura Tohe (Navajo)
Clifford E. Trafzer (Wyandot)
Mark Turcotte (Turtle Mountain
  Chippewa)
Alma Luz Villanueva (Yaqui)
Judith Mountain Leaf Volborth (Black-
  foot/Comanche)
Anna Lee Walters (Pawnee/Otoe-
  Missouria)
Eddie Webb (Cherokee)
Ron Welburn (Southeastern Cherokee
  Confederacy)
Lizbeth White (Mohawk/Seminole)
Luhui Whitebear (Chumash/Iroquois/
  Pueblo/Comanche/Hulciol)
Roberta Hill Whiteman (Oneida)
Diane Willie (Navajo)
Craig S. Womak (Muscogee, or Creek/
  Cherokee)
Richard E. Wood (Osage/Cherokee)

Elizabeth Woody (Warm Springs/
  Yakima/Wasco/Navajo)
Jack Wooldridge (Citizen Band
  Potawatomi)
Carole Yazzie-Shaw (Navajo)
Ray A. Young Bear (Mesquakie)
Greg Young-Ing (Cree)

INDEX

Page numbers in bold type refer to photographs.

Abeita, Louise (E-yeh-shur), 23, 273, 280
Abeita, Pablo, 29
Abel, Benjamin, 281
Abenaki Nation, 51, 54, 102, 106, 108,110, 132
Abiding Appalachia: Where Mountain and Atom Meet (Awiakta), 312
Abila y Ayala, Friar Pedro de, 74
Academic Squaw: Reports to the World from the Ivory Tower (Rose), 312
Achumawi People, 232
acid etching, 14
Acoma (Sky City), 24
Acoma massacre, 39, 50, 156
Acoma People, 46, 48, 60, 91, 255
Actor, The (Conley), 322
Adams, John C., 259
Adams, Vivian M., 317
Adario (Kondiaronk) (Huron leader), 61, 97, 119
Adawosgi (Swimmer Wesley Snell), **48**
Adena People (Mound Builders), 16
African Americans, 107
  Fort Gadsden ("Negro Fort"), 168–69
  and Native People, 40, 58, 133, 263
agriculture, 10, 12, 18, 21, 59, 65
  festivals honoring, 147, 154
  irrigation, 18
Aguilar (shipwreck survivor), 30
Ahatisistari (Huron leader), 65
Ahdoltay (Big Tree) (Kiowa leader), 219, 245, 251, 275
Ahookasoongh (Onondaga leader), 97
Ajoaste (Stadacona settlement), 34, 10, 40, 120
Akomen (Yukon River valley), 13
Akweks, Aren (Ray Fadden), 267
Alabama People, 40
Alarcón, Hernando de, 40
Alaska Federation of Natives, 302
Alaska National Interest Lands Conservation Act, 316
Alaska Reorganization Act, 280
Alaskan Native Claims Settlement Act, 306
Alcanfor (Tiguex settlement), 41

Alcatraz Is Not an Island (Aroniawenate), 306
Alcatraz Island, occupation of, 283, 304
alcohol and drug use, 121, 123, 150, 161, 263
Aleek-chea-ahoosh (Plenty Coup), **132,** 133
Aleut People, 118, 124
Alexie, Sherman, 303, **303,** 326
Alford, Thomas Wildcat. *See* Gaynwah
Algonkian Confederacy (Canadian), 25, 34, 64, 70, 128, 132
Alkosohit (the Subdivider), 15
All Indian Pueblo Council (AIPC), 48, 93, 272
Allard, Doug, 297
Allegheny Reservation, lease renewals, 324
Allen, Elsie, 261
Allen, Minerva, 279
Alokuwi (Poor One), 19
Alvarado, Hemando de, 41
Alwekon quarterly, 321
Ama Edohi (Moytoy), 111
American Book of the Dead (Barnes), 318
American Horse (Iron Shield) (Lakota leader), 183, 217, 253
American Indian Authors (Momaday), 306
American Indian Authors for Young Readers: A Selected Bibliography (Byler), 308
American Indian Education Policy Center, 304
American Indian Freedom of Religion Act, 312
American Indian Historical Society, 300
American Indian Holocaust and Survival: A Population History Since 1492 (Thomton), 322
American Indian in Graduate Study: A Bibliography of Theses and Dissertations, The (Dockstader), 298
American Indian Law Center, 302
American Indian Law Review, 312
American Indian Law Students Association, 304
American Indian Leaders: Studies in Diversity (Edmunds), 316
American Indian Movement (AIM), 302, 306, 308
American Indian Reader: Literature, The (Henry), 308

American Indian Research and Resource Institute, 318
American Indian Scholarships, Inc., 304
American Indian Science and Engineering Society (AISES), 312, 315
American Indian Stories (Zitkala-Sa), 270
American Indian Tribal Court Judges Association, 304
American Indian Wars, The (Tebbel), 300
American Indians, American Justice (Deloria), 318
American Museum of Natural History, 322
American Revolutionary War, 132
  Battle of Oriskany, 136, 137
  fighting methods, 136
  Native People and, 133, 134, 136, 137, 166, 168–69, 170, 171, 172
Americans Before Columbus (bimonthly publication), 300
Americans for Indian Opportunity, 304
Amherst, Jeffrey, 128
Anadaca Nation, 218
Anadu Iwacha; The Way It Was: Yakima Indian Legend Book (Beavert), 308
Anathareo (Gertrude Bernard Mottke), 267
Anasazi People, 12, 14, 18, 20, 22, 23
Anauta (Eskimo Woman), 284
ancestors, 19
...And with the Wagon—Came God's Word (Jumper), 320
Anderson, Anne, 267
Anderson, Robert A., 238
Andrade, Ron, **51**
Andros, Sir Edmund, 74, 88
Angle of Geese and Other Poems (Momaday), 308
animals and men (Inuit story), 14
Anishinabe Adioskan: Tales of the People (Vizenor), 304
Anishinabe Nagamon (Vizenor), 302
Anne (of England), 98, 99
Anne (of the Pamunkey). *See* Cockacoeske
Annenraes (Onondaga leader), 67
Annharte (Marie Baker), 287
Anoska Nimiwina (Jones), 260
Antell, Will, 279
Antonio, Juan. *See* Cooswootna
Aondiron People, 66

Apache Nation, 40, 75, 136, 214
  and municipal bonds, 320
  reservations, 250, 252
  treaties (U.S.A.), 224, 240
  wars (tribal), 74
  wars (U.S.A.), 197, 232, 250
Apache Nation (bands)
  Jicarilla Apache, **42–43,** 320
  Lipan Apache, 218
  Mescalero Apache, 40, 318
  Mimbreño Apache, 252
  White Mountain Apache, 74
Apalachee People, 34, 96
Apalachicola band, 208, 210
Apangassa People, 220
Apes, William, 181, 206, 210, 212
Apodaca, Raymond D., 291
Aquash, Anna Mae, 309
Arapaho People, 222, 232, 238, 240, 242
*Arapaho Way: A Memoir of an Indian Boy-
  hood, The* (Sweezy), 302
Arapoosh (Crow leader), 179, 211
architecture, 14, 16, 20, 41, 46
  pit houses (kivas), 18, 22
Area Redevelopment Act, 300
Argall, Samuel, 52
Arikara (Ricara) People, 202, 212, 222
Arkeketa, Annette, 299
Arlington National Cemetery, Native
  veterans memorial, 320
Armstrong, Bernice, 299
Armstrong, Jeannette C., 293, 318, 320
Arnett, Carroll. *See* Gogisgi
Aroniateka (Hendrick) (Machican/Mo-
  hawk leader), 99, 123
Aroniawenate (Peter Blue Cloud), 281,
  306, 312, 322, 324
Arpeika (Sam Jones) (Seminole leader),
  131, 214, 215, 235
artisans and workers, festival honoring,
  147, 154
arts and crafts, 10, 12, 16, 20, 28, 34
  basketry, 14
  beads, 10, 12, 22, 34
  ceramics, 12, 16, 18, 20, 22, 24, 257
  materials. *See* chalcedony; mica;
    rubber; shells, silver, tortoise
    shell, turquoise
  statues and figurines, 22, 24
  textiles, 14
  wood engravings, 16
  See also architecture; copperworking;
    metalworking; pottery; pottery culture
Ascending Red Cedar Moon (Niatum), 308
Ashiwi People (Zuñi), 12, 22, 30, 36, 74,
  110
  Spanish, dealings with, 40, 60, 83, 84,
    134
Ashkum Weesaw People, 214
Aspinet, 59
Assacumbuit (Abenaki leader), 93, 97, 109
assassination, 121, 129
Assimilative Crimes Act, 292
Assiniboin People, 78, 166, 212, 222, 266
*Assiniboines: From the Accounts of the Old

Ones Told to First Boy, The* (First Boy),
  300
Assiniwi, Bernard, 279, 308, 318
Association of American Indian Physi-
  cians, 306
Atakapa People, 40
Atchatchakangouen People (Illinois Na-
  tion), 66
Athabascan People (Upper Yukon), 19,
  136
Atsye, Meta, **256**
Attakullaculla (Onacona/Little Carpen-
  ter) (Cherokee leader), 111, 113, 127, 137
Attaquin, Helen, 273
*Attica: Official Report of the New York State
  Special Commission on Attica* (Harrison),
  306
Attucks, Crispus, 107, 133
Aunt Mary's Christmas Dinner (Reed), 260
Autobiography of a Papago Woman, The
  (Underhill/Chona), 280
Autobiography of a Winnebago, The
  (Radin/Crashing Thunder), 270
Autobiography of a Yaqui Poet, The (Savila),
  316
Autobiography of Black Hawk, The
  (Makatai-meshe-kiakiak), 210
Awalache People, 220
Awashonks (Sagkonate squaw sachem),
  73
Awiakta (Marilou Awiakta), 21, **34,** 35,
  105, 281, 312, 318, 326
Awonawilona (Zuñi/Ashiwi story), 30
Ayamek (Seizer), 13
Ayllón, Lucas Vásquez de, 33
Ayonwaeghs (John Brant) (Mohawk
  leader), 185, 199, 207
Aztec People, 32, 33
Aztec prophecy of obliteration, 33
Azure, Alice Hatfield, **29**

Babeshikit, **126**
Baca, Lorenzo, 291
Back to Malachi (Conley), 320
Bacon, Nathaniel, 76
Bacon's Rebellion, 76, 77
Baker, Marie. *See* Annharte
Baker, Odrik, 309
Ballard, Charles G., 275
Ballard, Louis Wayne. *See* Honganozhe
Banai, Edward Benton, 279
Banks, Dennis, 311
Bannister, Roger, 253
Bannock People, 232, 242, 252
Baranov, Aleksandr Andreyevich, 182
Barfoot, Van T., 289
Barker, George, 261
Barnard, Timpooche, 181
Barnes, Jim, 113, 227, 316, 318, 320, 322
Barnwell, Colonel John, 100
Barrett, John Adam, 321
basketry. *See under* arts and crafts
Bates, Russell L., **100,** 285
Batsi People, 222

Batsinas (Jason Betzinez), 235, 298, 301
battles. *See* war (battles)
beads. *See under* arts and crafts
Bear, Gail, 289
bear man (Pawnee story), 30
Bear River People, 92
Bears' Heart, James. *See* Nockoist
Beauharnais, Governor, 110
Beavert, Virginia, 308
Beavon, Daphne Odjig, 271
Beckwith, James. *See* Medicine Calf
Beckwith, Sir Jennings, 199
Bedagi (Big Thunder), 17
*Behind the Trail of Broken Treaties and The
  Indian Affair* (Deloria), 308
Belantse-eta (Minitaree) Nation, 202
Beltran, Bernaldino, 46
Bender of the Pine Bow, 33
Benedict, Salli M. K., 297
Bennett, Kay C., 273, 300
Bennett, Louis. *See* Hot'tsa-sodono
Bennett, Robert L., 303
Benpi People, 222
Benson, William R., 21
Bent, George, 219, **243,** 271
Beothuk People, extermination of, 132
Berkeley, Governor Sir William, 65
Berrendo, José, 253
Betrayed (Sneve), 308, 309
Betzinez, Jason. *See* Batsinas
BIA. *See* Indian Affairs, Bureau of
Bibo, Solomon, 257
Bidato (Big Eagle), 308
Big Bowl (Crow leader), 199
Big Crow, Moses Nelson, 281
Big Eagle, Duane, 291, 308
Big Eagle, Jerome. *See* Wamditonka
*Big Eagle's Story of the Sioux Outbreaks of
  1862* (Wamditonka), 258
Big Falling Snow (Yava), 312
Big Foot (Chief), 140
Big Foot (Si Tanka/Spotted Elk), 259
Big Winnebago. *See* Crashing Thunder
Bigjim, Fred, 285
Bigotes (Cicúye leader), 41
Biloxi People, 40
Birchfield, D. L.(Don), **76**
Bird, Gloria, 131
Bislahalani (Barboncito), 199, 237, 239,
  241, 245
Black Bear (Arapaho leader), 239
Black Bear, Ben, Jr., 310
Black Coal, 31
Black Dog, 132, 133
*Black Elk Speaks: Being the Life of a Holy
  Man of the Oglala Sioux*
  (Neihardt/Hehaka Sapa), 276
Black Hawk, 298
Black Hawk: An Autobiography
  (Jackson/Black Hawk), 298
Black Jack Davy (Oskison), 272
Black Jim, 251
Black Kettle, 11
Black River Chippewa. *See under*
  Chippewa Nation (bands)

Blackbird, Andrew J. *See* Mackawdebe-nessy
Blackened Ones (Native People), 13
Blackfeet. *See* Siksika People
Blackfeet Sioux. *See under* Sioux Nation (bands)
Blackfish (Shawne leader), 135
Blackfoot (Crow leader), 181, 245, 253
Blackfoot Nation, 230, 252, 253
Blackrobe (Kenny), 318
Blanchard's Fork Ottawa, 240
Blatchford, Herbert, 309
Blood People, 212, 252
blood quantum, 314–15
Blowsnake, Sam. *See* Crashing Thunder
Blue Cloud, Peter. *See* Aroniawenate
Blue Spruce, Beryl, 279, 301
Blunt, Colonel James, 236
Bobbie Lee: Indian Rebel (Maracle), 310
Bois Fort Chippewa. *See* Chippewa Nation (bands)
Bomazeen (Abenaki leader), 75, 91, 99, 101, 107
Bonga, George, 199
Bonilla, Francisco Leyba de, 48
Bonito Pueblo, 22
Bonnin, Gertrude Simmons. *See* Zitkala Sa, 270
Boone, Daniel, 135
Bosomworth, Mary Mathews Musgro. *See* Coosaponakeesa
Bosque Redondo, 236, 237, 239
Boston Massacre, 133
Boston News-Letter, 100
Bouchard, James. *See* Walomika
Boudinot, Elias. *See* Galagina
Bow, Clyde, 256
bow and arrow, adoption of, 18, 20
Bowen, Duwayne Leslie, 291, 324
Bowlegs, Billy. *See* Halpatter Miko
Boxley, David, **32**
Bozeman Trail, 238
Bradford, Governor William, 59
Brant, Beth, 285, **292**, 293, 320
Brant, John. *See* Ayonwaeghs
Brant, Joseph. *See* Thayendanegea
Brant, Molly. *See* Gonwatzijyanni
Brantly Blue, 209
Bras Coupe and Lexique des noms Indiens en Amerique, La (Assiniwi), 308
Brashear, Charles, 47, **47,** 275, 302, 312, 324
Brass, Eleanor, 267
Bright Eyes: The Story of Susette La Flesche, an Omaha Indian (Kidwell), 310
Brito, Sylvester J., 281, 320, 322
Brodhead, Colonel Daniel, 166
Broken Cord, The (Dorris), 322
Bronze Serpent, The (Bush), 326
Brother (Lenape reservation), 124
Brothers Three (Oskison), 278
Brotherton People, 208
Brown, Ed, 323
Brown, Emily Ivanoff. *See* Ticasuk

Brown, Joseph Epes, 276
Browne, Vee F., **240,** 299, 324
Browns Valley People, 10
Bruce, Louis R., 305
Bruchac, Joseph, III, 13, **118,** 119, 287, 310, 312, 316, 320, 322, 326
bubonic plague. *See* epidemics
Buckanaga, Jerome, 248
Buena Vista People, 222
Buffalo Bill, *See* Cody, William F.
Buffalo Bird Woman. *See* Waheenee
Buffalo Child Long Lance (Sylvester Long), 259
buffalo herds, extermination of, 254
Buffalo Horn (Bannock leader), 253
buffalo soldiers, 165
Bureau of Indian Affairs. *See* Indian Affairs, Bureau of
Burk Act, 266
Burnett, Robert, 273
Burns, Diane, 299
Bursum Bill, 272
Bush, Barney, 117, 291, 312, 318, 319, **319,** 320, 326
Bush, George, 322, 324
Bush, Mitchell L., Jr., 106
Business of Fancydancing: Stories and Poems, The (Alexie), 326
Bussell, Clara, 266
Butler, Raymond, 311
Butler, William, 175
Byler, Mary G., 308
Byrd, Colonel, 86

Cabeza de Vaca, Álvar Núñez, 34
Cabot, John and Sebastian, 28
Cabrillo, Juan Rodríguez, 44
Cacique (Cicúye leader), 41
Caddo People, 40, 88, 210, 218
Cahokia (Mound Builder city), 18, 22
Cahokia People. *See under* Illinois Nation
Cahuilla People, 224
Cahwais People, 220
Calanapo People, 222
Calapooia Nation, 226
Caldwell, E. K. (Kim), 199, **200**
Calhoun, John C., 196, 199
Calico People, 10
California State, 224
Callahan, Sophia Alice, 243
Calling Myself Home (Hogan), 316
Calusa People, 128
Cameahwait (Shoshone leader), 185
Campbell, Ben Nighthorse, **320**
Campbell, Maria, 285, 308
Canada
    Second Riel Rebellion, 254
    Seven Nations of, 180
    treaties (with Native Peoples), 252, 253
    wars (with Native Peoples), 254, 255
Canadian Born (Tehakionwake), 264
Canajoharie Mohawk. *See under* Mohawk

Canassatego (Onondaga leader), 59, 116, 117, 121
Canonicus (Narraganset leader), 47, 61, 63, 67
Cape Girardeau Deleware, 208
Cappel People, 222
Cárdenas, García López de, 41, 42
Cardiff, Gladys, 287, 310
Cardinal, Douglas, 279
Cardinal, Harold, 289
Car-io-scuse (Curly Bear), **236**
Carisis People, 222
Carius, Helen Slwooko, 312
Carlisle Indian School, **255,** 256
Carr, General Eugene, 242
Carr, Paddy, 187
Carson, Christopher "Kit," 236, 237
Carter, Jimmy, 316
Cartier, Jacques, 34, 35, 36, 40
Cassons People, 220
Castake People, 222
Catahecasasa (Black Hoof) (Shawnee leader), 117, 119, 207
Catawba People, 98, 120, 122, 298
Catches, Peter, 19
Catiti (Santo Domingo Pueblo), 85
Cattle Management (May), 316
Catua, Nicholas, 85
Caughnawaga Nation, 110, 132
Cayoni (Joseph F. Johns), 291
Cayuga Nation (Five Nations), 14, 48, 86, 88, 106, 134, 166, 168, 252
Cayuse Nation, 214, 228
"Celebration of Native American Life, A," 322
Century Clock: Story of a 49'er, The (Waterman), 270
ceremonial objects and costumes, 24
    breastplates, 24
    Cree sacred bundle, 322
    drums, **13,** 152
    headdresses, 24
    masks, 24, 70
    peace pipes, 16, 22, 50, 191
    peyote, sacramental use of , 324
    sacred objects, return of, 322, 324
    Spanish destruction of, 69, 70
    See also architecture: ceremonial buildings
ceremonies, 16, **32,** 60, 140 *See also* songs
Ceremony (Silko), 312
ceremony time (March), 140–42
    council fires, 141
    events, 141–42
    focus (family), 141
    prayer, 140–41
ceremony time (April), 142–43
    council fires, 142–43
    events, 143
    focus (environment), 142
    prayer, 142
ceremony time (May), 144–45
    council fires, 144
    events, 144–45

focus (heritage), 144
prayer, 145
ceremony time (June), 145–47
council fires, 145–46
events, 146–47
focus (education), 145
prayer, 145
ceremony time (July), 147–50
council fires, 148
events, 148–50
focus (government), 147–48
prayer, 147
ceremony time (August), 150–52
council fires, 151
events, 151–52
focus (culture), 150–51
prayer, 150
ceremony time (September), 152–54
council fires, 153
events, 153–54
focus (health), 152–53
prayer, 152
ceremony time (October), 154–56
council fires, 155
events, 155–56
focus (diversity), 154–55
prayer, 154
ceremony time (November), 156–58
council fires, 157
events, 157–58
focus (history), 156–57
prayer, 156
ceremony time (December), 158–59
council fires, 158–59
events, 159
focus (generosity), 158
prayer, 158
ceremony time (January), 159–61
council fires, 160
events, 160–61
focus (spirituality), 159–60
prayer, 159
ceremony time (February), 161–62
council fires, 161
events, 161–62
focus (community), 161
prayer, 161
cession. See under land
Cha People, 222
Cha-lahgee, 266
Chain of Friendship, 124
chalcedony, use of, 20
Chammakonee People, 222
Chammetco People, 222
Champlain, Samuel de, 52
Chamuscado, Francisco, 46
Chankai People, 222
Chappahsims People, 220
Charbonneau, Jean-Baptiste. See Pompey
Charbonneau, Toussaint, 185
Charger, Martin. See Wa-ana-tan
Charlatans (Native People), 13
Charles II (of England), 77
Charlot (Kalispel leader), 207, 251, 265
Chato (Apache leader), 235, **235,** 279

Chavers, Dean, 285, 313
Checom People, 222
Cheechawkose People, 214
Cheeshatemauck, 73
Chekilli (Muscogee leader), 111
Chemakum People, 226
Cheno People, 222
Chepoussa (Illinois Nation), 72
Chequawkako. See under Potawatomi
Nation (bands)
Cherokee Council of North America, 193
Cherokee Law Ways (Strickland), 306
Cherokee Nation, 28, 37, 102, 112, 120,
190
and the American Revolution, 137, 170
removal, 196, 204, 210, 214, 215, 216, 217
treaties (colonial), 104, 110, 118, 120, 122,
124, 126, 128, 132, 134,136
treaties (U.S.A.), 174, 178, 180, 184, 186,
192, 194, 204, 210, 214, 242
wars (U.S.A.), 174, 216, 236
See also Nuna-da-ut-sun'y
Cherokee Nation (bands)
Texas Cherokee, 216
Treaty Party Cherokee, 210, 218
Western ("Old Settlers") Cherokee, 218
Cherokee Indian Treaty, 192
Cherokee Spirit Tales (Strickland), 304
Cheraw People, extinction of, 131
Cheshahadakhi (Lean Wolf), **137**
Cheyenne Agency, 251
Cheyenne Memories, a Folk History (Stands
in Timber), 302
Cheyenne Nation, 86, 200, 222, 232, 238,
240, 242, 250, 292
See also Sand Creek Massacre
Chicago (Illinois leader), 107
Chickahominy Nation, 50, 52, 64, 72, 76,
112
Chickamauga People, 174
Chickasaw Nation, 214
cession and removal, 130, 170, 196, 208
treaties (colonial), 128, 130
treaties (U.S.A.), 182, 184, 194, 206, 208,
210, 214, 224, 226, 228, 240
wars (French), 116, 120
wars (Spanish), 40, 44
wars (tribal), 96, 102
wars (U.S.A.), 236
Chickataubut (House Afire), 59, 61
Chicks, Sheldon A., 309
Chicora, Francisco de, 33
Chief Big Foot Massacre (Wounded
Knee), 165, 233, 258, 259
Chief Eagle, Dallas, 273, 302
Childers, Ernest, 289
Chilili (Snow Bird), 13
China Lake (California), 10
Chingalsuwi (the Hardened One), 17
Chinkoa (Illinois Confederacy), 72
Chippewa Nation
French, dealings with, 78, 108
treaties (U.S.A.), 174, 180, 184, 186, 190,
192, 194, 198, 210, 212, 214, 218,

226, 228, 230, 236
wars (tribal), 132
Chippewa Nation (bands)
Black River Chippewa, 212, 230, 236
Bois Fort Chippewa, 240
Lac Courte Oreilles Chippewa, 318
Lake Superior Chippewa, 216, 218, 226
Lake Winnibigoshish Chippewa,
228, 236
Mississippi Chippewa, 216, 218, 226,
228, 236, 240
Pembina Chippewa, 236
Pillager Chippewa, 228, 236
Red Lake Chippewa, 236
Saginaw Chippewa, 214, 216, 230, 236
Sault Sainte Marie People, 228, 230
Swan Creek Chippewa, 230, 236
Chiricahua Apache Reservation, 250,
252
Chisholm, Jesse, 187, 243
Chisholm Trail, 187
Chiskiack People, 58
Chitanitis (Strong Ally), 19
Chitanwulit (Strong is Good), 19
Chitimacha People, 40
Chitomachen (Tayac), 61
Chitto Harjo (Wilson Jones), 219, 261,
264, 269
Chivington, Colonel John M., 242, 243
Chobahahbish People, 226
Chocorua (last of the Wamesit), 131
Choctaw Nation, 214, 254, 324
cession and removal, 128, 196, 206
French, dealings with, 108
treaties (colonial), 128, 130
treaties (U.S.A.), 174, 182, 184, 192, 193,
198, 206, 214, 226, 228, 240
wars (Spanish), 40
wars (tribal), 96
wars (U.S.A.), 236
Choctaws: A Critical Bibliography, The
(Kidwell), 316
Choenemnees People, 220
*Choice Collection of Hyms [sic] and Spiritual
Songs Intended [sic] for the Edification of
Sincere Christians of All Denominations, A*
(Occum), 134
Choinues People, 220
cholera. See epidemics
Chona, Maria, 280
Chookchanees People, 220
Chowchilla People, 220
Christian Native People, 225
Christianity (and Native People), 33, 37,
46, 61, 70, 71, 73, 85, 97, 199, 281, 323.
See also missionaries
Chunute People, 222
Church, Captain Benjamin, 77
Churchill, Ward, 237, 291
Chute, Robert, 275
Chyalpinish (Yokuts), 193
Cicúye People, 41
citizenship and Native People, 272
Civil War, 197, 232, 234, 236

Chippewa veterans, **239**
Clackamas People, 226
Clark, Carter Blue, **99**, 99, 291
Clarke, Frank, 295
Clarke, Peter Dooyentate, 242
Cleveland, Grover, 254
Cliff Palace, **11**
Clinton, General James, 166
Clinton, William J., 323, 328–29
Cloud, Henry Roe, 277
Cneenah People, 222
Coacoochee (Wild Cat) (Seminole leader), 31, 214
Coahuiltec People, 74
Cochise (Apache leader), 189, 251
Cochise, Ciye N., 306
Cockacoeske ("Queen" Anne of the Pamunkey), 75, 77, 107
Cockoman People, 222
Cocomcahras People, 224
Coconoon People, 220
Code Talkers, 143, 270, 283, 286, 288, 322, 326
Cody, Iron Eyes, 265
Cody, William F. (Buffalo Bill), 242
Coeur d'Alene People, 197
Coffee, Robin, 316, 324
Cofitachique People, 41
Cogewea (Sacagawea), 185
Cogewea, the Half-Blood: A Depiction of the Great Montana Cattle Range, by Humishu-ma, "Mourning Dove" (Humishuma), 274
Cohe, William. *See* Mohe
Cohena People, 222
Coiracoentanon (Illinois Confederacy), 72
Colbert, Levi (Chickasaw leader), 211
Cole, D. C., 281
Coleman Report on Indian Education, 302
Colfax and The Saga of Henry Starr (Conley), 322
Collus People, 222
Colorado, Pam, 241
Colored Man's Story of Providence and David and Jonathan, The (Gibson), 264
Columbus, Christopher, 27, 28, 29
Comanche Nation, 118, 189, 210, 214, 218, 224, 238, 240, 252
wars, 221, 250
Comcomly (Chinook leader), 131, 185, death and disfiguration of, 207
Commission on Indian Reservation Economics, 320
Comomo, 41
Compact History of the Indian Wars (Tebbel), 302
Complete Both Early and Late History of the Ottawa and Chippewa Indians (Mackawdebenessy), 260
Concha, Joseph L., 297
Conestoga Nation, 96, 97, 102, 104, 128
Confederated Umatilla Journal, 307
Conley, Robert J., 21, **22**, 63, 285, 320, 322,

324, 326
Conloy People, 132
Connecticut (British colony), 62
Connor, General Patrick, 236, 238
Conoy (Lenape) Nation, 39, 45, 61, 126
Contemporary Insanities, Short Fictions (Brashear), 324
Continental Congress, treaties with, 134
Conversations from the Nightmare (Sanchez), 310
Cook-Lynn, Elizabeth, 113, 275, 310
Cooper, Colonel Douglas H., 236
Coos People, 232
Coosaponakeesa (Creek Mary), 95, 97, 129
Cooso Cacique, 41
Cooso People, 41
Cooswootna (Juan Antonio) (Cahuilla leader), 171, 224, 237
Cooweescoowee (John Ross) (Cherokee leader), **179**, 179, 215, 241
copperworking, 10, 18, 20, 22, 24, 34
Copway, George. *See* Kahgegagahbowh
Coree Nation, 100, 102
Corn Tassel, 87, 127
Cornplanter (Seneca leader), 179, 181, 183
Cornstalk (Shawnee leader), 95
Coronado, Francisco Vásquez de, 40, 41, 42
Côrte-Real, Gaspar, 28
Cortés, Hernán, 29, 32
Costo, Rupert, 267
Cotoplaneniis People, 220
council fires
on treaty negotiations, 174
See also ceremony time (various months)
Council of Chota, 137
Council of Energy Resource Tribes (CERT), 310
County of Oneida, New York. v. Oneida Indian Nation of New York, 320
Courchene, Richard M., 271
Couro, Ted, 259
Coutu, Hector, 269
Covenant Chain treaties (1st and 2nd), 78, 86, 87, 98, 110, 124
Cow Creek Umpqua, 224
Cownanatico People, 226
Coyote, 75, 145
Ak-mul Au-authm (Pima), 10
Maidu legend, 32
See also Heyoka/Koshari
Coyote Stories (Humishuma), 276
Crashing Thunder (Big Winnebago/Sam Blowsnake), 270
Crawford, Colonel William, 170
Crazy Horse. *See* Tashunka Witco
Crazy Snake uprising, 264, 265
creation stories
Ak-mul Au-authm (Pima), 10
Athabascan (Upper Yukon), 136
Atse'hastquin and Atse'esdza (Diné/Navajo), 44

Wyandot, 170
Creative Writing: Fiction, Drama, Poetry, the Essay (Brashear), 302
Cree People, 25, 254
Cree First Nation (of Canada), 322
Creek Mary. *See* Coosaponakeesa
Creek (Muscogee) Nation, 21
cession and removal, 196, 201, 208
civil war, 168, 190
Swan Creek, 212
treaties (colonial), 96, 104, 110, 112, 118, 122, 128, 130, 132, 134
treaties (U.S.A.), 178, 180, 182, 184, 190, 192, 196, 198, 200, 202, 208, 209, 210, 214, 218, 226, 230, 240
wars (Spanish), 40,
wars (U.S.A.), 168, 191, 236
Creek-Seminole Spirit Tales (Strickland), 306
Cressap, Colonel, 133
Croghan, Catherine, 185
Crook, General George, 250
Crop Planting, Festival of, 141
Crow Nation, 136, 202, 211, 212, 222, 242
Crown of Columbus, The (Erdrich/Dorris), 324
Crying Wind (Stafford), 287, 310
Crystal Skull, The (documentary film), 293
Crystos, 291
Cuauhtémoc (Aztec leader), 33
Cuffe, Paul, 216
culture of the Native People, 150–51
Culu People, 222
Cuming, Sir Alexander, 111
Cuna, Juan, 67, 71
Curly Chief (Pawnee), 41, 97
Curtis, Charles, 235, 275, 281
Curtis Act (of 1898), 260, 280
Cusabo People, 40, 45, 78, 86
Cusick, David, 204
Custer Battlefield National Monument, 324
Custer Died for Your Sins: An Indian Manifesto (Deloria), 304
Custer's Last Stand, 252
Cuthand, Beth, 293

Da, Popovi, 273
Dade, Major Francis, 211
Dadgar, Maria Proctor, **286**
dam construction (and Native People), 292, 298, 300
dance (and dancers), 111
boy dancers (Wyandot legend), 28
festivals honoring, 150
Ghost Dance prayer song, 113, 257
Raven Dance, **32**
Sun Dance, 266
See also ceremonies; ceremony time (various months); Ghost Dance movement; legends and stories; literature; powwows; songs
Dance Around the Sun: The Life of Mary Lit-

tle Bear Inkanish, Cheyenne (Little Bear), 312
Dancing Horse of Acoma (Hunt), 300
Danohab People, 222
Dartmouth College, 134
Daspia People, 222
Dauenhauer, Nora Marks, 275
Daughters I Love You (Hogan), 316
Davidson, Florence E., 261
Dawes Commission, 258
Dawes Severalty (General Allotment) Act, 256, 258, 266, 274, 278
Dawn Land (Bruchac), 326
Daykauray, 53, 109
De Carrie, Sabrevior, 109
de la Balme, Colonel Mottin, 170
de Sosa, Gaspar Castano, 48
de Soto, Hernando, 36, 40, 41, 44
Death of Jim Loney, The (Welch), 312
Declaration of the All Indian Council in 1924, 325
Deer, Ada E., **278,** 279, 327
Degataga (Stand Watie), 187, 245
del Vallo, Martin, 255
Delaware. *See* Lenape Nation
Delaware Indian Art Designs (Tantaquidgeon), 294
Delaware map, **24**
Deloria, Ella Cara, 312
Deloria, Vine, Jr., 241, 277, 301, 306, 308, 310, 312, 318, 320
DeMézières, Athanase, 133
Denonville, Governor, 88
Department of the Interior. *See under* United States Government
Dial, Adolph L., 273
Dickson Mounds Museum, 326
Diegueño People, 224
Digging Out the Roots (Niatum), 312
Digueño, Jamul (Tipai-Ipai), 44
Dilemma for Indian Woman—Wassaja, The (Wauneka), 310
Diné People. *See* Navajo People
Dinwiddle, Lieut. Governor Robert, 123
discrimination
  by British colonists, 70
  Ku Klux Klan, 298
  U.S. government racism, 248–49
  See also massacres; murder
diversity, People and, 113, 154–55
Diwali (the Bowl), 123, 217
Docduc People, 222
Dockstader, Frederick J., 271, 298, 310
Dog Soldiers, 191, 243
Domagaya, 35, 37
Dominion of New England, 88
Dongan, Thomas, 84, 86
Donnacona (Stadacona leader), 35, 37, 40, 41
Dormer, Captain Thomas, 55
Dorris, Michael A., 289, 322, 324
Downing, Todd, 265
Doxtator, Honyery (Oneida leader), 137
Dozier, Edward P., 271, 304

Drake, Francis, 46
Drapeau, Darrell E., **109**
Dreamers, Season of, 156
Dreams of Jesse Brown, The (Bruchac), 310
Drinks Water (Lakota holy man), 136
drugs. *See* alcohol and drugs
Dull Knife. *See* Tah–me-la-pash-me
Duluth, Daniel Greysolon, Sieur, 78
Dunn, Martin F., 281
Durham, Jimmie, 29
Duwanish People, 226

Eadle Keatoah Toh (Big Morning Star) newspaper, 256
Eagle Bay (Moss Lake), Mohawk activists occupation of, 308
Eagle Man (Ed McGaa), 281
Earth Mother, 19, 23, 53, 55, 61, 93, 140
  week honoring, 143
Eastman, Charles A. *See* Ohiyesa
Echoes of Our Being (Coffee), 316
Echohawk, John E., 289, 309
Eclipse (Hogan), 318
education (by Native People), 100, 101, 300, 304, 315
  college, 304
  scholars and learners, festival honoring, 147
education (of Native People), 54, 122, 145, 196, 198, 201, **255,** 256, 302, 306
  Adult Vocational Training (BIA), 298
  BIA schools, 274, 312
  college, 73, 106, 117, 134, 219, 252, 253
  Indian Appropriations Act, 258
  and Native languages, 256
Edgar, Jim, 326
Edisto People, 40
Edmo, Ed, 291
Eeh People, 222
Eel River Nation, 180, 182, 184, 188, 204
effigy pipes, 22
Elangomel (Harmonizer), 29
Elderberry Flute Song: Contemporary Coyote Tales (Aroniawenate), 322
elders, respect for, 19
Elinipsico, 137
Eliot, John, 70, 93
Employment Division of Oregon v. Smith, 324
Empty Swings (Vizenor), 302
Enchanted Mesa, **25**
Enemy Way Music (McAllester), 296
Engles, William L., 321
Ensenore (Secotan), 47
Entering into the Silence—The Seneca Way (Nitsch), 310
Entering Onondaga (Bruchac), 312
environment, Native People and, 142
Enwhisteetkwa: Walk in Water (Armstrong), 318
Epallahchund (Calling Retreat), 47
Epanow (Apannow), 53, 55
epidemics, 27, 30, 34, 35, 36, 52, 54, 59, 61,

62, 73, 74, 85, 88, 110, 111, 112, 118, 136, 173, 180, 182, 183, 207, 212, 214, 215, 216, 217, 252, 264, 265
  as biological warfare, 128, 130
  See also smallpox
Episode of the Spring Roundup '77 (Jones), 260
Erdoes, Richard, 306
Erdrich, Louise, 103, 297, 320, 324
Erie People, 67
Escalante, Felipe de, 48
Escalante, Francisco Silvestre Vélez de, 134
Escorts to White Earth (Vizenor), 302
Eskimo Alaska Native People, 254, 264, 280
Eskimo First Nation of Canada, 318
Eskuin People, 222
Esopus People, 70
Espejo, Antonio de, 46
Espminkia (Illinois Confederacy), 72
Estevánico (African slave), 34, 36
Esther and Me, or "Just Relax" (Rogers), 274
Etowah (Cahokia settlement), 22
Eulogy on King Philip, as Pronounced at the Odeon, in Federal Street, Boston by the Reverend William Apes, an Indian (Apes), 212
events (and ceremonies). *See* ceremony time (various months)
Ex Parte Crow Dog, 254
Excerpts from a Mountain Climber's Handbook (Sanchez), 320
Experience of the Five Christian Indians of the Pequod Tribe; or the Indian's Looking-Glass for the White Man, The (Apes), 210
E-yeh-shur (Blue Corn), 23
E-yet-e-co (mother of all life), 10, 40

Fadden, John. *See* Kahionhes
Fadden, Ray. *See* Akweks, Aren
Fairy Take, A (Bow), 256
Fallen Timbers, battle of, 178, 185
family, Native People and, 141
Feeling, Durbin, 291
Fife, Connie, 301, 323
Fight Back: For the Sake of the People, for the Sake of the Land (Ortiz), 316
Finhioven (Kadohadacho leader), 133
Fire, John. *See* Lame Deer
First Boy (James Larpenteur Long), 300
First Hundred Years of Nino Cochise, The (Cochise), 306
Fish on Poteau Mountain, The (Bames), 316
fishing rights, 226, 228, 266, 300, 304, 312, 318
Five Nations. *See* Iroquois League of the Five Fires
Fixico, Donald L., 295
Flaming Arrow (James Paytiamo), 33, 59, 257, 276
Flaming Arrow's People, by an Acoma In-

dian (Flaming Arrow), 276
Flathead ("Confederated Tribes"), 228, 230
Flathead Reservation, 228
Flint and Feather (Tehakionwake), 268
Florida (state), 168, 169, 208
Flying Canoe Legend, The (Greenbrier), 266
Flying Hawk, 85
Folk Medicine in the Delaware and Related Algonkian Indians (Tantaquidgeon), 306
Folson-Dickerson, W. S., 261
Food and Gift Giving, Festival of, 159
Forbes, Jack D., 29, 61, 279, 296
Ford, Gerald R., 310, 313
Forsyth, Colonel George Alexander, 258
Fort Amsterdam (N.Y.C.), 64
Fort Ancient, 21
Fort Apache Scout newspaper, 300
Fort Dearborn massacre, 188
Fort Detroit, 128, 129, 131
Fort Duquesne, 122
Fort Gadsden ("Negro Fort"), 168–69
Fort Jackson. *See* Treaty of Fort Jackson
Fort Laramie. *See* Treaty of Fort Laramie
Fort McIntosh. *See* Treaty of Fort McIntosh
Fort Madison, 168
Fort Niagara, 128
Fort Orange (Albany, N.Y.), 58, 64
Fort Pitt, 128, 130, 134
Fort Saint Louis, 86
Fort Sasquesahanok, **24**
Fort Stanwix. *See* Treaty of Fort Stanwix
Fort William Henry, 122
Forty Years with the Cheyenne (Bent), 271
Four Corners region, 22
Four Mothers Society, 268
Fox. *See* Mesquakie People; Sac and Fox ("United") Nations
Fox Texts (Jones), 312
Foxwoods High Stakes Bingo and Casino, 326
fractionalization, 56–57, 58, 59, 136, 173, 185
France-Roy (Québec), 44
Francis, Ethel Gunn Haynes Gottlied. *See* Tdu-u-eh-t'sah
Francis, John C., 293
Francis, Lee, III, **288**
Francis, Lee, IV, 77, **85,** 289, 311, 313, 327
Franklin, Benjamin, 134
Fredericks, Tom, 317
Frémont, Captain John C., 218
French, Alice, 275
French and Indian War, 122, 123
Friday, Moses, 268
Friends of Thunder (Kilpatrick/Kilpatrick), 300
From Sand Creek (Ortiz), 316
From the Deep Woods to Civilization: Chapters in the Autobiography of an Indian (Ohiyesa), 270
Frontenac, Louis de Buade, Comte de, 74, 90

Fry, Maggie Culver, 265
Funmaker, Forest, 303
Future Is Now, The (Hillabrant), 308

Galagina (Buck Watie/Elias Boudinot), 185, 198, 217
Gallagher, Maym Hannah, 53
Galler, Cristal McLeod. *See* Humishuma
Ganadaio (Handsome Lake) (Seneca leader), 95
Ganienkeh (Land of Flintstone), 308
Garakontie (Moving Sun), 73, 78
Garangula (Otreouati), 87
Gatewood, Charles, 224
Gathering of Spirit (Brant), 285
Gattawisi (Near Fulfilled), 25
Gay American Indians, 318
Gaynwah (Thomas Wildcat Alford), 235, 281
Gelelemend (Killbuck) (Delaware leader), 95
General Allotment (Dawes Severalty) Act, 256, 258, 266, 274, 278
generosity, Native People and, 158
genocide of Native People, 196–97
Geoigamah, Hanay, 289
George II (of England), 111, 115
George III (of England), 115, 130, 132, 171
George, Charles, 297
George, Dan, 261
George Washington's America (Tebbel), 296
Georgia (British colony) , 110, 111, 112, 124, 134
Gerard, Forrest, 313
German Flats, battle of, 122
Germantown Flats (Shawnee Village) gathering, 132
Geronimo. *See* Goyathlay
Geronimo: His Own Story (Barrett/Goyathlay), 266
Ghigau, The (Beloved Woman of the Cheroke), 95, 111, 133
Ghost Dance movement (1st and 2nd), 231, 232–33, 248, 257, 258, 277
Ghost Dance prayer song, 113, 125, 257
Giago, Tim, 279
Gibson, Charles, 264, 266
Gieogamah, Hanay, 316
Gii-Ikwezensiwiyaan—When I Was a Little Girl (Kegg), 310
Gikenopalat (Trailblazer), 25
Gila Butte, 20
Gischenatsi, 37
Gish, Robert R., 285
Gist, George. *See* Sequoyah
Glancy, Diane, **116,** 117
Glooskap and Malsum (Algonkian story), 32
Gnaddenhutten Massacre, 170
God Is Red (Deloria), 308
Godfrey, Harriet, 227
Gogisgi (Carroll Arnett), 275
Going for the Rain (Ortiz), 310

gold (discovery and rushes), 250, 260
Gonwatzijyanni (Molly Brant) (Mohawk clan mother), 111, 181
Gonzales, Angela A., **112**
Good, Hiram, 238
Good Journey A (Ortiz), 312
Gordon, Roxy. *See* Toe Ga Juke Juke Gan Hoke Sheem
Gorky Park (Smith), 316
Gosiute People, 232
Gould, Janice, **62,** 293
Gourd Dancer, The (Momaday), 310
government, Native People and), 147–48
Goyathlay (One Who Yawns) (Geronimo), **31,** 37, 235, 266, 267, **267**
Grand Canyon, 40
Grand Pawnee People. *See under* Pawnee People
Grand Pueblo Revolt, 84, 85, 92
Grand River People, 228
Grand Traverse People, 228
Grandfather's Origin Story: The Navajo Beginning (Red Hawk), 322
Grandmother's Christmas Story: A True Quechan Indian Story (Red Hawk), 322
Grandmothers Knife, **132**
Granganemeo (Ensenore's son), 47
Grant, Lana, 287
Grasmick, Harold G., 318
Grasmick, Mary K., 316
Grass Woman, **243**
Grattan, battle of, 225
Grave Creek Umpqua People, 226
Grave of Goingsnake, The (Cha-lahgee), 266
Great Being, 13
Great Creator, 91
Great Jim Thorpe Longest Run, 320
Great Law of Peace, 14, 39, 48, 117, 137, 329
Great Mystery, 10
Great North American Indians: Profiles in Life and Leadership (Dockstader), 310
Great Revolt of 1680, 69
Great Sioux Nation, The (Ortiz), 312
Great Spirit, 11, 19, 23, 45, 53, 55, 61, 85, 89, 91, 97, 109, 121, 129, 131, 140, 173, 189, 255
See also ceremonial objects and costumes; ceremonies; ceremony time; Wakan Tanka
Green, Rayna, **96,** 97, 287, 316, 318, 320, 324, 325
Green, Richard G., 285
Greenbrier, Carlysle, 266
Gregory, Jack, 277
Grey Eagle (Kenneth Jackson), 273
Gros Ventre People, 214, 222, 266
Groseilliers, Médard Chouart, 66
Gross-Louis, Max, 277
Guarionex (Arawak), 31
Guerra, Friar Salvador de, 67, 71
Guerrero (shipwreck survivor), 30
Guess, George. *See* Sequoyah
Guests Never Leave Hungry: The Autobiog-

raphy of James Sewid, A Kwakiutl Indian (Sewid), 304
Gunitakan (Long-in-the-Woods), 21
Gunn, Agnes Atsye, 261
Gunokeni (Long Lineage), 15
Guyashuta (Seneca leader), 95

Haberman, Dorothy, 49
Habinapo People, 222
Hadley-Lynch, Regina, 291
Haida People, 13
Haida Reader (Lawrence), 308
Haigler (Aratswa) (Catawba leader), 119, 123, 127
Hail, Raven, 271, 302
Hale, Duane K., 287
Hale, Janet Campbell, 291, 308
Halfbreed (Campbell), 308
Hallett, William, 313
Halpatter Miko (Billy Bowlegs) (Seminole leader), 189, 216, 237
Halpatter Tustenugee (Alligator) (Seminole leader), 181, 211, 214
Hampton Normal and Agricultural Institute, 252, 253
Hanaholend (River Loving), 25
Hancock (Tuscarora leader), 101
Hansen, Annie, 45
Hansen, Terri C., **251**
Harjo, Joy, 265, **265,** 295, 308, 312
Harjo, William (Thomas E. Moore), 269
Harkins, George W., 51
Harlow, Captain Edward, 53
Harney trading post, 216
Harper's Anthology of 20th Century Native American Poetry (Niatum), 322
Harpoon the Hunter (Markoosie), 304
Harris, John, 123
Harris, LaDonna, 305, **305**
Harrison, David C., 306
Harrison, William Henry, 188, 189
Harquip (Chickahominy leader), 71
Harvard College, 73
Hastin (Manuelito) (Navajo leader), 193, 241, 243, 245
Hatchootucknee (Peter Perkins Pitchlynn), **198**
Hatikainye (Elaine Murphy Schroeter), **214**
Hattanwulaton (Having Possession), 21
Hatuay, 29
Haudenausaunee. *See* Iroquois Nation
Haw:kuh (Ashiwi village), 74
Hayes, Ira Hamilton, 299
Haynes, Agnes Gunn, **273**
Haynes, Robert B., **46,** 273
Hazelwood Republic, 225
headdresses, 24
Headley, Louis R., 313
health (of Native People), 152–53, 298, 302
   See also epidemics; medical resources
Heap Big Laugh (Madrano), 298

Heap of Birds, Edgar, 297
Heath, Charlotte W., 301
Hehaka Sapa (Black Elk) (Lakota holy man), 131, 136, 171, 181, 237, 276, 295
Hekoneck People, 222
Henry, Alexander, 129
Henry, Gordon D., Jr., 299, **313,** 313
Henry, Jeannette, 267, 304, 308
Henry, Patrick, 134
Hensley, William L., 303, 305
Henson, Lance, 289
heritage, 119, 144
   celebration of, 155–56
Herkimer, Nicholas, 136
Hewitt, John N. B., 231, 264
Heyoka/Koshari (Trickster/Clown) Solemn Time of, 145 *See also* Coyote
Hidatsa People, 136. *See also* Crow Nation
Hienwatah (not Hiawatha), 15, 63
high-steel construction, Native People and, 256
Highway, Thomson, 295
Hilbert, Vi, 271
Hilden, Patricia Penn, 73, **78,** 317, 326
Hill, Richard, 295
Hillabrant, Walter J., 287, 308
Hills, Norbert S., Jr., **313**
Hinmaton yalatkit (Chief Joseph) (Nez Percé leader), 217, **217,** 253, 265
Histoire des Indiens du Haut et du Bas Canada (Assiniwi), 308
history (Native People), 301
   celebration of, 156–57
   holocaust of, 248–49
History of the Ojebway Indians, with Especial Reference to Their Conversion to Christianty (Kahkewaquonaby), 234
History of the Ojebways, Based on Traditions and Oral Statements (Warren), 254
History of the Ottawa and Chippewa Indians of Michigan; a Grammar of Theirr [sic] Language and Personal and Family History of the Author (Mackawdebenessy), 256
Hitchiti People, 40
Hobomok, 59
Hobson, Geary, 285, 312
Hochelaga, 34, 35
Hogan, Linda, 125, 291, 316, 318, 324
Hohokam People, 14, 18, 20, 22, 24
Holcumas People, 220
Holoclame People, 222
Hololupi People, 222
holy men and women, 131, 136, 237, 257, 281
   season of, 156
Honanie, Gilbert, Jr., 285
Honey Springs, Civil War battle of, 236
Honganozhe (Louis Wayne Ballard), 277
Hoopa People, 222
Hoover, Herbert, 275
Hoover Commission on the Reorganization of Government, 292
Hope, Andrew, III, 293

Hopewell People, 18
Hopi Customs, Folklore and Ceremonies (Nequatewa), 296
Hopi People, 12, 17, 19, 39, 40, 60, 96
   Navajo-Hopi Land Settlement Act, 308
Hopi Roadrunner, Dancing (Rose), 308
Hopi Way, The (Mofsie), 304
Hopkins, Sarah Winnemucca, 254
Hose (Little Raven), 243, **243**
Hot'tsa-sodono (Deerfoot/Louis Bennett), 207, 235, 261
Houlton Nation, 316
Housatonic Nation, 110
House Made of Dawn (Momaday), 279, 302, 314
Housing and Community Development Act, 308
Howe, LeAnne, 295
Howechees People, 220
Howkuma People, 222
Hudson, Henry, 52
Huerta, C. Lawrence, 309
Hultgren, Marilou, 324
Humana, Antonio Gutiérrez de, 48
Humirdend (Hominy Man), 15
Humishuma (Morning Dove/Cristal McLeod Galler), 274, 276, 310
Hungry Wolf, Beverly, 295, 316
Hunkpapa Sioux. *See under* Sioux Nation (bands)
Hunt, Wolf Robe, 300
Hunter, Lois Marie, 294
Huron Confederacy, 34, 52, 60, 62, 64, 66, 97, 130, 132, 174
Hyde, Henry, 98

I Am a Pueblo Indian Girl (Abeita), 280
I Am Nokomis, Too: The Biography of Verna Patronella Johnston (Johnston), 312
I Fought with Geronimo (Nye/Batsinas), 298
Idakariwakaha People, 222
Ikaruck People, 222
Il n'y plus d'Indiens (a play) (Assiniwi), 318
Illasenor, David, 269
Illinois Confederacy, 72
Illinois (Lenape) Nation, 45, 66, 86, 194
   Cahokia People, 72, 182, 194, 208
   Kaskaskia People, 180, 182, 194, 208, 224, 240
   Michigamea People, 72, 208
   Peoria People, 72, 132, 194, 208, 240
   Piankashaw People, 66, 180, 182, 184, 190, 208, 224, 240
   Tamarois People, 182, 194, 208
   Wea People, 66, 180, 182, 184, 188, 192, 194, 198, 208, 224, 240
Illiterate Digest, The (Rogers), 272
In Search of Our Mother's Gardens (Awiakta), 318
In the Name of His Ancestor (Jones), 260
Indian Affairs, Bureau of (BIA), 89, 200,

268, 274, 278, 297
Adult Vocational Training, 298
blood quantum, 314–15
and health and medical care, 298
offices, AIM occupation of, 283, 306
Voluntary Relocation Act, 296
Indian Affairs, Department of (Continental Congress), 134
Indian Affairs, Office of (U.S. War Department), 200, 220
Indian agents, 258
Indian and the Devil, The (Gibson), 264
Indian Appropriations Act, 258
Indian Arts and Crafts Board, 278, 280
Indian Boyhood (Ohiyesa), 264
Indian Child Life (Ohiyesa), 268
Indian Child Welfare Act, 312
Indian Christmas (Pratt), 272
Indian Civil Rights Act (ICRA), 302
Indian Claims Commission, 208, 290, 294
Indian Country Today, 279, 316
Indian Defense League, 272
Indian Education: A National Tragedy—A National Challenge (U.S. Senate report), 304
Indian Education Act, 306
Indian Girl's Story, An (Waheenee), 270
Indian Heros and Great Chieftains (Ohiyesa), 270
Indian Historian, 300
"Indian John," 119
Indian Man: A Life of Oliver La Farge (McNickle), 306
Indian Music of the Southwest (McAllester), 300
Indian Nullification of the Unconstitutional Laws of Massachusetts, Relative to the Marshpee Tribe, or, The Pretended Riot Explained (Apes), 210
Indian Question (Unakuh), 254
Indian Removal Act (IRA), 196, 206
Indian Reorganization (Wheeler-Howard) Act, 277, 278, 279
Indian Rights Association, 254
Indian Self-Determination and Education Assistance Act, 310
Indian Story (Smith), 270
Indian Territory, 238
Indian To-day: The Past and Future of the First Americans, The (Ohiyesa), 268
Indian Tribal Governmental Tax Status Act, 318
Indian Tribes of the United States: Ethnic and Cultural Survival, The (McNickle), 300
Indian Voices (Henry), 304
Indian Youth of America, 312
Indiana Potawatomi. See under Potawatomi Nation (bands)
Indians of the Pacific Northwest (Deloria), 310
Indians, Superintendents and Councils: Northwestern Indian Policy, 1850–1855 (Trafzer), 320

Infants and Children, honoring time of, 141–42
Inherit the Blood (Bush), 320
Inheritors, The (Tebbel), 300
Inneck People, 222
Institute of American Indian Arts (IAIA), 300
intermarriage, 185, 327
International Human Rights Conference, 310
International Indian Fair, 250
International Indian Treaty Council, 308, 310
interpreters, 199, 219, 243. *See also* Code Talkers
Inter-Tribal Indian Ceremonial Association, 272
Intimpeaches People, 220
Inuit Circumpolar Conference, 318
Inuit People, 14
Ioni Nation, 218
Iouolumnes People, 220
Iowa (Ioway) People, 190, 200, 202, 206, 212, 214, 224
Ipellie, Alootook, 295
Iroquoian Cosmology (Hewitt), 264
Iroquoian vocabulary list, 34
Iroquois (Haudenausaunee) Nation, 13, 18, 19, 21, 36, 50, 52, 166
of Canada, 110
Stadacona Iroquois, 34, 35, 36, 39, 40, 44
Susquehanna Iroquois, 47, 66, 70, 74, 78, 96, 97, 102, 124
Wyandot Iroquois, 20, 21, 28, 44, 124, 128, 168, 170, 174, 180, 182, 184, 186, 188, 190, 192, 194, 216, 218, 220, 228, 240
See also Great Law of Peace
Iroquois Confederacy (League of the Five Nations), 14, 48, 52, 66, 74, 99, 100, 102
and the American Revolution, 168
treaties (colonial), 58, 60, 72, 74, 78, 84, 86, 90, 92, 96, 97, 98, 104
treaties (U.S.A.), 174, 178, 180, 182, 184
wars (tribal), 60, 66, 70, 78, 86, 88, 98, 137
See also Cayuga Nation; Mohawk Nation; Oneida Nation; Onondaga Nation; Seneca Nation
Iroquois Confederacy (League of the Six Nations), 101, 106, 134
Great Law of the Six Nations of the Iroquois Confederacy, 14, 39, 48, 117, 137, 329
treaties (colonial), 108, 110, 116, 117, 118, 120, 122, 124, 126, 130
treaties (tribal), 132
treaties (U.S.A.), 115, 134, 172, 178
Iroquois League of the Five Fires. *See* Iroquois Confederacy
Irving, Joe, 277
Isah-pomu'xika (Crowfoot) (Blackfoot leader), 213, 253, 259
Island Arawak (Taino) People, 27, 28, 29, 30

Isparhechar, 97, **98**
Itireitok, 13
Itachees People, 220
Iwo Jima, raising the flag, 273, 283
Iyanough, 59

Jackson, Andrew, 168, 169, 190, 196, 206, 211, 228
Jackson, Donald, 298
Jackson, Kenneth. *See* Grey Eagle
Jacobs, Alex A.. *See* Karoniaktatie
Jacobs, Kenneth, 271
Jacobs, Peter. *See* Pahtahsega
Jaimes, Annette, 291, 324
James, Overton, 301
Jamestown colony, 39, 50, 56, 58, 59, 60
Jamestown War, 64
Janotowi Enolowin (Keeping Guard), 13
Jay Treaty (of 1794), 272
Jefferson, Thomas, 69, 168, 183, 184, 196
Jémez People, 46
Jémez Pueblo Massacre, 90
Jersey People, 70
Jicarilla Apache. *See under* Apache Nation (bands)
Jicarilla Apache reservation, **42–43**
Jicarilla Chieftain newspaper, 300
Jim Whitewolf: The Life of a Kiowa Apache (Whitewolf), 304
Jimmy Yellow Hawk (Sneve), 306
Jligonsaseh (Iroquois woman), 15
Joe, Rita, 277
Johnny, "King" (Cheraw leader), 131
Johns, Joseph F.. *See* Cayoni
Johnson, Elias, 254
Johnson, Emily Pauline. *See* Tekahionwake
Johnson, Lyndon B., 302
Johnston, Basil H., 275, 310
Johnston, Robert, 297, 312
Johnston, Verna Patronella, 267, 312
Jojola, Ted, 295, 310, 321
Jolliet, Louis, 75
Jones, Peter. *See* Kahkewaquonaby
Jones, Sam. *See* Arpeika
Jones, William, 260, 264, 312
Jones, Wilson. *See* Chitto Harjo
Joseph, Chief. *See* Hinmaton yalatkit
Journal of the Reverend Peter Jacobs, Indian Wesleyan Missionary, from Rice Lake to the Hudson's Bay Territory and Returning Commencing May 1852 (Pahtahsega), 224
Juanita, **192**
Judge: The Life of Robert A. Hefner, The (Trafzer), 308
Jumper, Betty Mae, 293, 303, 320
Jumper, Moses, Jr., 295

Kabotie, Michael, 287
kachina masks, 70
Kahgegagahbowh (George Copway), 11,

193, 218, 222, 237
Kahionhes (John Fadden), 281
Kahkewaquonaby (Peter Jones), 234
Kahmiltpah People. *See under* Yakima Nation (bands)
Kahnawakeh (Mohawk citadel), 66
Kahweas People, 224
Kaianerekowa. *See* Great Law of Peace
Kaibah: Recollections of a Navajo Girlhood (Bennett), 300
Kaienkwahton (Old Smoke), 167, 175
Kalapuya People, 232
Kalifornsky, Peter, 269
Kamiaken, 73
Kanakuk (Kikapoo prophet), **90,** 91
Kancamagus (Pennacook leader), 75, 89
Kange'su-nka (Crow Dog), 211, 254, 255
Kanickhungo (Iroquois leader), 113
Kankakee Potawatomi People. *See under* Potawatomi Nation (bands)
Kansa (Kansas) Nation, 190, 200, 202, 218, 230
Kansas Potawatomi. *See* Potawatomi Nation (bands)
Karankawa People, 34, 36
Karnee: A Paiute Narrative (Lowry), 302
Karok People, 232
Karoniaktatie (Alex A. Jacobs), 171, 297, 321
Kaskaskia People. *See under* Illinois Nation
Kaskia (Illinois Confederacy), 72
Kataka Nation, 214
Kayete People, 222
Keechy Nation, 218
Keegan, Marcia, 287, 306, 308, 310
Keeshig-Tobias, Lenore, 295
Keewawnay. *See under* Potawatomi Nation (bands)
Kegg, Maude, 310
Kekewepellethe (Tame Hawk) (Shawnee leader), 175
Kennedy, Edward M., 304
Kennedy, John F., 301
Kennedy, Robert F., 304
Kennedy Report, 304
Kennerly, Joan Bullshoe, 277
Kenny, Maurice, **86,** 275, 318
Keokuk, **186,** 187
Keon, Orville, 275
Keon, Ronald, 297
Keon, Wayne, 291
Keres People, 10, 48, 92
Kerr-McGee Corp. v. Navajo Tribe of Indians, 320
Khapkhaponimi, 217
Kiantwa'ka (Cornplanter/John O'Bail), 111, 137, 213, 300
Kiawah People, 74
Kichitamak (Great Beaver), 23
Kichitamak II (Great Beaver), 29
Kickapoo Nation, 126, 180, 182, 188, 190, 192, 194, 198, 208, 216, 224
   Vermillion River Kickapoo, 194, 198

kidnapping, 27, 28, 32, 35, 36, 37, 38–39, 40, 41, 53, 70, 274
   See also massacres; murder; rape; slavery; starvation; torture
Kidwell, Clara Sue, **44,** 63, 285, 310, 316
Kieft, Governor Willem, 64
Kikiallus People, 226
Kilatika People (Illinois), 66
Killing Time, The Witch of Goingsnake and Other Stories, and Wilder and Wilder (Conley), 322
Kilpatrick, Anne Gritts, 271, 300, 302
Kilpatrick, Jack Frederick, 269, 300, 302
Kinehepend (Sharp One), 19
King, Bruce, 295
King, Jane (Odawa medicine woman), 131, 257
"King" Philip's War, 75, 76, 77
King, Thomas, 287
Kingsley, Normal, 240
Kintpuash (Kintpoos/Captain Jack), 217, 243, 250, 251
Kiosaton (Iroquois leader), 65
Kiowa Nation, 132, 214, 224, 240, 250, 252
Kiowa-Apache People, 252
Kit Carson Campaign: The Last Navajo War, The (Trafzer), 318
Kitche Manitou (Great Spirit), 55
kivas (pit houses), 18, 22, 69, 70
See also architecture
Klah, Hosteen, 286
Klamath People, 230, 222, 232, 236
Klikatat People. *See under* Yakima Nation (bands)
Klinquit People. *See under* Yakima Nation (bands)
Kolachuisen (Pretty Bluebird), 23
Kolawil (Noble Elder), 12
Konkapot (Mahican leader), 119
Konkapot, Levi, 119
Kootah-wecoot-soole-lehoola-shar (Big Hawk Chief), 221, 253
Kootenai ("Confederated Tribes"), 228
Korean War (and Native People), 291, 295, 297
Kosetah People, 222
Koshari. *See* Heyoka/Koshari
Kowwassayee People. *See under* Yakima Nation (bands)
Koyate People, 222
Krepps, Ethel Constance, 285, 316
KRNB-FM radio station, 310
KTDB-FM radio station, 306
Ku Klux Klan (Native People and), 298
Kuckeno (Cockenoe) (Montauk leader), 93
Kundera, Milan, 73
Ku-nugh-na-give-nuk (Rushing Bear/son of the Star), **213**
Kwitikwand (the Denouncer), 17

La Course, Richard Vance, 307, 309

La Flesche, Francis, 183, 231, 264
La Plata Cantata (Barnes), 322
La Salle and His Legacy: Frenchmen and Indians in the Lower Mississippi Valley (York), 318
La Villa Real de Santa Fe de San Francisco Assisi, 52
LaBarre, Governor, 87
Lac Courte Oreilles Chippewa. *See under* Chippewa Nation (bands)
Lacapa, Michael, 299
Lachine People, 88
LaClaire, Antoine, 210
lacrosse, 128
LaDuke, Vincent. *See* Sun Bear
LaDuke, Winona, 299
Lafayette, Marquis de, 201
Laguna Pueblo, 38, 92, 134
Laguna Woman (Silko), 308
Lake Calhoun (Minnesota), 221
Lake George, battle of, 122, 123
Lake Okeechobee, battle of, 214, 215
Lake Superior Chippewa. *See under* Chippewa Nation (bands)
Lake Winnibigoshish Chippewa. *See under* Chippewa Nation (bands)
Lakota. *See under* Sioux Nation (bands)
Lakota Times, 316
Lame Deer (John Fire), 306
Lame Deer, Seeker of Visions (Lame Deer/Erdoes), 306
land, 203, 205, 268, 276
   cession, 128, 130, 170, 196–97, 208, 224, 236, 248–49
   General Allotment (Dawes Severalty) Act, 256, 258, 266, 274
land claims, 304, 306, 308, 316, 318
   Navajo-Hopi Land Settlement Act, 308
   non-Native squatters, 272,. 298
   ownership and Native People, 56
   removal, 196, 201, 204, 206, 208, 210, 214, 216, 217, 228, 236, 237, 239, 251
   transfer, 266
   unassigned lands, 256
   See also Indian Removal Act; Long Walk; treaties
Land of Good Shadows: The Life Story of Anauta, an Eskimo Woman (Washburne/Anauta), 284
Land of the Spotted Eagle (Ota K'te), 276
language (Native People), 301
   Abenaki dictionary, 106
   celebrating, 143
   Cherokee syllabary, 198
   Iroquoian vocabulary list, 34
   Native American Languages Act, 324
   Navajo syllabary, 278
   repression of, 256, 283
   symbol writing, 14
   See also Code Talkers; interpreters; literature
Language of the Trees (Nitsch), 318
Langundowi (the Peaceful one), 15
Lapawin (Rich Again), 19

LaPeña, Frank, 281
LaPointe, James, 259
Laroque, Emma, 293
Larsen Bay People (Kodiak Island, Alaska), 324
Last Song, The (Harjo), 308
LaVatta, Emma, 268
Lawrence, Erma G., 308
Laylake, 231
Leaf Dweller, 23
League of the Five Great Fires. *See* People of the Longhouse
Leask, Janie, 293, 319
Leavitt Act, 276
Lederer, John, 72
Left Handed, 280
Left Handed, Son of Old Man Hat: A Navaho Autobiography (Left Handed), 280
Legacy: Engineering at Kansas State University (May), 318
legends and stories
    Atse'hastquin and Atse'esdza (1st man & woman) (Diné/Navajo legend), 44
    boy dancers (Wyandot legend), 28
    crows, legend of, 40
    Hahnunah the Turtle (Iroquois legend), 36
    Kochi-ni-nako (Keres legend), 48
    Kodoyanpe the Creator (Maidu legend), 32
    See also ceremony time (various months); Coyote; creation stories; Earth Mother; Great Spirit
Legends of Vancouver (Tehakionwake), 268
Legends, Traditions and Laws of the Iroquois or Six Nations and History of the Tuscarora Indians (Johnson), 254
Lekhihitin (the Author), 23
Lenape (Delaware) Nation, 10, 11, 12, 13, 16, 18, 19, 21, 25, 45, 47, 70, 170
    treaties (colonial), 74, 78, 84, 86, 90, 92, 100, 102, 104, 110, 112, 115, 116, 118, 122, 124, 126, 130
    treaties (U.S.A.), 134, 166, 174, 180, 182, 184, 188, 190, 192, 204, 218, 224, 240
    wars (U.S.A.), 178, 216
    See also Conoy Nation; Illinois People; Munsee People; Shawnee Nation; Turkey People; Unami People; *Wallam Olum*
Lester, David, 285
Letters of a Self-Made Diplomat to His President (Rogers), 272
Levier, Francis A., 295, 313
Lewis, Robert E., 269, **277**, 306
Lewis, Roberta M., **64**
Lewis and Clark expedition, 185
Liaywas People. *See under* Yakima Nation (bands)
Life and Adventures of Joaquín Murieta, Celebrated California Bandit, by Yellow Bird (Yellow Bird), 244
Life and Death of an Oilman: The Career of E. W. Marland (Mathews), 294

Life and Journals of Kahkewaquonaby (Rev. Peter Jones), Wesleyan Missionary (Kahkewaquonaby), 234
Life, History, and Travels of Kah-ge-ga-gah-bowh (George Copway), a Young Indian Chief of the Ojibwa Nation, with a Sketch of the Present State of the Ojibwa Nation, in Regard to Christianity and Their Future Prospects, The (Copway), 218
Life of America, The (Brashear), 302
Like Among the Piutes: Their Wrongs and Claims (Hopkins), 254
Lily of the Mohawks, 85
Linkwekinuk (the Beholder), 25
Linniwulamen (Truthful Man), 21
Lipan Apache. *See under* Apache Nation
Lippitamenend (Tamanend II), 29
literature, 327
    Algonkian Bible, 70, 93
    Mayan books, destruction of, 47
    See also language; legends and stories; songs; *Wallam Olum*
    Literature of the American Indian (Sanders/Peek), 308
Little Bear, Mary, 312
Little Bighorn, battle of, 252
Little Bighorn Battlefield National Monument, 324
Little Traverse People, 228
Little Warrior (Creek leader), 191, 253
Little Wolf, 111, **188**
Littlebird, Harold, 295
Littlecoon (Louis Oliver), 265, 325
Livingston, Robert, 90
Loclumne People, 222
Logan, Adelphina, 269
Logan, Colonel Benjamin, 174
Logan, James (Pennsylvania governor), 104
Logan, James (Tachnechdorus). *See* Tah-gah-jute
Lokwelend (Traveler), 25
Lololomai, 111
Lomatewama, Ramson, 297
Lone Star Ranger, The (Jones), 264
Lone Wolf, Louise, 300
Lonely Deer (Concha)
Long, James Larpenteur. *See* First Boy
Long, Sylvester. *See* Buffalo Child
Long Lance
Long Walk (of the Navajo), 156, 165, 236, 237, 239
Longest Walk (San Francisco/Washington, D.C.), 312
Longwha Nation, 218
Looking Glass, **252**
Lopez, Danny, 281
Lord Dunmore's War, 134
Lorenzo Tupatu (Picuris leader), 92
Lost Copper (Rose), 316
Louis, Adrian C., 291
Louis XIV (of France), 97
Louisiana (Spanish colony), 133
Lovato, José, 231

Love Medicine (Erdrich), 320
Low Dog, **103**
Lowaponskan (North Walker), 47
Lower Klamath (Pohlik) People. *See* Klamath People
Lowry, Annie, 302
Lucero, Richard, Jr., 289, 313, 321
Lucy and I as Missionaries (Reed), 264
Lummbee People, 298
Lusty, Terry, 287
Luther Standing Bear, 65
lynch mobs, 129
Lyng v. Northwest Indian Cemetery Protective Association, 322
Lyons, Oren, 63, 275

McAllester, David P., 292, 296, 298, 300
McCarthy, James, 259
Maccoa, 45
McCombs, Solomon, 312
McDonald, Arthur L., 303, 308
McGaa, Ed. *See* Eagle Man
McGary, Hugh, 175
Machapunga Nation, 100
Machigokhos (the Great Owl), 17
McInnis, John, 268
McIntosh, William, 185, 196, 201
Mackahtahmoah. *See under* Potawatomi Nation (bands)
Mackawdebenessy (Andrew J. Blackbird), 256, 260
Mackinac People, 228
McLaughlin, Marie L., 217
McLean, George. *See* Tatanga Mani
McLellan, Joseph, 289
McNickle, D'Arcy, 265, 280, 292, 296, 300, 306, 308, 312
Madison, James, 186, 189
Madrano, Dan C., 298
Magic Mirror, The (Tiger), 272
Magic of Balanced Living, The (Tebbel), 298
Magnus (Narraganset squaw sachem), 77
Maha People, 202
Mahican Nation, 29, 58, 60, 70, 72, 74, 124, 126
Máh-to-toh-pa (Four Bears), 215, 215
Mah-toio-wah (Whirling Bear/Conquering Bear), 225
Maidu People, 32
Maine Indian Claims Settlement Act, 316
Major Crimes Act, 254
Makah Nation, 228
Makatai-meshe-kiakiak (Black Hawk) (Sauk leader), 131, 185, 210, 211, 215
Makelomush (Much Honored), 35
Makhiawip (Red Arrow), 25
Maliseet Nation, 316
Malecite People, 116
Mallott, Byron, 287, 300, 305, 307, 311, 313, 319
man and giant crossing river (Wyandot story), 44
Mandan People, 202, 212, 222

Mangipitak (Big Teeth), 15
Manhattan Island, sale of, 56, 60
Manhattan People, 52, 56, 60
Mankiller, Wilma P., 49, 289, 319, 321, **321**, 322, 323, 325, 326
Mankiller: A Chief and Her People (Mankiller), 326
Mannahock People, 50
mano and metate, development of, 12
Manpower Development and Training Act, 300
Manuel, George, 275
Maracle, Lee, 295, 310
Marceau, Carmen Bullshoe, 279
March of Death, 89
Marhar Pawnee People. *See under* Pawnee People
Marionetta (Geronimo's wife), **267**
Markoosie, 287, 304
Marmon, Leslie, 308
Marpeya Wicas'ta (Cloudman) (Sioux leader), 221, 225, 235
Marquette, Père Jacques, 74, 75
Martin, Phillip, 299, 305, 317
Martinez, Maria Montoya, 257, 308, 317
Maryland (British colony), 62, 66, 74, 78, 84, 86, 130
Mashantucket Pequot Nation, 326
Maskansisil (Mighty Bison), 17
Mason, Captain John, 62
Mason, Velma Garcia, **58**
Massachuset People (Narraganset Nation), 29, 52, 54
Massachusetts (British colony), 62, 63, 65, 74, 78, 88, 99, 106, 108, 110, 112, 116, 118, 122
massacres, 38–39
    by British colonists, 58, 62, 76, 77, 106
    of British colonists, 100
    extinction and extermination, 131, 132
    by French colonists, 86, 108
    honoring the victims of, 15
    by Native People, 48, 64, 86, 88, 96, 108, 132, 188
    by settlers, 96, 128, 134, 226, 238
    by the Spanish conquistadors, 36, 42, 50, 90
    by the U.S., 165, 170, 218, 233, 248, 258, 259
    See also Chief Big Foot Massacre; kidnapping; missionaries (Roman Catholic); murder; rape; slavery; starvation; torture
Massacre of the Northern Shoshone, 236, 237
Massasoit (Wampanoag leader), 47, 56, 59, 61, 71
Massutakaya People, 222
Matchisjaws. *See under* Potawatomi Nation (bands)
Matemik (House Maker), 15
Mateo (Acoma leader), 91
Mathews, John Joseph, 259, 294
Ma-tih-eh-loge-go (Hollow Horn Bear), 255
Matoaka (Pocahontas), 53, 55
Mato-kuwapi (Chased-by-Bears), 125
Mattamuskeet People, 108
Mattaponi People, 50, 76
May, Cheryl, 293, 316, 318
Mayan books, destruction of, 47
Mayan People, 30
Mdewakanton Sioux. *See under* Sioux Nation (bands)
Me and Mine: The Life Story of Helen Sekaquaptewa as Told to Louise Udall (Sekaquaptewa), 304
Mean Spirit (Hogan), 324
Means, Russel, 281, 311
measles. *See* epidemics
Medamadec People, 222
medical resources (Native People), 35
    health, 152–53
    See also epidemics
Medicine Calf (James Beckwith) (Crow leader), 181, 199, 241
Medicine Crow. *See* Perits
medicine men and women, 131, **195**, 257, 314
Meeseequagulich People, 226
Mematway People. *See* Potawatomi Nation (bands)
Memoirs of an American Indian House (Jojola), 310
Mendoza, Dominguez, 85
Mendoza, Vicente de Zaldivar, 50
Mengakonkia People (Illinois), 66
Menominee Nation, 25, 108, 188, 192, 202, 204, 206, 208, 212, 220, 224, 230, 308
Menominee Restoration Act, 308
Menominee Tribe of Indians v. United States, 302
Me-ra-pa-ra-pa (Lance), **223**
Meredith, Howard L., 281, 308
Merriam Report, The, 274
Merrion v. Jicarilla Apache Tribe, 318
Mescalero Apache. *See under* Apache Nation (bands)
Mesquakie, 33
Mesquakie (Fox) People, 25
    removal, 196
    treaties (U.S.A.), 184, 190, 214
    wars (French), 108, 112
    wars (tribal), 132
    wars (U.S.A.), 188
    See also Sac and Fox ("United") Nations
Message Bringer Woman (Sanchez), 310
Messissuwi (Whole Hearted), 19
Metacomet ("King" Philip) (Wampanoag leader), 71, 73, 75, 77
metalworking, 10, 14
Metaphysics of Modern Existence, The (Delori), 312
metate and mano, development of, 12
Methoataske (mother of Tecumtha), 131
Mexico, conquest of, 32
Mi Ta-ku-ye: About My People (Walking Bull/Walking Bull), 312
Miami Nation
    treaties (colonial), 118, 126
    treaties (U.S.A.), 180, 182, 184, 188, 194, 204, 210, 214, 216, 226, 240
    war (colonial), 168, 170
    war (U.S.A.), 175, 178, 190, 191
    See also Eel River Nation; Illinois People
Miantonomo (Narraganset leader), 65
mica, use of, 18, 20
Michigamea People. *See under* Illinois Nation
Michikinikwa (Little Turtle) (Miami leader), 99, 168, 171, 175, 178, 179, 189, **190**
Micmac People, 28, 34, 132
Middle Five: Indian School Boys of the Omaha Tribe, The (La Flesche), 264
Miles, General A. Nelson, 252, 253
Mimbreño Apache. *See under* Apache Nation (bands)
Mingo People, 116, 168
Miniconjou Sioux. *See under* Sioux Nation (bands)
Minisink Nation, 124
Minnesota Chippewa Civil War veterans, **239**
Minnesota Uprising, 235
Minnetaree People, 212
Minuit, Peter, 60
Miracle Hill: The Story of a Navaho Boy (Mitchell), 302
missionaries, 87, 96, 193, 224, 234
    See also Christianity
missionaries (Roman Catholic), 46, 60, 67, 229
    child molestation, 71
    forced conversions, 134
    murder of, 74, 83, 84, 96, 211
    sacred objects, destruction of, 69
    torture and murder by, 67, 71
Missisauga People, 92, 132
Mississippi Chippewa. *See under* Chippewa Nation (bands)
Mississippi Choctaw Nation, 324
Mississippian culture, 22
Missouri Sac. *See under* Sac People
Missouria (and Otoe) "Confederated Tribes," 224, 226
Missouria People, 202, 206, 210, 212
Mistahimuskwa (Big Bear) (Cree leader), 201, 255, 257
Mitchell, Emerson Blackhorse, 99, 289, 302
Mitchigamia People (Illinois Nation), 182, 194
Miwok People, 46, 232
Moalkai People, 222
Mobile People, 40
Moccasin Maker and The Shagganappi, The (Tehakionwake), 268
Moctesuma (Aztec leader), 32, 33
Modoc People, 232, 236, 250, 251
Moffett, Walter L., 299
Mofsie, Louis, 301, 304

Mogollon People, 20, 22
Mohawk, John, 289, 311
Mohawk Nation (Five Nations), 14, 48,
  62, 65, 66, 72, 98, 100, 110, 256, 298, 308
  Canajohharie Mohawk, 132
  treaties, 62, 64, 70, 74, 88
  wars (American Revolution), 136, 166,
    168, 170, 172
  wars (tribal), 58, 60, 72, 74
Mohawk Trail (Brant), 320
Mohe (Cahoe/William Cohe), 225, 251,
  253, 273
Mohegan Nation, 60, 62, 110
  petition of, 176
Moingwena (Illinois Confederacy), 72
Moises, Rosalio, 261, 306
Mokatavato (Black Kettle) (Cheyenne
  leader), 183, 243
Mokolmokom (Canoe Master), 25
Molala People, 226, 230
Molin, Paulette Fairbanks, **255,** 289, 324
Molina, Felipe, 297
Moluntha (Shawnee elder), 175
Momaday, Natachee Scott, 269, 279, 302,
  306, 308, 310, 314
Moneda People, 222
Monks Mound, 22
Monongye, Don, 299
Monroe, James, 199
Monster Slayer (Browne), 324
Montagnais People, 34
Montaignais People, 25
Montana v. United States, 228
Montauk People, 29
Montejo, Victor, 297
Montezuma, Carlos. *See* Wassaja
Montmagny, Governor Charles-Jacques
  de Huault de, 65
Montoya, Alcario, 295
Moore, Thomas E. *See* Harjo, William
Moor's Charity School, 54
Moowhaha People, 226
Morlete, Captain Juan, 48
Morning and Evening Star, The (Friday),
  268
Moroney, Lynn, 279
Morriahs People, 222
Morton v. Mancari, 308
Mosack. *See under* Potawatomi Nation
  (bands)
Moses, Daniel Davis, 297
Mosionier, Beatrice Culleton, 293
Moss, Julie, 299
Mother Corn, 135
Mother Earth, Father Sky (Keegan), 308
Mottke, Gertrude Bernard. *See* Anahareo
Mottschujinga (Little Grizzly Bear), 50
Mound Builders. *See* Adena People
*Mountain Windsong: A Novel of the Trail of
  Tears* (Conley), 326
Mountain Wolf Woman, 101, 111, 300
*Mountain Wolf Woman, Sister of Crashing
  Thunder: The Autobiography of a Win-
  nebago Indian* (Mountain Wolf Woman),

300
Muckkose People, 214
Munsee (Lenape) Nation, 47, 184, 216,
  230
murder, 53, 232–33
  assassination, 121, 129, 132, 133, 171,
    217, 253
  executions, 77, 131, 132, 245, 251, 253
  lynch mobs, 129
  of Native People, 27, 40, 66, 71, 107, 137,
    165, 175, 240, 253, 306
  of whites, 74, 251
  See also discrimination; kidnapping; mas-
    sacres; rape; Sand Creek Massacre;
    scalping; slavery; starvation; torture
Murphy, Charles W., 293, 319, 321
Murray, John, 133
Muscogee. *See* Creek nation
Muscogee (or Creek) Indian Memorial
  Association, 268
Mushulatubbee (Mushalatubbee)
  (Choctaw leader), 135, 193, 199, 201,
  207, 215
Muskrat, Jeff W., 303
Mu-s-swont, **186**
My Horse and a Jukebox (Bush), 312
*My Indian Boyhood, by Chief Luther Stand-
  ing Bear, Who Was the Boy Ota K'te
  (Plenty Kill)* (Ota K'te), 276
Mysterious Being of the West (Seneca
  legend), 28
Myth and Prayers of the Great Star Chant
  (McAllester), 298

Naalye Scoton People, 226
Nah-ah-sa-na (Warluope/Gualoupe), **219**
Nahelta Chasta (or Shasta) People, 226
Nakomis *or* Sky Woman (Ojibwa story),
  30
Nakui-owaisto (Yellow Bear), **203**
Nambe Pueblo, **174–75**
Nanesmond People, 50, 78
Nanespasket (New Moon), 55
Nanticoke Nation, 23, 124, 126, 130, 132
Na'pi (Siksika legend), 36, 135
Narraganset Nation, 29, 32, 52, 61, 62, 64,
  72, 74, 75, 76
*Narrative of the Life and Adventures of Paul
  Cuffe, a Pequot Indian, During Thirty
  Years Spent at Sea, and in Traveling in For-
  eign Lands* (Cuffe), 216
Narvaez, Pánfilo de , 34
Nasnaga (Richard Rogers), 285
Nason, Bertha, 256
Naswawkee. *See under* Potawatomi Na-
  tion (bands)
Natchez Nation, 20, 40, 108
National Advisory Council on Indian Ed-
  ucation (NACIE), 306
National Congress of American Indians
  (NCAI), 283, 288
National Historic Trail of Tears, 322
National Indian Education Association

(NIEA), 304, 315
National Indian Health Board, 306
National Indian Youth Council (NIYC),
  300
National Indian Youth Council of Albu-
  querque (New Mexico), 300
National Museum of Natural History, 324
National Museum of the American In-
  dian (NMAI), 285, 322, 324
National Native News (Alaska Public
  Radio Network), 326
"National Native News" network pro-
  gram, 322
National Tribal Chairmen's Association,
  320
National Vietnam Era Veterans Inter-
  Tribal Association, 316
Nations Within, The (Deloria), 320
Native American Factor, The (Meredith),
  308
Native American Grave Protection and
  Repatriation Act, 324
Native American Journalists Association
  (NAJA), 320
Native American Languages Act, 324
Native American Press Association, 320
Native American Rights Fund, 304
Native American Substance Abuse
  (Mitchell), 318
*Native American Tribalism: Indian Survivals
  and Renewals* (McNickle), 308
Native American Women: A Bibliography
  (Green), 316
*Native American Women: A Contextual Bib-
  liography* (Green), 318
Nat-tai-ya (Blessed), **261**
Na-tu-ka (Two Medicine), **261**
Nature Chants and Dances (Nitsch), 320
Nauntenoo (Canonchet) (Narraganset
  leader), 75, 77
Navajo Business Preference Law, 320
Navajo Community College, 304
*Navajo Creation Myth: The Story of the
  Emergence* (Klah), 286
Navaho History (Yazzie), 306
Navajo (Diné) People, 21, 40, 44, 274, 294,
  323
  Long Walk, 156, 165, 236, 237, 239
Navajo-Hopi Land Settlement Act, 308
  treaties (U.S.A.), 242
  wars (U.S.A.), 193, 197, 232
  See also Code Talkers; Navajo Reserva-
    tion
Navaho Rehabilitation Act, 294
Navajo Reservation, 242
Navajo Times Today, 298
Navajo War (of 1863–66), 193, 232
Nawat (Left Hand), **258,** 259
Nbchopda People, 222
Neamathla (Seminole leader), 169
Near the Mountains (Bruchac), 320
Necotowance (Powhatan leader), 65
Neeboashs. *See under* Potawatomi Nation
  (bands)

Neekna and Chemai (Armstrong), 320

Neihardt, John G., 276

Nemshaw People, 222

Nenachihat (Watching Closely), 55

Neolin (the Delaware Prophet), 121, 123, 127, 129

Neptune, Francis Joseph (Passamaquoddy leader), 137

Nequatewa, Edmund, 296

Nerodchikov, Mikhail, 118

Neundorf, Alice, 287

Neutral Confederacy, 66

Neutral People (Huron Confederacy), 52, 62

Nevada Indians Speak (Forbes), 296

New Archangel (Russian Alaskan settlement), 182

New Corn, 181

New England Confederation, 64

New France, 58, 72, 74

New Jersey (British colony), 70, 74, 90, 122, 124, 130

New Mexico v. Mescalero Apache Tribe, 318

New Native American Dram: Three Plays (Gieogamah), 316

New Perspectives on the Pueblos (Ortiz), 306

New Voices from the People Named the Chippewa (Vizenor), 306

New York (British colony), 74, 78, 84, 88, 90, 92, 98, 104, 108, 110, 116, 118, 120

New York State Museum, 322

Newkumet, Vynola Beaver, 271

Newman, Patricia Tatsey, 293

Newtown, battle of, 167

Nez Percé Nation, 228, 230, 236, 242

Nez Percé Texts (Phinney), 278

Niantic People (Narraganset Nation), 52, 64

Niatum, Duane McGinnis, 119, 281, 308, 312, 316, 322

Nikinapi (Illinois leader), 75

Nine Poems (Tall Mountain), 312

Nipissing People, 66, 70, 132

Nipmuc People (Narraganset Nation), 29, 52, 65

Nisqually People, 226

Nitispayat (Friend Coming), 45

Nitsch, Twylah Hurd, 269, 310, 312, 318, 320

Nixon, Richard M., 308

Niza, Fray Marcos de, 36

No Turning Back: A True Account of a Hopi Indian Girl's Struggle to Bridge the Gap Between the World of Her People and the World of the White Man (White), 300

Noble Peace Mother, 166

Nockoist (James Bear's Heart), 221

Noel, Linda, 299

Noema People, 222

Noima People, 222

Noime People, 222

Nome People, 222

Nomee, Clara, **129**

Nompehwahthe (Carter Revard), 47, 117, 275

Nompeyo (Harmless Snake), **12**

Nonhelema (the Grenadier Squaw), 133

Nookchoos People, 220

Nookwachahmish People, 226

Norridgewock People, 112, 116, 118, 120, 122

North American Indian Women's Association (NAIWA), 304

North Carolina (British colony), 92, 100, 102, 122, 124

North Carolina State, 136, 170

Northern Drum, **13**

Northsun, Nila, 295

Northwestern Tribes in Exile: Modoc, Nez Percé, and Palouse Removal to the Indian Territory (Trafzer), 320

Notawkah. *See under* Potawatomi Nation (bands)

Notonotos People, 220

Notontors People, 220

Nottaway People, 78

N'Quentlmamish People, 226

Nu Mee Poom tit Wah Tit (Nez Percé Stories) (Shckpoo), 306

Nuchowwe People, 222

Numa-Nu: The Fort Sill Indian School Experience (Sumner), 316

Nuna-da-ut-sun'y (Trail Where They Cried), 156, 214, 216, 217

Nunavut (Eskimo First Nation), 318

Nuñez, Bonita. *See* Wa Wa Calachaw

Núñez, Diego, 48

Nye, Wilbur Sturtevant, 298

Oacpicagigua, Luis (Pima leader), 121

Oandasan, William, 127, 291, 317, 320, 321

O'Bail, John. *See* Kiantwa'ka

Obomsawin, Alanis, 277

Ocaninge (Chickahominy orator), 51

Occum, Samson (Mohegan leader), 95, 132, 134

Ochechotes People. *See under* Yakima Nation (bands)

Odawa (Ottawa) Nation, 25, 45
  treaties (colonial), 98, 130, 134, 174
  treaties (U.S.A.), 178, 180, 184, 186, 190, 192, 194, 198, 202, 204, 206, 210, 212, 218, 228
  wars (tribal), 52, 70, 74, 92, 132, 134

Odellah People, 222

Oeh-da the earth (Iroquois legend), 36

Of Utmost Good Faith (Deloria), 306

Office of Indian Affairs. *See* Indian Affairs, Office of

Office of Indian Education (OIE), 306

O-gî-mäw-kwè Mit-i-gwä-kî (Queen of the Woods) (Pokagon), 260

Oglala Sioux. *See under* Sioux Nation (bands)

Oglethorpe, James Edward, 111

Ohio Wyandot People, 212

Ohiyesa (Charles A. Eastman), 137, 231, 235, 259, 264, 266, 268, 270

0-hu-kah-kan: Poetry, Songs, Legends, and Stories by American Indians (Walking Bull/Walking Bull), 310

Ojibwa Heritage (Johnston), 310

Ojibwa Nation, 24, 30, 66, 70, 92, 178

Okahmause People. *See under* Potawatomi Nation (bands)

Oklahoma Human Rights Commission, 312

Oklahoma Indian Welfare Act, 280

Oklahoma State, 266

Okute (Shooter), 105, 121

Old Copper People, 10

Old Father, the Story Teller (Velarde), 300

Old Indian Days (Ohiyesa), 266

Old Indian Legends, Retold by Zitkala-Sa (Zitkala-Sa), 264

Old Man (Siksika legend), 36

Old Mexican, Navaho Indian: A Navaho Autobiography (Old Mexican), 290

Old Northwest, 188

Old Person, Earl, 297

Old Tassel, 55

Oledoska, 306

Oliver, Louis. *See* Littlecoon

Olmec People, 14

Olotaraca (Saturiba Timucua), 47

Olumapi (History Man), 15, 23

Omaha Nation, 182, 206, 212, 224, 238, 324

Oman, Lela Kiana, 269

Omtua, Pedro, 85

Oñate, Juan de, 48, 50

Oneida Nation (Five Nations), 62, 104, 110, 132

Orchard Onedia, 214
  treaties (colonial), 72, 86, 126
  treaties (tribal), 14, 48
  treaties (U.S.A.), 178, 214
  wars (French), 88, 92
  wars (American Revolution), 166

Oneko, 77

Only an Indian Girl (Reed), 264

Onondaga Nation (Five Nations), 62, 322
  epidemics and, 136
  treaties (colonial), 86, 96, 97, 106, 126
  treaties (tribal), 14, 48, 110, 120
  treaties (U.S.A.), 172
  wars (American Revolution), 166
  wars (French), 88, 90, 92

Onopoma People, 222

Onowutok (the Prophet), 23

Onpahtonga (Big Elk) (Omaha leader), 133, 181, 219

Opechancanough (Powhatan leader), 55, 59, 65

Opekasit (East Looking), 19

Oppeo People, 222

Oquillak, William, 261

Orator of the Plains. *See* Santanta Orchard Onedia. *See under* Oneida Nation

Oregon Trail, 238
Organization of North American Indian Students (ONAIS), 306
Origin and Traditional History of the Wyandotts (Clarke), 242
Oriskany, battle of, 136, 137
Ortiz, Alfonso, 304, 306
Ortiz, Roxanne Dunbar, 312
Ortiz, Simon J., 49, 75, 285, 310, 312, 316
Osage Nation (Great and Little), 184, 186, 190, 194, 198, 200, 202, 212, 216, 238
Osceola (Seminole leader), 59, 214
Oshkosh (Menominee leader), **180,** 181
Oskison, John Milton, 251, 264, 266, 272, 278, 280
Ota K'te (Luther Standing Bear), 276, 278
Other Side of Nowhere, The (Aroniawenate), 324
Otoe (and Missouria) "Confederated Tribes," 224, 226
Otoe People, 192, 202, 206, 210, 212
Otoh-hastis (Tall Bull), 191, 243
Ottawa. *See* Blanchard's Fork Ottawa; Odawa Nation; Roche de Boeuf Ottawa
Ottawa of Ohio, 206
O-wapa-shaw (Sioux leader), 217
Owen, Robert Latham, 231, 291
Owens, Robert M., **269**
Owl Song (Hale), 308
Oylacca People, 222

Paganchihilla (the Crusher), 21
Pahtahsega (Peter Jacobs), 224
Painier, Lenora, 15
Paiute People, 197, 232, 252, 316
Pakimitzin (Cranberry eating), 45
Pakwan People, 222
Palace of the Governors (Santa Fe), 52
Palmanteer, Ted, 287
Palmer, Gus, 287
Palmer, Lenora, 75
Palouse People. *See under* Yakima Nation (bands)
Palwisha People, 222
Pamlico Nation, 100
Pamunkey People (Powhatan Confederacy), 50, 75, 76, 78
Papago. *See* Tohono O'odham People
Papoonan (Delaware prophet), 121, 129
Parker, Arthur C., 255, 272
Parker, Ely Samuel, 243
Parker, Chief Everett, 306
Parker, Quanah, *See* Quanah Parker
Parrilla, Governor, 120
Parrish, Rain, 318
Parra-Wa-Samen (Ten Bears), 104, 105
Passaconaway (Pennacook leader), 47, 61, 65
Passamaquoddy Nation, 116, 137, 316
Paul I (Czar of Russia), 180
Paul Wihelm (Prince of Württemberg), 199
Pavich, Paul, 312

Pawanami (Rich Turtle), 25
Pawnee Loups, 210
Pawnee People ("Confederated Bands of), 30
    Grand Pawnee People, 192, 210, 220
    Marhar Pawnee People, 192
    Pawnee Loups, 220
    Pawnee Republic, 192, 210, 220
    Pawnee Tappaye, 210, 220
    Pitavirate Noisy Pawnee People, 192
treaties (U.S.A.), 192, 202, 230
Pawtucket People, 54
Paxton boys, 128
Payouska, **182**
Paytiamo, James (Flaming Arrow), 33, 59
peace pipes, 16, 22, 50, 191
Peacemaker, 14, 15, 91, 99, 117, 137
Peek, Walter W., 308
Pelletier, Wilfrid, 273
Peltier, Leonard, 308
Pematilli (Always There), 23
Pembina Chippewa. See under Chippewa Nation (bands)
Pemoholend (Constant Love), 15
Pencille, Herbert W., 299, 307
Pend d'Oreilles. *See* Upper Pend d'Oreilles
Penkwonwi (Drought), 15
Penn, W. S. (Bill), **274,** 275
Penn, William, 84, 85, 96
Pennacook People, 58, 67
Pennsylvania (British colony), 84, 86, 90, 96, 97, 98, 100, 102, 104, 110, 112, 116, 118, 120, 122, 124, 126, 130
Pennsylvania State, 181
Penobscot Nation, 112, 116, 118, 120, 122, 316
Penoi, Charles R., 269
Penoi, Jon R., 293
People of the Longhouse. *See* Iroquois Confederacy
Peoria People. *See under* Illinois Nation
Pepicokia People (Illinois), 66
Pepinakaw. *See under* Potawatomi Nation (bands)
Pepomahemen (Navigator), 23
Pequot People, 29, 60, 318
Pequot War, 62, 63
Peralta, Pedro de, 52
Perea, Robert L., 291
Perits (Shenakpas/Medicine Crow), **195**
Persian Gulf War ("Desert Storm"), 324
Peters, Russell M., 275
Petroglyphs (Bush), 318
peyote, sacramental use of , 324
Peyote Music (McAllester), 292
Phinney, Archie, 278
Piankashaw People. *See under* Illinois Nation
Piapot (Flash in the Sky), 171
Picotte, Agnes, 312
Piegan People, 212, 252
Pigwacket People, 116
Pilgrims, 47, 71. *See also* Plymouth Plantation

Pillager Chippewa. *See under* Chippewa Nation (bands)
Pilsohalan (Chaste Loving), 15
Pima. *See* Ak-mul Au-authm People
Pima Indian Legends (Shaw), 302
Pima Past, A (Shaw), 308
Pima Remembers, A (Webb), 298
Pimokhasuwi (Stirring), 21
Pine Ridge Reservation
    AIM occupation, 283, 308
    AIM/FBI confrontation, 308
Piñeda, Alonso Alvarez de, 32
Piper, Lee. *See* Ugidali
Piscataway People, 86
Pisquouse People. *See under* Yakima Nation (bands)
Pit River People, 231
Pi'ta Le-shar (Big Bow), 251
Pitavirate Noisy Pawnee People. *See under* Pawnee People
Pitcachees People, 220
Pitchlynn, Peter Perkins. *See* Hatch-ootucknee
Pitenumen (Mistaken), 31
Pitseolak, 306
Pitseolak: Pictures out of My Life (Pitseolak), 306
Pius XII, 281
Pizarro, Francisco, 29
Plain, Ferguson, 301
Platero, Dillion, 111, 273
Pleyel, Egon, 67
Plymouth People, 66
Plymouth Plantation (British colony), 47, 56, 58, 59, 66, 72
Pocahontas (Matoaka), 53, 55
Pochanawkwoip (Buffalo Hump) (Comanche leader), 221
Poems of Alexander Lawrence Posey, The (Posey), 266
Pohlik-lah (Jacque Winter), 35
Pohoneechees People, 220
Point Pleasant, battle of, 135
pony soldiers, 165
Pokagon, Simon, 260
Pokowwe People, 222
Polingaysi Qoyawayma. *See* White, Elizabeth Q.
Pomo People, 222, 232
Pompey (Jean-Baptiste Charbonneau), 185, 199
Ponca (Poncarar) Nation, 192, 200, 230, 238
Ponce de León, Jaun, 30, 31, 32
Pontiac (Ponteach) (Odawa/Ottawa leader), 105, 127, 128, 129, 131, 132, 133
Pooleyama, Violet, 65
Poor Sarah, or Religion Exemplified in the Life and Death of an Indian Woman (Galagina or Elias Boudinot), 198
Popé (San Juan Pueblo prophet), 85
Popé's Rebellion. *See* Grand Pueblo Revolt

population (of Native People), 180, 258, 263, 264, 270, 316
   California, 132
   Huron Confederacy, 62
   Illinois Confederacy, 72
   "Indian" Slaves, 98
   Northwest, Alaska and Canada, 212
   Taino (after Columbus), 30
   Wappinger, 64
Porter, Osway, 45
Posey, Alexander Lawrence, 251, 266
Poskesas People, 220
Post, Wiley, 279
Potawatomi Nation, 25, 174 and French colonists, 62
   treaties (colonial), 130
   treaties (U.S.A.), 180, 182, 184, 186, 188, 190, 192, 198, 202, 204, 208, 210, 212, 214, 240
   wars (tribal), 132
   wars (U.S.A.), 178
Potawatomi Nation (bands)
   Chequawkako People, 212
   Indiana Potawatomi, 218
   Kankakee Potawatomi People, 208
   Kansas Potawatomi, 240
   Keewawnay People, 212
   Mackahtahmoah People, 212
   Matchisjaws People, 212
   Mematway People, 212
   Mosack People, 212
   Naswawkee People, 212
   Neeboashs People, 212
   Notawkah People, 212
   Okahmause People, 212
   Pepinakaw People, 212
   Prairie Potawatomi People, 208, 218
   Quashquaw People, 212
   Quiquito Potawatomi People, 214
   Wabash People, 174, 212, 218
Potomic Nation, 102
Potoyunte People, 220
pottery, 12, 16, 18, 22
   Estrella red-on-gray, 20
   Hohokam red-on-buff, 24
pottery culture, 12
Poverty Point People, 12
Powhatan Confederacy, 50, 52, 56, 58, 59, 60, 63, 64, 75, 76
powwows, 250, 315
   festivals honoring, 150
   See also ceremonies; ceremony time (various months): events; dance; songs
Prairie Potawatomi People. See under Potawatomi Nation (bands)
Pratt, Jennie, 272
Pratt, Richard H., 253
prayers. See ceremony time (various months); songs
Pretty-Shield Medicine Woman, 276
Problem of Old Harjo and Making an Individual of the Indian, The (Oskison), 266
prophets, 23, 33, 85, **90,** 91, 121, 123, 133, **166,** 185, 187

season of, 156
Prophetstown (Ohio), 187, 188
Prouville Tracy, Marquis Alexandre de, 72
Providence Plantations (British colony of Rhode Island), 62, 63, 64
Psychology and Contemporary Problems (McDonald), 308
Public Law 280, 296
Pueblo Indian, The (Sando), 310
Pueblo Indians of North America, The (Dozier), 304
Pueblo Nations, 48, 93, 304
   AIPC, 48, 93, 272
   Spanish Crown land grants, 88
   Supreme Court and, 252
   voting rights, 292
   See also Bonito Pueblo; Grand Pueblo Revolt; Jemez Pueblo Massacre; Laguna Pueblo; Nambe Pueblo; San Ildefonso Pueblo; San Juan Pueblo
Pueblo Nations: Eight Centuries of Pueblo Indian History (Sando), 326
Pullar, Gordon L., 289, 317, 319
Pushkareff expedition, 126
Pushmataha (Choctaw leader), **130,** 131, 187, 189, 199, 201, 205, 211
Pustsmoot (Keres legend), 48
Puyallup People, 226

Qeya pu kowak migration (Keres story), 40
Quaker Promise Kept: Philadelphia Friends' Work with the Allegany Senecas, A (Bowen), 324
Quanah (Quanah Parker), **218,** 219, 269
Quapaw Nation, 40, 192, 200, 210, 240
Quarterly Journal of the Society of American Indians
Quashquaw. See under Potawatomi Nation (bands)
Quatie (Elizabeth Brown Henley Ross), 215
Queen Anne's War, 102
Quileute Nation, 228
Quilsieton People, 226
Quinault Nation, 228
Quinney, John. See Waun-na-con
Quintano, Santiago, 254
Quiquito Potawatomi. See under Potawatomi Nation (bands)
Quitting Time and Go-Ahead Rider (Conley), 324
Quivira (Wichita) People, 40

racism, 312
   "Little Red" mascot, 308
   See also discrimination
Radin, Paul, 270
Radisson, Pierre Esprit, 66
Raising the Moon Vines (Vizenor), 300
Rale, Father Sebastian, 106

Raleigh, Sir Walter, 48
Randolph, Richard, 119
rape, 38–39, 40, 107, 165, 232
   See also kidnapping; massacres; murder; slavery; starvation; torture
Rappahannock People, 50
Rasmussen, Knud, 253
Raven (Tlingit legend), 18
Raven and the Redbird, The (Hail), 302
Raven Dance, **32**
Reagan, Ronald, 316, 318
Real People: The Dark Way and The Real People: The White Path, The (Conley), 326
Real People: The Way of the Priests, The (Conley), 326
Red Cedar Warrior (Brito), 320
Red Cloud, 31
   stamp honoring , 322
Red Cloud, Mitchell, 295
Red Fox, 259
Red Hawk, Richard. See Trafzer, Clifford E.
Red House, John, 291
Red-Horse, Valerie, 70
Red Hunters and Animal People (Ohiyesa), 264
Red Lake Chippewa. See under Chippewa Nation (bands)
Red Man in the New World Drama (Deloria), 306
Red Man newspaper, 256
Red Mother (Pretty-Shield Medicine Woman, 276
Red Paint People, 12
"Red Power," 283
Red Stick Creek. See Creek civil war
Redsky, James, 261
Reed, Bill, 271
Reed, Ora V. Eddelman, 260, 264
Reifel, Benjamin, 311
Remembered Earth: An Anthology of Contemporary Native American Literature, The (Hobson), 312
removal. See under land
Renegade Tribe: The Palouse Indians and the Invasion of the Inland Pacific Northwest, The (Trafzer/Scheuerman), 320
Republican River Expedition, 242
Reservation, The (Williams), 310
reservations, **42–43,** 124, 194, 226, 232, 242, 250, 252, 254, 288, 292
   and gambling, 326
   and dam construction, 292, 298, 300
   Pine Ridge Reservation (AIM occupation), 283, 308
Returned Prodigal, A (Reed), 260
Returning the Gift Festival, **327**
Revard, Carter. See Nompehwahthe
Revery, A (Young Beaver), 204
revolts, 69, 218, 232
   African Americans, 40
   against British colonists, 100, 102
   against Spanish colonists, 66, 120, 121, 193

against the U.S. government, 167, 232, 252
See also Crazy Snake uprising; Grand Pueblo Revolt; Minnesota Uprising; Tecumseh's Rebellion; treaties; wars
Rhoades, Everett Ronald, 299, 301, 307
Ribault, Jean, 45
Richardson, Dawn, 277
Ridge, John, 217
Ridge, Major, 217
Riding the Earthboy (Welch), 306
Riggs, Lynn, 261
Rilatos, Selene, **191**
River Saint Peter's Sioux. *See under* Sioux Nation (bands)
Roanoke Island colony (North Carolina), 48
Roanoke People, 78
Robertson, Nellie, 258
Roche de Boeuf Ottawa, 240
Rock, Howard, 269
Rock River Sac. *See* Sac People
Rocque de Roberval, Jean-François de La, 44
Rodríquez, Friar Augustin, 46
Roessel, Robert A., Jr., 301
Roessel, Ruth, 279
Rogers, Richard. *See* Nasnaga
Rogers, Ronald, 293
Rogers, Will, 253, 270, 272, 274, 279
Rogers, Will, Jr., 269, 287, 327
Rogersisms: The Cowboy Philosopher on Prohibition (Rogers), 270
Rogersisms: The Cowboy Philosopher on the Peace Conference (Rogers), 270
Rogue River People, 224, 226
Rokwaho (Daniel Thompson), 287, 297, 321
Rolf, John, 53
Rollin, John. *See* Yellow Bird
Roosevelt, Theodore, 266
Rose, Wendy, 293, 308, 312, 316
Ross, A. C. (Allan "Chuck"), 285
Ross, Elizabeth Brown Henley. *See* Quatie
Ross, John. *See* Cooweescoowee
Rough Rock Demonstration School, 300
Round Valley Songs and Moving Island (Oandasan), 320
rubber, use of, 18
Rudolph, Sergen, 64
Runner in the Sun: A Story of Indian Maize (McNickle), 296
Running Sketches of Men and Places, in England, France, Germany, Belgium, and Scotland and The Traditional History and Characteristic Sketches of the Ojibwa Nation (Copway), 222
Russell, Norman, 271
Russians (in Alaska)
    Native People and, 182, 227
    traders and exploration, 118, 124, 126, 180

Sac and Fox "Confederated Tribes," 214

removal, 196
treaties (U.S.A.), 198, 200, 202, 204, 206, 208, 212, 214, 216, 224, 230, 240
Sac People
    Mississippi Sac and Fox, 230
    Missouri Sac, 214
    removal, 196
    Rock River Sac, 192
    treaties (U.S.A.), 184, 190
    wars (tribal), 132
    wars (U.S.A.), 168, 188
    See also Sac and Fox ("United") Nations
Sacagawea. *See* Cogewea
Sacheriton People, 226
Sacred Drum, Solemn Time of, 152
Sacred Fire, Solemn Time of, 157–58
sacred objects
    return of, 322, 324
    See also ceremonial objects and costumes; ceremonies; ceremony time; Wakan Tanka
Sacred Pipe: Black Elk's Account of the Seven Rites of the Oglala Sioux, The (Brown/Hehaka Sapa), 276
Sacred Time, Solemn Time of, 162
Sacumna People, 222
Sadongei, Alyce, 299
Saginaw Chippewa. *See under* Chippewa Nation (bands)
Sagoyewatha (Red Jacket) (Senaca leader), 71, 89, 123, 199
Sahehwamish People, 226
Sahgandeoh (Lucille Winnie), 265, 302
Sah-gan-de-oh, the Chief's Daughter (Sahgandeoh), 302
Sahkumehu People, 226
Sainell People, 222
St. Augustine (Florida), 46
Saint Francis People (Abenaki), 116, 132
St. Leger, Colonel Barry, 136
Saint Regis People, 132
Sainte-Marie, Buffy, 287
Sakonnet People, 72
Salisbury, Ralph, 273
Salish ("Confederated Tribes"), 228
Saludes, Quentin, **295**
Saluskin, James, 279
Saluted. *See* Wahunsenacawh
Samahmish People, 226
San Carlos Reservation, 252
San Gabriel de los Espanoles, 48
San Gabriel de Yongue, 52
San Ildefonso Pueblo, 48
San Imirio Uvas People, 222
San Juan Pueblo, 48
San Luis Rey People, 224
Sanapia, 306
Sanapia, Comanche Medicine Woman (Sanapia), 306
Sanchez, Carol Lee, 19, **125**, 125, 167, 174, 279, 310, 320
Sanchez, Miguel Rashid, **167**
Sand Creek Massacre, 140, 156, 165, 242, 243

Sandefur, Gary D., 318
Sanders, Thomas E., 308
Sando, Joe S., 273, 310, 326
Sandusky River Seneca, 206
Santa Adiva (Caddo leader), 89
Santanta (White Bear) (Orator of the Plains), 207
Santee Sioux, *See under* Sioux Nation (bands)
Santiago (Cuba), settlement of, 30
Sarcee People, 252
Sarris, Greg, 297
Sassacus (Pequot leader), 63
Satana (White Bear), 75, **206**
Saubel, Katherine Siva, 271
Sauk People, 25
Sault Sainte Marie People. *See under* Chippewa Nation (bands)
Savageau, Cheryl, 295
Savila, Refugio, 316
Savonra People, 222
Scaghticoke Nation, 110
scalping, by whites settlers and soldiers, 175, 237, 240, 253
Scarouady (Oneida leader), 119, 121
Scattameck (Delaware prophet), 45, 133
Scheuerman, Richard D., 316, 320
Schodelick (Skagit legend), 18
Scholder, Fritz, 281
Schroeter, Elaine Murphy. *See* Hatikainye
Scioto meeting, 132
Scott, Colonel Samuel, 127
Scruniyatha (Half-King) (Seneca leader, 123
Seale, Doris, 281
Sealey, D. Bruce, 275
Seapocat People. *See under* Yakima Nation (bands)
Sears, Vickie, 285
Season of Broken Treaties, 143
Season of Loss, A (Barnes), 320
Secettu Mahqua (Black Beaver), **184**, 187, 255
Secret of No Face: An Ireokwa Epic, The (Parker/Oledoska), 306
Sekaquaptewa, Helen, 304
Seloso, Juaquin, 217
Selu: Seeking the Corn-Mother's Wisdom (Awiakta), 326
Seminole Nation, 168, 200
Second Seminol War, 211, 215
    treaties (U.S.A.), 198, 208, 210, 218, 230, 240
    wars (U.S.A.), 210, 214, 216, 236
Senachwine, 21, 89
Senahuow People, 222
Seneca Myths and Folktales (Parker), 272
Seneca Nation (Five Nations), 14, 28, 48, 66, 70, 74, 86, 88, 110, 280, 298, 324
    treaties (colonial), 106, 116, 128, 130
    treaties (U.S.A.), 180, 182, 190, 192, 194, 206, 208, 216, 240
    wars (American Revolution), 136, 166, 168, 172

See also Sandusky River Seneca; Tonawanda Seneca
Seneca and Shawnee ("United Nations"), 206, 208, 240
Seneca, Martin, Jr., 313
Senungetuk, Joseph, 285
Sequoyah (George Gist/George Guess), 198
Seragoines People, 222
Sermon Preached at the Execution of Moses Paul, An Indian Who Was Executed at New Haven, on the 2nd of September 1772 (Occum), 132
Sesseton Sioux. *See under* Sioux Nation (bands)
Set-angya (Satank/Sitting Bear), **244,** 245, 251
Seven Golden Cities of Cihola, 36, 40
Sevenka, 61, 135
Sevukakmet: Ways of Life on St. Lawrence Island (Carius), 312
Sewid, James, 269
Shabonee (Shabonna), 135
Shakagapewi (Righteous), 21
Shamokin People, 118
Sharitarish (Pawnee leader), 199, 255
Shateroronhia (Leatherlips) (Wyandot Huron leader), 95
Shaw, Anna Moore, 302, 308
Shawamet People (Narraganset Nation), 52
Shawnee (Lenape) Nation, 23, 34, 39, 45, 168, 174
    treaties (colonial), 96, 97, 98, 102, 104, 112, 116, 118, 119, 122, 124, 126, 127, 130, 132, 134
    treaties (U.S.A.), 134, 174, 180, 182, 186, 190, 192, 194, 202, 206, 208, 224, 240
    wars (U.S.A.), 174, 175, 179, 188, 190, 216
    See also Seneca and Shawnee ("United-Nations")
Sheldrake (McInnis), 268
shells, use of, 22, 24
Shining Arrows, 41
Shinnecock Indians, The (Hunter), 294
Shiwape (Shriveled Man), 15
S'Homamish People, 226
Shongopovi. *See* Hopi People
Short Haida Stories (Lawrence), 308
Shoshone People, 25, 232, 236, 237, 242
Shoshone-Goship People, 236
Shoulderblade, James, 267
Showeway, Paul, 229
Shu-Hai, 12
Shyiks People. *See under* Yakima Nation (bands)
Siksika (Blackfeet) People, 36, 134, 211, 212
Silko, Leslie Marmon, 293, 312, 316
Simon, Edwin, 261
Simsawa People, 222
Sin-a-paw (Don Whiteside), 277
Sinte Gleska (Spotted Tail), 211, 254, 255

Sinte Gleska College, 318
Siouan-speaking People, 19
Sioui, Eleanor, 273
Sioui, Georges, 295
Sioux Nation, 25, 108, 216, 292, 316
    treaties (U.S.A.), 200, 202, 204, 212, 214, 222, 242, 250
    wars (tribal), 78
    wars (U.S.A.), 184, 190, 191, 232
Sioux Nation (bands)
    Blackfeet Sioux, 238
    Brulé (Lakota) Sioux, 238
    Hunkpapa Sioux, 202, 238, 254
    Mdewakanton Sioux, 206, 212, 222, 230
    Miniconjou Sioux, 238, 252
    Oglala (Lakota) Sioux, 166, 200, 238, 322
    River Saint Peter's Sioux, 190
    Sans Arc Sioux, 238
    Santee Sioux, 212, 232
    Sesseton (Sisseton) Sioux, 206, 212, 222, 230, 240
    Sioune Sioux, 200
    Sioux of the Broad Leaf, 192
    Sioux of the Lakes, 190
    Sioux of the Leaf, 192
    Sioux Who Shoot in the Pine Tops, 192
    Teton Sioux, 190, 200, 222, 252
    Two Kettle Sioux, 238
    Wahpekute Sioux, 206, 212, 222, 230
    Wahpeton Sioux, 206, 222, 230, 240
    Yankton Sioux, 190, 200, 212, 214, 230, 238
Sitadin (Stadacona settlement), 34
Sitting Bull. *See* Tatanka Iyoyake Siuslaw People, 232
Siwah People, 222
Siyante People, 220
Skagit People, 18, 226
Skaiwhamish People, 226
Sketches of Ancient History of the Six Nations (Cusick), 204
Sketches of Other Indian Tribes of North America: True Traditional Stories of Tecumseh and His League, in the Years 1811 and 1812 (Clarke), 242
Skinner, Linda, 293
Skinpah People. *See under* Yakima Nation (bands)
S'Klallam People, 226
Skokomish People, 226
Skopeahmish People, 226
Sktahlejum People, 226
Sktahimish People, 226
slavery (of Native People), 27, 28, 29, 30, 32, 36, 38–39, 42, 44, 55, 59, 62, 76, 77, 96, 98, 100, 108, 110, 119, 126, 175, 199, 230, 248
    See also kidnapping; massacres; murder; rape; starvation; torture
Slickpoo, Allen P., 273, 306
Slim Buttes, battle of, 253
Slipperjack, Ruby, 297
Smalhkamish People, 226
smallpox and infected blankets, 140, 156,

128, 130, 165, 248
    See also epidemics
Smith, Kenneth, 317
Smith, Martha, 270
Smith, Martin Cruz, 316
Smithsonian Institution, 324
Smohalla, 255
Snake "government," 261
Snakes People, 13, 19
Sneve, Virginia Driving Hawk, 277, 306, 308, 309
Snohomish People, 226
Snoqualmoo People, 226
Snow, John, 277
Snug Little Purchase: How Richard Henderson Bought Kaintuckee from the Cherokees in 1777, A (Brashear), 312
Snyder Act, 270
Somethings I Did (Gordon), 306
songs (and singers), 111, 117, 199
    Ashiwi (Zuñi) offering song, 53
    Arapaho, 109
    Aztec prayer song, 239
    festivals honoring, 150
    Luiseño death song, 91
    Tohono O'odham death song, 215
    See also ceremonies; ceremony time (various months); dance; legends and stories; literature
songs (prayer)
    Dakota prayer song, 103
    Ghost Dance prayer song, 113, 125
    Ho'Chunk prayer song, 25
    Ojibwa prayer song, 53, 93
    Pawnee prayer song, 87
    Tlingit prayer song, 93
songs (war)
    Dakota warrior song, 133
    Five Nation war song, 109
    Lakota war song, 97
    Ojibwa battle song, 79
Songs and Dances of the Lakota (Black Bear/Tbeisz), 310
Songs for the Harvester of Dreams (Niatum), 316
Society of American Indians, 268
society of peace, 211
Sociology of American Indians: A Critical Bibliography (Thomton/Grasmick), 316
Sohonuts People, 222
Solís, Padre Gaspar José de, 89
Solomon, Madeline, 267
Son of the Forest: The Experience of William Apes, a Native of the Forest, Comprising a Notice of the Pequod Tribe of Indians, Written by Himself, A (Apes), 206
Soul of the Indian: An Interpretation, The (Ohiyesa), 268
Souligny, **108**
South Carolina (British colony), 74, 78, 84, 86, 96, 104, 118, 120, 122, 127
Speaking of Indians (Picotte/Pavich/Deloria), 312
Speckled Snake, 85

Spirit Woman (Wa Wa Calachaw), 316
spirituality, Native People and, 159–60
Spiro (Cahokian center), 24
Squawskin People, 226
Squiaitl People, 226
Squinahmish People, 226
Ssipsis, 285
Stadacona Iroquois. *See under* Iroquois People
Stafford, Linda. *See* Crying Wind
Stalker, Alfred, 19
Standing Bear, trial of, 252
Standing Bear, Luther. *See* Ota K'te
Standish, Miles, 59
Stands in Timber, John, 302
Stands in Timber, Liberty, 302
Stanwix, General, 124
Starblanket, Noel V., 291
Starnatum (Stadacona settlement), 34
Starr, Emmet, 243
Starr, Jean, 279
Starr's History of the Cherokee (Strickland), 302
starvation, 27, 36, 65, 130, 156, 232, 274
   See also kidnapping; massacres; murder; rape; slavery; torture
State and Local Fiscal Assistance Act, 306
State of Native America, The (Jaimes), 324
Stehchass People, 226
Steilacoom People, 226
Stkahmish People, 226
Stockbridge Nation, 178, 216, 220, 230
Stolen Girl, A (Bussell), 266
Stoluckwhamish People, 226
Stone Giants (Shawnee story), 34
Stony Ones (Native People), 13, 19
Stories of the Sioux (Ota K'te), 278
Story of a Vision, The (La Flesche), 264
Story of an American Indian, The (Martinez), 308
Story of Deerskin, The (LaVatta), 268
Story of Polly's Life (Nason), 256
Storyteller (Silko), 316
storytellers and storytelling, 13, 51, 112, 271, 303, 326
   honoring time of, 159
   See also legends and stories; literature
Strange Company and Ned Christie's War (Conley), 324
Strange Journey: The Vision Life of a Psychic Indian Woman (Lone Dog), 300
Strickland, Rennard J., 285, 302, 306
Strong Medicine Wind, A (Krepps), 316
Strong Stone, 19
Struck by the Ree, 107
Stump, Serain, 304
Stung Arm (Chief Sun's mother), 109
Stuyvesant, Peter, 70
Stylistic Development of Navajo Jewelry, The (Parrish), 318
Succaahs People, 220
Sullivan, General John, 166
Summer, Delores T., 316
Summit Springs, battle of, 242, 243

Sun, Chief, 109
Sun Chief: The Autobiography of a Hopi Indian (Talayesva), 286
Sun Bear (Vincent LaDuke), 275
Sunus People, 222
Suquamish People, 226
Surrounded, The (McNickle), 280
Survival of American Indians Association, 300
Survival This Way: Interviews with American Indian Poets (Bruchac), 322
Susquehanna. *See under* Iroquois Nation
Swan Creek. *See under* Creek
Swan Creek Chippewa. *See under* Chippewa Nation (bands)
Swanson, R. A., 291
Sweet Medicine (Cheyenne legendary hero), 86, 87
Sweezy, Carl, 302
Swimmer, Ross 0., 287, 319, 321
Swinamish People, 226
symbol writing, 14

Tabegauche Utah Nation, 236
Tac, Pablo, 87
Ta-Chang, 12
Taches People, 220
Tafoya, Terry, 297
Tah-gah-jute (Mingo leader), 107, 133, 134, 171
Tah-me-la-pash-me (Dull Knife) (Cheyenne leader), **188**, 189, 243
Tah-se-tih's Sacrifice (Walker), 266
Taignoagny, 35, 37
Tailla (Stadacona settlement), 34
Taino (Island Arawak) People, 27, 28, 29, 30
Takelmeo People, 197
Talayesva, Don C., 61
Talcot, Major, 77
Talega People, 18, 19, 21, 25
Tales of Okanogans, The (Humishuma), 310
Talhnchees People, 220
Taliaferro, Leftwich, 259
Talking Indian: Reflections on Survival and Writing (Walters), 326
Tall Candle: The Personal Chronicle of a Yaqui Indian, The (Moises), 306
Tall Mountain, Mary, 113, 271, 312, 316
Tamaganend (the Pathmaker), 21
Tamaha (One Eye) (Sioux leader), 135
Tamakwi, 19
Tamanend I, 17, 18
Tamanend II (Lippitamenend), 29
Tamanend III (Tammany), 85
Tamaroa (Illinois Confederacy), 72
Tamarois People. *See under* Illinois Nation
Tamaskan (Mighty Wolf), 19
Tammany Society, 85
Tanaina Tales from Alaska (Vaudrin), 304
Tankawon (Little Cloud), 23
Tantaquidgeon, Gladys, 261, 294, 306
Tano People, 90

See also Tewa People
Taos Indians and Their Sacred Blue Lake, The (Keegan), 306
Taos People, 218, 304
Tapahe, Loren, 313
Tapahonso, Lucy, 297
Tapouaro (Illinois Confederacy), 72
Taquachi (Frozen One), 15
Tashawinso (Quite Ready), 47
Tashunka Witco (Crazy Horse), 217, 252, 253
Tasukamend (the Blameless One), 15
Tatanga Mani (Walking Buffalo), 53, 303
Tatanka Iyoyake (Sitting Bull), 37, 254
Tatanka Ptecila (Short Bull), 105
Tatnah People, 222
Tatobam, 63
Tatsey, June Bullshoe, 277
Tavaibo (Numataivo), 232
Tawacarro Nation, 218
Tawakaro Nation, 214
Tayateduta (Little Crow), 235
Taylor, Drew Hayden, 301
Taza (Apache leader), 251
Tbeisz, R. D., 310
Tdu-u-eh-t'sah (Like-A-Song), **16**, 17, 93, 271
Te Ata, 65, 259
Tears and Despair, Season of, 161
Tebbel, John, 287, 296, 297, 298, 300, 302
Tecumseh and His Times: The Story of a Great Indian (Oskison), 280
Tecumseh's Rebellion
Tecumtha (Tecumseh) (prophet/Shawnee leader), 23, 47, 168, 175, 183, 187, 189, 191
Teedyuscung (Delaware leader), 95, 97, 121, 129, 189
Tehakionwake (Emily Pauline Johnson), 235, 258, 264, 268
Tekakwitha, Keteri (Lily of the Mohawks), 85, 281
ten brothers (Haida story), 24
Tenchekensit (Breaking Open), 21
Tenochtitlán (Aztec capital), 32
Tenskwatawa (The Shawnee Prophet/Open Door), **166**, 167, 168, 185, 187, 188
Teton Sioux. *See under* Sioux Nation (bands)
Teukakas (Wallamwatkin leader), 217
Texas (Republic of), 216
Texas (Spanish colony), 133
Texas Cherokee. *See under* Cherokee Nation (bands)
Texas Titan: The Story of Sam Houston, A (Oskison), 274
Texon People, 222
Tewa People, 90
   See also Tano People
Tewa World: Space, Time, Being, and Becoming in a Pueblo Society, The (Ortiz), 304
textiles. *See under* arts and crafts
Teyarhasere (Abraham/Little Abraham)

(Mohawk leader), 123, 135, 171
Thamesville, battle of, 191
That's What She Said: Contemporary Poetry and Fiction by Native American Women (Green), 320
Thayendanegea (Joseph Brant) (Mohawk leader), 117, 135, 137
Then Badger Said This (Cook-Lynn), 310
There Is My People Sleeping: The Ethnic Poem-Drawings of Serain Stump (Stump), 304
There Is No Word for Goodby (Tall Mountain), 316
There's Not a Bathing Suit in Russia and Other Bare Facts (Rogers), 274
They Came Here First: The Epic of the American Indian (McNickle), 292
Thom, Melvin, 300
Thomas, David, 58
Thompson, Daniel. *See* Rokwaho
Thompson, Earle, 295
Thompson, Morris, 309
Thornton, Russell, 265, 287, 316, 318, 320
Thorpe, James Francis (Jim), 257, 268, 269, 297, 318, 320
Thorvald, 22
Ticasuk (Emily Ivanoff Brown), 265
Tiger, Eunah J., 272
Tiguex massacre, 42
Tiguex People, 39, 42
Tiller, Verornica Velarde, 293
Timucua People, 30, 32
Tionontati People (Huron Confederacy), 62, 66
Tipai-Ipai (Jamul Digueño), 44
Tippecanoe, battle of, 188
Tisquantum (Squanto), 47, 51, 59
Tiwa People, 46
Tlingit People (Alaska), 13, 18, 180, 182
To Frighten a Storm (Cardiff), 310
To Lead and to Serve: Indian Education at Hampton Institute, 1879–1923 (Molin/Hultgren/Green), 324
Toanhooch People, 226
tobacco, 101, 111, 191
Tocde People, 222
Tocia People, 222
Toe Ga Juke Juke Gan Hoke Sheem (Roxy Gordon), 289, 306, 327, **326**
Tohe, Laura, 297, **297**
Tohono O'odham People (Papago), 40, 318
Tolowa People, 232
Tolumnes People, 220
Tomeches People, 220
Tomochichi, **110**, 111, 113, 261
Tonawanda Seneca, 230, 280
Tongue River, battle of, 238, 239
tools, Stone Age, 10
Toomnas People, 220
Toova People, 224
tortoiseshell, use of, 18
torture, 41
    by Native People, 170

by the Roman Catholic Church, 67, 71
    See also kidnapping; massacres; murder; missionaries (Roman Catholic); rape; slavery; starvation
Toto People, 222
T'Peeksin People, 226
Tracking (Bruchac), 320
trade andbarter, 18, 34, 45, 52, 56, 60, 62, 64, 78, 96, 104, 110, 112, 116, 118, 250
traditions, celebration of, 160–61
Trafzer, Clifford E. (Richard Red Hawk), **50**, 51, 293, 308, 316, 318, 320, 322
Trail of Broken Treaties caravan, 306
Trail of Tears. *See* Nuna-da-ut-sun'y
Translator's Son (Bruchac), 316
treaties (Native Peoples), 56, 59, 83, 167
    as "agreements," 242
    and fishing rights, 226, 228, 318
    ratification of, 248
    recognition, 244
    tribal, 64, 70, 74, 106, 120
    with British colonists, 50, 54, 62, 63, 65, 66, 70, 72, 73, 74, 86, 90, 92, 96, 97, 98, 100, 101, 102, 104, 106, 108, 110, 112, 113, 116, 118, 120, 122, 124, 126, 135, 136
    with Dutch colonists, 64, 70, 74
    with French colonists (Canada), 62, 66, 72, 84, 112
    with Great Britain, 96, 98, 106, 110, 116, 122, 124, 126, 128, 130, 131, 132
    with Spanish colonists, 133
    with the U.S. Government, 115, 130, 134, 164–65, 166, 168–69, 172, 174, 175, 176, 178, 180, 182, 184, 186, 187, 188, 190, 192, 194, 196–97, 198, 200, 202, 204, 206, 207, 208, 209, 210, 212, 214, 216, 218, 220, 222, 224, 226, 228, 230, 234, 236, 238, 240, 241, 242, 244, 248, 250, 252, 253
    See also Chain of Friendship; Cherokee Indian Treaty; Continental Congress; Covenant Chain; Jay Treaty; land: cession; land: removal; revolts; Season of Broken Treaties; wars
Treaty Ground, 198, 199, 200
Treaty of Amity (Plymouth), 58
Treaty of Camp Moultrie, 198
Treaty of Charleston, 127
Treaty of Choctaw Trading House, 192, 193
Treaty of Dancing Rabbit Creek, 206, 207
Treaty of Doak's Stand, 198, 199
Treaty of Dover, 67
Treaty of Fort Gibson, 210
Treaty of Fort Jackson, 190
Treaty of Fort Laramie, 222, 243
Treaty of Fort McIntosh, 174
Treaty of Fort Stanwix, 115, 130, 134, 172
Treaty of Fort Wayne, 188, 189
Treaty of Ghent, 168
Treaty of Greenville, 168, 180
Treaty of Hard Harbor, 130, 132
Treaty of Hell Gate, 228
Treaty of Hopewell, 174

Treaty of Lochaber, 132
Treaty of New Echota, 210
Treaty of Paris, 115, 168, 170
Treaty of Payne's Landing, 208, 210
Treaty of Sycamore Shoals, 134
Treaty of Three Rivers, 64
Treaty of Utrecht, 102
Treaty of Washington, 201
Treaty of Westminster, 74
Treaty Party Cherokee. *See under* Cherokee Nation (bands)
Treaty with the Creeks, 208
Treaty with the Nisqually, 226
Treaty with the Omaha, 224
Treaty with the Ottawas and Chippewas, 228
Treaty with the Western Cherokee, 204
Tremblay, Gail, 123, 289
Tribal Tribune, 298
"tribe" as a term, 265
Trickster (Clown). *See* Heyoka/ Koshari. *See also* Coyote
Trimbel, Charles, 279
Trip to the Moon, A (Robertson), 258
Trout, 107
Truman, Harry, 291
Tryon, William, 132
Tsalagi (Arnett), 310
Tsiyugunsini (Dragging Canoe), 111, 137, 167
Tso, Tom, 323
tuberculosis. *See* epidemics
Tuckabatchee Micco, 203
Tuhucmaches People, 220
Tumwater People, 226
Tundra Times newspaper, 300
Tupatu, Lorenzo (Picuris leader), 85
Turk (Pawnee guide), 40, 41
Turkey (Lenape) People, 47
Turnica People, 40
turquoise, use of, 20, 22
Turtle Island, 10
Tuscarora Nation (Six Nations), 98, 100, 101, 102, 106, 166, 178
Tustunnuggee Thulucco, 191
Tutelo Nation, 37, 126, 132
Tutuni People, 197, 232
Tuup-weets (Colorow/Colorado), 189, 257
Twightwee People, 124, 174
Twist, Glenn J., 271, **271**
Two Kettle Sioux. *See under* Sioux Nation (bands)

Ugidali (Lee Piper), 273
Umatilla Nation, 228
Umpqua Nation, 226
Unaduti (Dennis Wolf) (Cherokee leader), 203, 219, 261
Unakuh, 254
Unami (Lenape) People, 47, 124
Uncas (Mohegan leader), 61, 65
Underhill, Ruth M., 280

United States v. Winans, 266
United States Courts
  Court of Claims, 228, 254
  Montana v. United States, 228
  right to sue, 252
  Voight decision, 318
  voting rights, 292
  See also United States Supreme Court
United States Congress, 268
  Alaska Reorganization Act, 280
  Alaskan Native Claims Settlement Act, 306
  American Indian Freedom of Religion Act, 312
  Assimilative Crimes Act, 292
  Burk Act, 266
  Curtis Act (of 1898), 260, 280
  Dawes Commission, 258
  General Allotment (Dawes Severalty) Act, 256, 258, 266, 274, 278
  Indian Appropriations Act, 258
  Indian Civil Rights Act (ICRA), 302
  Indian Education Act, 306
  Indian Reorganization (Wheeler-Howard) Act, 277, 278, 279
  Indian Tribal Governmental Tax Status Act, 318
  Major Crimes Act, 254
  Navajo-Hopi Land Settlement Act, 308
  Public Law 280, 296
  Snyder Act, 270
  State and Local Fiscal Assistance Act, 306
Voluntary Relocation Act, 296
United States Department of the Interior, 220, 270, 272, 280, 288, 292
  assistant secretary for Indian affairs, 310, 313
United States Government
  citizenship and Native People, 272
  and economic development, 300
  Eskimo Alaska Native rights, 254
  House Concurrent Resolution 108, 296
  Leavitt Act, 276
  and Native languages, 256
  and Native People, 164–65, 244
  severance taxes and sovereignty, 318
  termination of the trust relationship, 292, 296, 298
  treaty ratification, 248
  unassigned lands, 256
  See also Indian Affairs, Bureau of; Indian Affairs, Office of; Indian Claims Commission; U.S. Army Corps of Engineers; war (Native People vs U.S. Government). *Also under* treaties
United States Postal Service, 322
United States Senate
  Select Committee on Indian Affairs, 320
United States Supreme Court, 164
  County of Oneida, New York. v. Oneida Indian Nation of New York, 320
  Employment Division of Oregon v. Smith, 324
  Ex Parte Crow Dog, 254

  jurisdiction on reservations, 254
  Kerr-McGee Corp. v. Navajo Tribe of Indians, 320
  Lyng v. Northwest Indian Cemetery Protective Association, 322
  Menominee Tribe of Indians v. United States, 302
  Merrion v. Jicarilla Apache Tribe, 318
  Morton v. Mancari, 308
  New Mexico v. Mescalero Apache Tribe, 318
  and Pueblo People, 252
  United States v. Winans, 266
  Washington v. Confederated Tribes of the Colville Indian Reservation, 316
  Washington v. Washington State Commercial Passenger Fishing Vessel Association, 312
  water rights, 266
Uppagoines People, 222
Upper Pend d'Oreilles ("Confederated Tribes"), 228
Urbanization of American Indians: A Critical Bibliography, The (Thomton/Sandefur/Grasmick), 318
Usen, 37
U.S. Army Corps of Engineers, 292, 300
Usurper of the Range, The (Jones), 264
Ute Nation, 232, 242, 252, 256
Utchapa People, 222
Uvavnuk (Eskimo holy woman), 17

Valenzuela, Mimi, 291
Vallejo, Don Ignacio, 193
Vargas, Governor de Vargas, 90, 91
Vaudrin, Bill, 304
Velarde, Pablita, 271, 300
Velázquez, Diego de, 30
Vermillion River Kickapoo. *See under* Kickapoo Nation
Verrazano, Giovanni da, 32
Vice President's Council on Indian Opportunity, 302
Victorio, 252
Vietnam War (Native People and), 302
Village of the Great Kivas (Ashiwi/Zuñi), 22
Virginia (British colony), 50, 51, 52, 54, 63, 64, 78, 84, 86, 116, 120, 122, 130, 134
Virginia State, 136
Vizcaíno, Sebastián, 50
Vizenor, Gerald, 279, 300, 302, 304, 306
Voices of the Heart (Coffee), 324
Voight decision, 318
Volborth, Judith Mountain Leaf, 295
Volga Germans: Pioneers of the Pacific Northwest, The (Trafzer/Scheuerman), 316
Voluntary Relocation Act, 296
voting rights, 272, 292, 296

Wa-ana-tan (Martin Charger), 211, 225,

265
Wa Wa Calachaw (Bonita Nuñez), 316
Wabash. *See under* Potawatomi Nation (bands)
Wabasha (Red Leaf) (Mdewakanton Sioux/Chippewa leader), 95
Wachaets People, 220
Wacksache People, 222
Waco Nation, 218
Wagomend (the Assinsink Prophet), 121, 121
Wahashaw (Wausau) People, 212
Wahcheehahska (Man Who Puts All out of Doors) (Winnebago leader), 215
Waheenee (Buffalo Bird Woman), 270
Wahpekute Sioux. *See under* Sioux Nation (bands)
Wahpeton Sioux. *See under* Sioux Nation (bands)
Wahunsenacawh (Powhatan), 39, 51, 53, 55, 85
Waindance, 65
Waioskasit, 107
Wakaholend (Beloved One), 17
Wakan Tanka, 121, 125, 131
  See also Great Spirit
Wakely, David, **88**
Wakely, Lela Northcross, 89
Walk in Your Soul (Kilpatrick/Kilpatrick), 302
Walker, Bertrand, 266
Walker River Reservation, 232, 233
Walking Bull, Gilbert, 310, 312
Walking Bull, Montana, 310, 312
Walking Hail, 225
Walla Walla Nation, 228
Wallam Olum (Red Record), 10, 11, 12, 23, 27, 32, 55, 62
Wallama (Painted Red), 19
Wallis, Michael, 326
Walters, Anna Lee, 291, 326
Walwaskik Wappinger People, 64
Wamditonka (Jerome Big Eagle), 258
Wamesit People, extinction of, 131
Wampanoag People (Narraganset Nation), 29, 32, 52, 54, 64, 72, 76
wampum, 50, 66, 322
Wamsutta (Wampanoag leader), 71
Wanatee, Adeline, 35
Wanatshapam People. *See under* Yakima Nation (bands)
Wangomend. *See* Wahunsenacawh
Wannalanset (Pennacock leader), 67
Wannuck People, 222
Wapachikis (White Crab), 53
Wapagamoshiki (White Otter), 45
Wapagokhos (White Owl), 13
Wapahakey (Dawn Ground), 29
Wapallanewa (White Eagle), 13
Wapameepto (Big Jim), 211, 251, 265
Wapashum (White Horn), 45
Wapashuwi (White Lynx), 21
Wapkicholem (White Crane), 17

Wappo People, 232
Wappinger People, 60, 64
Waptipatit (White Chick), 19
War of 1812, 168, 188
War of Spanish Succession, 102
War of the Grand Alliance, 88
Warren, Whipple William, 201, 254
Warrior, Clyde, 300
Warrior Who Killed Custer: The Personal Narrative of Chief Joseph White Bull, The (White Bull), 302
wars (battles)
    Little Bighorn, 252
    Fallen Timbers, 178, 185
    German Flats, 122
    Grattan fight, 225
    Honey Springs (Civil War), 236
    Lake George, 122, 123
    Lake Okeechobee, 214, 215
    Lame Deer, 306
    Newtown, 167
    Oriskany, 136, 137
    Point Pleasant, 135
    Second Seminol War, 211
    Slim Buttes, 253
    Summit Springs, 242, 243
    Tascaluza vs de Soto (Mabila), 40
    Thamesville, 191
    Tippecanoe, 188
    Tongue River, 238, 239
    Wolf Mountain, 252
wars (French vs British), 102, 122, 123
wars (Native People), 63, 75
    vs American colonists, 173
    vs British colonists, 63, 73, 75, 76, 77, 78, 84, 86, 99, 100, 128, 134
    vs Dutch colonists, 62, 64
    vs French colonists, 44, 72, 88, 92, 112, 116, 117, 120, 123, 171
    vs Native People, 20, 21, 37, 52, 58, 60, 62, 66, 70, 72, 74, 96, 108, 110, 127, 132, 168, 184, 211, 230, 231
    vs Spanish conquistadors, 40, 42, 48, 50
    See also American Revolutionary War; Civil War; French and Indian War; Korean War; Lord Dunmore's War; Navajo War; revolts; treaties; (colonial); Vietnam War; War of 1812; World War I; World War II
wars (Native People vs U.S. Government), 174, 178, 179, 188, 190, 191, 210, 214, 215, 221, 238, 239, 250, 252, 254, 256, 258
    Bannock War, 252, 253
    Comanche Wars (1830–50), 221
    Modoc War, 250, 251
    Red River War, 250
    Second Seminol War, 210, 211, 214, 215, 216, 232–33
    Ute War, 252
    See also Continental Congress; treaties (U.S. government)
Ward, Nancy. *See* Ghigau
Wasechun-tashunka (American Horse), 217, 267

Washburne, Heluis Chandler, 284
Washinga Sakba (Black Bird), 181, 183
Washington, George, 123, 178, 179, 199
Washington v. Confederated Tribes of the Colville Indian Reservation, 316
Washington v. Washington State Commercial Passenger Fishing Vessel Association, 312
Washo People, 232
Wassaja (Carlos Montezuma), 270
Wassaja: Freedom's Signal for the Indians monthly, 270
Water Spider (Cherokee legend), 28
Waterman, Charles E., 270
Watie, Buck. *See* Galagina
Watomika (James Bouchard), 199, 229, 257
Watsahewa People, 222
Waubun (Ojibwa legend), 24
Wauneka, Annie Dodge, 295, 301, 310
Waun-na-con (John Quinney), 33, 97, 107, 137
Wawatam, 129
Wawequa, 65
Way of a Peyote Redman, The (Brito), 322
Way to Rainy Mountain, The (Momaday), 304
Waymouth, George, 51
Ways of My Grandmothers, The (Hungry Wolf), 316
We Are All Fullbloods (Gibson), 266
We Can Still Hear Them Clapping (Keegan), 310
We Shall Live Again: The 1870 and 1890 Ghost Dance Movements as Demographic Revitalization (Thornton), 320
We Talk, You Listen: New Tribes, New Turf (Deloria), 304
Wea People. *See under* Illinois Nation
Weather Smokey, 215
Webb, Eddie, **221**
Webb, George E., 298
Weber-Pillwas, Cora, 289
Wechillas People, 220
Weiser, Conrad, 120
Wekwochella (Exhaustion), 15
Welbum, Ron, 289, **289**
Welch, James, 285, 306, 308, 312
Wemalchees People, 220
Wemilches People, 220
Weninock, 105
West, Thomas, 52
Westbo People, 78
Western ("Old Settlers") Cherokee. *See under* Cherokee Nation (bands)
Western Writers Association of America, 285
Wetamoo (Wampanoag squaw sachem), 73, 77
Wetchpeck People, 222
We'wha, 55
Weyapiersenwah (Blue Jacket), 168, 173, 185
What Moon Drove Me to This (Harjo), 312

Wheeler, Bernelda, 281
Wheeler-Howard (Indian Reorganization) Act, 277, 278, 279
When the Grass Grew Long (Oskison), 264
White, Elizabeth Q. (Polingaysi Qoyawayma), 13, 300
White, Felix, 277
White Bull, Joseph, 302
White Calf, 11
White Corn Sister and Back Then Tomorrow (Aroniawenate), 312
White Eagle—Green Corn (McCombs), 312
White Hat, Albert, 281
White House Task Force on Indian Health, 302
White Mountain Apache. *See under* Apache Nation (bands)
White Stick Creek. *See* Creek civil war
White Wampum, The (Tehakionwake), 258
Whitecloud, Tom, 269
Whitehorn v. State: Peyote and Religious Freedom in Oklahoma (Johnston), 312
Whiteman, Henrietta V., 101, 111
Whiteman, Roberta Hill, 291
Whiteside, Don. *See* Sin-a-paw
Whitewolf, Jim, 107, 304
Whitt, Shirley Hill, 279
Whusi People, 222
Wiccahunes People, 220
Wichita Nation, 104, 118, 133, 210, 218, 252
    See also Quivira People
Wild Harvest: A Novel of the Transition Days in Oklahoma (Oskison), 272
William and Mary College, 106
Williams, Agnes, 49
Williams, Lorna, 291
Williams, Roger, 63
Williams, Ted C., 275, 310
Williamson, Colonel David, 170
Wilson, Jack. *See* Wovoka
Wilson, James, 134
Wilson, Peter, 101
Wimbee People, 84
Winelowich (Hunter-in-Snow), 25
Wind from the Enemy Sky (McNickle), 312
Wingandacoa People, 48
Wingenund (the Willing One), 17
Wingina (Ensenore's son), 47
Winnebago Nation, 128, 188, 192, 202, 204, 208, 214, 218, 228, 230
Winnepurget, 61
Winnie, Lucille. *See* Sahgandeoh Winter, Jacque (Pohlik-lah), 35
Winter Count (Dallas Chief Eagle), 302
Winter in the Blood (Welch), 308
Winter of the Salamander (Young Bear), 316
Winters, Henry, 266
Winters doctrine, 266
Wintun People, 232
Wirasuap (Bear Hunter), 237
Wisdom of the Senecas (Nitsch), 312
Wisham People. *See under* Yakima Nation (bands)

Wo Ya-ka-pi: Telling Stories of the Past and the Present (Walking Bull/Walking Bull), 310
Wodziwob, 232
Wolassi People, 222
Wolf, Dennis. *See* Unaduti
Wolf Mountain, battle of, 252
Wollpahpe Snake People, 238
Wolumenap (Good Inscribed), 29
Womack, Craig S., 61, **67**
women (Native People), **192,** 198, 325
  importance of, 63, 65, 134
  medicine women, 131
  sachems and leaders, 55, 65, 73, 75, 77, 89, 109, 111, 133, 289
Women in American Indian Society (Green), 324
Women, Work, and Politics: Belgium, 1830–1914 (Hilden), 326
wood engravings. *See under* arts and crafts
Wooden Leg, 276
Wooden Leg, a Warrior Who Fought Custer (Wooden Leg), 276
Woody, Elizabeth, 299, **299**
Wootonekauske (Wetamoo's sister), 77
Wopohwahts (White Shield), 213
Wopumnes People, 222
Wordcraft Circle of Native Writers and Storytellers, 285, 326
World War I (and Native People), 270
World War II (and Native People), 273, 143, 270, 283, 284, 285, 286, 288, 299
  See also Code Talker
Wounded Knee, occupation of. *See* Pine Ridge Reservation
Wounded Knee Massacre, 165, 233, 258, 259
Woven Holy People (Parrish), 318
Wovoka (Jack Wilson), 231, 232–33, 257, **276,** 277
Wowol People, 222
Wulakeningus (Well Praised), 37
Wulitpallat (Good Fighter), 29
Wulitshinik (Fine Forests), 23
Wyandot Iroquois. *See under* Iroquois Nation
Wynepuechsika (Cornstalk) (Shawnee leader), 135, 137

Yagawanend (the Lodge Man), 19
Yahi Yana People, 240
Yahooskin Snake Nation, 236
Yakima Nation, 197, 228, 306
Yakima Nation (bands)
  Liaywas People, 228
  Palouse, 228
  Pisquouse People, 228
  Kahmiltpah People, 228
  Klikatat People, 228
  Klinquit People, 228
  Kowwassayee People, 228
  Ochechotes People, 228
  Seapocat People, 228
  Shyiks People, 228
  Skinpah People, 228
  Wanatshapam People, 228
  Wisham People, 228
Yalumne People, 222
Yamado People, 222
Yamasee People, 40, 102
Yana People, 218, 232
Yankton Sioux. *See under* Sioux Nation (bands)
Yanktonai Dakota, 212
Yassi People, 222
Yava, Robert, 312
Yavapi People, 250
Yawilchine People, 222
Yazzie, Ethelou, 306
Yeagley, David, 295
Yellow Bird (John Rollin), 224
Yellow Creek Massacre, 134
yellow fever. *See* epidemics
Yellow Robe, Rosebud, 267
Yellow Robe, William S., 301
Yellow Thunder, Raymond, murder of, 306
Ylacca People, 222
Yokuts People, 220, 232
Yolamir People, 222
Yoo Pescha Pallaguianna (Quintano), 254
York, Kenneth H., 293, 318
Young Bear, Ray A., 20, 316
Young Beaver, 204
Young Chief, 61
Young-Ing, Greg, 301
Ysopete or Sopete (Wichita guide), 40, 41
Yuchi (Chisca) People, 40, 66, 110
Yuki People, 222, 232
Yuma: Frontier Crossing of the Far Southwest (Trafzer), 316
Yuma People, 40, 197
Yurok People, 232

Zaepkoheeta (Big Bow), 207, 265
Zah, Peterson, 319
Zaldivar, Captain Juan de, 48
Zepeda, Ofelia, 297
Zia People, 46
Zitkala-Sa (Gertrude Simmons Bonnin), 253, 264
Zuili Tales (Lewis), 306
Zuñi. *See* Ashiwi People